THE ESSENTIAL MAYHEW

BERTRAND TAITHE

THE ESSENTIAL
MAYHEW

REPRESENTING AND COMMUNICATING
THE POOR

RIVERS ORAM PRESS
LONDON

First published in 1996 by
Rivers Oram Press, 144 Hemingford Road, London N1 1DE

Published in the USA by
Paul and Company
Post Office Box 442, Concord MA 01742

Set in Baskerville
by N-J Design Associates, Romsey
and printed in Great Britain by
T.J. Press (Padstow) Ltd

British Library Cataloguing-in-Publication Data
A catalogue record for this book is available from the British Library

ISBN 1 85489 046 8
ISBN 1 85489 047 6 (pbk)

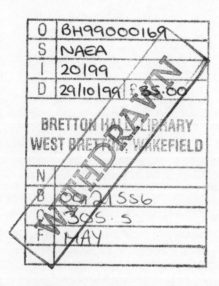

CONTENTS

═══════════

PART I

Acknowledgments

Introduction   3

1 Henry Mayhew 1812-1887   9

2 The Genesis of *London Labour and the London Poor*   13

3 Open Letters: Mayhew and his Correspondents   22

4 Cracking the Hard Nuts   33

5 History in their Own Words   45

Postscript   58

Appendix   60

Notes   61

PART II

Answers to Correspondents   85

Index   252

ACKNOWLEDGMENTS

This book has a long history and owes its existence to many people: François Crouzet first supervised the M.Phil. dissertation which was my first encounter with Mayhew. Later, while I was working on my PhD thesis, Carolyn Steedman advised me to gather this material into a book. She also introduced me to Elizabeth Fidlon who believed in this project. Other friends and colleagues read and influenced this book, I must thank, in chronological order, Philippe Girard, Duncan Steer, Ceri Riley, Ray Taylor and Mark Jenner. I also thank David Vincent who read the manuscript at an early stage and whose useful comments helped me, I hope, to amend some of the shortcomings of this book and make it more user-friendly. Mark Jenner read large chunks of the text and advised me on many aspects of this work. Librarians in the Birmingham University Library, the British Library, Bibliothèque Nationale, and Guildhall have also been very helpful. Yet, in spite of owing all this, no one but me is responsible for any defects in this work.

Editorial note: The relevant references to *London Labour and the London Poor* (1861) (LLLP), the *Morning Chronicle Survey* (MCS) (Razzell's edition, 1981), or the Correspondence appended in this volume will be notified as such: [LLLP (volume), (page)], [MCS (volume), (page)]; [C (page)].

To Vicky

"But this dedication is for others to read:
These are private words addressed to you in public."

T. S. Eliot.

PART 1

INTRODUCTION

Mayhew, Henry, author of *London Labour and the London Poor*, born in London, November 25 1812. He was sent for his education to Westminster School, but not taking with [he rebelled against] the discipline in force & [he] ran away [off them]. He was then placed as midshipman on the last of the East India Company's service [on board of a ship of war, but left the navy], but left the sea to embrace the law.

Returning to London from a sojourn in Wales he projected "Figaro in London", and, in partnership with the late Gilbert A'Beckett became manager of the Queen's theatre (where his farce of the Wandering Minstrel was produced) but the speculation was a failure.[1] In 1841 he was one of the principal agents in establishing [he projected and obtained the cooperation of the principal writers in] *Punch*, which he edited for some years when he had differences with the proprietors and vacated his offices.[2]

He was editor of the *Comic Almanac* [and] after leaving *Punch*, contributed to numerous magazines and periodicals.[3] In 1842, he published a small work entitled *What to Teach and How to Teach It* in which he contended strongly against task work, flogging and prizes in schools. From 1846 to 1850, several works of a broadly, almost farcical character appeared "by the Brothers Mayhew", George Cruikshank being the illustrator. His chief work is *London Labour and the London Poor* showing the condition and earnings of those that will work, those who cannot work and those who will not work.[4] In 1856, Mr. Mayhew struck out the idea of an association for the reformation of criminals, and towards promoting his object he chaired meetings of the thieves of London of whom several narrated their experience of the world and its ways. The association does not seem to have prospected further than the prospectus. Mr. Mayhew's latest publication is *The Great World of London*[5] [but owing to the sudden death of Mr. Bogue the publisher, the book remains incomplete]. Mr. Mayhew is also the author of the *Peasant Boy Philosopher* a novel founded upon the boyhood of Ferguson, the shepherd astronomer.

A Dictionary of Contemporary Biography: handbook of the peerage of rank, worth and intellect, G. Griffin and Co., 1860, corrected proof.[6]

This short notice, written for a biographical dictionary of contemporary figures, was corrected by Mayhew himself. Most existing short biographies of Henry Mayhew draw upon the main elements of this (auto)biography and are often similarly limited.[7] But, in Mayhew's case, a biographical approach will never cast a new light on his major work since he has left us very little writing about himself. This project reinterprets Mayhew's work through the study of his readers and correspondents of the 1851–2 serialization of *London Labour and the London Poor* and enables us to understand the significance of *LLLP* within its original context. Few texts have such an indistinct image and require such urgent re-evaluation. Karel Williams alone has analyzed the complex bibliography and historiography of *London Labour* and also its gradual acceptance as a canonical Victorian text.

Mayhew wrote a number of different texts called *London Labour*, at different periods, and aimed at different readerships. In 1849 the *Morning Chronicle* employed him as the London correspondent of their survey of the condition of the working classes in Britain. Then, in 1850, as the result of a conflict with his employers, Mayhew left or was fired. Immediately he set up his own periodical entitled *London Labour and the London Poor*. For Mayhew, this move into the unknown entailed a change of readership, of substance and style. The enterprise folded in 1852, however, and it was not until 1856 that Mayhew embarked upon another project of such breadth. This was a work entitled *The Great World of London*, which, serialized like his previous project, remained unfinished, this time following the death of the publisher. In 1861, however, another publisher, Griffin, Bohn and Co., undertook to gather together and publish the serialized text of the 1851–2 journal. They completed it with a collection of texts of various origins and formed a new third volume.[8] *London Labour* therefore became a triple decker. *London Labour* was a great success and the publishers followed it a year later with a scandalous fourth volume on prostitution and crime. Meanwhile, they issued a "completed" *Great World of London* under the title *The Criminal Prisons of London*. However, in this fourth volume of *London Labour*, Mayhew had written only the first 37 pages [LLLP, 4, 37], a chosen "collaborator" having written the other 155 pages of the volume, leaving it unfinished in 1852. Another ten years passed before a team of young journalists completed the text for Griffin, Bohn and Co. Among these journalists, Hemyng, previously known for a lightweight comparison of women in London and Paris, completed the part on prostitution. Binny and Halliday wrote from scratch on the theme of thieves and beggars, and finally the Reverend Tuckniss made a complimentary survey of various charitable agencies in London, thereby lending a veneer of philanthropic respectability to this sensationalist piece of journalism.

This "saucy", and now much quoted, fourth volume was poorly received. Some, like Florence Nightingale, who was familiar with the earlier edition of *London Labour*, deplored its assumptions with regard to prostitution.[9] This may have been the reason that most later nineteenth-century editions comprised just the three first volumes of 1861. Mayhew may have refused to put his name on a volume he had not written, or it may be that the publishers did not think that such a book on prostitution was appropriate for popular reading (thus exemplifying the self-censorship practised on cheap editions from the 1860s onwards). However, the four-volume hardback edition of 1862 is the one that is most well known now, having become the version of *London Labour and the London Poor* that has been most commonly published in the twentieth century.

It can be seen, therefore, that Mayhew's project was polymorphic: it had several lives. Unlike a purely literary text, or a complete text, there is no clear progression, no sense of achievement. The task itself had no beginning and no end. *London Labour* was perceived in various ways at every stage of its existence. It was read according to how it was presented: as part of an expensive newspaper; as a cheap, penny periodical sold alongside "penny dreadfuls", and as an expensive, four-volume book. Similarly historians and literary critics have used different periods of the book, different material, to assess Mayhew's work and "canonical" importance. Williams found a number of contradictions in Mayhew's intentions and style, mainly because Mayhew's historiography is almost as complex as the genesis of *London Labour* itself.

In his lifetime, Mayhew enjoyed only temporary fame. When he died in 1887, a few of his friends described him as the "great and shamefully ignored compiler of that amazing document".[10] This back-handed homage reduced his authorship of the work to the status of "compiler". It also narrowed the definition of *London Labour* to that of a document, albeit "amazing". Subsequent works on poverty, such as those by Charles Booth, Rowntree, Mass Observation[11] and Orwell, never mention him.[12] It was not until after the Second World War that Mayhew and his work emerged again. R.J. Cruikshank [13] was perhaps the earliest to compare him, although negatively, with Dickens.[14] Then, between 1949 and 1951, Peter Quennell edited three volumes from the 1862 edition. This was a rediscovery of Mayhew, and portrayed "the other side of the Dickensian coin". While Dickens was a writer of fiction, Mayhew was described as "the painter of reality". Occasionally he achieved prominence in Dickensian studies as the potential inspiration of the master, a footnote to *Our Mutual Friend*.[15] It appears that the talent and imagination that was thought to inspire the social criticism in Dickens remained unacknowledged in Mayhew. Yet there is the paradox that "the realist" Mayhew made his social denunciation with such a degree of "objectivity" that realism implied social criticism. Scholars have played down Mayhew's role and skills as mediator to extract merely the nicely framed portraits and interviews that feature in parts of his work.[16] This angle has informed the selection from Mayhew's "characters" that have seen the light regularly since the 1950s under various titles.[17]

At the end of the 1960s, Cass and Dover published the unabridged 1862 edition of *London Labour and the London Poor*. This interest in Mayhew's apparently complete text followed a revival of Dickensian studies.[18] Mayhew was still used as a source of information, usually presented as a mere collector of 1851 common utterances. His texts were perhaps the closest thing to an oral history tape recording and his tales of poverty and long-lost London life may have appealed to prosperous 1960s readers. This combination of voyeurism and sentimentality could be compared to the original impact of Mayhew's work among his contemporary readers.[19] E.P. Thompson was alone in politicising Mayhew, a message with few reverberations at the time.[20]

The breakthrough in "Mayhew studies" came in 1971. Ann Humpherys in the USA, and Thompson and Yeo in the UK, simultaneously edited Mayhew's articles from the *Morning Chronicle* under the respective titles of *Voices of the Poor* and *The Unknown Mayhew*.[21] Both editions intended to re-establish Mayhew as an important writer and his work as a fundamental sociological text. However, while these works shared an identical project, their political agendas could hardly be further apart. Thompson and Yeo rehabilitated Mayhew, while Humpherys generally agreed with the assessment of Gertrude Himmelfarb. Mayhew nevertheless re-entered the arena of social studies after a decade of sentimentalization. A few years later Raphael Samuel emphasized further Mayhew's importance as a pre-Marxist theoretician of exploitation.[22] Meanwhile Himmelfarb repeatedly and powerfully presented *London Labour* as a middle-class ideological construction marginalising poverty.[23] This debate re-established *LLLP* both as an important work and a matter of controversy.

The usefulness of Mayhew's work was thought to have been exhausted with the publication of the full collection of the *Morning Chronicle* articles; it was promoted as a theoretical and ideological text while undermined as a valuable source of information.[24] The basis of Thompson and Yeo's claim to have made a discovery was that they contrasted *their* Mayhew with the *known* Mayhew.[25] It was *London Labour* sociology v. *London Labour* entertainment.[26] This discrepancy between two modes of reading has persisted. Mayhew as historian, sociologist, radical, conservative, journalist, racist, literary fraud...the polymorph *London Labour and the London Poor* seemed to elicit all manner of interpretation.

Karel Williams usefully summed up these approaches in his radical criticism of all these readings.[27] Paradoxically, his own work marked the conclusion of a period of intense reflection on Mayhew. In the 1980s fewer people appeared to be ready to embark upon further reflection on Mayhew's importance, and he seemed to fade in the mass of Victorian literature. Significantly his work has recently been coupled or compared with a range of other authors' work: so there has been, for example, Mayhew and Conan Doyle,[28] Mayhew and Malthus,[29] Mayhew and Freud,[30] or, more traditionally, Mayhew and Dickens.[31] This list is not exhaustive and the pre-eminence of Mayhew in each of the pairs varies. This reflects not only Mayhew's loss of identity but also the difficulty of defining his work.

London Labour had doubled in size and had grown to prominence among Victorian texts but it has not become any easier to read in its entirety. *London Labour* is now a core text, almost a textbook in its own right, often quoted, often partially studied, always deemed worthy of attention but difficult to use. It is therefore one of the least studied texts of the "canon" of Victorian literature.

Mayhew's own words are perhaps the best defence against "the enormous condescension of posterity".[32] *The Essential Mayhew* consists mainly of another of Mayhew's texts: his correspondence. This was a public correspondence printed on and within the covers of the weekly issues of *LLLP* between 1851 and 1852. In this context, the sociologist/journalist wrote more openly about his work, his methods and hopes. There he claimed his authorship over his survey in spite of his readers' claims: the correspondents-subject of his work. This correspondence fitted within the periodical and was, *per se*, the readers' published correspondence. It remains a literary document in its own right. In the process Mayhew learnt about his readers and, in turn, they influenced the writing of his prose. Some of Mayhew's "Answers to Correspondents" became a short-lived weekly work standing on its own, under the title *Low Wages*. The readers' letters illustrate not so much the daily practice of literacy[33] but they define what we will call "early sociology", for convenience, as an open cultural artefact.[34] The correspondence surrounded the text of the 1851–2 edition of *London Labour and the London Poor*, the most productive and the most radical years. These letters were a favourite for the readers. They often do not derive from Mayhew's text, but were at the origin of its most interesting features. They are interesting as a distorted reflection of "socio-ethnographic" writing by the readers themselves, by the subject of the enquiry itself. The aims of this edition are to broaden *London Labour and the London Poor*; to provide modern readers with a long missing undertext, with a key to its understanding. No particular knowledge of *LLLP* is needed to understand or use them. This correspondence works as an exchange; it is reflexive and contains internal debates using *London Labour* as a backdrop. Mayhew's complete sociological works are: the *Morning Chronicle* articles, the 1851–2 incomplete books with the following correspondence, the 1856 *Great World of London*, the elements added later by Griffin and Mayhew, and *The Shops of London*, which was the swansong of Mayhew's encyclopaedic ambitions.[35]

This introduction, divided into six parts, analyses different aspects of the letters collected in the second half of this book, without exhausting the rich potential for further research. Chapter one examines the social context of the Fleet Street "scene" at the time preceding the publication of *London Labour and the London Poor*. It is a general introduction to Mayhew, followed by an introduction to the literary underclass of which he was a part, and which provides the backdrop to his publications. The third attempts to tackle the question of authorship in a periodical, engaging with the difficulty in analyzing readerships of the past. The fourth and fifth chapters treat issues debated in these letters. Three major themes emerge from this long correspondence: political economy considered theoretically and practically; questions of philology, linguistic, sociological and moral questions concerning the life of prostitutes and, above all, the possible causes of the "fall" into prostitution. The aspects of philology and prostitution are treated together because they belong, at different levels, to the same contemporary concern with purity and "the order of things".[36]

1

HENRY MAYHEW 1812-1887

Mayhew was born in 1812 into a wealthy London family, one of seventeen children of Joshua Mayhew, of the Mayhew firm of Carey Street.[1] Henry's professional existence crossed with that of some of his brothers at various times in his life: Thomas (1810-1834), a poet and editor of the *Poor Man's Guardian*[2] who, bankrupt after the failure of his popular encyclopaedia, committed suicide in 1834;[3] Edward (1813–1868) wandering actor and dramatist, who became a sports journalist;[4] and three other younger brothers who worked with Henry at different periods: Horace (1816–1872), Augustus[5] (1826–1875) and Julius.

Even among his eccentric brothers, Henry Mayhew managed to be the least stable. In 1827 he ran away from Westminster School in the company of Gilbert Abott A'Beckett. (1811–1856)[6] On his return, his father sent him as a midshipman on an East India Company boat (and not into the Navy as he stated in 1860) bound for Calcutta. Joshua Mayhew, a harsh man from all accounts, expected him to come back dead or disciplined. While Dickens and Martineau modified their biographies in the Griffin's dictionary to minimize the hardship of their youth, Mayhew put emphasis on his rebellion. When he returned from India in 1829, Mayhew became a lowly trainee lawyer in Wales for a brief period. Ill-suited for this career,[7] he then settled as a freelance journalist and *The Thief*, a digest edited with A'Beckett, was his first venture,[8] followed by the comic *Figaro in London* (1833), modelled on Philipon's Parisian *Charivari*. Mayhew initiated the venture but, as was his wont, left most of the work to associates. With A'Beckett again, Mayhew when he was twenty-two years old, managed the Queen's Theatre for a short while.[9] When this failed the two young men fled abroad to escape their creditors.

In 1835 Mayhew found himself vegetating in Paris,[10] in the company of a number of associates, such as John Barnett,[11] and a group of penniless literary talents: Douglas Jerrold (1803–1857) and William Makepeace Thackeray (1811–1863). Thackeray, Mayhew and Jerrold all belonged to the first generation of English Bohemians[12] who started a fashion for migrating to Paris[13] and, ten years later, some of Henry's brothers followed in his footsteps.[14] According to family stories, often our only source, Jerrold himself was in Paris in flight from a ferocious solicitor, Joshua Mayhew. Henry Mayhew took it upon himself to assist Jerrold; he managed to obtain a rescheduling of Jerrold's debts and in doing so secured his friendship.

In the 1850s Augustus Mayhew, G.A. Sala, Tinsley and Vizetelly lived in Paris under Charles Dickens's patronage. These "Bohemians" mostly belonged to the middle class (with a few exceptions such as Mark Lemon, who was the son of a publican, or Thackeray, described as a "gentleman" in the parlance of the day). Their attitudes towards work, politics and money defined a controversial collective identity. They were poor and in debt, borrowing both money and ideas freely from each other. Their field was the common literary production of Fleet and Grub Streets.[15] British Bohemians were mostly journalists struggling in the limited market of the 1830s and 1840s. This group of novelists, radicals and literary young Turks smoked, drank and speculated heavily. The equation between radicalism and bohemianism forged a strong source of identity.[16] In Henry Mayhew's case, his difficult youth and the suicide of his brother Thomas at a young age may have had a bearing on his politics.[17] After his time in Paris, Mayhew was involved in several literary ventures. Two of his plays, *But, However* and the *Wandering Minstrel* were successful, while *Figaro in London* ran short both of money and inspiration. Mayhew and a few friends then launched plans for a new comic weekly to be called *Punch, or the London Charivari*. Comic weeklies offered the only field open to youth and creativity.[18] The combination of *The Times*'s domination over the daily press and the Bohemians' lack of money and prestige limited their opportunities. They seized their chance in the much freer market of the 1850s, the most prominent among them editing or establishing substantial periodicals. Mayhew's *London Labour and the London Poor*, Dickens's *Household Words*, Thackeray's *Cornhill Magazine* and Jerrold's editing of *Lloyd's Weekly London Newspaper* illustrate the achievements of a whole generation.[19]

Punch was an unexpected success,[20] yet, two years later, Mayhew resigned his editorship and ownership in exchange for a trifling sum of money. He had thus sold the rights to his one financially successful venture, while his brother Horace Mayhew stayed on the board of *Punch* until his death and Douglas Jerrold left over a conflict with Thackeray and A'Beckett.[21]

The *Punch* years had been formative and they had given Mayhew the opportunity to meet talented illustrators whom he later employed to work from daguerreotypes on *London Labour and the London Poor*.[22] In 1842, Mayhew and his brothers contributed to Ingram's revolutionary

Illustrated London News. This first illustrated periodical claimed to be "didactic and graphic" even in the text. This constituted a major shake up in Fleet Street journalism. Within a short time, the engravings that appeared in the *Illustrated London News* gradually came to play the role previously established by the broadsheets.[23] The text became less descriptive, the substance of the journalistic language modified with arguments increasingly built on the mechanically reproduced images. Engravings from daguerreotypes complemented this process in the late 1840s. Readers expected realistic illustrations and texts could afford to be more metaphorical and analytical. [C, 102; 134; 159] Unlike the brutal expressionism of the early woodcarvings of the Seven Dials broadsheets, these reproductions "from life" involved a more subtle technique of expression, a blend of artistic convention and innovation. Mayhew made full use of these developments in his weekly *London Labour and the London Poor*.

Once he became financially secure, Mayhew married Douglas Jerrold's eldest daughter, Jane (1825–1880). The marriage had important consequences for his career. She was the origin of his philanthropic interest and passim references suggest that she may have been a source of his social concerns. The "Crippled Street Seller of Nutmeg Graters" [C, 134; 160; 175] always addressed his thanks to her, and later she received prisoners on ticket of leave into her home. She wrote much of Mayhew's work under his dictation.[24] In spite of Mayhew's various activities, however, the couple lived beyond their means and, in 1847, after the failure of his railway periodical, *The Iron Times*, Mayhew was bankrupt.[25] At the same time, his literary production peaked with six new books in three years written with Augustus under the collective name "the Brothers Mayhew". Mayhew's financial troubles caused a rift with Douglas Jerrold that ended in permanent estrangement. Jerrold died in 1857 and Henry was notably absent at the funeral.[26] In his will, Jerrold left £2 a week to Jane Mayhew,[27] and most of his estate to his unmarried daughter, Mathilda. In the 1860s Mayhew initiated an unsuccessful legal pursuit to contest Jerrold's will. Unfortunately for Henry, his brother Horace, the most respectable of the Mayhew brothers, inherited their father's estate.[28] Henry was, then, left to survive on the verge of bankruptcy from 1847 to the end of his life.

After the 1852 failure of *LLLP*, Mayhew, Jane and their two children, Athol and Amy, left for a long, creditor-free trip on the Rhine. They stayed in Germany for most of the following decade. We know virtually nothing of Mayhew's life between 1867 and his death in 1887. In all those years, his output was limited to three miserable attempts at a come-back: when he appeared as a mercenary enquirer for publicans, when co-authoring a play with his son, with a single issue comic periodical, and with a poor collection of sketches and articles in 1881. His exile in Germany began the period during which references in books or in the press to Mayhew are rare.[29] Only a few scenes escape from oblivion: we find him living with his son in London in 1867. Athol, then a professional photographer, begged Professor Owen to assist him.[30] At that time Henry Mayhew still used the British Library although he suffered from rheumatism and could hardly walk.

Mayhew's state of continual bankruptcy was associated less with the romantic Bohemian improvidence of youth than with the dishonesty of an ageing crook. Unlike other prominent Bohemians of the 1840s, about whom secondary Bohemians and biographers were keen to write whole chapters, Henry Mayhew did not manage to turn his talent and his early fame into middle-class respectability and wealth. "By turns sanguine and despondent—now in all the ecstasy of a prospective fortune, and anon down in the dumps of impending bankruptcy—he lacked the even balance of mind that goes to make success last" wrote his son in 1895.[31] *London Labour* in 1852 represented the peak of his fame and intellectual respectability, yet it did not ensure financial stability.

2

THE GENESIS OF
LONDON LABOUR AND THE
LONDON POOR

THE INTELLECTUAL ORIGINS OF *LONDON LABOUR*

Mayhew's life's work was quantitatively important and qualitatively diverse. In common with many bohemians Mayhew was notoriously versatile,[1] a successful wit making, at times, large sums from his humour. Two of his brothers, and particularly Augustus, co-authored many of the more lightweight books with him. Mayhew conceived the ideas and plots while his brothers and wife did most of the writing alone or under his dictation.[2] His restless character meant that he was more eager to launch ventures than to develop them. His interests in the creation of new plots and situations were the literary counterparts of his interest in experimental sciences.[3]

An important phase of thinking on inductive and heuristic pedagogy followed his chemistry experiments of the 1830s. His long pamphlet *What to Teach and How to Teach It*, as well as an article on surprise, rationalized the failures of his own education.[4] His inductive and mind-broadening educative ideas bore the deep scars of his youth and of ill-suited strict schooldays. While Mayhew's theories might appear anecdotal and personal, vaguely following the argument in Rousseau's *Émile*,[5] they provided the structure for his successful novelisations of the youth of such figures as Humphry Davy, Benjamin Franklin and Martin Luther. With regard to education he developed the idea of starting with "natural philosophy" (sciences), graduating to "mental philosophy" (arts and knowledge of the self) and finally to "moral philosophy" which mixed the knowledge of social and divine laws. According to his pedagogic precepts, the practical teaching of these broad themes was through a strictly heuristic awakening of the child's curiosity and memory. Nothing was imposed on the child, all knowledge was imparted by means of induction, so that:

> the mode of education, on means of imparting a knowledge of these subjects, should commit in bringing before the pupil all the most *extraordinary circumstances* connected with the particular fact or truth

13

which the teacher wishes to communicate—leading him to expect a certain result which is conforming with his limited experience—producing some other result which is in direct opposition to that experience—thereby exciting his surprise and wonder, together with his curiosity—and thus creating in him a desire to learn that which the tutor desires to teach.[6]

This philosophy justified his pedagogic novels of the 1850s and was behind his whole output. *London Labour and the London Poor* combined the style of the *Illustrated London News* new journalism with Mayhew's pedagogic theories. The hallmark of this inductive education was the recourse to staged discoveries and laborious, repetitive explanation. Stylistically "that is to say" signalled a pedagogic step-by-step unmasking of the complex vocabulary used. The method of teaching was to expose facts in a dramatized sequence. New words and terms were introduced in a rehearsed sequence, and what appeared to be repetition itself usually contained novel elements. The discrepancy between two sequences was provocative and induced the reader to reconsider his or her previous conclusions. It became a stylistic choice. In his correspondence Mayhew often chose to express his assertions mathematically. He would put a sequence of numerical examples and symbols repeating each other in two different modes.

Mayhew applied his method to various types of marketable literature. Most of his work thus contained an element of surprise and social reform as can be seen in his children's stories or pot-boiling novels, in which these ideas were subtly developed. *The Greatest Plague in Life*, for example, highlighted the middle classes' exploitation of servants.[7]

Mayhew's reflection on literary techniques went further than pure pedagogy. His idealization of literature remained an aspiration and was not consistently evident in the bulk of his prose.

Of all painting, word painting is perhaps the most difficult and subtle. It is worse than 'writing on poster', being indeed a species of drawing in the air—a style of spectral landscape sketching where sounds, ideas and imagination have to do duty for pencil, colours and canvas. It can only attain its ends suggestively—That is to say, by making the reader conjure up in his own mind the image that the author desires to present to it. High-class literary description is, so to speak, a continual series of ghost raising—the excitation of a succession of pictorial opposition; so that a kind of phantom panorama, or visionary drama (according as we are treating of men or places) shall flit before the 'mind's eyes' with all the 'counterfeit presentment' and illusive reality of a dream.

There are three ways, apparently, of describing unknown objects:
(1) by detailing the qualities or circumstances in connection with them;
(2) by comparing them to some known objects; and
(3) by setting forth the effects or feelings produced by them.

The first constitutes, in its literal phase, the cataloguing process, and belongs rather to the plainness of science than to the coloured rhetoric of literature, whilst in its picturesque aspect, it not only approaches the conciseness of logical definition, but in seizing upon the literary 'essence', as it were, or signal peculiarity of an object, discovers the precise point of cognition and re-cognition in connection with it—that is to say, the one particular quality by which it is immediately apprehended in the mind; and thus, instead of clouding the idea with a mass of words, conjures up in the fancy a sudden and vivid image of the thing, scene or character intended. Shakespeare and Milton possessed this picturesque power of description to a wondrous degree.

The second mode of description, or that which conveys an idea of unknown objects by comparing them to known ones, is at once brilliant and striking. The survile, [sic] indeed is essentially a figure of enlighten- ment as well as beauty. Not only is there an exquisite charm in discovering some unexpected resemblance (and this indeed, is the main source of pleasure produced by imitative arts in general), but the very vividness of the 'gay surprise' which is excited by the cunning of the com- parison serves also to intensify the perception of the idea sought to be conveyed, and thus at once to illuminate and colour the text—like a flood of light suddenly let in through some bright painted window.

The last descriptive process, of that which deals with the effects rather than the object itself, is, however, the highest and most artistic of all. This constitutes the mythical and poetic method of representation, conveying a sense of the objects by means of the feeling it inspires. Thus the fields are made to 'smile', the brooks to 'murmur' and the 'jocund morn to stand *tiptoe* on the mighty mountain top', whilst the gladdening and reddening sprint of wine is typified as a youthful god wrapped in a tiger skin and attended by a train of dancing satyrs.

There is, indeed, a high and low style of word painting, as with all the representative forms of art. The literal, or cataloguing method of literary description, hardly ranks as an artistic process any more than pictures of 'still life', or 'railing adventure', or farm-yard symphonies—or any mere- ly initiative rather than species of rendering—can be regarded as aesthetic performances—For as the photograph gives but the *particular* and accidental look of an individual for the mere moment that he is in front of the camera, whilst high class portraiture depicts the *general* expression distinctive of the character of the man, and thus points his very spirit as it were—even so the 'inventory taking' style of literature, which is so popular at the present day, utterly fails in rendering the pic- turesque features and feeling of a scene and a place—the genius loci, as it were—the mythical and unseen spirit, haunting the landscape as the dryad of old were supposed to do, and lighting it up like a soul....The author is well aware how signally he has failed in reaching the standard of excellence he has laid down.[8]

This extract from the preface of one of Mayhew's most ambitious literary works illustrates the literary theories that lie behind most of his earlier writings. Mayhew adopted Platonist theories of representation: his ambition was to convey the *idea* of a character or a place, its eternal essence and not only its appearance. Therefore the concept of "realism" is not useful in analysing Mayhew's work, because, as he pointed out himself, realism was neither aesthetic, nor artistic, nor fundamentally valid as a rhetorical tool. When one experiences the catalogue of characters evoked in Mayhew's prose, one must not forget that Mayhew intends to work the "ghost raising" to the level of an aesthetic experience. In *LLLP*, the ghost rising from his enquiries is that of exploitation. His characterization had an aesthetic as well as a social purpose. All of his writing aimed to provoke sentimental affinities and sympathy. Any typification was above all an idealization and a conceptualization. Mayhew's "characters" condensed the reality around them and perceived reality of their inner nature.[9] Mayhew also wrote that his interviews and his descriptions were a mere reflection of the real. [C, 118] This might appear contradictory to us, yet glancing, for example, at a contemporary portrait of the royal family, one understands well how such portraits drawn from a living model can also reflected the essence of the royal function.

Nineteenth-century readers were actively involved in the moral and sentimental order of representation. [C, 92] Ainsworth or Reynolds' novels abounded with dramatic typification of the inner reality. Readers attempted to identify the *LLLP* illustrations, and the subject of those descriptions themselves occasionally wrote to claim this resemblance. [C, 134; 159] In popular literature there was little fundamental dichotomy between the inner truth and appearances, between behaviour and character.[10] When there was one it was characteristically repulsive and frightening;[11] "girls...who can blush and look as modest as a maid, who are nothing but sly whores." [C, 218–19]

The picturesque was meant to provoke a shock of cognition. The importance Mayhew gave to the picturesque in his scale of aesthetic forms is fundamental to understanding the manner in which he wrote about life in London. The alienation from the situation described and the "colour" of the attitudes, speech and characters were not sufficient on their own to create the conditions of a "vivid mental picture". This style was also the commercial prerequisite to reach a market for this established type of travel literature. Mayhew's views on style, extracted from a book of travel on the Rhine, enable us to reconsider *London Labour and the London Poor* as a form of travel narrative—partially at least. The "discovery" of the unknown had to be framed as a form of heterology, or science of the Other.[12] Though London was not a distant Celebes Island, the reader's position towards the text was the same: [LLLP, 4, 107-108] as the narrative formal types followed ethnological models.[13] Distance was in the eye of the reader, and this distance empowered the reader with a panoptic gaze. Mayhew made a physical experiment of this distance with his balloon observations of London. This rhetoric estranged the readers from a world not so far apart from their own lived experience as we might believe.[14] With readers, often artisans, writing to the journal, this became a self-deluding rhetorical tool, an estrangement to oneself, which, in turn, enabled a form of scientization or objectivization of their existence.[15]

A SHORT HISTORY OF *LONDON LABOUR*

Mayhew's approach was the consequence of the circumstances of the *LLLP*. The *Morning Chronicle* commissioned Mayhew and a few others to assess the nation, to survey and understand the country in the turmoil of the age. A year after the peak of the 1848 Chartist agitation,[16] a social epidemic of political unrest together with an epidemic of cholera, raged in London.[17]

Mayhew was chosen (or volunteered) to enquire into the condition of the working class in London, while Angus Reach (1821–1856), their parliamentary reporter and a *Punch* editor, coordinated the enquiries on rural and industrial England.[18] The *Morning Chronicle* was then a new platform for Peelite ideas uniting Tory defectors, but it was losing money.[19] The editors took the risk of investing large sums to provide their readers with the largest survey of Britain since Chadwick's *Report on the Sanitary Condition of the Labouring Population of Great Britain*, in 1842,[20] and the first private venture of its type. Among all correspondents, Henry Mayhew was quantitatively the most important contributor as well as the most controversial. His articles on circumstantial prostitution among needleworkers shocked readers just as the "song of the shirt" had done earlier in *Punch*. It was through this activism that Mayhew came to share a platform with the Chartists.[21] Perhaps as a result of exchanging ideas with Chartist groups, he became radical in his criticism of employers such as the Nicol Brothers. [C, 94; 109; 116; 153] Unfortunately for Mayhew the Nicols advertised in the *Morning Chronicle* and, having to choose between the two, the journal placed greater value on free trade than on Mayhew's contributions. The editors censored Mayhew's work, publishing substitute articles which opposed his ideas. This conflict ended with Mayhew's departure from the newspaper.

Mayhew's initial aims had been to investigate the new political working class and the infectious corners of the capital, mixing politics and sanitary concerns.[22] In a way, the cholera was a medical equivalent to Chartism in politics; both were monsters reflecting recurrent fears. Yet both were unique: the spread of cholera contradicted miasmatic theories,[23] while Chartism was essentially different from famine riots or "Captain Swing".[24] Mayhew denied that the Chartists belonged to the Dangerous Classes (a then recent French concept prefiguring Marx's *Lumpenproletariat*), yet he rhetorically adopted Frégier's style while uncovering layers of poverty.[25]

Among Christian socialists,[26] interest was expressed in two types of political situation: France post-1848[27] and Mayhew's account of the lower classes in London. Mayhew gave a much needed dramatic dimension to their pessimistic appreciation of the consequences of the Industrial Revolution.[C, 29–134] In Gertrude Himmelfarb's words, Mayhew's readers had, to some extent, a shock not of discovery but of recognition.

Mayhew also reworked older traditions of urban representation. His picture of the street-seller class seems to echo the "Cries of London" from the early eighteenth century.[28] Like Mayhew's classification of street-sellers, the "Cries of London" classifications were according to the product sold. They also depended on appearance and symbolic importance and did not mirror the relative economic importance of London retailers. [C, 155] Mayhew's classes were descriptive and illustrative in the tradition of eighteenth-century natural science.

This eighteenth-century illustrative system of classification[29] accounts for the structural form of the first series of *London Labour and the London Poor* (published independently as two volumes in 1851). Mayhew's task was to create a readership out of nothing. He also had to create a network of retailing. *London Labour and the London Poor*, published every Saturday, was sold in railway stations in London and in the provinces, Ireland included. The latter network of retailing was not very regular and many correspondents complained about delays. Mayhew headed a journalistic venture with an acquired readership different from the inherited readership of the *Morning Chronicle*. Sold in popular instalments (two pennies for the normal text and three when treating prostitution[30]) *London Labour and the London Poor* claimed to be a serious work to be bound at the end of each volume. [C, 119–20; 144; 158; 163] This mode of publication was common and many consequent works of that period were presold as a serial before appearing under hard covers. [C, 120] The first volume, mostly dealing with street-sellers, was the most eye-catching of the three, and probably played the role of an introduction to the rest of the work. The first volume completed, Mayhew started to publish two more volumes simultaneously on alternate weeks. These two volumes were on different but related subjects. The first began as a logical extension of the first volume with yet more street-pedlars. It later contained a survey of the London streets, traffic, pollution and cleansing. [C, 206; 216] The other volume published over the same period began with Mayhew's prospectus and system of social classification in function of work, "Those that work, those that will work, those that cannot work and those that will not work" and a laborious approach to prostitution. This study of prostitution (for more details see chapter 6), was not written by Mayhew himself but by a young ethnographer and author, Horace St. John (1832–1888). His survey of the existing literature covered the history of prostitution since the beginning of mankind on the six continents. During the period August 1851 to February 1852, weekly readers of *London Labour and the London Poor* were presented alternately with a survey either of prostitution abroad or of the London sewers.[31]

To follow such an association and juxtaposition, the reader was faced with darker and more disturbing issues while losing on the local colour that made Volume One such an entertaining book, or even a "charming book" [C, 162] Simultaneously, Henry Mayhew published his thoughts on political economy taken from "Answers to Correspondents", under the title *Low Wages*. Mayhew did not limit his prodigious productivity to *LLLP*. He also wrote articles for various journals, a novel, and several pamphlets. One was an article on the problem of the housing of the poor in Viscount Ingestre's *Melliora*. A committee of London tailors published Mayhew's speeches on the industry and against the closure of Crystal Palace on Sundays.[32] Ranging from philanthropy to the promotion of culture, [C, 118–19] these pamphlets signalled the peak of Mayhew's political activities.[33]

Mayhew was gradually breaking away from his own class, and although he had planned another five years of his work, he had to abandon it before time. [C, 163] Various problems and disputes with his publisher hastened the end of the first edition of *London Labour and the London Poor*;[34] a decline in sales may well have been another contributory factor.[35] Publication ceased in February 1852, with the second volume already completed and the third, on prostitution, interrupted in the middle of a sentence. [C, 39–40]

LONDON LABOUR IN 1851

The 1851 edition is not the only one valid for the reader of Victorian literature, but it is the only one published under Mayhew's sole editorship and control. Later editions were certainly also widely read but not by the same people and not in the same way. The difference in price between the cheap editions of 1851, or even 1865, and the edition of 1861 and 1862 in hardcover volumes was significant. Moreover, reading *LLLP* as a serial, published over two years, was quite different from reading a bound, multi-volume book. The serial required less effort and had greater impact. The intertwining of lived experience and reading taking place over a two-year assiduous, but interrupted, weekly reading cannot be compared with reading an easily discarded tedious text. The serial format spread an often difficult text over time and imposed a rhythm on the reading; it also built up expectations and momentum.[36] The correspondence reflects strongly this attentive and expectant way of reading. The greatest attraction of *LLLP* was its potential, the sense of anticipation it created.

In Mayhew's 1851 environment, *LLLP* was considered a novelty and a dramatic masterpiece. Many Bohemians worked on it. The Mayhew workshop counted about a dozen of them and friends dropped by while work was in progress. This was a collective effort under Henry's direction. In turn there was a collective appropriation of Mayhew's work. Augustus wrote a novel inspired by it, *Paved with Gold*, which was later turned into a melodrama. Charles Dickens certainly used some details of Mayhew's work in the writing of *Our Mutual Friend*. Reynolds, Ludlow, Kingsley and Beames all borrowed from Mayhew and occasionally advertised on his covers.[37] William Thackeray and Douglas Jerrold advertised *LLLP* as a masterpiece, "more romantic than any romance". With its approximately 400 "verbatim" interviews, *London Labour and the London Poor* was a vast source of quotations, a dictionary of street language usable for other forms of dramatization.[C, 157–8] Mayhew's peers regarded the work as a modern drama and a source of literary inspiration. A melodrama entitled *The London Labour and the London Poor* appeared on stage four years after the end of the series, revealing the long-term influence the book had on representations of urban life in the 1850s. The play, set in a cheap lodging-house kitchen described in *LLLP* [LLLP, 1, 250], contrasted a suffering mother with her persecutors from the New Poor Law administration.[38] The people who often went to cheap theatres, particularly the costermongers, were the very people depicted in the play. Mayhew did not provide the plot of the play but its mode of expression, the details of the setting and many constitutive elements of the pathos. This play was not created for a middle-class audience willing to learn about poverty, but for a large East End theatre where, for the price of a few pennies each, several hundreds of working men and women piled in to see the show. [C, 91] As in all melodrama the play comprised a conflict of good and evil, a universal message but, beyond this, there was a strong political element —a depiction of the class struggle.[39] The mass of the people, as portrayed in *LLLP*, clearly sympathized with the heroine. While there was a strong element of self-definition through middle-class eyes, Mayhew only reflected the image they had chosen. He was the medium through which the people could see themselves represented but through this process he modified and altered the very words and terms of that self-representation. The melodrama of *London Labour and the*

London Poor was a distorted mirror of working-class reality with a clear political agenda. Working-class readers of *LLLP* knew the book for what it was: a struggle and a drama.

CONCLUSION: THE PATHOS OF A MELO-SURVEY

Out of the structure of the classification, often the juxtaposition of several complementary interviews, the character of a London type developed. Mayhew was constantly constructing generalizations because they empowered his heuristic pedagogy with a more general pathos. [C, 121–2] The drama of the people appealed more than individual fate. In reading Mayhew's work at the end of the twentieth century we lack the contexts of the work existing at the time, and these are difficult to re-create. The media dimension of the work is difficult to evaluate: how much of this information was new or surprising to the reader? How much was scandalous or unacceptable?[39] How much was even too difficult to believe?

In the context of the time, *London Labour and the London Poor* embodied a polemical dimension hard to appreciate for the modern reader, since it is easy to view the book as uni-dimensional. London in 1851 is at least as distant as the Celebes Islands are now to the average British reader. Was it to the 1851 readers? Did they have the feeling that they were reading a comprehensive and analytical work in the making or was this dimension entirely obscured by anecdotal stories? These few questions end this chapter, which represents a simple introduction to Mayhew's work and conditions of production. Correspondents and author shared a project of interactive communication. It is perhaps a surprise to see that, as in ancient philosophy, a type of science, a sort of "sociology", was born through the dialogue of two entities: the author, master and teacher, the correspondent, pupil and rebel disciple. Of this process only one thing has survived and it is the result of a Socratian intercourse, the delivery of a collective soul: *London Labour and the London Poor*.

3

OPEN LETTERS

MAYHEW AND HIS CORRESPONDENTS

Letter-writing is one of the least studied fields of common literacy in the nineteenth century. Roger Chartier's recently edited study stands almost alone as an anthropological analysis of the most common types of letter-writing in nineteenth-century France. This study is nevertheless fragmentary; it relies mostly on manuals, samples of letters collected for their stamp value by the French post office, and the 1847 survey of the post in rural France.[1] However, the quantitative methods and techniques used by Chartier's team are unfortunately not very useful here where we examine the epistolary documents which make up the second half of this book. These letters were not for the most part private but they often formed a short, complete correspondence which was printed in *LLLP* as a periodical.

Letters to periodicals are not part of common epistolary practice. They form a unique activity in their own right but have not yet been the subject of much academic study.[2] This is somewhat curious since writing to periodicals has always been (and remains) a popular pastime. This kind of letter is the result of a specific literary effort, [C, 122] which can be analyzed according to the author's intention. Who wrote to a periodical, particularly to a periodical like *London Labour and the London Poor*? From initial identification we can establish a general pattern for this type of letter-writing, at least in the limited context of 1850–1852. A quick look at the various, clearly identified trades and professions shatters several myths instantly, for Mayhew's readership was diverse and contradictory. If we believed in the idea that letter-writing was a practice only adopted by those who clearly mastered literacy, or that others suffered from a block or were ashamed of their difficulties in communication, we are at once proven wrong. A semi-literate pauper, like the poor harp player, managed to send or to bring his petitions to Mayhew's office, [C, 199] for, if London correspondents could not afford the penny post stamp, they could always bring the letter

22

personally to the office. There, Mayhew kept his books and records of the received monies and evidence open to any inquirer. [C, 164–6] Among the correspondents, we also find a letter from the two poor needleworkers whom Mayhew had used for his article on circumstantial prostitution. [C, 88] In each case the semi-literate correspondents' letters were reproduced in their original spelling that supposedly validated their authenticity.[3]

We could close the debate here on the authenticity of the letters sent to Mayhew. It seems unlikely that Mayhew himself had to write parts or the whole of letters reproduced in his "Answers to Correspondents". Forging letters to create another platform for the editors' ideas was (is) perhaps a common trick among editorial boards, but in Mayhew's case there was a certain lack of motive.[4] Some readers' queries and letters, mostly the ones reproduced in their entirety, argued against Mayhew and sometimes with no less logic and forcefulness than Mayhew's answers. Mayhew himself considered readers' forgeries possible and misidentified two readers as the same individual. [C, 175] Yet, after examination, Mayhew's suspicions seem to have been unjustified. There is no proof of forgery as such; hence, this correspondence is examined as if there were none.[5]

The diversity of the readership presents a difficulty. Mayhew did answer, however briefly, every letter addressed to him. These answers often took less than a sentence and did not take up any of the correspondents' arguments. We are therefore left with replies such as "yes, in 1828", with nothing to indicate the correspondents' identity in the periodical itself. We have to judge Mayhew's readership from a sample edited by Mayhew himself. [C, 160] The rule of Mayhew's editing, emphasising the content more than the social origin of the writer, still enables us to hope for a fairly representative sample. Yet if we return to our initial concern about the "uses of literacy", the degree of education and therefore the social origin of the correspondent would have dictated a logical order familiar to middle-class readers. This is an unavoidable interpretative vicious circle: the editor selected what he could best comprehend. This certainly modified the representativeness of our "sample".

In general, Mayhew's active readership (those who wrote letters) mainly comprised working-class and lower-middle-class men and women. Within that group, however, women writers are in a minority, along class lines. Whereas the middle-class woman may have read *LLLP* as a quaint text and wrote out of curiosity, the governess and the street-seller have a clearer purpose in writing. We also find many "collective" readers, for example members of the model lodging house library, unions and societies,[6] who often corresponded through their president. [C, 147] We find the educated artisan, [C, 120] some small masters, [C, 91–2] and some impoverished working-class people such as the needlewomen. Among educated employees (are they working-class?), most of whom considered themselves as part of a larger entity, the "London Labouring classes" are clerks, shopkeepers, the governess. [C, 93][7] Among the lower-middle classes we find the socially involved Anglican lower clergy, [C, 119][8] and the educated specialists of "political economy" collecting statistics.[9] We also find the wealthy officer writing to defend the morality of army officers in general. There is no evidence that most of the readers enjoyed a large income. Neither is there any evidence that readers (apart from one exception) had followed the previous series in the *Morning Chronicle*, rather the opposite. Readers often enquired whether a topic in which they were interested had previously appeared in the newspaper. [C, 92] On the other hand, we do have some evidence that most readers were new readers. They came into contact with Mayhew's work from his prospectus, [C, 103; 179] from an accidental purchase at the station, or from hearsay.[10] The letter-writers were generally in control of their craft. Only a few examples reflect a poor mastering of literacy. Among the better skilled, there was the working-class poet dying in misery [C, 156; 158–9] or the literary society of coal whippers. [C, 95–7][11] Indeed, the level of literacy in most letters approached Mayhew's own. Later in this chapter, we will consider the various modes of correspondence practised in "Answers to Correspondents" in *LLLP*.

What was the purpose of this correspondence? What were Mayhew's aims in publishing these open letters? Was the practice common in that kind of work? Dickens did not publish letters in *The Pickwick Papers* nor in any of his other serialized works. Who were the readers? What role did such correspondence play in their lives? What was the fundamental value of such an exchange of ideas and information? The "Notice to Correspondents" was published at the readers' request. *London Labour and the London Poor* was only in its infancy when readers asked Mayhew to answer their letters publicly, thus he created the notice printed on wrappers. [C, 87] These new protective covers provided a title page and space for advertising and the "Answers to Correspondents". The latter originally occupied spare space among the few advertisements but soon took up most of the available room. To control this invasion, Mayhew tried to apply certain rules regarding the correspondence. [C, 89–90; 217] He attempted to impose various prerequisites for publication. Mayhew tried to establish the correspondence as a collaboration in which the readers played an ancillary part sending statistics, facts and information. To some extent, letter-writing became a form of extended self-help. Readers were supposed to share their experiences with the author or another reader. [C, 89–90] Mayhew only wanted to enlarge his team. However, the author's wishes do not necessarily coincide with those of the reader.

From the beginning the author and the readers had different aims. Mayhew understood the "Notices" as a platform for information while most of the readers viewed it as an opportunity to air calls for justice [C, 144; 155–6], ideas, debates [C, 154; 215–16; 242] and denunciations [C, 186; 210–11; 246] inspired by the facts which formied the core text. These letters asked fundamental questions of an abstract order regarding Mayhew's methods and techniques, and while Mayhew saw the correspondence as an appendix to his own work, readers and correspondents used it to contradict, complement, correct, suggest and modify this work. Soon letters became more engaged in their own debates; they became exchanges referring less and less to the core text and more to the previous correspondence. [C, 106–8; 128–9] The debate focused on Mayhew's answers and concentrated less on the "facts" collected in *LLLP*. Readers also showed a growing interest in "Answers to Correspondents" and its preservation for posterity. [C, 119; 157] Mayhew had mixed feelings about the correspondence and downplayed its importance, while using it as source material for *Low Wages*, his theoretical approach to political economy [C, 119] or even in the text of *LLLP*. [LLLP, 2, 222]

Readers requested and soon obtained more continuity in the publication of the letters, and greater prominence. They wished to have them printed separately so that they could be bound at the end of the volume, not forming an insignificant wrapper but as a meaningful part of the work. [C, 121; 173] The binding was left to the initiative of the readers. Significantly, the three remaining examples of the work used as the source of the text of this book were differently bound. The British Library copy contained a selection of "Answers". The one at the Bibliothèque Nationale in Paris contained the answers selectively cut away from advertisements and title pages. Meanwhile, the Guildhall's library copy was bound with the title pages, and advertisements! None of these three copies contained the complete text.

This relation to the printed text is interesting. The readers (here conservationists of the above libraries) exerted an editorial choice on the material. Mayhew structured the debates and edited readers' letters and occasionally intervened using brackets within a reader's letter. [C, 102] In other cases, he undertook to find other correspondents wishing to answer a letter to which he did not feel qualified to respond. The "Notice" thus became an autonomous platform, almost independent from *London Labour and the London Poor*. Its role as a complementary text justifies its separate publication in this book.

"Answers to Correspondents" formed an enjoyable part of Mayhew's sociology. Readers valued the short texts and the liveliness of the opinions expressed. For the modern reader it is necessary to understand the material circumstances of reading *LLLP* in 1851. In the weekly, the "Answers to Correspondents" framed the text, providing the subtext that clarified the underlying theories of *London Labour* and opening them up for public debate. Yet even the most violent opponent of Mayhew's ideas never sought to deny him mastery of the main narrative, the one between the covers. Critiques addressed to Mayhew-correspondent were not addressed to Mayhew-author. [C, 171; 185; 215] The two entities were dissociated.[12] Umberto Eco's notions of open and closed texts seem to apply quite well to Mayhew's text: the main text, *London Labour and the London Poor*, was too complex and diverse to be analyzed comprehensively and criticized by the readers. Meanwhile the more specific, closed texts, coming in answer to the readers' enquiries, were more accessible and reducible. *LLLP* was therefore a text with two dimensions: one open and one closed to analysis. Following Eco's paradoxical definition, it was the open text, the more diverse in inspiration, which was less accessible, while the closed text, dealing specifically with only one issue at a time, was the one which authorized an equal relationship with the author.[13] The whole literary status of *London Labour and the London Poor* was therefore defined through this paradoxical dual writing. Mayhew as a writer was respected, while Mayhew as a thinker was contested. This was the dynamic of this early sociology firmly anchored in literature and journalism.

Mayhew was aware of this ambivalence and, in the first stages of the correspondence, signalled his status through the exclusive use of capital letters for his own name. Later he alternated lower and upper case according to whether he wrote as a correspondent, as the author or just as the editor of the notice, occasionally using initials, like his readers. [C, 88; 173; 229]

On the other hand, suggestions were often addressed to the social explorer. These exhortations were associated with a call to the author to investigate the class of the correspondent himself. So we find the draper asking Mayhew to probe his own class, and the clerk asking when Mayhew will expose the conditions of life common among the underpaid clerks of the city. [C, 100; 154; 179] In short, the correspondence turned into a call for public attention. This added another dimension to *London Labour and the London Poor*. The core text was a way of bringing to light subjects known within one's class but not to another's. Mayhew, in the correspondence at least, re-created the universal project of the *Morning Chronicle* articles, not wishing to limit his enquiries to marginal groups of paupers. [C, 190] He intended to become the mediator of information within and throughout the working class. His information travelled horizontally within the class structure and not vertically anymore. [C, 174] His universal project was revived, but with a different purpose. The *Morning Chronicle's* readership had been mainly composed of the well-to-do. In E.P. Thompson's words, Mayhew's early articles revealed poverty to the middle class. In the penny weekly, Mayhew built links between isolated groups and pointed out parallels among the living and working conditions of different groups, a form of class consciousness. [C, 89–90] Because he had this role, Mayhew represented more to his correspondents than being merely a 'travel' writer, as described above. The role of mediator was thrust upon him—he did not actively seek it. He did not fulfil his universal programme either. Meanings were attributed to *London Labour and the London Poor* throughout the correspondence. These meanings reveal themselves only if we approach the act of reading a text, as innovative which this one was, and as a consciousness-raising experience. The communication between the author and his readers was an active way of "belonging" to a community: belonging to the object of the investigation, to the subject of the investigation. In Saussure's famous triangle, readers became "signifier" contributing to "signifying" while they were actually the "signified".[14] The terms of a correspondence being based at least on the recognition of each other's identity, if not on equality, the act of writing a letter to a magazine was a way of constructing and defending one's identity *vis-à-vis* the author and the wide community of readers.

The modes of communication varied enormously according to the recipient of these letters. Readers sometimes addressed their letters to Mayhew alone, building intimate and privileged links with the creator of this all-encompassing narrative. We only know the content of these letters through fragmentary answers. This privileged mode of correspondence was private. Mayhew himself answered some of these letters or gave short, printed answers, unintelligible without the correspondent's query.

Considering Mayhew's project—to write the history of the people in their own words—this almost intimate correspondence involved a great deal more than the simple exchange of news between people who know each other, as letters usually are. To write to the creator of such a wide-ranging history of "ourselves", was to venture into history in the making. Unlike most journalistic forays, Mayhew's project was historical, a fact of which he was conscious. His perspective was also, perhaps unwittingly, reforming most ideas of history. It negated the dogma of progress, the study of changes or any form of teleological anticipation. Mayhew was writing a text that presented itself as an ideological slice of reality, as the transcription of the real fixed in a-temporal immediacy. What was then good historical practice: distance from the subject, work on archives, the choice of a political chronology, was not part of Mayhew's project. He wrote history without chronology, history that did not stretch further than human memory, history that virtually ignored politics and favoured economics. In this "imitation" of daily life, so much like daily life synthesized, the reader had the unique opportunity of entering by way of a letter. The letter framed this intervention.

The intervention grew more powerful when the letter was addressed to Mayhew by name, and, through him, to all the readers. [C, 97–8; 209–10] For a reader-writer it was a rare opportunity to enter posterity and the possibility of being published in such a widely distributed magazine was a powerful incentive to writing a letter. Cast in the role of the severe critic or of the working-class economist, the reader-writer was an individual author editing his copy [C, 196] and part of Mayhew's narrative. Even if "Answers to Correspondents" were only framing—metaphorically and physically—the text of *London Labour and the London Poor*, it was still (at least for the 1850s readers) part of it.

This intervention worked in several ways. It could be part of a communication with a fellow reader-writer on Mayhew's platform but without Mayhew himself. The tone could be of a counter-critic: the second reader-writer applying the same methods the first had used. The letter could be a pamphlet. [C, 94; 107–8; 206–8] Like a fully developed correspondence, there could be a philosophical conversation, or a narrative reminiscent of epistolary novels. Readers apologized for their poor style, their lack of knowledge or manners, while immediately contradicting these apologies by a demonstration of superior literary proficiency of encyclopaedic or sophisticated writing which was particularly significant in the philological debates of the notice. These letters established themselves as useful lessons. They assumed a *de facto* equality between Mayhew and his readers. [C, 197] If *LLLP* were a piece of research on life and the world, then the researcher needed enlightening on facets he could not have known about, since they were outside his experience. [C, 120–2]

Many letters were actually constructed as eyewitness accounts, like a journal or diary, which might form the basis of an autobiography. "My life was a street showman, from an early age having a crippled arm." The distance between the narrator and the subject, "my life was" extended his experience to that of a whole group, becoming more than a biographical sketch. [C, 122] Many works written on working-class journals and autobiographies have shown how the authors of those texts felt about being read by others, how they assumed external and posthumous readings. These works also demonstrate how writing could become an exercise in political consciousness. Structuring the narrative of one's life implied the realization of a class *fatum* or the consciousness of a collective, be it professional or gendered, political history.[15]

Mayhew had called for journals, or at least for their outline: account books. [C, 89–90; 226–7] If Chartier is right, the practice of the journal dates from the early ages of literacy. Each literate family kept a book of events, credits, debits, birth and deaths. From Pepys to Harriet Martineau, journal writers have gradually dissociated those activities into different forms of literature. The gap widened between distinct genres: the accounts were separate from the journal itself and, while the administration took charge of most of the registrations, public events became the bread and butter of the press. Those activities seemed increasingly gendered within the family unit: to men the books of account, to women the journals. Of course such a dichotomy is but an illusion. Poor needlewomen kept accounts books while many working men kept their journals carefully up to date. [C, 88]

Mayhew focused more on economics than on feelings and mediated reality. He wanted another sort of material than the type he could gather from interviews. Taking the account books, Mayhew read into them most of the details of a life and reconstituted an existence from them. Gathered in the form of statistics, the details would acquire a scientific and aesthetic dimension, a sense of collectiveness. The authority and the beauty of a statistical table matched its evocative power. Mayhew trusted these carefully kept columns of numbers, a journal would even be redundant. Yet, he gave careful attention to the circumstances in which they were created and often wished to make the books of accounts more specific. [C, 193–5; 208–9; 228] Details of an individual's "productivity", conditions of work and practices had to be added. The individual circumstances had to be expressed with the tools used to judge large quantities. Mayhew sought to establish detailed statistics rather than to make generalisations.

Readers sent their books to Mayhew. They also sent statistics which already formed several individual account books. These were collective biographies. [C, 184] The role of "Answers to Correspondents" was, once more, to provide a platform for this exposition of collective life stories, often through the deliberate use of reiterated and repetitive collective biographies. In 1850 when Mayhew attempted to unionize the young thieves of London and thus redeem them collectively, he invited them to speak on the platform, one after the other. [MCS, vol. 1, 418/ C, 195] He let them understand "in their own words", through the similarities of their unfortunate experiences that they shared enough to form a mutual-help society, while he sat quietly through most of the meeting. This collective catharsis gave a structure to chunks of *LLLP* and to his notice to correspondents. Because *London Labour* was supposedly "in their own words", the reader-subject had a right to authorship. This also illustrates the meaning of the gifts and books sent to Mayhew. Some readers wanted to add other printed material. [C, 88] Others tried to promote themselves as independent writers, [C, 97–8] which gives another dimension to letter-writing.

Some letters effectively begged help from Mayhew and other readers who might offer the help required. [C, 119] Some, such as the poor harp player, used their temporary fame to sell their services to the public. When dealing with gifts of money, Mayhew refused to be the "alms provider" and left the task to his publisher. [C, 92] He thus avoided being branded a philanthropist and repeating the mistake he had made by distributing £800 when he worked for the *Morning Chronicle*. [C, 164] Mayhew selected letters from the "deserving poor" (in the "New Poor Law" meaning of the words) who could not work. The column thus had alternate purposes as an employment agency, a loan office or a charity. Through these materialist letters, "Answers to Correspondents" affected the text itself: *London Labour and the London Poor* also had an implicit political agenda. Its appeal lay as a literature of reform, sometimes of combat, animated by the author-reader pamphleteers. The sub-text enabled readers to intervene and help, to provide comfort or to change the fate of the characters of the core text. History was there, the techniques of sociology were there, and the author mediated social answers. Mayhew had addressed society with a description of poverty that his readers took to heart to change. [C, 134] He did not mediate sums of money like an indiscriminate charity but according to his own version of self-help.

"Answers to Correspondents" thus became a channel for social reform and "philanthropy". The choice was the readers'. Mayhew himself was not a philanthropist. He shared to a certain extent the Benthamite creed of "lesser eligibility" practised in workhouses [C, 92] and refused to see in seasonal charity (winter kitchens) [C, 102] an answer to structural difficulties in society.[16] He believed in individual enterprise. This Liberal view justified his loan fund at 5 per cent interest, paying 3 or 4 per cent to shareholders,[17] which meant that the "Answers to Correspondents" gradually acquired an economic and social dimension. This primitive associative banking went in the direction of sophisticated forms of mutual sick-fund societies developed during the period. [C, 92; 101–2; 158; 164–6; 171]

Economic initiatives taking place in the correspondence gave a practical dimension to *LLLP*. *London Labour and the London Poor* became a book of information, advice and news: the undeclared programme of Mayhew's readers. Historians ignored these aspects because the "Answers to Correspondents" sub-text was not available and because they accepted Mayhew's declared intentions on historical writing too literally. They unequivocally reduced *LLLP* to a fine example of middle-class representation of the poor, not perceiving that readers might appropriate the text differently. When Mayhew awarded them the space for personal expression, he authorized, perhaps for commercial reasons, this shift of focus. Although editing the letters, the control he exercized over this creative process was limited. Notably, he authorized the inclusion of some characters who gave the "human" and sentimental weight to his text on the London paupers. The readers' sentimental intervention contrasted with the sometimes brutal rhetoric of *LLLP*, and the materiality of the lives he described gave weight to his understanding of pauperization. Readers went behind the curtain of literature, to verify the content of the book and modify it, thus leaving the text on its own. Readers wanting to rescue the little watercress girl from an unbearable fate of vice, melodramatized the girl who had no childhood.[18] [C, 92] Immediately following the readers' help, the watercress girl might not be a watercress girl any more and Mayhew's literature alone rescued her from oblivion. The text was not reflecting anything anymore. Like an ethnologist who comes with all his or her cultural apparatus to observe and to hasten the last days of a civilization, Mayhew modified what he saw. His enquiry modified the condition of the enquired. It became history in the making since the "historian's gaze" was, like Medusa's gaze, petrifying life into literature.

CONCLUSION: THE TERMS OF LITERATURE

Literature of combat, sentimental literature, reformist and polemical literature, *London Labour and the London Poor* encompassed all these factors. Yet, only the readers' letters gave it a theoretical edge, a sharp social and critical facet, confirming its practical and journalistic dimension. These letters and their various impacts on the writing of the book also explain the commercial argument of *London Labour and the London Poor*. It provided slices of serious literature, without the moral slant of novels, in a journalistic format. In this shape it contained, through the letters, a series of improvised essays and announcements on practical action and help. The simple "sociology" was a complex piece of literature and served complex purposes.[19] The combination of literature, journalism, and socio-history helped the readers to reflect on their lives. The pedagogic "Answers to Correspondents" fitted with Mayhew's ideological educational concepts: the surprise of the text was followed by the reader's curiosity and the teacher's explanation and new problems. Yet, more than that, it led Mayhew to consider further what he would perhaps have only stated as evidence. His answers to confrontational queries took on such vivid importance to their author that he soon felt confident enough to publish his own contribution in *Low Wages*. In the correspondence, we find his theories in their infancy.

More than simple intercommunication, *LLLP* formed a true interaction between inquirer and inquiry, taking place publicly through the medium of the press. It provided a platform for a unique experiment of reflective social investigation and the creation of a conceptual framework to take place simultaneously within one periodical. Though London was the principal subject, the correspondence represented a sample of all humanity. When readers communicated their experience of Edinburgh, Glasgow or Stockport, they undermined the specificity of London, thereby also reinforcing the universality of the text. [C, 121–2; 157]

The book was a global project based around the consent and participation of all the readers, all the purchasers. It was only possible with their help: help in founding the work, help in advertising it, help in conceptualising it and eventually help in creating it. The readership *was* the book. Mayhew achieved fame as a literary man but only his specific and paradoxical relations with his readers gave his work a sociological dimension. His dual identity, that of thinker and sociologist, was the subject of debate and dependent on the readership's views. Mayhew as a writer pre-dated *London Labour and the London Poor* while Mayhew as a thinker only existed within "Answers to Correspondents". These letters were the sole foundation of his intellectual endeavours, and it was the readers' expectations which anticipated future developments. With such a fragile intellectual, social and financial basis, the sociological exploration was carried out by putting a mirror up to society. It had to please, to follow the path taken by the readers' mind; to fulfil their expectations or to disappear.

4

CRACKING THE HARD NUTS

POPULAR POLITICAL ECONOMY

When considering the broad readership of *LLLP*, the emphasis on political economy—often in technical language—calls for analysis. Political economy traditionally belongs to what many have called élite culture. In the first half of the nineteenth century, political economy was considered the modern and predictive science *par excellence*.[1] It structured the knowledge of the present economic progress and that of the future. Quintessentially a product of the industrial revolution, political economy outgrew its historical origins to become a system of concepts akin to natural laws or natural sciences.[2] [C, 172] Retrospectively, political economy also became one of the favourite intellectual tools of historians.

In its early nineteenth-century phase, the political economy of crisis had Malthusian implications. Smith, Ricardo, Mill and Babbage's works had achieved canonical importance, penetrating the press and parliamentary debates. Economic forecasters reiterated the hypotheses and principles of these theorists, and cited their examples in a confidence-building litany.[3] The popularization of classical political economy was fundamental to the establishment of its respectability. People like Harriet Martineau undertook to explain to the workers themselves the complex systems that operated around them showing how they provided them with work, food and clothes, or deprived them of all these things.[4] The methods used to assert the authority of political economic argument were almost worthy of a religious mission, a characteristic Mayhew was keen to denounce. [C, 95–6]

The works of Samuel Smiles first appeared and gained popularity in the 1850s.[5] Although also read by the poor, there is a huge epistemological gap between Smiles's work of the 1850s, which fitted perfectly with the orthodoxy and the earlier popular economy formulated in the 1830s as an open revolt against classical economy. "The Popular Science", as Noel Thompson calls it, was dying with

Chartism and could no longer present a coherent alternative to political economy.[6] In Mayhew's correspondence, the nature of political economy was one of the main subjects debated. It was in this area that the reflexive debate between reader-subject and author-analyst became a conflict. Two poles of popular political economy faced each other: orthodox political economy and Mayhew's Utopian sociological and reformist agenda. Mayhew owed his denunciations of the arbitrary causes of poverty to Chartist popular economy. He also pointed out the inconsistencies of the old Poor Law such as the custom of paying agricultural labourers according to their family circumstances. This approach transgressed intellectual and social boundaries and struck a raw nerve. He went even further when he hailed the trade unions as saviours of the nation in the unfair class "scramble". "Assuredly if it were not for the trade societies, the country would have been destroyed by the greed of the capitalists long ago." [C, 205]

Mayhew made his plea for social equality mainly by challenging the main contradiction within orthodox political economy, the hardest nut of post-Ricardian political economy: the conceptualization of the value of labour and the relations between employer and employee. [C, 125–8]

Henry Mayhew's thinking did not belong to the classic literature of popularized political economy but appealed to people who had some knowledge of the alternative political economy of the 1830s. Many of his statistics actually dated from that period and reflected earlier debates on the value of wages. It was also reminiscent of Christian economics of the first half of the century.[7]

It is not surprising in the atmosphere of the late 1840s, overheated with political and social problems, that Mayhew turned to concepts and ideas developed a decade earlier in almost similar circumstances. He returned to a moral evaluation of the value of labour. He posited justice and fair reward for skilled labour against the brutalization associated with machinery, unregulated competition and sweatshops.[8] He wished "to make the public aware of the infamies that can be practised upon the labourer when the trader is allowed to use him as his own brutalizing love of gain may dictate". [C, 97] The years following the repeal of the Corn Laws and the opening to free trade were a triumph for free-trade policies and doctrines. Prominent propaganda enterprises such as the Anti-Corn Laws League had established political economy as a paradigm of basic education. The movement reflected northern interests, free trade being thought to be of most benefit to large factories and powerful industries. London industries faced a crisis different from the one afflicting handloom weavers.[9] Their crisis was not machinery-related but the consequence of sheer exploitation. "The more work there is to do the less the workpeople will get for it." [C, 127] The long declining silkweaving, tailoring or cabinet-making industries first suffered from foreign competition and sweatshops, and only subsequently from the introduction of machinery. Mayhew's foremost experience was of London's sweatshops not of Manchester's manufactures. Yet Mayhew could not avoid thinking that machinery was the cause of a "global crisis". The "global" crisis was an extrapolation from his London enquiry, but his explanations were in contradiction to his own observations. [C, 115; 125–34; 153; 161–2; 167–9]

Mayhew witnessed an economic decline in many artisan trades that was not the result of surplus production. In cabinet-making he could argue that lower salaries paid for the purchase of raw materials but the expansion of the textile industry was technology based.[10] There was therefore a double tension in his text: a tension between his own experience and global changes in British industrial production and a tension within his own approach to political economy.

As Karel Williams has pointed out, Mayhew's economic theories were those of an outsider in the context of traditional economic thinking. Mayhew's economic ideas as articulated in the correspondence were formulated within the framework of classification elaborated in the theoretical part of London Labour and the London Poor itself. His first problem was to assess society in relation to production. In 1850 natural science classifications had not yet spread to the social sciences.[11] Mayhew needed an intellectual tool of the kind used to classify a world of commodities at the Universal Exhibition of 1851. [LLLP, Vol. 4, 6] Facing a mass of incomplete data, he wished to classify in order to describe, to organize in order to prove, to invent in order to understand. Few models were available, save Villefosse in Babbage; [C, 111; 141–3] Prince Albert's system absurdly separated materials according to the amount of work that each one required; hence steel was described as "raw material" and leather as manufactured. The 1841 Irish and English census methods were also imprecise and unsystematic.[12] Mayhew was seeking an operational system encompassing the whole of society. It also had to be a moral system, incorporating the value of work in order to establish a moral hierarchy. He seems to have used Utilitarian precepts only to invest them with a moral significance.[13] Mayhew did not classify society according to wealth, utility, or the physical nature of work but on the amount of creativity involved: a worker could be creative or parasitic. His original norm differentiated between the workers and the idle, and among the idle between "those who will, will not or cannot work". Among the producers, his system then categorized separately those who extract, produce, or improve. Distributors and consumers stood apart.

In parallel to this physiocratic system, [C, 150–1] Mayhew had established a moral pyramid at the top of which were people working for the improvement of humanity.[14] The superior class (N, III) contained religious clergies (Anglican, Nonconformist and Catholic—in that order), educators, and medical practitioners. Below were the producers, artists, "extractors" (miners, fishermen) or workers (artisans and industrial labourers). Under them were the ancillary classes helping to oil the wheels of society, the "Auxiliaries", that is, all those who made a profit from the work of others by developing, financing or distributing their production. The lowest category, the servant class, contained the entertainers, the army, lawyers, politicians, Queen and house servants.

This frequently cited classification served several purposes in Mayhew's view of society.[15] It first appeared in his prospectus prior to the periodical of 1851, to be reprinted later in *LLLP*, [Vol. III, 1851] and Mayhew always emphasized its ideological importance. It rearranged the moral order of society. The emphasis was on the role of producers in a familiar religious order of merit. Finally, Mayhew attempted to forge a solidarity of class between himself and working people that would not have existed were his pyramid based on wealth. [C, 112–13] This was perhaps also a lucid statement on his own inability to make a stable, middle-class living. The concept of "fair shares" follows on from Mayhew's system of division.[16] Yet while this system was used to justify a moral stance, Mayhew's own sociological practice made classifications according to trade, and had only loose connections with this ideological scaffolding. [17]

THE SCRAMBLE FOR LOW WAGES

Mayhew contrasted his idealization of merits with actual rewards and examined the question of social injustice. He used the word "scramble" to describe the negotiation of wages between employers and employees. [C, 197–9] While he has an almost Marxist approach to class relations and labour, he also differed substantially from Marx.

Mayhew's fundamental assumption was that all profit was the result of skilled work applied to materials. In this view the allocation of wealth was simply unfair and to be corrected. Labour—although occasionally presented as evil—was not regarded as dehumanizing. The model of society that Mayhew adopted was one of individual exploitation. [C, 110–12; 115–16] Even though he studied what Marx qualified as the *Lumpenproletariat*, he never identified the underpaid workers as class enemies. He perceived the fluidity of their economic situation and clearly refused to analyze class relations within a purely political framework. Mayhew did not write about April 1848; he did not have his Eighteenth Brumaire.[18] He nevertheless understood the paradoxes of

36

this productive exploitation as it created underconsumption and necessarily a crisis. Workers made more for less but could, in turn, buy less of the expanding mass of commodities. "We have made up more commodities than the great mass of the people have the means of purchasing and thus produced, at one and the same time more and more clothing, and more and more nakedness—too many shoes, and too many bare feet—too many shirts and too many shirtless." [C, 136] While he idealized surplus value and somewhat overestimated the consequences of profit on wages, he clearly recognized the dangers of an underconsuming mass-producing society. The manifestation of this situation was on his doorstep: the Crystal Palace Exhibition assembled the wealth of the world in a huge display of consumerism, but workers could hardly afford the entrance fee and a day off during the week.[19] Meanwhile pickpockets relieved richer visitors of their watches and handkerchiefs. Mayhew, more than most of his contemporaries, linked injustice, crime and poverty. [C, 168; 189–91][20]

There is also a difference of scale with Marx. Mayhew studied exploitation through micro-economics—his correspondence had been established with that purpose in mind. He sought to collect as many "diaries", journals and accounts as possible, his first experience of the brutalization of economic exchange came from reading this type of document. His interviews also extracted this sort of information. They illustrated best the gap between the capacities of production and consumption. Mayhew's generalizations were based on individual experiences, not on large economic statistical series. [C, 128; 143] Macro-economy to him was just the reflection of domestic economy, a notion implied in his inductive philosophy.[21]

Mayhew viewed the economy as static. Areas of growth merely compensated for areas of depression. Only the uneven distribution of wealth created the appearance of change. The long-term consequences of free trade and of steam-powered production in this physiocratic approach to the national economy seemed catastrophic. This prediction of impending doom had a strong appeal. A period of fast growth brought about an increase of production in many sectors of society and, as a side-effect, created a crisis in others. It was a growth lived like a disaster. "How is it possible for working men and women to avail themselves of the superabundance of material and shirts, shilts [sic] and petticoats when the only thing they have to give in exchange is their labour?" [C, 106] The fluid market, expanding in some areas and experiencing overproduction in others, left workers with few certainties.

Although the price of bread, for instance, had gone down, so had real incomes in some industries. [C, 111] And, in London, which was Mayhew's main field of study, a crisis had arisen as a result of changes in the modes of production and consumption. Small production, like cabinet-making, had to meet greater demand at lower cost: this was achieved through higher productivity paid at the same global rate. "The fallacy [of Political economy] is in taking no notice of the duration of the daily labour." [C, 116] The same concern can be found in Marx [*Capital*, Vol. 1, Chapter X] yet, even if such parallels do occur in their ideas, Mayhew failed to construe exploitation as anything more than injustice. He noted the qualitative decline of some production and how the minimal salaries paid in sweatshops undermined average incomes.[22] [C, 116] His economic model remained close to an artisan's romanticization of fair competition. He then attributed the brutalization of this competition to greed, the same greed that had replaced the inconsistent old Poor Law with a "minimised and terrible" one.[23] [C, 238]

The sweaters' "social dumping" affected Mayhew's model and divided producers into qualified and unqualified workers competing for survival with each other and with the "steam men". Mayhew used here the flawed Malthusian concept of "steam men" to denounce the concentration of wealth in the overgrown productive sector. [C, 105–6] Meanwhile he demolished Malthus's argument in the manner of a platform speaker:

> the population question in which F.B.B. seems to go the whole hog like Stewart [sic] Mill,—declaring that there is no hope for the workmen of this country until they imitate the Catholic priests and register vows in heaven of perpetual celibacy ... [C, 105]

and demonstrated a sharp understanding of the importance of increasing demand in the market:

> Every fresh pair of feet that come into the world do [sic] not create a demand for an extra pair of shoes—nor each new back want clothing— nor each new head require additional shelter ... Certainly not. The steam man is the greatest of our national blessings. Our fellow man the greatest of national curse. [C, 106]

In addition to subverting Malthusian paradigms, Mayhew adopted the powerfully sentimental Chartist rhetoric of domesticity and family values while stressing the benefits of increased human demand.[24]

Yet, in contradiction with this exposition of an expanding market, Mayhew held the view that the allocation of wealth to machines was at the expense of the workers, and that part of the latter's loss financed industrial investment. Overproduction only made goods cheaper for those who could afford to consume. [C, 131; 136–7]

Mayhew's main problem in these pages was that the nature of industrial investment contradicted his static representation of the production and distribution of wealth. Some of his readers soon accused him of being a rearguard Luddite and a Chartist. [C, 161] This aspect of his thought is confused. Mayhew seldom considered emigration as a solution. [C, 163] He believed enrichment would reduce the risk of a natural Malthusian trap while he condemned industrial investment for creating an artificial one. [C, 105–6] This contradictory approach was self-defeating and one cannot account for its appeal.

The attraction of Mayhew's modelizations and theories was not only their simplicity but also the way they matched working-class experience of the economic situation in London. They were theories that applied specifically to a period of change and of devaluation: the fall in production costs, the simplification of production in a number of activities and the phasing out of traditional crafts. Mayhew emphasized the value of the possession of skills,[25] and compared the obsolescence of a skill with an expropriation, such as the ones ordered to let the trains through working-class neighbourhoods. [C, 245] The loss was real for workers but this concept of rights to the ownership of skills conflicted with established property rights.[26] Mayhew did not develop this critique of property rights along the lines followed by Proudhon, however and, in many other instances, the question was left pending. At the same time it is condescending and incorrect to dismiss Mayhew's views on this theme as another instance of sentimentalism. Their powerful and provocative appeal to his readers should not be ignored. [C, 157]

TRADE UNIONS AND SELF-HELP

Mayhew's arguments contained the seeds of political change. Yet Mayhew refused to discuss either Chartism, co-operation, socialism or communism in isolation. [C, 97] Nevertheless, from the very first appeal for documentary evidence, Mayhew sought to assess the potential of trade unionism and more precisely its economic viability. Internal viability was the first concern at a time when many mutual-help societies and trades unions had failed. External viability related to the chances of trade unionism and co-operation affecting the fate of the nation. [C, 89–90] Mayhew sought and obtained some of the material he wanted. Small trade societies across the United Kingdom, Ireland included, subscribed to his periodical and contributed to "Answers to Correspondents"which subsequently became a platform for union campaigns in Sheffield and in the Midlands with the "Anti-Truck" society. [C, 93–4; 107–8; 156]

Mayhew was committed to good buying practices [C, 160–1] and to a small loan-fund complemented by the Mutual Investment Society, of which his younger brother Horace was a director. This created a conflict of interest, for the bank advertised in the magazine and contributed to the small fund created to help paupers described in *London Labour and the London Poor*. This financial joint-venture helped to present *LLLP* as a model for practical self-help, reinforcing this impression by the publication of statistics on the increase of work resulting from a teetotal lifestyle. [C, 206–8] This was a classic theme in the literature of reform and a dangerous development. Did Mayhew wish to set an example that would persuade the masses to change their ways? Did he intend to become one of those pedagogic philanthropists he so often criticized? The fate of the bank and Mayhew's fund is unknown. What is important is that this practical model of co-operative self-help continued all through the period the magazine was published. [C, 164–5]

Mayhew's aim was to convince his readers that working-class people could be capitalists and should invest in themselves. His close friends subscribed to this cross-class movement, becoming involved in his politically innocuous project to change society. This association based on respect for work was reminiscent of Christian Socialist ideals.[27] It was, in other terms, the pattern for most of the non-revolutionary radical struggles of the century that united lower-middle class and working-class men into an holistic reform project.[28] [C, 95–6; 198–9]

Mayhew appeared at Chartist meetings of the time, if only as a "friend" of the working class; his struggle was elsewhere. He tried repeatedly to unionize all kinds of people: young thieves, ballast heavers' wives and needlewomen. These lost causes appealed to him because they were all extreme cases of brutal pauperization. Thieves were stealing out of poverty, needlewomen were prostituting themselves out of poverty and neglect, ballast heavers' wives were starving because their husbands were drinking the middlemen's beer.[29] Mayhew believed in unions to attenuate the violent consequences of the law of supply and demand. [C, 136–8]

DEBATING WITH READERS

From Mayhew's letters, the gradual build-up of conviction into revolt becomes evident. If "Mr. Mayhew himself believes that the working men of England are grossly wronged by capitalists", what did Mayhew say about capitalism? [C, 95] Mayhew did not conceive the system tele-ologically, yet he ranked social relations historically from slaves, to "villeins", to exploited workers (hirelings)... [C, 195] His proposals for change were similarly inspired by romantic historical views.[30] Significantly the term he chose to define fair exchange was "the tribute" system, by which he meant that workers were partners and not servants. [C, 112] As partners in production, workers should be paid according to the results of the whole enterprise and obtain a share of the profits. The question then asked by his readers was: why would any capitalist invest in participative ventures? Mayhew's social answer to this problem was that capitalists and workers would become complementary—to the point where differences would disappear and every worker investing in a loan bank would become a small capitalist helping another working-class person.[31] [C, 171] Mayhew concluded that the exploitation of individuals by profiteers might then come to an end through the empowering of the former. Readers were also keen to give a political agenda to loan funds, emphasizing that they did not wish to benefit a state that "would in any period of political commotion probably make of our money arms to crush us". [C, 102] Mayhew emphasized that the whole scheme implied spontaneous and gradual reforms and excluded revolutionary action. [C, 95] The Manchester Bolt-Makers Society's aims of competing financially with their employers appealed more to him. [C, 158] Was it more than a middle-class daydream? Was Mayhew anything more than a *bricoleur*?[32]

Perhaps because he was insecure on the subject, Mayhew's stance was most violent when debating political economy, and it was this subject that was debated more than any other. Against his readers, he used all the weapons available to him: sarcasm, insult and contradiction among them. [C, 176–7; 181–2]

Yet they carried on writing. The vitality of this debate gives an indication of its importance. Mayhew insulted his readers with sarcasm, by making fun of them and refusing to debate their ideas (a refusal contradicted by more letters). [C, 171–2; 191–2] He apologized, made friends with faithful readers, analyzed their statistics and mellowed in his opposition. He faced strong opposition from the very first letter he wrote on political economy. Readers whom he quickly identified as partisans of the "Manchester school of economics" wrote furiously to defend the existence of morally neutral economic laws. These defenders of the "free market" did express similar views in remarkably similar terms and Mayhew could be forgiven for thinking that many of the letters were the work of one and same person. These readers usually defended the need for sacrifice, the doom of uncompetitive producers and above all the supreme law of supply and demand. [C, 103–5] Most of them repeated Ricardo's arguments on wages, usually confidently repeating the current canon of political economy. It is clear that some of the readers had internalized this particular economic model.

Self-taught readers attacked the self-taught writer on points of theory that Mayhew had failed to master or understood. Readers used digests and encyclopaedias. Mayhew claimed that only the unabridged texts and statistics were of any value. He expressed the wish that "a gentleman with a taste for desultory readings will not occupy his time by repeating to him for the thousandth time the old opinions touching supply and demand". [C, 172] Yet his own references to Mill, [C, 105; 114; 132; 140; 172] De Quincey [C, 168], Ricardo [C, 131; 171] or Babbage [C, 112; 140; 141] are usually highly selective and mainly concern machinery.[33] In contrast, his readers' dense and usually coherent letters accept the whole corpus as equivalent to "Natural Laws". Political economists had forced through their respectability on the wave of optimism created by the anti-Corn Laws campaigns. Protectionists like Mayhew held the opposite view. They feared most of the social costs of competition.[34] [C, 176] By taking the case of artisans as his example, Mayhew was mostly investigating modes of production in which productivity gains were at the expense of quality. This experience was not typical of other types of industrial production involving technological innovation.

The evidence he brought forward only highlighted the case of obsolete industries such as the work of handloom weavers and sawyers. [C, 133–4; 162; 168; 172] Mayhew's arguments therefore failed to convince devotees of political economy: he refused to argue on their terms. He was aware of the implications of the terminology used within political economy and tried to neutralize it by introducing an element of moral values, such as fairness or justice. He admitted being a convert to justice.

> Mr. Mayhew should add, that previous to his inquiries he believed in Supply and Demand, and Free Trade, as religiously as R.H. himself does. Let R.H. go through the same course of education, and, as a honest man he will assuredly arrive at the same result. [C, 179]

His writing shaped his political opinions and he eventually rejected political economy as strongly as he had rejected the *Morning Chronicle*'s censorship. [C, 110]

The conflict was one of logic. Readers argued that fairness or justice were not consequent parts of the logic of the market. Mayhew answered that since justice ruled most other human activities, it was at work that it needed to be defended most vigorously. To the readers, the world of economics was a sphere of activity entirely separate from the family, the church, and from philanthropy. Mayhew judged economics according to its impact on the family, on the increased need for palliative philanthropy and on the sacrifice of individuals. He was also weary of the political economists' use of the term "community" which he denounced as a bias that favoured the rich.

> The fallacy of the whole appears to consist in ignoring the existence of the labourer and not paying the same regard to his interests as to those of the capitalist class. [C, 234]

Following this, he argued for an understanding of the word community which would affect the interests of the majority—the labouring class. The social undertone of the concept of "community" tied him to Christian Socialist and co-operationist ideologies.[35]

Mayhew defended his idiosyncratic reasoning, using scientific metaphors as well as Christian arguments. He deployed the laws of science as a rhetorical tool, but was also ready to abandon them. Thus political economy could only justify its scientific credibility if it were as morally acceptable for an individual as for the whole of society. This was essentially an individualistic analysis lacking scope and power. Mayhew had to use demagogic language by, for example, comparing greedy capitalists with Ikey Solomon, a notorious fence. [C, 96; 192] Like the "Jew fence" (a note of common radical anti-semitism) the capitalists lived on the proceeds of poverty. [C, 191] This appears closer to Proudhon than to Marx. Thieving is a form of exploitation that does not entail a wider theory of exploitation. Mayhew's choice of metaphor and his alarmist demagoguery [C, 205] make him closer to Cobbett, Carlyle or even the French socialists[36] than to the German socialists.[37]

CONCLUSION: MAYHEW, HIS READERS AND THE "IDEA OF POVERTY"

The reader of the time read Mayhew's *London Labour and the London Poor* and the sub-text "Answers to Correspondents" on political economy and clearly associated the narrative on London with the ideas of its author. Meanwhile the letters became so important to Mayhew that he published them independently as a separate work. In the editing of *Low Wages*, Mayhew ignored the readers' letters that had inspired his political development, and clouded even more of his ideas in a rhetorical mist. There were only six issues of this pamphlet produced. The series on economy made sense to contemporary readers only through the dialectic of the correspondence. The correspondence provided a background for the main body of the text on London poverty and demonstrated the principles that lay behind it. It worked like the moral conclusion to a tale.

Mayhew's knowledge of poverty and "penny capitalism" gave strength to his ideas on low wages and his involvement as an intellectual *engagé* scornful of Adam Smith's retreat to a Scottish village. [C, 172] Himmelfarb attributes to him major changes in the general perception of the urban poor, while, paradoxically, she minimizes the importance of his examples or his empathy with the poor. Hers does not constitute a valid appreciation of *LLLP*; Mayhew did a great deal more than simply list commonplace characters in an entertaining way.

It is true, however, that Mayhew's rhetoric often included ethnological analogies. As pointed out earlier, there was an element of romance and exoticism in the work, that was part-stylistic, part-aesthetic. To imply that Mayhew's intention was to indulge in a taste for the repulsive is misleading. He included costermongers—street-pedlars—in his class of distributors, for he knew them to be an important part of the distribution of good. This knowledge was compatible with classifying them as nomads, using a system of double referencing, in social, ethnographic terms and in economic terms. The relation between these categories presented no difficulty and this was perhaps aided by the reading of "Answers to Correspondents".

LLLP was a powerful text that provided a very strong argument in favour of reform. It was sufficiently articulate for Chartists and Christian Socialists to claim it as a masterpiece and for *The Economist* to denounce it as propaganda.[38] It therefore had a dual role: it was unquestionably a genuine literary enterprise and a political pamphlet. This dual function is also the mark of Dickens's work.[39] Both writers, like other early Victorians, chronicled with growing unease the brutal social changes taking place at the time. *London Labour and the London Poor* should be read avidly as much for the understanding that it facilitates as for the knowledge it imparts. It is not a gallery of portraits, rather the Domesday book of the industrial revolution.

5

HISTORY IN THEIR
OWN WORDS

Can any of my etymological friends point out the derivation of the slang term "*mort*"[1] or "*mot*", a low woman and thence a prostitute? The word mot, indeed, seems to be the generic term for prostitute, as a flash mot (a court-esan), a coolie's mot (a soldier's woman), a legger's mot (a sailor's woman), and so on. The prostitutes are occasionally called "marms" or "ma'ams"; this appears to be an abbreviation of "madams", which would seem to have been formerly used for "mistresses" or kept women. Can any one oblige Mr Mayhew with proof of this, or to the contrary? Is the term mot (or mort) connected with mother? The Russian for mother is *mat*; and the Sanscrit [sic], *mata*; the Welsh is *mam*, (query, ma'am). [C, 218]

This was one of Mayhew's public queries, belonging to a cycle of letters written on the subject of philology, in this case the sexually loaded etymology of "mot". There were several philological debates running at once; "Bunmaree", [C, 101; 169–70] "mot" and "haberdasher" provided an abundance of discussion in "Answers to Correspondents". [C, 155; 162; 171] A close examination of the philological debate within *London Labour and the London Poor* approaches culture from an unusual angle. The recent debate on the construction of popular culture, following the work of Gareth Stedman-Jones and Patrick Joyce, has been conducted in terms which are difficult to apply here. The forms of cultural appropriation debated here are closer to what Norbert Elias and later Roger Chartier have exposed in their respective works.[2] The inspiration for my analysis is to be found in Olivia Smith's *Politics of Language* which emphasized the connections between grammar, etymology and politics (as Malcolm Deas did later).[3] On the one hand, the appropriation of complex and difficult intellectual tools built a language of self-education, while on the other philology became associated with ethnology, a shortcut to intellectual social climbing and a discursive conceptualization of social anxieties. Mayhew's debates do not attain the political explicitness of the 1790s' discourse on language, but it could be argued that *LLLP* was nevertheless, deeply engaged in a project to achieve political reform.

The first part of this chapter analyses the readers' efforts to approach the language historically, while Mayhew used dialectic philology and attempts to broaden his sociology. The second half of this chapter will examine the implications of this discrepancy, and address how the different ways in which philology was used affected approaches to prostitution.

PHILOLOGY–ETHNOLOGY

Mayhew had launched the philological debate in his "Answers to Correspondents" and contributions soon abounded. In the context of the time this was quite surprising. The London Philological Society dated only from 1842, and readers of *London Labour* may not have been aware of its activities.[4] The year *LLLP* was published (1851) was well before philology in Britain was popularized by the conferences of Max Müller.[5] The first chair in philology was inaugurated only in 1868 and Mayhew's extensive knowledge of the subject contrasts with the slow pace of translation and acceptance of German philology in Britain. As Cary Plotkin has pointed out[6] German concepts were slowly imported into Britain.[7] Were Mayhew and his readers part of the avant-garde in philological matters? Why should he and his readers devote so much time to reading dictionaries, foreign grammars and manuals of ancient literature?[8] In sum, what was the purpose of philology in a project of this kind?

These basic questions are made even more crucial by the emphasis placed by Foucault on Grimm and Bopp's works in an early nineteenth-century, fundamental epistemological change.[9] These philological matters might appear anecdotal if they were not so important in the writing and the reading of *London Labour and the London Poor*. Earlier dictionaries, particularly eighteenth-century ones, were often a collection of rare words. Mayhew was aware of this tradition which fitted with some aspects of his work. The queries on odd words that he initiated belong to this old epistemological order. At the same time his emphasis on new philologists indicates an intellectual awareness of recent developments. [C, 162; 169–70; 173] Moreover, Mayhew used philology in his exploration of the most scabrous aspects of London. [C, 228–32; 250–1] The above etymology of "mot" presents strong similarities with Mayhew's classifications. The prostitutes were defined according to their customers: they were either "soldiers' women", or "sailors' women". Mayhew's philology structured his linguistic and social exploration of prostitution.

If philology were a useful rhetorical tool in the writing of difficult aspects of *London Labour*, its relevance to Mayhew's readers is more intriguing. Readers did not become involved simply to contribute to this compilation of urban folklore. They also aimed towards "high culture" and the processes of acquisition of knowledge.[10] [C, 120] Philology was the new science that turned language into a subject of study. It analyzed words as elements within the mechanics of expression, their meaning being less important than their history. This history could either be ethnic and to a large extent national (historic derivation) or come from much further within a family of languages (dialectic derivation). The latter theory was contributed by Bopp and Grimm.

In 1851, Mayhew's knowledge of the work of Grimm and Bopp placed him among the few initiates of the new science. Mayhew was fluent in German and French. He had also travelled through parts of the British empire while still young.[11] His personal skills probably helped his understanding of complex linguistic issues. When entering the field of social exploration, Mayhew loosely identified his work with that of the many antiquarians who collected English dialects, or reinvented Celtic languages.[12] He wished to write a "history of the people in their own words".[13] Surprisingly, he chose to adopt the most far-reaching theory of language. Words haunted his work and their history gave clues to the hidden history of the crowd. Yet this history was not necessarily national—it constitutes a schematic yet plausible introduction to Mayhew's preoccupations, but there remain other points to address.

The philological project in which Mayhew and his readers were engaged had an insistence on purity and universality. There are two separate issues involved. On the one hand, there is a concern with the purity of the language, [C, 230–2] and on the other with the moral purity of the object of social exploration. [C, 101] This latter aspect appears particularly in the correspondence on prostitution. For there was only one all-encompassing quest for purity that questioned both words and sin.

POPULAR PHILOLOGY

The idea of popular philology is somewhat alien to established philology, which has always been an intellectually elitist discipline. This elitist image is associated particularly with the original masters of the field, Bopp (1791–1867) and Grimm (1785–1863). Both were exemplary German scholars who compared the grammars of Sanskrit, Old Slav, Latin, Lithuanian and Old German. Grimm's work may suggest how philology permeated into popular culture. Between 1811 and 1829, Jakob, with his brother Wilhelm, published the most famous tales of German folklore, including Hansel and Gretel, and Snow White. These hugely popular stories were deeply concerned with issues such as the origins of legends. Universal in theme and an example of the common Indo-European roots of European languages and legends, they complemented Bopp's grammar.[14] It was this publication, therefore, that accounts for the interest devoted to antiquarian discoveries in Britain. This was also a period of Celtic revival[15] and of interest in the Arthurian legends common in French and German.[16] Sagas, legends and folklore were more than myths needed to assist in the making of nation states. They also provided evidence of the common origin of all the cultures of Europe. This discovery of an ancient white man's culture can be set alongside other uses of philology during this period of colonial expansion.[17] By finding similarities among a large family of European languages and cultures, philology played an important role in highlighting perceived differences between European and other dominated "native" cultures.

Philology and ethnology were used as a means of establishing a European identity in the colonial era.[18] Ethnological elements can also be seen in Mayhew's cultural project.[19] Mayhew was attempting to create an ethnology turned inwards, one that would also be a history of the people and, by extension, a history of humankind. Mayhew distanced the subject of his observation from his readers; yet, as noted before, the readers and the subject were often one and the same. This distancing conformed to specific genres in vogue at the time: travel literature and of the two new sciences already mentioned, ethnology and philology. Ethnology was the science of description and the acquisition of knowledge of cultural "inferiors". Philology traced the complex history of language, in this case the evolution of English from primitive "Sanskrit". [C, 218] Both sciences chartered the chronology of a civilizing process.[20]

Mayhew's categorization created broad stereotypes associated with various attributes, including, perhaps principally, language. [C, 157–8] By this method he dealt with words and rules in the same way that Darwin dealt with living fossils during his travels to the South Sea islands.[21] Darwin, Bopp, Grimm, Müller, Wedgwood and Mayhew were all producing work contemporaneously. There is no doubt that Bopp and Grimm had the most significant influence on Mayhew. Mayhew's *LLLP* was encyclopaedic in character. It included an extensive reference index and errata section [C, 103;145] at the end of each volume, and in many ways functioned as a dictionary of the underworld[22] (including, literally, the sewers).[23] This dictionary-like precision and encyclopaedic exhaustive nature were probably what made it most attractive to contemporary readers. [C, 224]

Within *LLLP*, there was a demand for debates on words. Dictionaries appeared at regular intervals and sold in large numbers. Comparative philology increasingly shaped the presentation of word definitions and bilingual dictionaries. Dictionaries were a central feature of self-education and few other items except the Bible were to become so central to lower-class high culture. The foundation stone of a personal library was, and remains, a dictionary. When Mayhew launched his inquiries on words, he created a stimulating challenge for the reader. It was a cultural experience perhaps similar to completing crosswords. [C, 228–30] The discovery of these words and the subsequent search for histories and derivations created an intriguing and fascinating exercise—a gratifying cultural test. The appearance of pedantic answers formulated from dated etymological paradigms demonstrated the readers' tremendous enthusiasm in this minor quest for knowledge.

The words that were to become the subject of so many letters were not prevalent by their sole meaning, or in relation to the object represented. Their importance lay in the role they had as words, as elements, in the history and logic of the language. They signalled affinities between languages and cultures. They conveyed the burden of history, of ideal and cultural meanings. Mayhew did surrender to some of the nationalistic ideology latent in philology when he recognised that the language of the working class was probably Saxon in origin.[C, 224] The old issue of the "Norman yoke" lurks in this debate. The purification of language alluded to earlier could have involved an awareness of the element of class—a struggle against the language of the "Ol' Corruption". Mayhew did not pursue this line of argument, however. While it is very likely that he and his readers were aware of Horne Tooke's political struggles, they do not in fact allude to it.[24]

It would be extremely symbolic if Mayhew's apparent rejection of Horne Tooke's etymology were accompanied by a similar rejection of early radicalism. His openness towards German ideas would become even more interesting. Alas, the evidence at our disposal does not enable us to make such bold claims. It is moreover not certain that Mayhew viewed philology so much as a political tool than as a rhetorical and epistemological one. It was in examining words that Henry Mayhew sought the roots of his own investigations. It is fundamental to observe that *London Labour and the London Poor* worked alternately within two different intellectual frameworks: (1) within political economy and the theory of exploitation, [C, 180] and (2) within philology and the exploration of meanings. The link was made by readers and author alike. Statistics and economic concepts rubbed shoulders with philological debates in one letter. Both discourses needed to be appropriated and they complemented each other. Philology held the key to mastering the means of expressing oneself; political economy held the key to power beyond politics. In both cases Mayhew's work dealt with empowerment and the people's appropriation of "their own words". Mayhew's sociology was based around language itself not Charles Booth's sociology of numbers.[25]

For Mayhew himself, philology was perhaps also a way of dominating the vast and almost impossible project that he had set himself. "Really the subject he has undertaken is so vast it becomes almost fearful to contemplate." [C, 190]

THE MEANINGS OF PURITY

Readers and author agreed on using philology at its lowest etymological denominator to purify language. Yet they disagreed over exactly what in the language should be purified. Mayhew's correspondents mostly checked the origins of words to determine their ethnic purity, that is, their Saxon roots, and sought to clarify their meanings. Mayhew more often checked the grammar, as in his analysis of John Stuart Mill's text, or in his analysis of his correspondents' letters. [C, 135–6] He kept philology for more thorough investigations of selected words. There was also a fundamental discrepancy between Mayhew and his readers on the type of philology to use. On the readers' part this quest for national and political linguistics extended to defending "traditional" English philologists:

> In your estimate of the value of Richardson's *Dictionary* on accounts of the copious examples it contains from the earliest authors, and also of his notions as to the historic mode of Etymology, you concur in, I believe the general opinion. I am aware the work has been censured as wholly deficient in what you term "dialectic Etymology through the medium of cognate languages". But it is only fair to keep in mind that the author considered Researches into the Affinities of the Indo-Germanic tongues (the cognate languages, to which I presume, you allude) to be the peculiar province of Comparative Philology and quite out of place in an English dictionary...I am sufficiently national, notwithstanding my pride and joy in the Crystal Palace Exhibition, to wish the names of Sir Wm. Jones and John Horne Tooke not to be overlaid by those of Geisner and Bopp, great as they undoubtedly are. [C,196]

The readers stuck to Johnson's order of things, and the more adventurous to Horne Tooke's. Their philology was often pure etymology.[26] They sought a class-based and nationalist purification of the language according to historical evidence. Mayhew, on the other hand, worked to propagate the new ideas of comparative philology. He sought to establish a comparative approach to language and society, a relativist way of tackling sensitive issues. This was partly the influence of contemporary ethnology and partly a convenient rhetorical tool. Lacking the intellectual coherence of Bopp's project, Mayhew's use of comparative philology involved an even greater distancing from the subject. Dialectical philology had universalist claims. Mayhew also sought a common sociological and political idiom: philology was the cornerstone of this quest.

In spite of seeking common ground between politics and linguistics, Mayhew held an elitist view on the use of words only in their "literal" sense and with perfect knowledge of their "primitive" meaning. Characteristically this conservative position revealed itself during a debate on political economy, and he used it to assert his literary prominence. [C, 181–2; 184] In this particular case the meaning incorporated the history of the word from its most distant and foreign past. This quest for a refined language was also part of the transition into modernity which permeates the entire corpus of Victorian literature. Through their letters, Mayhew's readers were expressing these changes. The debate on usable sources to analyze the language illustrates the gap between ancient and modern, between eighteenth-century style national etymology and international, ethnological philology.

The divide between Mayhew and his readers appears to diminish as the debate runs its course through the columns of "Answers to Correspondents". Assuming a teacher-like position, Mayhew led the debate and structured it around his concepts, while the interpretations reflected his readers' concerns. [C, 229] The readers' letters were generally articulate and not stylistically different from Mayhew's. Those readers who expressed a particular interest in philology seem to have belonged more to the lower-middle class or upper-working class,[27] while letters on political economy were often from artisans, workers and "small masters". This might suggest more than one audience for the work, reflecting perhaps the different occupations of the various categories of readers. Workers had something to say about wages and the value of labour. Clerks and clergymen—workers of words—had much to say about education, etymology and philology. [C, 185]

A number of letters contradicts this generalization. We must accept that political economy and philology together provided the basic framework of analysis for all the topics discussed in the correspondence. These two modes of analysis were linked not only by proximity in "Answers to Correspondents" but also by strong similarities in their inner mechanics.

Readers showed an awesome etymological imagination and inventiveness. [C, 211] Returning to the word "Mot" still used around 1850 to signify a "punk", vagrant or prostitute, we find the most obsessive patterns of analysis. Various etymologies were put forward by readers: "amourette" [a flirt], "Morta" [a Parcæ, daughter of Night and Darkness], "Mot" [the Dutch for prostitutes: "It is therefore, there applied to this class of women as a vituperative term, designating them as foul agents of corruption and destruction, even as the moth is to woollen clothe".]; and "Motte" ["an old French word I can only translate as vulva"]. Other hunting metaphors added to the etymology a strong sexual connotation. Whether it be originally the Parcæ, a part of female genitals, an insect, fair game, a prostitute or an innocent flirt, the word "Mot" had a rich etymology stretching almost to the queen herself with "ma'am". Extremely rich was the fruit of these weird juxtapositions in Spain, Greece, France, Holland and France again. France was the country of vice, the land of venereal disease[28] and regulated prostitution.[29] The French etymology was therefore quite strong on cultural grounds even if fanciful on philological ones. The metaphorical and mythological origins of the word, the Parcæ and the pest, betrayed their fears and morbid fascination. The Dutch origin of the word was linked to sailors and gave an exogenous origin to sin. There were more than some purely nationalistic clichés in this constant reminder of the foreign origin of vice. The history of a slang word belonging to the most debased vocabulary betrayed an obsessive fear of the taint. This debate highlighted these impure origins. Even if their complex history were sheer invention, the readers defined "mot" as alien. [C, 229–30] It brought back into the debate the notion of purity at two levels. Debated scientifically it became legitimate to discuss such a word as "mot". A deferential use of Latin, for example, covered voyeurism and hints of pornography.[30] [C, 232] A cathartic analysis of obscure etymologies took place as a way of purging the language. The rituals of purification implied the virtual death of a word.

This discussion purified the vocabulary of the readers and made careless use of words unacceptable. Mayhew strongly emphasized the empowerment given by mastery of the literal meanings of philology. Combining philology with political economy in approaching critical issues such as prostitution provided Mayhew with one answer to a conceptual tangle.

Prostitution could be set within the context of political economy. Mayhew could incorporate "vice" into the category of labour and cite purely environmental causes for the common "fall". Alternatively he could borrow analytical frameworks from religious writers. An economic analysis was weak in several aspects, making it too difficult to use. No economist attempted to identify a coherent pattern of "fall" into prostitution. Because prostitution was viewed in moral terms it was not the business of the secular researcher to explore it, even less to publish his findings on a weekly basis. [C, 185–6] Mayhew presented an alternative way of debating the problem: he employed philology and ethnology, the twin disciplines, and, through a careful process of building distance from the subject, sought origins and comparative reference points.

If a family of languages shared some common roots, Mayhew argued, then perhaps some behaviour, some functions, recurred similarly in every culture. The placing of prostitution in a context of comparative history on a global scale clarified its real "nature", and reduced it to its common denominator. It also extracted it, however gently, from a conventional Christian system of values.

THINKING PROSTITUTION

In the core text of *London Labour*, Mayhew approached prostitution reluctantly, after months of resistance to readers' demands. [C, 113; 175; 202] Significantly his introduction to the topic was etymological and as broad as possible.

> The term *whore* has strictly the same signification as that of *prostitute*; though usually supposed to be from the Saxon *Hyrian*, to hire, and consequently to mean a woman whose favours can be procured for a reward. But the Saxon substantive Hure, is the same word as the first syllable of *Horrowen*, which signifies literally a filthy quean, a har-lot...Prostitution and whoredom, then have both the same meaning, viz. perversion to vile or filthy uses; and consist in the surrendering of a woman's virtue in a manner that excites our *moral disgust*...as in the marriage of a young girl to an old man for the sake of his money, as much as an act of prostitution as even the grossest libertinism.[30]

This definition discharged the emotional impact of the subject through a clever disquisition on etymological origins while substantially broadening the field of common uses of the word. At the same period Mayhew took some distance with the topic and entrusted most of the core text to Horace St. John.[31] St. John treated prostitution like a philologist, from the ancient times, from abroad, from the primitive cultures until the present day. His history of prostitution fitted well with

Mayhew's relativist philology, neutralizing the moral impact of the theme and establishing a chronology of progress.

While St. John constructed a polymorphic image of prostitution on the five continents since biblical times, Mayhew treated the correspondence on the subject carefully. The correspondence often treated the subject much more explicitly than the core text, either using philology, or violently confronting lived experiences. [C, 218–19] Horace St. John compiled a mountain of secondary evidence from all sorts of travellers, from historians, from the Bible and from classic authors. Fastidiously dwelling on details, he built a chronicle of daily prostitution turned towards exotic countries or a distant past. The point made clear was that prostitution was ubiquitous and a-historical. Describing prostitution in detail showed only that prostitution had no history in the nineteenth-century meaning of the word, no beginnings and no end, even if social approaches to prostitution had. This lack denied it any intention, any project, even evil, and only depicted it as a repulsive (according to common sense) behaviour.

During this enquiry Horace St. John built an ideal Victorian reference library considered in the annex to this chapter. The "library" did not contain any book specifically dealing with prostitution. Most of the opuses referred to were ethnologists' accounts of otherness, of various "primitive" civilizations in which they encountered a sour reflection of European vices. Many undermined the myth of original innocence by exposing the "immorality" of "primitive" societies. These books had a hidden agenda. They assessed white men's moral equality or even superiority the better to assert their material superiority. The state of nature lost its classical appeal. Yet none of them was devoted to the subject of "prostitution" as such; prostitution remained a vague concept. The economic argument with which we now qualify prostitution, the momentary selling of one's body to a customer, was not the only definition. Any sexual activity out of wedlock could be thus named. On the other hand, Mayhew compared some marriages to prostitution. Concubines and women in common-law marriages were also prostitutes according to him.[32]

In the early Victorian era, a handful of studies had begun to describe prostitution as a "commercial" activity. The true pioneer was the French doctor Alexandre Parent-Duchâtelet, a hygienist, obsessed with the consequences of pollution. Mayhew knew his major work with its logic and reassuring set of preventive control measures. Parent-Duchâtelet inspired other social writers like Michael Ryan[33] in 1839 or, the most famous of all, William Acton in 1857.[34] Except among social commentators like Mayhew, prostitution was seen as a sanitary issue. Prostitutes were described as agents of contagion who could be contained with the regulation of their "commercial" activities.[35]

Mayhew was also aware of evangelical "explorers" of the "under-world". Though he explicitly rejected philanthropy and most of the work done through the distribution of tracts, [C, 211–13] he could not ignore the rising tide of evangelical writings from missionaries. Many, such as the work of William Logan, provided a good exploration of the social causation of prostitution.[36] The main difference of focus was the moral tone of descriptions. Medical analysts defined prostitution as an ahistorical evil,[37] a simple consequence of social rules on late male marriage and of male sexual impulses, while preachers equally (if not simultaneously) apportioned the sin between the prostitute and her customer.[38] [C, 124]

Prostitution in 1851 was not clearly defined. In the whole set of reinterpreted ideas concerning vice, it had a limited role to play. The idea of "dangerous classes" coined by the French policeman Frégier was relatively new [C, 94] and permitted repressive interpretation of the popular turmoil of the 1830s and 1840s.[39] It also authorized a differentiation between classes eligible to vote. Yet, in 1851, Mayhew insisted that prostitution did not really belong to the world of the dangerous classes (if indeed Mayhew accepted the idea) but originated from all strata of society. [C, 219–20; 240–2] The world of prostitution was ambiguous in his analysis. He clearly identified upper-class prostitution and the *demi-monde* with the "Ol' Corruption" of the aristocratic classes. Mayhew raised the old banner of radicalism once again. [C, 220]

After long and careful philological preliminaries, Mayhew and his readers faced the problem of the "fall" into prostitution. Medical analysts did not really present the problem of the "fall" in moral or economic terms but related it to the inclinations of some women towards easily made money. They also pointed out the high rate of atonement into the "moral society" through the acquisition of a little business. Preachers on the other hand used the concept of vice, temptation, etc. to analyze the "fall" and often pointed out that prostitutes died young.[40] To the former, prostitution was a transient phase of impoverished women's lives; to the latter, prostitution was the doom of vicious impoverished women.

Mayhew used a different framework. Even if he admitted that more poor women were prostitutes, he refused to admit that *only* poor women were prostitutes. He apportioned guilt according to the prostitutes' social origins. Some were born in it. Their proximity was such that no sin was involved. They inherited a business for which their whole education prepared them. [C, 213–15] Some were driven to prostitution to complement insufficient wages. Mayhew described the scandalous conditions of needlewomen, who had suffered such a loss of income that many had to find complementary wages in prostitution. This case inspired the most scandalous of Mayhew's articles in the *Morning Chronicle* and it was the one that led him to radicalize his anti-political-economy discourse. [MCS, Vol. 1, 158]

Their "fall" was the archetypal case of prostitution caused by economic pressure and in Mayhew's analysis it also had the value of an excuse. The only ones for whom Mayhew refused to present any apologies were prostitutes who originally had an honest alternative. Among these, upper-class prostitutes were the ones he considered truly "vicious".

Mayhew's uneasy attitude to prostitution varied between the two sources of his inspiration: religious condemnation and scientific analysis. He reluctantly answered his female readers' queries on the purity of the flowers sold as a cloak by young prostitutes. To the naïve question Mayhew replied that the subject was not exactly feminine. Prostitution was a woman's crime, but the crime was not fully gendered in middle-class terms (as these were women, not middle-class ladies). This illustrates further the difficulty of tackling such an elusive concept. [C, 99] Philology proved useful to find a third way in analyzing words of slang or cant, [C, 157–8] and this analysis in itself provided documentary evidence on prostitution in older times and a key to the opprobrium surrounding the issue.

The main text meanwhile, published alternately every other week with the study of London streets and sewers, contained Horace St. John's step-by-step critical review of the history and geography of prostitution. Most letters on the other hand dealt with philology and personal experiences.

The most important letters were those of W.G. [C, 211–13] from Glasgow, who represented the religious perspective and a general exaggeration of the problem, and that of "A Clerk in the City". [C, 247–8] The former was ambiguous about prostitution. He frequented casinos and tried to redeem a prostitute with a pocketful of tracts,[41] but his morbid fascination with prostitution betrayed the curiosity of a voyeur under a religious cover. In his account he included the story of the "fall" of the girl, an officer's daughter led into prostitution by her father's mistress, etc. This pattern of "fall" fitted in with the "Ol' Corruption" theory. The following week two readers criticized and convincingly denounced the story's conventional pathos and melodramatic details. [C, 240–2] Readers detected cheap melodramatic plots in these evangelical denunciations of the "fall".

Another letter was more unusual and Mayhew was very cautious in publishing it. He sought the identity of the man and checked his references. The story is that of a middle-class man chosen by a prostitute. Later the woman was driven out of her lodging by her pimp[42] and she found herself with the "clerk", living with him, abandoning her business for him. The story presents two interesting features. It gives a greater importance to the woman's free choice and gives some flesh to the usual narratives of prostitution in the Victorian era. It shows her climbing up the social ladder to a limited extent since she remained the clerk's concubine. The second aspect is Mayhew's answer. He began with a definition of prostitutes' "fancy men" and denounced the clerk as one of them. He then advised him to marry the woman. [C, 249]

There was no room there for the stereotype of the "fallen" woman's redemption. This example stands almost alone in the vast literature on prostitution and confronts some recent academic generalizations on Victorian prostitution. Mayhew's sociology of prostitution was wider ranging than most of his contemporaries'. The range of views over the problem seems to have narrowed through the Victorian era. As the concept of prostitution became more detailed and systematized, attitudes in the 1860s became increasingly radical on the paradigms of the Contagious Diseases Acts. In other words, the increased opposition between the two possible attitudes towards prostitution, the medical and the evangelical, left little room for Mayhew's third stance. The 1862 edition of *LLLP* contained the scandalous fourth volume which rested on sensational approached to prostitution and crime. It totally ignored the subtle class analysis of prostitution Mayhew wished to use.

Mayhew's step towards systematic sociology was ignored and remained unpublished, because of the general commercial failure of *London Labour*. Mayhew sent a form to various local and police authorities across the country to collect the general data about prostitution in the United Kingdom. He obtained many answers but unfortunately never published them. The method he used belonged half to the great statistical tradition, but was, for the other half, purely behavioral. [C, 195–6] Mayhew sought to know how many well-dressed prostitutes there were. The emphasis on dress reflects the importance of clothes as the commonest form of social recognition. His language on this occasion was revealing of his own double standard: upmarket prostitutes were said to "walk the streets" while the lowest "infest". He also sought to look at the factors of concentration, brothels or lodgings, to be able to build up a geography of urban prostitution, built on comparisons and metaphors, like a nest, a hell of prostitution, which would instantly relate modern prostitution to other and older cultural phenomena.

CONCLUSION: THE GRAMMAR OF CIVILISATION?[43]

The role of such a cautious sociology of prostitution was to frame and integrate new patterns within the old imagery of vice and crime. In that "Grammar of Civilisation", "history in their own words", Mayhew sought to establish his own position in the same manner a philologist would position himself towards languages: as an explorer and as a grammarian. The use of both economic causation for the fall and philology for the social status defined new research paradigms. One explained some of the most legitimate causes of prostitution, poverty, the other investigated the social and moral side. This dual approach had cleared the ground for a double condemnation of prostitution as both a crime and a form of exploitation. What this study of a handful of cases and few pejorative terms achieved is rather unique for the period. The issue was frankly laid out under its multiple guises, from the point of view of the prostitute choosing her "beau", from the traditional moral condemnation of the sin, from the economic and exploitative point of view and from the class issue. This *tabula rasa* of Victorian morality was no mean achievement when one considers the ideological straitjacket in which later observers remained. The unfortunately unpublished great survey of prostitution would have been unique. It would have positioned prostitution within society and attempted to make the hidden visible. Emphasis was put on the dress, on the class market of prostitutes, on their habits. Both the medical emphasis on contagion and the religious emphasis on sin were absent. In its place there was a view of a parallel society attached organically at every level to the damaged fabric of Victorian society. Marriage, divorce, education, poverty, crime were entangled as a set of causes. Such a complex representation of prostitution did not admit the preaching of nineteenth-century panaceas, be it medically controlled police regulation or police enforced repression. The correspondence stopped, as often with Mayhew, at the preliminary stage of demolition but there were potent promises in this correspondence.

Mayhew was fully conscious of working within and against large "systems" of representation. With ethnology and philology he crafted an alternate way out of history and his position towards history was ambiguous. He claimed to be an historian but he worked "from below" against the entire contemporary historiography. Mayhew was close to antiquarians but was not collecting to save and classify. He collected and classified to explain, to penetrate the logic of social changes and evolutions.

In Mayhew's project, philology was also the framework which enabled him to construct an historical dimension even to current

58

words. Mayhew used philology as a discursive means of exploring mass history and contemporary moral issues. While on the one hand etymology reified the language of the street, dialectic philology opened its historical potentiality on the other. The author-readers used etymology and philology to learn something about themselves. Meanwhile Mayhew used philology morally to disarm sensitive issues such as prostitution and personal behaviour, while politically approaching them.

POSTSCRIPT

"Answers to Correspondents" with its confused authorship (chapter 4), its conflicting approaches to political economy (chapter 5), its unusual handling of philology to approach prostitution (chapter 6) offers a very different view on Mayhew's sociological work. This shamble was creative. The correspondence was organized and theorized well above the main text of *London Labour and the London Poor* of 1851. Mayhew, I believe, comes out better from this constant interaction with his readers than in the subsequent historiography. Mayhew was a Victorian, an uneasy one, not *the* "Victorian" bourgeois voyeur. His work was not part of a Benthamite conspiracy to define and outcast the poor. His sociology was not preconceived, in fact, if Mayhew's work belonged to sociology it was a weird animal, a cross breed of ethnology, philology, history, journalism and political economy. Mayhew's work so clearly open to his correspondents, was sociology open to anybody, a narrative "science" in want of a name in which everything that was then Modernity had a role to play.

APPENDIX

THE WORLD OF PROSTITUTION AND VICE ACCORDING TO HORACE ST. JOHN'S BIBLIOGRAPHY

Horace St. John's bibliography of prostitution and vice was mostly compiled on second-hand accounts of either exotic countries or dead civilizations like Ancient Egypt of Ancient Rome. He chose to expose his "facts" in chronological order. He set prostitution in the fabric of human history, breaking any geographical boundaries, he claimed that even "natural" cultures from the pacific islands knew the "Social evil". His sources shifted from eighteenth-century material insistent on the philosophical qualities of "primitive cultures" and particularly to the absence of "shame" of native women, to evangelical and colonialist literature that considered these cultures as ignorant, if not essentially evil. The great centres of interest were the "natives" of the rising British Empire, including aborigines of Australia and New Zealand, Indians and Northern Americans. The survey also covered many African countries, and China that remained *terra incognita*. Nordic cultures considered in their pagan past were also included as were many nations of the Russian Empire. Japan, still closed to Europeans, was not even mentioned.

NOTES

INTRODUCTION

1. *The Wandering Minstrel* was a success but the Queen's had to wait for Marie Witton to enable it to become a respectable establishment when it took the name "The Prince of Wales". E. Yates, *Recollections and Experiences*, Bentley and Son, 1884, p.204.

2. Mayhew founded *Punch* and edited it for the first year; he then sold his shares to Mark Lemon. See M.H. Spielmann, *The History of Punch*, Punch, 1895, pp.4-17, and A. Mayhew, *A Jorum of Punch, With Those Who Helped to Brew It, Being the Early History of the London Charivari*, Downey and Co., 1895, pp.91-124.

3. Mayhew worked on Ingram's *Illustrated London News*. He also wrote for several newspapers, including the *Edinburgh News* in 1851.

4. The theoretical part of *London Labour and the London Poor* including Mayhew's classifying method and ideas on society was the only one constantly reprinted.

5. *The Great World of London*, David Bogue, 1856.

6. Griffin and Co. compiled a dictionary of biographical notices of the great men and women of the time. The publishers sent proofs of these notices to the people concerned who usually corrected some minor details or protested or who had their notices rewritten several times (such as Harriet Martineau). All text between square brackets is by Mayhew. The dictionary was reprinted late in 1861 as *The RANK and Talent of the Time*.

7. See for example the *Dictionnaire Encyclopédique Larousse du XIX Siècle* or *Everyman's Encyclopedia* of 1913. Among the eighteen notices listed in the *British Biographical Archive*, 1989, this one comes third and is the only one we know Mayhew was free to correct.

8. Augustus Mayhew probably. His *Paved With Gold* portrayed him and his brother visiting a low lodging house at night. This novel became a melodrama sometime later in the 1850s. A. Mayhew, *Paved with Gold, or the Romance and Reality of the London Streets: An Unfashionable Novel*, Chapman and Hall, 1854; new edition, Cass, 1971, pp.12-17. G.J. Howerd, *Paved with Gold*, Victoria Theatre, Sept. 1858–Feb. 1859.

9. See the letter to the publisher, below, which predated the Contagious Diseases Acts debate. See J. Walkowitz, *Prostitution and Victorian Society*, Cambridge University Press, 1980; B.O. Taithe, "From Danger to Scandal", PhD thesis,

Manchester University, 1992.

To Griffins and Co (1860)
Gentlemen,
   I beg to thank you very much for your kind present of Mayhew's work connected with the London poor.
   I have been obliged, as a rule, to decline presents, but the gracious way in which you offer this makes me feel it would be ungracious to do otherwise than accept, with many thanks.
   The "extra volume", which I had not yet seen, heave upon a subject, which, as regards the army, has attained a fearful importance, and upon which we are now at this time engaged. I regret however to see Mr Mayhew lending his powerful voice, p.210 etc. in favour of the French discipline of regulation by Police.
   He would perhaps find, on further enquiry, that there is no proof that discipline of "regulation" succeeds even in its object, i.e. the diminution of disease *from* vices, the only object which it professes to obtain—That it greatly increases national indifference to immorality, that foreigners are themselves beginning to see this and see also that Parent-Du-Châtelet's [sic] doctrine is the curse of nations by professing to give vice immunity from the consequences assigned to it by natural law,
   Faithfully yours,
   Florence Nightingale

10. See W. Tinsley, *Random Recollections of an Old Publisher*, Simpskin, Marshall and Co., 1900, p.73; the quotation is from G.A. Sala, *Things I have Seen and People I Have Known*, Cassell and Co., 1894, Vol.I, p.iii.
11. See G. Woodcock, "Henry Mayhew and the Undiscovered Country of the Poor", *Sewanee Review*, 1984, Vol.92, 4: 556-73, which relates how ex-members of Mass Observation encountered Mayhew's text for the first time after the war, too late for Orwell. See P. Summerfield, "Mass Observation: Social Research or Social Movement?", *Journal of Contemporary History*, 1985, Vol.20, 3:439-452.
12. C. Booth, *Life and Labour of the People in London*, Final Volume, Notes and Conclusion, Macmillan, 1902, and *Labour and Life of the People in London*, Macmillan, 1907; R. O'Day and D. Englander, *Mr Charles Booth's Inquiry: The Life and Labour of the People in London Reconsidered*, Hambledon Press, 1993. O'Day and Englander argue that Booth knew Mayhew's work but rejected his methods and style.
13. See R.J. Cruikshank, *Charles Dickens and Early Victorian England*, Pitman, 1949, p.233.
14. See also the strangely titled S. Rubinstein (ed.), *The Street Trade's Lot, London 1851, being an account of the lives, miseries, joys and chequered activities of the London Street-Sellers, as recorded by their contemporary Henry Mayhew and now recalled for the edification of the public by Stanley Rubinstein*, c.1945, seemingly the first selection from *LLLP* [1861 edition].
15. H.S. Nelson, "Dickens' *Our Mutual Friend* and Henry Mayhew's *London Labour and the London Poor*", *Nineteenth Century Fiction*, 1965, 20:207-222. P. Sucksmith, "Dickens and Mayhew: A Further Notice", *Nineteenth Century Fiction*, 1969, 24:345-349. R.J. Dunn, "Dickens and Mayhew Once More", *Nineteenth Century Fiction*, 1970, 25:348-353.
16. With the exception of A. Hookham, "The Literary Career of Henry Mayhew", MA, Birmingham University, 1962.
17. See P. Quennell, *Mayhew's London*, Springbooks, 1952 and *London's Underworld*,

W. Kimber, 1950. K. Chesney, *The Victorian Underworld*, Maurice Temple-Smith, 1970.

18. Among others: P. Ackroyd, *Dickens' London*, Headline, 1987; R.J. Cruikshank, op.cit., 1949; C.M. Mackay (ed.), *Dramatic Dickens*, Macmillan, 1989; N. Philips and V. Neuberg, *Charles Dickens, A December Vision: His Social Journalism*, Collins, 1986; G. Smith, *Dickens, Money and Society*, University of California Press, 1969.

19. This morbid fascination enables a contemporaneity with Mayhew's common readers of his times, quite close to Kierkegaard's notion of contemporaneity. See *Philosophical Fragments* [1843], Princeton University Press, 1942.

20. E.P. Thompson, "The Political Education of Henry Mayhew", *Victorian Studies*, 1967, 11:41-62.

21. See E.P. Thompson, "Henry Mayhew and the *Morning Chronicle*", in E.P. Thompson and E. Yeo, *The Unknown Mayhew*, Merlin Press, 1971, pp.11-50.

22. R. Samuel, "Mayhew and Labour Historians", *Society for the Study of Labour History*, 1973, 26:47-52.

23. G. Himmelfarb, "Mayhew's Poor: A Problem of Identity", *Victorian Studies*, 1971, xiv:307-329; "The Culture of Poverty" in H.J. Dyos (ed.), *The Victorian City*, Routledge & Kegan Paul, 1973, pp.707-36; *The Idea of Poverty, England in the Early Industrial Age*, Faber & Faber, 1984. Himmelfarb's main arguments are: that the numerical sample of *LLLP* is insignificant (this excluding the *Morning Chronicle* articles), that Mayhew exploited the poor for his own aims, which in turn led to a greater marginalisation of the poor in society. There is a deep and unresolved contradiction in this argument.

24. See G. Himmelfarb's review in *American Historical Review*, 1973, pp.1467-8; and the answer of Gareth Stedman-Jones in the 1983 preface of *Outcast London*, 2nd edition, Peregrine, Penguin Books, 1984.

25. See R. Maxwell, "Henry Mayhew and the Life of the Streets", *Journal of British Studies*, Vol.17, 2:87-105, pp.89-92. Maxwell criticised Thompson and Yeo's division of Mayhew's text into good or bad sociology and advocated a more global approach to Mayhew's *oeuvre*.

26. R. Kent, *A History of English Empirical Sociology*, Gower, 1981, pp.31-52. Kent valued Mayhew's empiricism which he opposed to theorists of sociology as in R. Aron's *Les Étapes de la Pensée Sociologique*, Gallimard, 1967.

27. K. Williams, *From Pauperism to Poverty*, Routledge, 1981, pp.237-77.

28. A. Joffe, "Detecting the Beggar: Arthur Conan Doyle, Henry Mayhew and 'The Man with the Twisted Lip'", *Representations*, 1990, 31:96-117.

29. C. Gallagher, "The Body Versus the Social Body in the Works of Thomas Malthus and Henry Mayhew" in C. Gallagher and T. Laqueur, *The Making of the Modern Body*, University of California Press, 1987, pp.83-106.

30. C. Herbert, "Rat Worship and Taboo in Mayhew's London", *Representations*, 1988, 23:1-24.

31. C. Crosby, *The Ends of History: Victorians and the Woman Question*, Routledge, 1991, pp.69-109.

32. E.P. Thompson, *The Making of the English Working Class*, Penguin, 1966, p.11.

33. Wide studies of the impact of literacy among one class seems to be out of fashion in historical studies, yet if we must refer to old works on the topic, our investigation of literacy would be more concerned with elements pointed out in Webb and Altick than with Hoggart's sentimental reinvention of the working class. See: R.K. Webb, *The British Working Class Reader: Literacy and Social Tension 1790-1848*, Allen and Unwin, 1955; R.D. Altick, *The English Common Reader: Social History and the Mass reading Public*, University of Chicago Press, 1957; R. Hoggart, *The Uses of Literacy: Aspects of Working-Class Life, with Special References to Publications and Entertainments*, Chatto & Windus, 1957.

34. The nature of sociology is another debate historians do not often face. When tackling Mayhew, historians often use the concept of sociology in a simplified and positivist manner. The idea defended in this book is that Mayhew was a proto-sociologist as much as he was a novelist, a journalist etc. The fact that his sociological work might have been a "dead end" does not matter. On the origins of sociology, see W. Lepenies, *Between Literature and Science: The Rise of Sociology*, Cambridge University Press/Editions de la Maison des Sciences de l'Homme, 1988, translated from *Die Drei Kulturen*, 1985; A. Swingewood, *A Short History of Sociological Thought*, Macmillan, 1991; P.J. Simon, *Histoire de la Sociologie*, Presses Universitaires de France, 1991.
35. *The Shops of London*, March–September 1865, was a sort of analytical directory aimed at a niche market.
36. The notion of purity among the Victorians belongs to several fields of research. See: F. Mort, *Dangerous Sexualities: Medico-Moral Politics in England since 1830*, Routledge & Kegan Paul, 1987; J. Weeks, *Sex, Politics and Society: The Regulation of Sexuality since 1800*, Longman, 1981, new edition, 1989, pp.19-89; *Against Nature: Essays on History, Sexuality and Identity*, Rivers Oram, 1991; E.J. Bristow, *Vice and Vigilance: The Purity Movements since 1700*, Gill and Macmillan, 1977; G. Himmelfarb, *Marriage and Morals Among the Victorians*, Faber & Faber, 1986; J. Walkowitz, *City of Dreadful Delight*, Virago, 1992.

1

HENRY MAYHEW

1. For more detailed (although sometimes contradictory) biographies, see: E.P. Thompson, "Henry Mayhew and the *Morning Chronicle*" in Thompson & Yeo, *The Unknown Mayhew*, Merlin Press, 1971, pp.11-50; N. Cross, *The Common Writer, Life in Nineteenth-Century Fleet Street*, Cambridge University Press, 1985, pp.93-102; A. Humpherys, *Travels in the Land of the Poor*, University of Georgia Press, 1979. Humpherys' psychological biography is still the most complete on Mayhew.
2. Thomas Mayhew replaced Hetherington temporarily as the editor of *The Poor Man's Guardian*, the most important Radical newspaper of the 1830s.
3. Thomas Mayhew's suicide associated political despair with financial troubles, estimated perhaps exaggeratedly at £10,000. (See *Men of the Time: Biographical Sketches*, D. Bogue, 1856.) Thomas Mayhew's short and desperate life associated poetry and Radicalism. On suicide, see B.T. Gates, *Victorian Suicide: Mad Crimes and Sad Stories*, Princeton University Press, 1988. A. Humpherys, op.cit., pp.1-30; E.P. Thompson, op.cit., pp.13-14.
4. Edward Mayhew, *Make Your Wills*, Cumberland, c.1845; *The Illustrated Horse Doctor*, W.H. Allen & Co., 1860; *Dogs, their Management* [1859], 30th edition, Routledge & Son, 1934.
5. Augustus was also a playwright in collaboration with H. S. Edwards: *The Poor Relation*, 1851; *My Wife's Future Husband*, 1851; *The Goose with the Golden Eggs*, Strand Theatre, 1859; *Christmas Boxes*, Strand Theatre, 1860, etc.
6. See A. Mayhew, *A Jorum of Punch*, Downey and Co., 1895, pp.10-25 and A. A'Beckett, *The A'Becketts of Punch*, Constable & Co., 1903.
7. A. Mayhew, op.cit. p.9.
8. H.R. Fox-Bourne, *The English Newspapers, Chapters in the History of English Journalism*, Vol.II, Chatto & Windus, 1887, pp.116-17.
9. See E. Yates, *His Recollections and Experiences*, Bentley and Son, 1884, p.204.

10. See A. Mayhew, op.cit. 1895, pp.1-10. The *hôtel meublé* was in the rue d'Amboise near the red light district of the Palais Royal.
11. John Barnett (1802-1890) composer, author of the "Mountain Sylph" (1834).
12. The name Bohemian came from an association with gypsies (*bohémiens* in French). The term became particularly popular in the 1850s after the publication of Henry Murger's *Scènes de la Vie de Bohème*, Michel Lévy Frères, 1851. See E. Yates, *Recollections*, op.cit., p.285.
13. The Paris stage of Mayhew's life is debated. Mayhew's own son ascertained it to be the founding stage of his friendship with Jerrold. As on many other occasions, one has to rely on family legends (like Mayhew's alleged "one-man show") without much evidence of their truths. Athol Mayhew seemed better placed than one of Mayhew's niece. See A. Humpherys, op.cit., p.14 and note 18.
14. On exile in Paris see L.S. Kramer, *Threshold of a New World: Intellectuals and the Exile Experience in Paris 1830-1848*, Cornell University Press. 1988.
15. See N. Cross, *Common Writer*, op.cit., p.32. Bohemians in Paris were well placed to describe the political turmoil of 1830 and 1848.
16. See W. Tinsley, *Random Recollections*, op.cit., Vol.II, p.68. "His emphatic declaration that he was not a Bohemian surprised me the most, because I thought he was rather radical in his politics."
17. See E.L. Blanchard (1820-1889), *The Life and Reminiscence of E.L. Blanchard*, Hutchinson and Co., 1891, Vol.II, p.171; A. Mayhew, op.cit., p.xiv.
18. H.R. Fox-Bourne, op.cit., p.117; M.H. Spielmann, op.cit., pp.17-34. Both authors insist that after the closure of the Radical titles in the 1830s (the *Poor Man's Guardian* closed down in 1835), humorous journals were fashionable. The people joining the Punch staff already worked on other titles such as Jerrold's *Punch and Judy*, *The Charivari*, etc.
19. *Lloyd's London Weekly Newspaper* was a popular weekly created by the famous penny dreadful author, Lloyd, who converted it into the radical press and thus into a form of respectability. V. Berridge "Popular Journalism and Working-Class Attitudes, 1854-1886", University of London, PhD, 1975. Jerrold assumed the editorship until his death in 1857 and, despite his son's claims, did not manage to make it profitable. See W.E. Adams, *Memoirs of a Social Atom*, Hutchinson, 1903, p.103.
20. J.A. Sutherland, *Victorian Novelists and Publishers*, University of Chicago Press, 1976, pp.4-5.
21 A.W. A'Beckett, op.cit., pp.98-121. G.A. A'Beckett, *The Comic History of England*, Punch, 1848. Douglas Jerrold objected to a comical treatment of history.
22. Mayhew did not use George Cruikshank but illustrators of a more "photographic" style. They used the journalistic manner they would have adopted for the *Illustrated London News*. Richard Beard, the first British professional photographer, was the author of most of the daguerreotypes which formed the basis for the *London Labour and the London Poor* engravings. His work was done in a studio but the diversity of the poses and the quality of the background show a constant effort to portray the character in his or her context. The background might have been left to the draughtsmen, also talented people. Henning was one of the artists Mayhew met at Ingram's newspaper while Henry George Hine was the leading illustrator. Hine was a true Pre-Raphaelite artist who had worked earlier with the Mayhew Brothers and who produced some of the best illustrations from Beard's daguerreotypes. Engravers Mason, Meason and Whimpers, were also artists. Thus we have three creative stages between the posing model and the engraving: the photographer, the artist and the engraver.
    If we had to compare the illustrations of Mayhew's work with contempora-

neous work it should be with the most avant-garde techniques of illustrated journalism. See *La Lumière*, 25 February 1854; C. Mackay, *Through the Long Day: Or the Memories of a Literary Life during Half a Century*, Macmillan, 1887, p.356; M. Bortram, *The Pre-Raphaelite Camera: Aspects of Victorian Photography*, Weidenfeld & Nicolson, 1985; H. Gernsheim, *The History of Photography*, Thames & Hudson, 1988.

23. The iconographic dimension of ballad prints is not often studied yet those engravings were a constant feature. Prints were not exclusively associated to one particular song or story but rather used on several sheets covering similar topics, being a form of trademark signalling the romance or the penny dreadful better than the title of the song. On ballads see J.S. Bratton, *The Victorian Popular Ballad*, Oxford University Press, 1975; on the Catnach and Seven Dials publishers see C. Hindley, *The Catnach Press, a collection of books and woodcuts of John Catnach, publisher at Seven Dials*, Hindley, 1862; *The Life and Times of John Catnach*, Hindley 1878; P. Joyce, *Vision of the People*, Cambridge University Press, 1991, pp.230-55; L. Shepard, *The History of Street Literature*, David and Charles, 1973.

24. Henry Mayhew, *German Life and Manners as Seen in Saxony at the Present Day*, Vol.I, Allen and Co., 1864; dedication "To my wife, literally my right hand, scribbling to my dictation".

25. Mayhew owed more than £2,000 spent on various improvements to his household, he incriminated Mark Lemon as owing him large amounts of unpaid rights over *Punch. The Times*, 12 February 1847.

26. Details of Jerrold's burial have been narrated by W. Jerrold, *Douglas Jerrold, Dramatist and Wit*, Macmillan, 1914, pp.654-7.

27. M.H. Spielmann, op.cit., p.268.

28. W. Jerrold, op.cit., pp.658-9.

29. A.W. A'Beckett, op.cit., p.358.

30. The letter was written in a much altered handwriting:

> 230 Regent Street,
> December 5, 1867.
>
> My dear professor Owen
>   My son, whose place of business is at the above address, has just brought me your very kind letter. It is a convincing proof of how rightly I had judged you. With true greatness you know as well as I do that real goodness is almost always allied; and permit to say (without a suspicion of the meanness of flattery) that it was this feeling which enured me to apply to you as a friend in my need.
>   It is the hardest of all literary task to express gratitude gracefully for sincere thankfulness is, like longitude only to be ascertained and measured by *Time*; but profession is still empty words, so do no more think me thankless, if I say not what *Others* might expect on such an occasion.
>   Unfortunately I am powerless with the rheumatism in my feet, from which I have been suffering for some time or I would come to the Museum gladly + shake you by the hand; but Mrs Mayhew, who was going to the reading room for me today, kindly offers to bring you this letter + to wait for your reply. Believe me to be my dear, professor, Yours most cordially.
> HM
>
> PS My son, I would add, is a young photographer of no mean a skill, he has just photographed the Shakespeare Cast for Miss Burdett Coutts—It strikes me you might, in your position, have it occasionally in your power to do him

a good turn + and if i were not assured that if you could you would, I would not have ventured to have taxed your friendship further by the addition of this postscript.

31. A. Mayhew, op.cit., p.91.

HENRY MAYHEW'S CREATIONS AND COLLABORATIONS

DATE	TITLE	TYPE
1832	*The Thief.* Ends 1832 *Figaro in London.* Ends 1839	Newpaper Comic magazine
1834	*The Wandering Minstrel*	Play
1835	*But... However*	Play
1841	Punch –1845	Comic magazine
1842	Coll.* in *Illustrated London News* –1849	Newspaper
1842	*What to Teach and How to Teach It*	Pedagogy
1843	Brothers,** *Comic Almanac* –1853	
1844	Brothers,** *The Prince of Wales Library*	Pedagogic stories
1847	Brothers,** *The Good Genius* *The Greatest Plague in Life*	Humorous novels
1848	Brothers,** *The Image of his Father,* *Whom to Marry, The Magic of Kindness*	Humorous novels
1849	Coll. to *Morning Chronicle* –1850 *Fear of the World* and *Acting Charades* Speech 28 Oct 1850 by Mr Mayhew at the Committee of Taylors of London	1st series of articles, LLLP Pamphlet against the Nicol Brothers
1851	*London Labour and the London Poor* to Feb. 1852 Coll. to *Edinburgh News*, 1851 Coll. to Melliora *Life Among the Mormons,***1851 or the Adventures of the Sandboy Family*	Vols I, II, and first 193 pages of Vol. IV Reportage Pamphlet Ethnology Humorous novel
1854	*The Stories of the Peasant Boy Philosopher*	Pedagogic child story
1855	*The Wonders of Science*	Pedagogic child story
1856	*The Morning News* –1859 *The Great World of London* *The Lower Rhine and its Picturesque* *Scenery*, 2 Vols	LLLP reprint Criminal study Travel account
1858	*The Upper Rhine*, 2 Vols	Travel account

1861	*Young Benjamin Franklin* *London Labour and the London Poor* Reprint Vols I & II (1851), new Vol. III	Pedagogic child story LLLP reprint & added material
1862	*London Labour and the London Poor* Reprint Vols I, II & III (ed. 1861) and completed 1851 Vol. III as Vol. IV	LLLP reprint & added material
	The Criminal Prisons of London Reprint of *The Great World of London* finished by John Binny	Treatise on prisons
1863	*The Boyhood of Martin Luther*	Pedagogic child story
1864	*The German Life and Manners as seen in* *Saxony*	Ethnology/ travel account
1865	*London Labour and the London Poor* Cheap reprint of 1861 edition	LLLP reprint
	The Shops and Companies of London	LLLP reprint with added material
1870	*Only Once a Year*	Comic magazine
1871	*Report concerning the hours of closing usual* *among the unlicensed Victualling* *establishments*	Commissioned Investigative journalism
1873	*Mont-Blanc* with Athol Mayhew	Play
1881	*The London Characters*	LLLP reprint

Coll.   Collaboration
–1853   Until 1853
Brothers** Brothers Mayhew (Augustus, Henry and sometimes Horace)
LLLP   *London Labour and the London Poor*
***   The authorship of this anonymously published book is debated, see
     A. Humpherys, op. cit., p. 210
****   1862 edition, reprint, Dover 1968

2

THE GENESIS OF *LONDON LABOUR*
 AND THE LONDON POOR

1. G.N. Ray, *W.M. Thackeray's Contribution to the Morning Chronicle, 1844-1848*, Illinois University Press, 1955.
2. Spielmann, op.cit., p.268.
3. See A. Mayhew, op.cit., p.10.
4. H. Mayhew, "What is the Cause of Surprise? And What Connection Has It With the Laws of Suggestion?", *Douglas Jerrold's Shilling Magazine*, 1847, VII:561-564.
5. Education had become one of the topics of the day and the experiments developed concretely by people like Owen were far more teaching-orientated,

69

compared with Mayhew's ideas, which were only applicable in a strictly individual relationship of master to disciple. See P. McCann, *The Educational Innovators*, Macmillan, 1967; *Socialization and Social Science in Popular Education in the Nineteenth Century*, Methuen, 1977.

6. H. Mayhew, *What to Teach and How to Teach It*, 1842, p.43.

7. See E.P. Thompson, "Henry Mayhew and the *Morning Chronicle*" in Thompson and Yeo, op.cit., p.17.

8. Mayhew, preface to *The Upper Rhine: The Scenery of its Banks and the Manners of its People*, Routledge, 1858.

9. See A. Lees, *Cities Perceived: Urban Society in European and American Thoughts, 1820-1940*, Manchester University Press, 1985; Alex Potts, "Picturing the Modern Metropolis: Images of London in the Nineteenth Century", in *History Workshop Journal*, Autumn 1988, 26:28-56.

10. The typification in Ainsworth's *Jack Sheppard* or in most penny dreadfuls is quite close to what one would find later in "comics". On "low" literature see F. Moretti, *Signs Taken For Wonders: Essays in the Sociology of Literary Forms*, Verso, 1983; revised edition, 1988.

11. See A. Joffe, op.cit.

12. See L. Giard, "Epilogue: Michel de Certeau's Heterology and the New World" and M. de Certeau, "Travel Narratives of the French to Brazil: Sixteenth to the Eighteenth Century", *Representations*, 1991, 33:212-26.

13. The ethnological and colonial narrative became quite common later in the century. Colonized cultures provided a model of underdeveloped civilization, for the most primitive of them without a history, to which the poor of the country could easily be assimilated in one rhetorical racist and atemporal stereotype: Gal. Booth, *In Darkest England and the Way Out*, Headquarters, 1890, pp.9-17; R.N. Lebow, *White Britain and Black Ireland, The Influence of Stereotypes on Colonial Policies*, Institute for the Study of Human Issues, 1976; N. Thomas, *Out of Time, History, and Evolution in Anthropological Discourse*, Cambridge University Press, 1989, pp.9-16.

14. G. Stedman-Jones, *Outcast London*, Clarendon Press, 1971; Lees, op.cit.; Gertrude Himmelfarb, op.cit., 1984.

15. A similar process took place recently in P. Bourdieu, *La Misère du Monde*, Le Seuil, 1993, pp.903-25.

16. On London Chartism, see D. Goodway, *London Chartism, 1838-1848*, Cambridge University Press, 1982.

17. On cholera there see C. Cowdell, *A Disquisition on Pestilential Cholera*, Samuel Highley, 1848; R.J. Morris, *Cholera, 1832*, Croom Helm, 1976; M. Pelling, *Cholera Fever and English Medicine*, Oxford University Press, 1978; W. Luckin, "The Final Catastrophe: Cholera in London, 1866", *Medical History*, 1977, 21: 32-42.

18. P.E. Razzel and R.W. Wainwright, *The Victorian Working Class: Selections from the Morning Chronicle*, Frank Cass, 1973.

19. See: H.R. Fox-Bourne, op.cit., pp.156-7. The Whig newspaper was virtually bankrupt in 1848 and was bought from Sir John Easthrope in February. P.E. Razzell and R.V. Wainwright, op.cit., p.iii. Mayhew's manifesto was very upfront and prefigured the following conflicts:

> I aim to reveal the economic and social causes of poverty—I shall consider the whole of the Metropolitan poor under three separate phases according as they will work, they can't work and they won't work. While treating of the poorly paid, I shall endeavour to lay before the reader a catalogue of such occupations in London...to ascertain, by positive inspection the conditions of their homes to learn by close communion with them not only how little they subsist on but how large a rate of profit they have to pay for the little upon

which they do subsist...to calculate the interest the petty capitalist reaps from their necessities.

20. On Chadwick and his major survey see B. W. Richardson, *The Health of Nations: A Review of the Work of Edwin Chadwick with a Biographical Dissertation*, Longman, Green and Co. 1887; P. Besses, "Science Sociale et Idéologie Bourgeoise selon Bentham dans le *Report on the Sanitary Condition of the Labouring Population of Great Britain*", *Villes et Santé*, Clermont Ferrand University Press, 1988, pp.47-120; R. Lewis, *E. Chadwick and the Public Health Movement, 1832-1854*, Longman, Green & Co, 1952; A. Brundage, *England's Prussian Minister, E. Chadwick and the Politics of Government Growth, 1832-1854*, Pennsylvania University Press, 1988.

21. Chartist circles also provided him with revenge on the *Morning Chronicle* after an article written by another as the Committee of Tailors of London published his speech under the title:
    REPORT OF THE SPEECH OF OCT. 28 1850 AT ST MARTIN'S HALL, LONG ACRE printed by the Committee of Tailors of London for the purpose of exposing the falsehoods contained in an article that appeared in the Morning Chronicle of Friday 4th 1850 on the sweating or domestic system and to exhibit to the public the terrible evils engendered by this system whether regarded in a moral, physical, religious, social or sanitary point of view.

22. On slums see E.C. Midwinter, *The Victorian Social Reform*, Longman, 1988; P. Garside, and Y. Ken, *Metropolitan London, Politics and Urban Changes 1837-1981*, Edward Arnold, 1982; J.H. Treble, *Urban Poverty in Britain 1830-1914*, St Martin's Press, 1979; J.A. Yelling, *Slums and Slum Clearance in Victorian London*, Allen and Unwin, 1986.

23. There is a large bibliography on miasmatic theories but a non-specialist view at the subject can be completed through the reading of A. Corbin, *Le Miasme et La Jonquille: L'Odorat et L'Imaginaire Social aux XVIIIème-XIXème Siècles*, Flammarion, 1982.

24. J. Burnett, *Idle Hands: The Experience of Unemployment, 1790-1990*, Routledge, 1994, pp.10-41.

25. Various attitudes existed, from the most conservative who coined the words "Dangerous Class" and who implied that poverty and vice were mutually explanatory to phrenologists like Combe who considered vice and crime a form of congenital madness. Others like Beames, Hill or Buret explained both misery and vice through the lack of education. This was close to Mayhew's views. See H. Frégier, *Des Classes Dangereuses de la Population dans les Grandes Villes*, Baillière, 1840; F. Hill, *Crime: Its Amount, Causes and Remedies*, John Murray, 1853; T. Beames, *The Rookeries of London*, Thomas Bosworth, 1850 and *A Plea for Educational Reform*, James Ridgway, 1856, E. Buret, *De la Misère des Classes Laborieuses en Angleterre et en France*, Paulin, 1840; G. Combe, *The Principles of Criminal Legislation; and The Practice of Prison Discipline Investigated*, Simpskin Marshall and Co. 1854.

26. See B. Colloms, *The Victorian Visionaries*, Constable, 1982, p.69.

27. See M. Agulhon, *1848, ou l'Apprentissage de la République*, Le Seuil, Paris, 1973.

28. See L. Shepard, op.cit., pp.10-25.

29. On the epistemological break of the late eighteenth century, see M. Foucault, *Les Mots et les Choses*, NRF, 1966, pp.293-305.

30. At 2d. per week or between 8 and 10 pence a month, when each of Dickens's instalments for *Dombey and Son*, Bradbury, 1846-1848 sold for 1 shilling, Mayhew's work was "very good value for money".

31. On the subject, albeit for an earlier period, see M. Jenner, "Early Modern English Conceptions of Cleanliness and Dirt as Reflected in the Environmental

Regulation of London, c. 1530-c.1700", D.Phil, University of Oxford, 1991, forthcoming as a book.

32. See J. Hall, *The Sons of Toil and the Crystal Palace: In Reply to Mr Mayhew*, John Snow, 1853.

33. Of this later attempt there exists only a letter (in the British Library Manuscript Dept.) sent to Leigh Hunt (1784-1859) on 12 September 1856.

Dear Sir,

I beg to enclose...a few papers relating to a society in which I feel a lively interest. I send you also a lithographed letter of Bulwers in connection with the same subject. I know you will cordially approve of this first practical attempt to give the masses some little sense of the beauties which encompass them on every side and to teach them the high and cheap luxury of Art enjoyments—I am sure you think as I do the only sane way of taking working men from pit houses is to teach them to delight in Higher and Better pleasures since a taste for such matters is incompatible with the love of sensual gratifications.

I know you will gladly give your name as a patron of such a society especially when I tell you that I desire to link about the institution all the most earnest and graceful minds of the present day, if too we could prevail upon you to deliver a brief address upon the use of the beautiful in art + nature to working men we should be able to inaugurate the society in a most honourable + memorable manner.

Pray do not let any idle modesty keep you from such an undertaking—believe me no man is so highly praised by the great mass of workers as yourself + none would they think as a greater reason to listen to + and none let me add could they hear more graceful and comforting things, Believe me with great esteem too.

Yours very Truly
HENRY MAYHEW

34. *London Labour and the London Poor* failed as with most of Mayhew's ventures at the Court of Chancery. His publisher had changed addresses during the publication and probably went bankrupt.

35. Several hypotheses have been put forward and it is not impossible that Mayhew lost some of his credibility after he attacked the London ragged schools movement. See Biographical Notice in C. Knight, *The English Cyclopaedia*, C. Knight, 1856.

36. See L.K. Hughes and M. Lund, *The Victorian Serial*, University Press of Virginia, 1991, pp.1-14.

37. G. Reynolds' *Sempstress*, J.M. Ludlow, "Labour and the Poor", in *Fraser*, 1850, 41:1-18; C. Kingsley, *Cheap Clothes and Nasty*, William Pickering, 1850 all took on board much of Mayhew's material and pathos.

38. See E. Kaplan, *Motherhood and Representation: The Mother in Popular Culture and Melodrama*, Routledge, 1992. On *East Lynn*, see: pp.76-106.

39. On melodrama see: C.H. MacKay (ed.), *Dramatic Dickens*, Macmillan, 1989; P. Brooks. *The Melodramatic Imagination*, Yale University Press, 1976; M.R. Booth, *English Melodrama*, Herbert Jenkins, 1965.

40. On scandalous journalism see D.J. Gray, "Early Victorian Scandalous Journalism" in J. Shattock and M. Wolff, *The Victorian Periodical Press: Samplings and Soundings*, Leicester University Press, 1982, pp.317-48. Gray seems to argue that scandalous journalism was a thing of the past by 1842 in the new clime of Victorian respectability.

3

OPEN LETTERS: MAYHEW AND HIS CORRESPONDENTS

1. R. Chartier (ed.), *La Correspondance, les Usages de la Lettre au XIX Siècle*, Fayard, 1991. P. Lebrun-Pezerat "La Lettre au Journal", pp. 427-49, deals specifically with letters written to a news magazine for French post office employees.
2. Major texts on the subject do not make mentions of it: see R.D. Altick, *The English Common Readers*, Chicago University Press, 1957; L. Brown, *Victorian News and Newspapers*, Oxford University Press, 1985.
3. This use of "original spelling" may be assimilated to that of the "original pronunciation" to render the "accent". Mayhew and Dickens often use this technique to comic or verisimilitude effect.
4. See Lebrun-Pezerat, in Chartier (ed.), op.cit., p.447.
5. In any case a forgery would be just as "truthful" to our study. We cannot identify each and every one of Mayhew's readers but need to work on the existing printed exchange; were the correspondents fake, Mayhew's dependency on such a correspondence would be even more revealing.
6. Among others, see the Universal Anti-Truck Society, The Training Institution for Nurses, several reclaimed prostitutes' societies, the National Philanthropic Association, the *Arts Union Journal*, the *Dublin Commercial*, the *Journal of Industry*, etc. Journals or newspapers either advertised *London Labour and the London Poor* or reproduced some of its articles.
7. Mayhew's readership seems to have been predominantly urban. On the general patterning of literacy in Britain and the problems *London Labour* encountered with distribution in the rural districts, see W.E. Stephens, *Education, Literacy and Society, 1830-1870: The Geography of Diversity in Provincial England*, Manchester University Press, 1987.
8. The view that Mayhew's work was potentially dangerous had been expressed on other authors' work after the repeal of the stamp duty. See J. Collinge, *The Probable Results of Immoral Publications on the Youth of this Country*, Heywood, 1846.
9. On the vitality of provincial statistical research see, among many others, T.S. Ashton, *Economic and Social Investigations in Manchester*, 1833-1933, London Statistical Society, 1934; J. Koren, *The History of Statistics: Their Development and Progress in Many Countries*, 1918, Burt Franklin, 1970; S. Stigler, *The History of Statistics: The Measurement of Uncertainty before 1900*, Harvard University Press, 1986.
10. This sets *London Labour and the London Poor* in the normal lot of serialized books. It had the same uses as a magazine, a review or a penny dreadful with the same extensive expectations and lengthy reading time. L. K. Hughes and M. Lund, *The Victorian Serial*, University Press of Virginia, 1991, pp.9-33.
11. B. Brierley, *Home Memories and Recollection of a Humble Life*, Heywood & Son, 1886, represents very well the class of self-taught literary men who flourished in Britain as well the vitality of literacy among the working class. See P. Joyce, *Visions of the People*, Cambridge University Press, 1991, pp.193-211; M. Vicinus, *The Industrial Muse*, Croom Helm, 1974; B.G. Worral, "Self-Taught Working Men: The Culture and Ideology of Autodidacticism, with Special Reference to Lancashire, 1790-1930", PhD, Manchester University, 1985.
12. G. Dillon, *Rhetoric as Social Imagination: Explorations in the Interpersonal Function of Language*, Indiana University Press, 1986, pp.145-7.
13. The theme is recurrent in Eco's life work and is explored in the following texts: *Opera Apta*, Bompiani, 1962; *The Role of the Reader*, Indiana University Press, 1979; *The Open Work*, Hutchinson/Radius, 1989.

14. Saussure and Barthes would be useful here to explore that privileged relationship between reader and author. Unlike the mediation of novels which is largely symbolic, in this instance it is tangible. Between two entities the reader—author often change roles and write about one another; here readers and authors and writings are combined. There is a full simultaneity between the author, the reader and the writings: they seem to collide into one space, forming *London Labour and the London Poor*. See R. Girard, *Mensonges Romantiques et Vérités Romanesques*, Le Seuil, 1961, pp. 15-67.

15. See C. Steedman's brilliant analysis of a journal kept by a working-class soldier and policeman: *The Radical Soldier's Tale*, History Workshop Series, Routledge, 1988; J. Burnett, D. Mayall, D. Vincent, *The Autobiography of the Working Class: An Annotated Critical Bibliography*, Vol.I, 1790-1900, Harvester, 1984; D. Vincènt, *Bread, Knowledge and Freedom: a Study of Nineteenth Century Working Class Autobiography*, Europa, 1981; R. Garnier, *Subjectivities, A History of Self-Representation in Britain, 1832-1920*, Oxford University Press, 1991, pp.138-58; V. Sanders, *The Private Lives of Victorian Women: Autobiography in Nineteenth Century England*, Harvester Wheatsheaf, 1989, pp.7-20.

16. See Viscount Ingestre, *Melliora, or Better Times to Come, Being the Contribution of Many Men Touching the Present State and Prospect of Society*, John W. Parker, for the General Society for the Dwelling of the Working Class, 1853.

17. Colin G. Pooley recently made a useful communication on the "self-help" dimension at the origin of building societies which combined useful savings, mythical valorisations of ownership with model lodgings planning. "Building Societies, Self-Help and Home-Ownership in England and Wales, circa 1850-1940", Self-Help Conference, Lancaster University, July 1991.

18. Carolyn Steedman, for instance, used the "Little Watercress Girl" as the type of inverted childhood convention and as a trademark in our understanding of the past in *Landscape for a Good Woman*, Virago, 1986, p.30.

19. T. Bottomore and R. Nisbet (eds) *A History of Sociological Analysis*, Basic Books, 1978; See: R. Aron, *Les Étapes de la Pensée Sociologique*, Gallimard, 1969; W. Lepenies, op.cit., pp.1-5, 108-20, 183.

4

CRACKING THE HARD NUTS

1. See M. Berg, *The Machinery Question and the Making of Political Economy 1815-1848*, Cambridge University Press, 1980, pp.32-42.

2. See A.J. Blanqui, *Histoire de l'Economie Politique depuis les Anciens jusqu'à nos Jours*, Guillaumier, 1882; K. Marx, *Das Kapital, Kritik der Politischen Oekonomie*, Otto Meisner, 1867. T. Hodgskin, *Popular Political Economy: Four Lectures Delivered at the London Mechanics Institute*, Charles Tait, 1827, p.3: "That *natural* Science, which has received the erroneous name of Political Economy".

3. The moral dimension of political economy in the early nineteenth century is particularly obvious in Bentham's work but also in Mill's or even in Ricardo. Collections of examples were the work of popular writers like Samuel Smiles who certainly gave the genre its greatest standard with *Self-Help: with Illustrations of Conduct and Perseverance*, John Murray, 1859. Morality itself was presented as quantifiable and therefore entered the field of political economy, although it was not a product, it was a value added to human stock. See J. Fletcher, *Summary of the Moral Statistics of England and Wales*, private circulation, 1849.

4. See Harriet Martineau's popular series, a novelization of political economy, such as, *Illustrations of Political Economy; N 1 "Life in the Wilds"; A Tale*, Charles Fox, 1832. This first volume took the "natural state" hypothesis into the context of pioneering South Africa. Ideas were naturally debated among people who returned to the most absolute poverty after an attack. Martineau's talented narrative made the message of political economy extremely readable.

5. Smiles' work was one of the bestsellers of the century and his later works also sold well. They are characterized by a strict individualism put forward in the examples developed. In terms of economic theory the concept of self-help is understood in its narrowest meaning as very orthodox and only prone to improve competitiveness on the labour market. A human being seen as a commodity is advised to improve in order to be more readily consumable. S. Smiles, *Workmen's Earnings and Strikes*, 1861. Reprinted from the *Quarterly Review*.

6. See N. Thompson, *The People's Science: The Popular Political Economy of Exploitation and Crisis 1816-1834*, Cambridge University Press, 1984, and the most important among the 1830s theoreticians, John Ramsay McCulloch, *The Principles of Political Economy*, London, 1825. Thompson's argument is based on the vitality of economic debates in the unstamped press of the 1830s including Hetherington's *Poor Man's Guardian* on which Mayhew's brother worked. This active anti-political economy reflection ended up as a failure for reasons seen also in Mayhew's work: the inability to transcend moral definition when tackling the question of the value of labour. Owen, Gray and Hodgskin turned to free tradism, monetarism or sectarianism respectively.

7. B. Hilton, *The Age of Atonement: The Influence of Evangelicalism on Social and Economical Thought, 1795-1865*, Clarendon Press, 1988, pp.36-70.

8. J. Burnett, *Idle Hands: The Experience of Unemployment, 1790-1990*, Routledge, 1994, pp.82-7.

9. J. Burnett, op.cit., pp.42-77.

10. Even if earlier organisational mutations had modified these industries. See A. Randall, *Before the Luddites: Custom, Community and Machinery in the English Woollen Industry 1776-1809*, Cambridge University Press, 1991.

11. Colin Clark's division into three sectors, primary, secondary and tertiary had not been theorized. See C. Clark, *The National Income*, Macmillan, 1931, and *National Income and Outlay*, Macmillan, 1937.

12. See H. Mayhew, *London Labour and the London Poor*, Vol IV, 1851, pp.5-7. Mayhew judged the census definitions to be too imprecise and too unsystematic.

13. R. Gagnier, *Subjectivities*, pp.90-1. Gagnier links Mayhew's classification to Mill's Utilitarianism. Yet I feel it is closer to traditional moral classifications than to a much altered Utilitarian system.

14. Social definitions of what a caring society should be, putting enlightened educators at the top, were relatively common among Christian Socialists of that period; B. Colloms, op.cit., p.4.

15. As pointed out in the introduction, this theoretical part of *London Labour and the London Poor* was printed in every edition of the book but never separately. This suggests that Mayhew saw it as central to his study but only comprehensible when located at the heart of the work. K. Williams, *From Pauperism to Poverty*, Routledge & Kegan Paul, 1981, pp.240-5.

16. Mayhew's adopted the 1830s view which ruled in Noel Thompson's words that "labour [was] exchanged below and commodities above their natural values" (N. Thompson, op.cit. p.235).

17. R. Gagnier, op.cit., p.63.

18. P. Stallybrass, "Marx and Heterogeneity: Thinking the Lumpenproletariat",

Representations, 1990, 31:69-95.

19. See T. Richard, *The Commodity Culture of Victorian England: Advertising and Spectacle, 1851-1914*, Stanford University Press, 1990, pp.3, 7-8, 24-5.

20. Mayhew later spent more time on criminology in his *Great World of London* and worked with many others on the early paradigms of that early social science. See among his contemporaries T. Beggs, *Juvenile Delinquency and Reformatory Institutions*, Social Science, 1857; G. Combe, *The Principle of Criminal Legislation*, Simpskin Marshall and Co., 1854.

21. Foreign trade is almost an alien concept to him, the notion of free trade is only seen through the narrow limits of bread pricing. Mayhew was a genuine "little Englander" when it came to considerations about world economy. The Irish famine was not one of his concerns either. Even if he did allude to the Irish problems he did not try to extend his views beyond the slums of London.

22. Mayhew analyzed well the problems encountered by workers who had to resort to sweat shops for their employment. According to whether they were slow or quick hands they could or could not make up the difference between hourly wages and wages by the piece. The precariousness of employment with strong seasonal differences was another aspect he treated.

23. At least on paper, many studies now demonstrate that the Poor Law was not implemented as rigidly and as systematically as originally thought. See M.E. Rose (ed.), *The Poor and the City: The English Poor Law in its Urban Context 1834-1914*, Leicester University Press, 1983. On popular resistances see J. Knott, *Popular Opposition to the 1834 Poor Law*, Croom Helm, 1986. P. Wood, *Poverty and the Workhouse in Victorian Britain*, Alan Sutton, 1991.

24. See A. Clark, "The Rhetoric of Chartist Domesticity: Gender, Language, and Class in the 1830s and 1840s" in *Journal of British Studies*, 1992, 31:62-88.

25. On skill see C. More, *Skill and the English Working Class, 1870-1914*, Croom Helm, 1980.

26. Mayhew understood the 1840s crisis as the consequence of the loss of statutory rights against entrepreneurs at the beginning of the century. See I. Prothero, *Artisans and Politics in Early Nineteenth Century London*, Dawson, 1979.

27. B. Colloms, op.cit.; John C. Cort, *Christian Socialism, an informal history*, Orbis, 1988. At the same period Ludlow published his important *Politics for the People*, Augustus Kelley, reprint, 1971.

28. See D.G. Wright, *Popular Radicalism: The Working Class Experience, 1780-1880*, Longman, 1988; T. Tholfsen, *Working Class Radicalism in Mid-Victorian England*, Clarendon, 1976.

29. Gangs were organized by middlemen who would receive a sum from the entrepreneur for a specified work. Middlemen chose their gang labourers and paid them. There was therefore no contact between the capitalist and the workers. Middlemen were often publicans who could take advantage of the situation by paying late on Saturdays or by only employing drinkers. Dockers had been freed from that system by an Act of Parliament but ballast heavers had not. A similar gang system existed for street-sweepers. Christian Socialists attempted to help them in the 1850s. See B. Colloms, op.cit., pp.97-106.

30. Contrast with Marxian historical materialism. See R.F. Hamilton, *The Bourgeois Epoch, Marx Engels on Britain, France, and Germany*, University of North Carolina Press, 1991, pp.1-12.

31. See Proudhon, *Qu'est ce que la Propriété?*, Garnier Frères, 1848.

32. *Bricoleur* as opposed to *ingénieur* is a concept which suits Mayhew well. The dilettante could not operate the same conceptualization as the professional intellectual and revolutionary theorist.

33. C. Babbage, *On the Economy of Machinery and Manufactures*, Charles Knight, 1832.

34. See E. Demaré, *London 1851, the Great Exhibition*, Folio Society, 1972.
35. R. Williams, *Keywords, A Vocabulary of Culture and Society*, Fontana Press, 1988, pp. 75-6.
36. G. Stedman-Jones made this point clear in his review article "The Labours of Henry Mayhew, Metropolitan Correspondent of the *Morning Chronicle*", *London Journal*, 1984, Vol 10, 1:80-85, p.83.
37. See E.P. Thompson, *William Morris, Romantic to Revolutionary*, Pantheon, 1976, pp.22-39.
38. *Economist*, "Distressed Populations", 16 November 1850, pp 1264-5. This review addressed the MCS rather than LLLP, but Mayhew kept referring to it in "Answers to Correspondents".
39. Dickens' reform writings were more powerfully expressed in *Household Words* in the 1850s after *London Labour and the London Poor*, see P. Ackroyd, *Dickens*, Minerva, 1991; N. Philips and V. Neuberg, *Charles Dickens, A December Vision: His Social Journalism*, Collins, 1986.

5

HISTORY IN THEIR OWN WORDS

1. Mayhew's emphases.
2. See: G. Stedman-Jones, *Outcast London*, 2nd edn, Peregrine, Penguin, 1983; P. Joyce, *Visions of the People*, Cambridge University Press, 1991; N. Elias, *Uber den Prozess der Zivilisation.: Soziogenetische und Psychogenetische Untersuchungen*, Haus zum Falken, 1939, particularly volume I; R. Chartier, "Culture as Appropriation: Popular Culture in Early Modern France" in S. Kaplan (ed.), *Understanding Popular Culture: Europe from the Middle Ages to the Nineteenth Century*, Ritmeyer, 1984, pp.229-54.
3. M. Deas, "Miguel Antonio Caro and his Friends: Grammar and Power in Columbia", *History Workshop*, Autumn 1992, 34:47-71; O. Smith, *The Politics of Language, 1790-1819*, Oxford University Press, 1984, pp.110-53.
4. The Philological Society decided to compile a dictionary complementing Richardson's (1836) in the summer of 1857. It was helped in its endeavour by the Early English Text Society (1864). *The New English Dictionary* was sent to publishers in 1882. (*OED*, New Edition, pp.xxxv-xliv.) Earlier dictionaries, particularly eighteenth century ones, were more often a collection of rarer words. The origins of words explored in Mayhew's correspondence remain debated.
5. Philology is an historical science which not only tries to create chronological landmarks in the language itself but also to some extent, to exercise a reflexive exploration of itself. See: H. Haarsleff, *The Study of Language in England 1780-1860*, Princeton University Press, 1967, and *From Locke to Saussure: Essays on the Study of Language and Intellectual History*, University of Minnesota Press, 1982. A more literary approach also gives interesting accounts of growing philological concerns in Victorian England: C.H. Plotkin, *The Tenth Muse; Victorian Philology and the Genesis of the Poetic Language of Gerard Manley Hopkins*, Southern Illinois University Press, 1989. A social history of language is still in limbo but one can say that the language problem is at the heart of any research in cultural history, see P. Burke, and R. Porter, *The Social History of Language*, Cambridge Studies in Oral and Literate Culture, Cambridge University Press, 1987; P. Joyce, op.cit., pp.193-214; L. Hunt (ed.), *The New Cultural History*, University of California Press, 1989.
6. C. Plotkin, op.cit., pp.14-17.

7. Horne Tooke and *The Diversions of Purley* in 1786 had a long-lasting influence and kept Britain immune to the new philology. See H. Haarsleff, op.cit., 1967, p.73.
8. The following books are often quoted in the correspondence: *The Standard Library Cyclopaedia*; Chaucer's *Prologue*; F. Bopp, *Vocalismus*, 1836; Joseph Bosworth (1789-1876), *A Dictionary of the Anglo-Saxon Language*, Longman & Co. (1838); Robert Kelham (1717-1808), *A Dictionary of the Norman Old French Language*, E. Brooke, 1779; Napoléon Landais, *Dictionnaire Général des Dictionnaires Français*, Bureau Central, 1834; John Ramsay McCulloch (1789-1864), *The Dictionary of Commerce*, 1832-1839; John Horne Tooke (1736-1812), *The Diversion of Purley*, 1786; Charles Richardson (1775-1865), *A New Dictionary of the English Language*, William Pickering, 1836, 1839, 1844.
9. See M. Foucault, *Les Mots et Les Choses*, NRF, 1966, pp.293-305. Changes in attitudes towards language form one of Foucault's most convincing arguments for a radical break in the epistemology between the "classical age" (C17th-C18th) and the nineteenth century.
10. The processes of the acquisition of knowledge are very complex and can be tackled in different ways. Self-taught men, like Ben Brierley in Manchester, recalled in their memoirs the process of acquisition of "high" culture, social position and self-respect. The vitality of autodidacticism and the interest in dictionaries are complementary. See B. Brierley, *Home Memories and Recollection of a Humble Life*, Heywood, 1886; M. Vicinus, *The Industrial Muse*, Croom Helm, 1974; B.G. Worral, "Self-Taught Working Men: The Culture and Ideology of Autodidacticism, with special reference to Lancashire, 1790-1930", PhD, Manchester University, 1985; B. Maidment, *The Poorhouse Fugitives*, Carcarnet, 1987.
11. Mayhew had travelled to India, across France and Germany. He had therefore been confronted with Latin, Germanic and the (then considered primitive) Indo-European languages of India. His linguistic encounters reflected most of the actual field of philological research at that time. Carolyn Steedman also recently reflected on the linguistic encounters of John Pearman whose diary she edited as *The Radical Soldier's Tale*, Routledge & Kegan Paul, 1988.
12. See H. Trevor-Roper, "The Invention of Tradition: The Highland Tradition of Scotland" and P. Morgan, "From Death to a View: The Hunt for the Welsh Past in the Romantic Period" in E. Hobsbawm and T. Ranger (eds), *The Invention of Tradition*, Cambridge University Press, 1983, pp.15-100.
13. See H. Mayhew, *London Labour and the London Poor*, Vol I, 1851, Preface, p.xv. This free space given to those forgotten in history is certainly the most generous aim of Henry Mayhew and it inspired feminist writers who see Mayhew's attempt as an early opening to alternative ways of writing history. See C. Crosby's *The Ends of History, Victorians and the "Woman Question"*, Routledge, 1991, pp.69-109
14. See F. J. Newmeyer, *The Politics of Linguistics*, University of Chicago Press, 1986, p.20. The national dimension of any linguistics or philology could not be better exemplified than through this parallel creation of philology and folklore; both dig deeply into the roots of the *Kultur* and although universal in content (techniques of philology, universality of tales) both can be interpreted within the strictly nationalistic framework of nations in the making.
15. See P. Burke, *Popular Culture in Early Modern Europe*, Maurice Temple-Smith, 1978, pp.15-19.
16. Arthurian legends are common to French Brittany, Spanish Galicia and British Cornwall. They represent the best example of the spreading of similar tales, tales have also been fruitfully used in psychoanalysis, according to K. Jung or to B. Bettleheim.

17. See C. Plotkin, op.cit.; C. Bolt, *Victorian Attitudes to Race*, Routledge & Kegan Paul, 1971.
18. On a controversial contribution to a study of literary imperialism, see E. Said, *Culture and Imperialism*, Chatto & Windus, 1993, pp.1-15.
19. K. Williams, *From Pauperism to Poverty*, Routledge & Kegan Paul, 1981, pp.265-7.
20. On variations in the meaning of civilisation, see N. Elias, op.cit., pp.11-77.
21. Charles Darwin's only published works at the time of *London Labour* was his *Journal of Researches into the Natural History and Geology of the Countries Visited during the Voyage of HMS "Beagle"*, Henry Colburn, 1839, and his *Zoology*, Smith Elder and Co., 1840.
22. Various dictionaries of the Underworld were published in the nineteenth century. See J. Duncombe, *Sinks of London Laid Open*, 1848; Ducange Anglicus, *The Vulgar Tongue*, 1857 which uses Mayhew's definitions and inquiries in "the wandering tribes of London"; J.C. Hotten, *The Dictionary of Modern Slang*, 1859. There was already a tradition of such dictionaries in Britain, as of the 1700s, which belonged to criminology rather than philology. The use of slang by criminals was always over-emphasized and contributed to create a criminal "character".
23. *London Labour and the London Poor*, Vol. II, pp.181-247.
24. See A. Stephens, *Memoirs of John Horne Tooke* [1813], Burt Franklin, 1968, and the chapter devoted to Horne Tooke in O. Smith, op.cit., pp.110-53.
25. R. O'Day and D. Englander, op.cit.; C. Booth, *London Labour*, 1902, 1907.
26. See O. Smith, op.cit., pp.15-19.
27. R. Chartier, *Cultural History: Between Practices and Representations*, Cambridge University Press, 1988; and "Culture as Appropriation" in S. Kaplan (ed.), op.cit., pp.229-54.
28. On the history of V.D. see F. Mort, *Dangerous Sexualities: Medico-Moral Politics in England since 1830*, Routledge & Kegan Paul, 1987; R. Davenport-Hines, *Sex, Death and Punishment: Attitudes to Sex and Sexuality in Britain since the Renaissance*, Collins, 1990.
29. A. Parent-Duchâtelet, *De la Prostitution dans la Ville de Paris*, Baillière, 1836; A. Corbin, *Les Filles de Noce: Misère Sexuelle et Prostitution*, Aubier Montaigne, 1978; J. Sole, *L'Age d'Or de la Prostitution*, Plon, 1993.
30. Ronald Pearsall, *The Worm in the Bud: the World of Victorial Sexuality*, 2nd edn. Pimlico, 1993, pp.380-1 on a similar use of French. Also see Richard Mason, *The Making of Victorial Sexual Attitudes*, Oxford University Press, 1995.
31. Horace Stebbing Roscoe St. John (1832-1888), son of James Augustus St John (1801-1875) the famous author and traveller. He was leader writer on the *Daily Telegraph* when very young and used literary references to build the most extensive possible history of prostitution. He later published accounts on the life and customs in the Dutch Indies all from secondary sources and family connections. See: *London Labour and the London Poor*, 1852, Vol.III, p.37.
32. "She who confines her favours to one may still be a prostitute", *London Labour and the London Poor*, 1851, Vol.III, p.36.
33. M. Ryan, *Prostitution in London with a Comparative View of that of Paris and New York*, Baillière, 1839.
34. W. Acton, *Prostitution Considered in its Moral Social and Sanitary Aspects in London and Other Large Cities*, John Churchill, 1857. In the historiography of medicine and prostitution, Acton was held as the best British equivalent to Parent-Duchâtelet but it appears from more recent studies that he was marginal among the professional world of medicine and that his work might not have received the uncritical attention it was believed to have encountered. See J. Peterson,

"Dr Acton's Enemy: Medicine, Sex and Society in Victorian England", *Victorian Studies*, 1986, 29:569-90; R. Porter and L. Hall, *The Facts of Life, the creation of sexual knowledge in Britain, 1650-1950*, Yale University Press, 1995.

35. England was never a fully regulationist country but the lobby in favour of the Contagious Diseases Acts (1864) and its extension showed a deep support among the establishment.

36. W. Logan, An Exposure from Personal Observation of Female *Prostitution in London, Leeds, Rochdale and Glasgow*, 1843. Logan had a long and influential career among the non-conformist northern preachers and more particularly as a temperance preacher. The fight against prostitution was an associated cause for teetotallers who believed prostitution was created and sustained by alcoholism. See B. Harrison, *Drink and the Victorians: The Temperance Question in England 1815-1872*, Faber & Faber, 1971; *Dictionary of British Temperance Biography*, Society for the Study of Labour History, 1973.

37. Syphilis has a complex history. There were two opposing theories on its origins: either it came from America or it was a native disease. In any case, prostitutes were seen as a-historical, without a clear social status and were marginalised on the borders of the criminal world. See L.P.A. Gauthier, *Recherches Nouvelles sur l'Histoire de la Syphilis*, J.P. Baillière, 1842.

38. The apportionment of responsibility between the prostitute and the customer was traditionally not favourable to the former but the tendency was reformed during the Contagious Diseases Acts debate which took place between 1869 and 1886. The sentimentalized vision of the prostitute replaced that of the fallen woman. See J. Walkowitz, op.cit., 1980; "Male Vice and Feminist Virtue: Feminism and the Politics of Prostitution in Nineteenth-Century Britain", *History Workshop Journal*, spring 1982, pp.77-93; Bertrand Taithe "From Danger to Scandal: Debating Sexuality in the Victorian Era and the Morbid Imagery of Victorian Society", PhD, Manchester University, 1992, ch.4.

39. See M. Agulhon, *1848, ou l'Apprentissage de la République*, Le Seuil, 1973; H.A. Frégier, *Des Classes Dangereuses de la Population dans les Grandes Villes*, Baillière, 1840, p.203; J. Greenwood, *Unsentimental Journeys, Byways of the Modern Babylon*, Ward Lock and Tyler, 1867; *The Seven Curses of London*, Stanley Rivers and Co., 1869; *Odd People in Odd Places, or the Great Residuum*, Frederick Warne and Co., 1883; *Ragged London in 1861*, 1861, p.9.; G. Sims, *How the Poor Live and Horrible London*, 2nd ed. Chatto & Windus, 1889, p.44. All these titles belonged to a repressive literature drawing racial limits between deserving and unredeemable individuals.

40. F. Finnegan, *Poverty and Prostitution, a Study of Victorian Prostitutes in York*, Cambridge University Press, 1979; Frances Finnegan infers from her study that such a high mortality was effectively the case in York.

41. Casinos and theatres, as well as parks, gin palaces or any other public space with limited policing were hunting grounds for prostitutes. These places were notorious and the very act of going to one indicated a sexual purpose. Harmless occupations were therefore not only a moral aim, to get the workers out of drinking places but also a geographical delimitation of virtue by creating pure spaces where virtuous working-class people might go and express their self-respect. See P. Bailey, *Music Hall: The Business of Pleasure*, Oxford University Press, 1986; *Leisure and Class in Victorian England*, Methuen, 1987; J.S. Bratton, *Music Hall: Performance and Style*, Oxford University Press, 1986; P. Bailey, "Conspiracies of Meaning: Music Hall and the Knowingness of Popular Culture", *Past and Present*, August 1994, 144:138-170.

42. The word "pimp" might be anachronistic since historians like Judith Walkowitz

80

maintain that prostitutes did not have pimps in the modern meaning of the word as their activities were not fully criminalized until the 1885 Act. Naturally, they did have friends, lovers and sometimes protectors and the distinction between the gigolo, "fancy man", and the pimp is thin. Even if prostitution were not yet a part of the criminal networks in the 1850s, men did exploit prostitutes or, at least, established relationships which were close to pandering.

43. This phrase is borrowed from Braudel's last published book title: *Grammaire des Civilisations*, A. Colin, 1987.

PART II

ANSWERS TO CORRESPONDENTS

EDITORIAL NOTE

Some letters were acknowledged too briefly to be worth reproducing, others were not judged worth reproducing, either because they were simple queries to which Mayhew answered privately, donations, or relatively less interesting communications. They are listed for each number in the edited-out section with a short summary of the communication if necessary.

Mayhew's spelling, typography and punctuation have been respected in the transcript of the text below. However the sign for the conventional sterling pound, £, has been used rather than Mayhew's "l." For the same reason d. and s. signs standing for pence and shillings have not been put in italics.

Advertisements	First appearance
Mutual Investment Society	No 6
The Adventures of Mr and Mrs Sandboy	No 7
Gutta Percha tubing and lining	No 7
Call for a secretary for the Costermonger association	No 7
Thomas Beames, *The Rookeries of London*	No 8
Heal and Son, bedding	No 15
Mutual Pension Society	No 17
The Magic of Kindness	No 20
Keating's cough lozenges	No 22
Mayhew's articles in *Edinburgh News*	No 22
J. T. Wood's illustrations	No 22
Rowland's "Aqua d'Oro"	No 31
Diorama of the cities and scenes of Europe	No 38
Cooperative agency	No 38
Reprint of *LLLP* back numbers	No 42
The Shabby Farmerly	No 45
Rimmel's "toilet vinegar"	No 46
Low Wages	No 46

Mayhew advertised "those that will not work" to appear on 19 July 1851, postponed publication to 2 August, then the 16 and 23 August when the first number appeared. "Mr. MAYHEW purposes commencing as soon as the preliminary arrangement can be made, an inquiry into the causes, extent and consequences together with the means at present in operation for the mitigation or prevention of prostitution in London, the result of this inquiry will be published in the present work every alternate weeks so that the current number of LONDON LABOUR AND THE LONDON POOR will be devoted one week to the London street folk and the next to the London prostitutes the number upon the latter will be differently paged so as to admit being bound up as a separate volume.

Mr. MAYHEW needs hardly add that any information in connection with the subject will be considered as strictly confidential; and that the names and descriptions of the persons making any communications are never at any time published by him but at their own request."

TO CORRESPONDENTS.
[No.5, 11 JANUARY 1851]

IN compliance with the request of many Subscribers, the outer pages of this periodical will, in future, be used as a wrapper, intended to be cut off in binding, [Sic] This will not only keep the work from being soiled, but enable Mr. Mayhew to answer the inquiries of his several Correspondents.

Concerning the order in which the several divisions of "London Labour and the London Poor" will make their appearance, Mr. Mayhew begs to state that the first six Monthly Parts will be devoted to an exposition of the condition and earnings of the several varieties of the London Street-folk. A Title, Preface, and Index will then be issued, so that the whole of the Numbers on that subject may be bound up into a Volume, in which it is hoped, will be found a full and minute account of the numbers, income, experience, habits, and tastes of every class of person getting his or her living in the public thoroughfares; whether Street-seller, Street-buyer, Street-finder, Street-performer, Street-artizan, or Street-labourer; including accounts of the Street-Irish, Street-Jews, Street-Italians, Street Blind and Maimed, Street Mechanics, Pedlars, Costermongers, and Gipsies,—and thus constituting Vol.I. of the first real History of the People that has ever been attempted in any country whatsoever.

This done, Mr. Mayhew purposes directing his attention to the Producers; beginning with the Workers in Silk, Cotton, Wool, Worsted, Hair, Flax, Hemp, and Coir, as well as the Workers in Skin, Gut, and Feathers, comprising both the Manufacturer and Makers-up of these Materials. Under these two heads will be

I. WORKERS IN SILK, COTTON, WOOL, WORSTED, FLAX, HEMPEN OR OTHER MATERIALS.

1. *Manufacturers of Materials.*

Silk, ribbon and lace manufacturers.	Factory workers.	Flock manufacturers.	Lint makers.
Lace menders.	Spinners.	Mop makers.	Tape makers.
Gauze makers.	Weavers.	Worsted manufacturers.	Hemp dressers and manufacturers.
Braid makers.	Knitters.	Carpet and rug manufacturers	Canvass weavers.
Gimp spinners and weavers.	Candle and lamp-wick makers.	Hair manufacturers.	Rope and cord spinners.
Fringe manufacturers	Stocking makers.	Wig makers.	Net makers.
Tassel makers.	Woollen and cloth manufacturers.	Hair dressers.	Mat makers.
Trimming makers.		Artists in hair.	Sail and sailcloth makers.
Coach-lace makers.	Cloth pressers.	Brush and broom makers	Tarpaulin makers.
Gold-lace weavers.	Shawl makers.	Flax and linen manu-facturers.	Ship's caulkers.
Cotton manufacturers.	Crape makers.	Thread makers.	Tilt makers.
Wadding makers.	Felt manufacturers.		Sack and bag makers and weavers.

2. *"Makers up" of Materials.*

Tailors and breeches makers.	Dress makers and milliners.	Stay and corset makers.	Quilters.
Slop workers.	Robe makers.	Belt makers.	Bed and mattress makers.
Accoutrement makers.	Satin and silk workers.	Stock makers.	Hatters.
Sempstresses.	Embroiderers.	Umbrella and parasol stitchers.	Bonnet makers.
Shirt makers.	Berlin wool makers.	Purse makers.	Cap makers.
Baby-linen makers.			Cloth-cap makers.
			Artificial-flower makers.

II. WORKERS IN SKIN, GUT, AND FEATHERS.

1. *Manufacturers of Materials.*

Skinner and skin dressers.	Curriers and leather sellers.	Catgut makers.	Goldbeater's-skin makers.
Parchment makers and dealers.	Strop makers.	Gut blowers and spinners.	Feather manufacturers.
Tanners.	Furriers.	Musical string makers.	Pen makers and dealers.
		Bow-string makers.	Quill dressers.

2. *"Makers up" of Materials.*

Boot and shoe makers.	Leather case makers.	Glove makers.	Whip makers.
List shoe makers.	Leather pipe makers.	Saddlers.	Coach trimmers.
Ball makers.	Cap peak makers.	Harness and collar makers.	

** *Answers to Letters received will be given in the next Number.*

ANSWERS TO CORRESPONDENTS.
[No.6, 18 JANUARY 1851]

Edited out:

J.T. (*WHO PAYS THE TAXES?*); J.S. SOCIETY OF CABINET MAKERS; THE REV. J.E.H.; "THE BRISTOL TAILOR"; G.J.H.; J.P.; BRISTOL; PIMLICO SOCIETY OF CARPENTERS (*REPORT OF*); EDITOR OF *THE JOURNAL OF INDUSTRY*; J.I.G.; T.R. MILK-STREET.; A PURCHASER; PENSION SOCIETY OF CLICKERS (*REPORT OF*), A.B.C.; D.P.M.; P.C., *IMPORTATION INTO HULL*; F.W.; C.B.; J.R.; T.D.; THE LOOKER-ON; E.J.B. DRURY-LANE.

Several anonymous communications have been received, some of them evidently curious and (if duly authenticated) valuable, but it is impossible to attend to any statement unless means are afforded of testing its accuracy by the names and addresses of the parties forwarding the information being communicated in confidence.

"THE DISEASE AND THE REMEDY," a valuable Essay, has been received. It is heartily wished that the example of Mr. E. Edwards's industry and research in collecting statistics and other information concerning the printing trade may be followed by the secretaries of other trade societies.

TWO POOR NEEDLEWOMEN.—Agnes M.—and Jane W.—, who, in my inquiries among the needlewomen, had become known to me as persons of good character, have written to me stating: "Our circumstances are very bad, we have only earnt a few shillings for the last twelve weeks." MR. MAYHEW can vouch for the worthiness and for the poverty of those two poor women. Toiling from morning till night, they have had but twopence-halfpenny a day to live upon for several years, after paying their rent. This Mr. MAYHEW proved in the *Chronicle*, by extracts from their account-books.[1]

CAROLINE G., the widow of a railway-guard, writes to describe her extremely distressed condition.

PUBLIC BATHS, &c.—Thanks are due for the ticket and documents. The establishment will be noticed in due course.

THE SWANSEA HERALD, DUBLIN COMMERCIAL JOURNAL, STOCKPORT ADVERTISER, and other papers, containing notices of "London Labour and the London Poor," have been received.

THE PROFILIST is thanked, and will be communicated with.

---

[1] See Peter Razzell (ed.), *The Morning Chronicle Survey of Labour and the Poor: Metropolitan District*, Caliban, 1980, Vol. I, p. 158. This six-volume definitive reprint of Henry Mayhew's *Morning Chronicle* articles will thereafter be referred to under the initials MC.

ANSWERS TO CORRESPONDENTS.
[No.7 & No.8, 25 JANUARY 1851.
1 FEBRUARY 1851][2]

An account has been given among the notices to correspondents of the several occupations which will be treated of in this work, on the completion of the volume concerning the street-folk. In the meantime, the several operatives, trade societies, and employers, will do the Author, and it is hoped themselves and the public, a considerable service by forwarding such *facts* connected with their trade, as may have come under their own *personal* experience.

MR. MAYHEW would feel obliged by the name and address of the writers being added to all communications—not with a view to publication, but as a guarantee of respectability and good faith. MR. MAYHEW (for obvious reasons) never prints the names of those from whom he receives his information, but leaves the public to look to him alone as the person responsible for the truth of the statements here published; it is therefore necessary for his own credit sake, that he should be furnished with the means of ascertaining the credibility of his informants, before pledging himself to the authenticity of any facts with which they may supply him. All anonymous communications will henceforth be unattended to.

The statistical information that MR. MAYHEW desires is of three kinds— First, concerning the earnings of individuals—Secondly, the income and expenditure, objects and government of trade societies—and Thirdly, the *kind* of cheap labour by which the "cutting" masters in the several trades are enabled to undersell the more liberal employers.

1st. The earnings of individual operatives should be proved by the account-books of the employers or employed both of which will be

highly valuable, especially if extending over a series of years. Each of the account-books of the operatives, however, should be accompanied by a statement as to whether it represents the earnings of a person who is *fully, partially,* or only *casually,* employed; also, whether the workman is a *quick, average,* or *slow* hand. Of course all such books (or statistical documents of any kind indeed) as may be entrusted to MR. MAYHEW for the purposes of this work, will be carefully preserved, and when done with faithfully returned.

2nd. The trade society statistics that MR. MAYHEW would be thankful for, are statements of the number of members in and out of society for a series of years—the wages of society men during the same time, specifying the cause of any rise or fall—the subscriptions paid by members, and how much of these is devoted to trade purposes, and how much to "philanthropic" (if any)—the income and expenditure of the society for each year as far back as possible— the sums paid annually to the unemployed, as well as the yearly number of unemployed members—the amount given every year to the sick, (specifying if possible the prevailing diseases of the trade)—the sums disbursed to the superannuated, as well as the gross amount paid at death of the members, setting forth the number of individuals in each case—the sums paid for insurance of tools, if any—the amount disbursed to tramps—the number of employers who pay society prices, and if possible the number of those who do not (the last items especially, should be given for as long a period as possible, so that an estimate may be formed as to the prospects of the trade). MR. MAYHEW would also be glad to know what are the trade regulations concerning apprentices—the term of apprenticeship—the number usually taken—the premium paid— and the remuneration of the apprentice. The hours of labour recognised by the Society, and the duration of the brisk and slack seasons, would likewise be useful, as well as whether the men are paid day-work or piece-work. It would further be desirable to know the cost and causes of any strikes that may have taken place, and

---

[2] This notice was printed consecutively on No. 7 and No. 8 of the periodical accompanying different personal notices.

the opinion of the more intelligent members of the trade thereupon. MR. MAYHEW wishes moreover to be furnished with facts as to whether the late reduction in the price of food has been followed by a commensurate reduction in the rate of wages, and whether at the time of the imposition of the income or any other tax, the wages of the operatives were reduced to an equal extent. MR. MAYHEW is aware that such has been the case in many trades, but he is desirous of ascertaining whether the reduction has been general, and if not, of learning the nature of the exceptions.

3rd. As to the nature of the cheap labour by which the cutting master in the different trades are enabled to undersell the more liberal employers. MR. MAYHEW wishes to know; first, whether the cheap labourers employed belong to the less skilful portion of the trade—as boys, "improvers,"—old men, &c.; or to the less respectable—as the drunken, the idle, and the dishonest; or the less expensive—that is to say, those who will put up with a coarser diet, as foreigners, Irishmen, &c., and those who have their subsistence found them, either by the State, as paupers and criminals, or by their connections and relations, as wives and children. Also whether there are any "aids to wages" among the cheaper labourers in the several trades, as "allotments," "relief," &c. &c. Moreover, it would be advisable to make known whether the cheap workers are obliged to find security, and if so, to what extent—whether they are bound to provide any and what articles that it is usual for the more liberal employers in the trade to find for their workpeople— whether they are bound to buy their materials, tools, or food, of their employers, and if so, the prices charged by them compared with others. If they are boarded or lodged by their employers, the quality and quantity of provisions, and style of accommodation found them. If there are fines, the nature of the offences for which they are imposed, and the amount exacted. If middlemen are customary, then should be stated the sum paid *to* such middlemen by the employer, and the sum paid *by* them to the employed; if, on the other hand,

there be a large number of small working masters in the trade, it would be desirable to know the lowest sum required by an operative to commence manufacturing on his own account—the usual hours of labour among the small masters—the rate of working, that is to say, the quantity of work done by them in a given time—the number who work on the Sunday—the time lost in finding a market for the goods when finished—the advantages taken of their necessities by the tradesmen to whom they sell—the kind of assistants the small masters employ, and the wages they pay.

Statistical information on the above points, in connection with any of the trades (specified in No.5), or indeed in connection with any other trade, will be of the utmost value. Such information need not concern London alone, but the provinces as well, for it is MR. MAYHEW's intention not to confine the work to the artizans and labourers of the Metropolis solely.

MR. MAYHEW would further be thankful for accounts as to the individual expenditure of operatives. These would be of the greatest service, as the means of arriving at the number of ounces of solid food consumed by working men in particular trades, so that the quantity may be contrasted with other trades, as well as with the dietaries of paupers and prisoners.[3] A statement of the sum spent in intoxicating liquors would do good in tending to check a most pernicious custom.

In conclusion, MR. MAYHEW begs to state, that he would likewise be glad to be furnished with a brief account of the experience, privations, and struggles of those working men whose lives have been unusually chequered, and the publication of which is likely to prove interesting or useful to their fellow-workmen, or the public generally.

---

[3] See C. Dickens, *Household Words*, 27 April 1850, for a similar approach of diets in prisons and workhouses. N. Philips & V. Neuberg, *Charles Dickens: A December Vision*, Collins, 1986, pp. 70-84.

ANSWERS TO CORRESPONDENTS.
[No.7b]

Edited out:
P.L.; W.B.; A BOOTMAKER; AN INVESTIGATOR; A GREENGROCER; B.H.R.W; E.C.M.; J.R.; W.P.; F.R.S.; T.W.R.; T.W.P.; W.T.; A PLAIN SPEAKER; P.P.; A.R.

Mr. W.H. FORMAN writes to point out "a slight error respecting the number of people that can be accommodated in the Gallery of the Victoria Theatre," in the first number of this work. [LLLP, Vol. 1, p.18] Mr. Forman states that 1,000 is (what is termed among the fraternity) "a fizzer," but 900 is the full number the gallery will hold, the other hundred hang about the beams, &c., as described in the first number. Mr. Forman is thanked for his correction, and for his concluding remarks.

E.B., PORTLAND TOWN. See p.219 of M'Culloch's "Dictionary of Commerce" (1844). [2nd edition] The orthography used is that of the leading fruit brokers—though there are certainly doubts on the subject—but in such matters custom is often the only recognized authority.

L.A.—The number cited was on the authority of a government table. L.A.'s censures, though complimentary, collaterally, to the importance of such a work as "London Labour and the London Poor," are hardly borne out by the facts.

T.R. suggests a Grand National Labour League.

M.N.L.—On the authority of a Report of the Poor-Law Commissioners.

MENTOR. The fulness of a Parliamentary Inquiry, by a Select Committee, can hardly be questioned.

ANONYMOUS COMMUNICATIONS have been received but they cannot— it seems again necessary to announce it—command any attention.

ANSWERS TO CORRESPONDENTS.
[No.8]

Edited out:
FAIR DAY'S PAY FOR A FAIR DAY'S WORK; RECTUS IN CURIA; L.L.A.; R.F.; A BOOTMAKER; L.M.N.; T.P.; T.W.P.; P.P.; R.S.A.; D.; "LAUDATOR TEMPORIS ACTI"; WHOLESALE DEALER; A FORMER SUFFERER.

TO CORRESPONDENTS.—Letters received later than Saturday morning cannot be attended to in the Number published on the following Wednesday. [In fact the other way round]

B.B.—The Plumber's trade was not the subject of any Metropolitan Letter on Labour and Poor in the *Morning Chronicle*.

A.Z.—The answer to B.B. applies to this querist also.

AN ADMIRER.—The question of democracy and aristocracy cannot be discussed in "London Labour and the London Poor," in the way which "An Admirer" recommends.

A GARDENER.—Of such things the costermongers know and care nothing. The tariff of 1842 reduced the duty on foreign pears to 6d. per bushel (3d. from British possessions); it was formerly 7s. 6d.

E.L.—POOR NEEDLEWOMEN.—A letter has been received, from which the following is an extract, the name and address being given, and to be learnt at the Office, 69, Fleet-street.—"I am an employer of female labour in the ill-paid trade of shirt making, and also in the Berlin brace trade. In your last Number I perceive an account of two poor needlewomen; my object in writing is to offer them work, which is continual, winter and summer, and also to lay before you my scale of wages. I have an opening for ten or twelve good hands in either of the above trades. My system is a division of labour. I pay 4s. per dozen for stitching, 3s. 2d. for the plain work, and 6s. for the fitting, which I fix myself, thereby relieving the hands of the most difficult part of the trade. I have the whole of the latter part done upon the premises, under my own inspection, paying every attention to the comfort of the work-people. They have an airy work-room, with fire and candles, cotton is found, and a comfortable tea provided; so that their earnings are free from deductions. I am also in want of a good button-hole worker, wages 3d. a dozen button-holes. I have not been able to see your letters in the *Morning Chronicle*, but am anxiously waiting their appearing in your weekly paper. I am told there are thousands making shirts at 2¹/₂d. each; if this is really the case, I think it must be in consequence of their being extremely inferior hands. The great fault appears to be, that poor girls are not properly instructed in the use of the needle, very few make really quick and clever needlewomen; while the many are so very inferior, that they are compelled to accept any wages that may be offered. The above wages are far less than I should like to be able to pay, but the very utmost I can afford under present circumstances, leaving but a very trifling profit for my own labour and superintendence."

F.S.—The question will be treated in due course, and F.S. shall be communicated with. The subject was very briefly alluded to in the *Morning Chronicle* about a twelvemonth ago.

LAW WRITERS' APPRENTICES.—Such communications are of great value, and may prove of great usefulness, as many abuses cannot possibly be corrected, for they have never been exposed. The correspondent in question—it is better not even to give his initials—will be written to when the condition of the Clerks, Assistants, &c. of London is, the important subject of inquiry.

ANSWERS TO CORRESPONDENTS.
[Nos 8b & 9, 1 FEBRUARY 1851,
8 FEBRUARY 1851]

Edited out:
J.R., LIVERPOOL A.F.F.

—————————

"L.C.F. presents her compliments to Mr. MAYHEW, and begs to enclose half a sovereign, to be disposed of as he may think proper, to any of the distressed persons mentioned in his

account of the "LONDON POOR." She heartily wishes that she could make it more, but her circumstances do not admit of it at present, though she trusts ere long, to be able to send another donation; and will also when possible, subscribe to the 'Friendly Association of Costermongers,' as described in Mr. MAYHEW's work. Should the two Young Flower Girls, or the little Cress Girl, [LLLP, Vol 1, pp.135, 151] mentioned by Mr. MAYHEW, be still in distress, her own sympathies go first with the *young* in sorrow. So much sin as well as misery may be prevented, by timely aid in supplying them with stock to pursue their honest trading, that one might hope whilst assisting them in their means of support, to be also aiding, (however humbly), in 'saving souls alive.' But Mr. MAYHEW will be, of course, the best judge where so sadly small a sum can be made of the most avail."

[Mr. MAYHEW has handed over the half-sovereign, kindly forwarded by L.C.F. to his Publisher, Mr. JOHN HOWDEN. Mr. MAYHEW has, in his dealings with the poorer classes, seen too many instances of the evils of promiscuous charity, to consent to become the dispenser of alms. The most dangerous lesson that can possibly be taught to any body of people whatsoever is, that there are other means of obtaining money than by working for it. Benevolence, however kind in its intentions, does oftentimes more harm than even the opposite principle. To bestow alms upon a struggling, striving man, is to destroy his independence, and to make a beggar of one who *would* work for his living. It is to teach such an one to trust to others for his subsistence, rather than to convince him that he himself contains within his own frame the means of providing for his own sustenance—indeed, it is to change the self-supporting animal into the mere vegetable; for the main distinction between animal and vegetable life is, that the one seeks its own food and the other has it brought to it. Mr. MAYHEW while he wishes to arouse the public to the social necessity of enabling every person throughout the kingdom to live in comfort by his labour, has no wish to teach the humbler classes that they can possibly obtain a livelihood by any other means. All that the better part of the working-classes desire is, to live by their industry; and those who desire to live by the industry of others, form no portion of the honest independent race of workmen in this country whom Mr. MAYHEW wishes to befriend. The deserving poor are really those who *cannot* live by their labour, whether from under-payment, want of employment, or physical or mental incapacity; and these Mr. MAYHEW wishes, and will most cheerfully do all he can, at any time and in any way, to assist. If the poverty arise from unfair payment, we should demand from the employers a fair living price for the work. If, on the other hand, it arise from want of employment, then we should seek to obtain work for those who cannot themselves procure it; and if from disability, we should use our influence to get them admission to some asylum specially devoted to the alleviation of their particular sufferings; or, if there be no such asylum, then we should endeavour to found some one of the kind wanted.

Mr. MAYHEW has been thus explicit as to the principles which guide him, because he wishes it to be known that, for several reasons, he has no desire to fill the post of dispenser of alms. In the first place, it is necessary that, for the honour of the office he has taken upon himself, he should be placed beyond even the remotest suspicion. He has therefore determined to accept no place of pecuniary trust whatsoever; and in accordance with this resolve, he has handed over such money as has been forwarded to him for distribution among, the poor, to Mr. JOHN HOWDEN, with the view of making it the nucleus of an institution that he is most anxious to see established, viz., a "Loan-Office for the Poor," where small advances may be obtained on approved security, at a moderate rate of interest. This appears to Mr. MAYHEW not only to overcome all the objections to almsgiving, but to afford the same pecuniary assistance to those who stand in need of it without degrading them into beggars. Such an institution would also go far to put a stop to the exorbitant rates of interest now charged by those who trade upon the necessities and destitution of the indigent,—such as the dolly-shops, pawnbrokers, stock-money lenders, tally-shops, and many like iniquities.[4] Those gentlemen and ladies who would not object to serve upon the committee of such an institution, are requested to forward their names to the Office, 69, Fleet-street, and those who think sufficiently well of its objects to contribute towards its capital, will oblige by making their post-office orders payable to Mr. JOHN HOWDEN, who has kindly consented to act as Honorary Secretary for the time being. It is proposed to pay three, or, if possible, four per cent. interest for all contributions made to the institution, the sums contributed by the subscribers being lent out at five per cent., and the difference devoted to the expenses of the institution.]

LUCY L., of Bedford-square, sends the subjoined:—

"Sir,—I am a governess, anxious to provide for my old age, and save all I can for that purpose. The difficulty is, how to invest these savings—the savings'-banks give such a small interest. In No.6 of your admirable work on LONDON LABOUR AND THE POOR, I see an advertisement of the 'Mutual Investment Society,' wherein they proffer 5 per cent. for money deposited with them. I hope you will excuse the liberty of my inquiring whether you know anything of the Managers of the Society, and would you advise my depositing my savings there? my apology for this intrusion is, that I look upon myself as one of the Labourers of London. A notice in your next Number will greatly oblige, your sincere admirer, LUCY L."

[The lady is informed that Mr. HENRY MAYHEW himself has no connection whatever with the Institution referred to; his brother, Mr. Horace Mayhew, is, however one of the Directors. The "Mutual Investment Society" appears to be a very valuable Institution.]

---

[4] See David Vincent, *Poor Citizens: The State and the Poor in Twentieth-Century Britain*, Longman, 1991, pp. 5-22.

Mr. J. BRIGGS, 28, IRONGATE, DERBY, the Chairman of the "Universal Anti-Truck Society," forwards a printed Appeal for subscriptions to obtain an Act for carrying out the objects of the excellent institution over which he presides. The proposed Act is to prohibit the stoppage of any portion of a workman's wages under any pretence whatsoever. This is most needed. The revelations published by Mr. MAYHEW, in the *Morning Chronicle*, show the iniquities now commonly perpetrated upon working men through such means as those Mr. Briggs and his friends seeks to abolish. The sufferings of the poor ballast-heavers—[MCS, Vol. 2, Letter XXII, 1 Jan 1850, pp.232-36] the miseries of the workmen for "sweaters"—the injustice of the fines imposed by Messrs. Moses, Hyams, Samuels, Nicoll, and all the other *slop* tailors of the metropolis—the "pence" demanded from the sawyers for the use of their tools—the stopping system, as practised in the cabinet trade—the security system, as carried out among the needlewomen at the East-end of London—all show how necessary it is that some Act of Parliament should be immediately passed to put a stop to such infamies.[5] Mr. MAYHEW will be happy to co-operate with Mr. Briggs and the Derby Society in any way he can.

G.P. writes as follows.—The thanks of the community are due to your unwearied exertions in searching out and laying before the public the state of these small traders in London; but the knowledge of the low, ignorant, depraved, and heathenist condition of the costermongers of London, only increases our responsibility, and calls upon all, not only the Christian and Benevolent, but on even the most careless to stretch forth a helping hand to raise them out of this, for they undoubtedly belong as you have well shown to the *classes dangereuses* and for this reason an appeal is made to the selfish; for if something is not done to alter the condition of this and such like

classes, our country may soon be overwhelmed by them. It may with truth be urged that there are many schemes of benevolence and that all cannot be overtaken. But if on no higher ground, it must be done in self-defence, and depend upon it, by expending money in improving the condition of such, and in teaching them the laws of God and man; you not only do the great good of making them better subjects, and better men, but also save your pocket; for the hundreds thus spent will save thousands now expended on pauperism and crime. There is a difficulty in persuading men of this; but the statistics of Ragged Schools &c., tend to prove this most emphatically. The mode of procedure with such a class is very difficult, and the great means is to use as much as possible not repressive but inducive measures. I fully agree with you, that a blow must be struck at their amusements—by offering for the same price a better and more rational entertainment. Also, by endeavouring, to make them cultivate habits of saving; and a good mode, I think, would be to lend money at a small rate of interest, the principal payable by instalments. Education must not be omitted, and the only way to induce them to this would perhaps be by a sort of Ragged School specially for them. If you could set up a Society for the reformation of the costermongers, with their habits of industry, I really think much good might be done at very little expence. I beg to inclose you a Post-office order for 1£ to be applied as you think proper for the benefit of the costermongers, of which be so good as acknowledge its receipt. I am now engaged in trying to establish coffee-shops and stalls in Edinburgh, chiefly in the neighbourhood of the public-houses, with the object of drawing off the working man from frequenting these. Two which have been established in Dundee have been most successful. If you could give me information, or any suggestions, I would esteem it a great favour.

[The 1£ has been handed over to Mr. JOHN HOWDEN.—G.P. appears to be working in the right direction with the coffee-shops and stalls in Edinburgh. Were the same steps, however, to

---

[5] A similar act protecting coal whippers had been passed in 1843. MC, Vol. 2, p. 153.

lessen the use of spirituous liquors to be taken in London, the police would interfere—for a stall pitched in the streets of the metropolis no matter with what view, is an infringement of the Street Act. *To endeavour to live honestly is (in London street-life) contrary to Act of Parliament.*[6] Let those who object to street-trading think, for one moment, what would-be the cost to the community in "poor rates" alone, if the street-sellers were obliged to declare upon the parish funds for their subsistence. The enormous sum of money spent yearly in the streets will give us some faint idea of the amount that would be required of the several parishes of London to keep the street-sellers.

The arrangements of the "Costermongers' Friendly Association" will be published in a few days; subscriptions, in the mean time, should be forwarded to Mr JOHN HOWDEN. A list of subscribers will be printed shortly.

H.M.W. says, in a letter, "In your valuable publication of LONDON LABOUR AND THE LONDON POOR, mention is made, more than once, of a clergyman, I presume of the Established Church, who is now gaining a living by selling stenographic cards in the streets. [LLLP, Vol.1, pp.260-1] Now it has occurred to my mind, that, instead of trying to obtain a livelihood in such a precarious way, that person, if of an age and competent abilities, and, moreover, not averse to such an undertaking, might not only benefit himself; but also his fellow-creatures, by becoming a Missionary. Judging from the manner in which you have expressed your opinion on the system of sending out missionaries to convert the heathen, whilst thousands of our poor are perishing for lack of knowledge at our own doors, I am touching on a delicate subject; but knowing as I doubt not you also do, that thousands of our fellow countrymen are leaving these lands, year after year, for our distant colonies, who, on arriving there, find no, or very few, ministers to supply their

spiritual wants, which, no one can deny, are not *less* needed there than they were here; and knowing, too, that the great Societies, who have the spiritual welfare of souls under their special care, are crying out for more helpers in the work, my proposal may not, perhaps, be worthy of your attention. 'The Society for the Propagation of the Gospel in Foreign Parts' I should especially recommend, for the reason that it is more particularly devoted to the welfare of our fellow-countrymen and brethren in the colonies. The 'Church Missionary Society' is also equally deserving of support."— MR. MAYHEW will shortly have occasion to see the gentleman above referred to, and will then mention to him the proposal made in H.M.W.'s letter.

AN INQUIRER.—The street-seller's statement forwarded to us on the subject of the police, is comprised greatly in what the man "has heard say;" and only direct statements of facts are inserted, unless incidentally.

ANSWERS TO CORRESPONDENTS.
[Nos 9 & 10, 8 FEBRUARY 1851, 15 FEBRUARY 1851]

The London coal-whippers have forwarded a Prospectus of a new journal which is about to be published by some members of their own body. These labouring men have long been celebrated for the many classical scholars included among their ranks; but curious as classical scholarship may be when found among such a class, still intelligence in a periodical will prove of much greater value. It is hoped therefore that the coal-whippers will not be so anxious to display their learning as their sense. If they will but avoid a perhaps pardonable demonstration of their scholastic acquirements, and determine to deal with the labour question judicially rather than emotionally, eschewing all that may savour of the platform— if they will but adhere to plain matters of fact, collecting and making known the statistics of labour, and so contribut-

[6] See James Winter, *The Teeming Streets of London*, Routledge, 1993, p. 43 on the 1839 Police Act.

ing their mite of truth to the general knowledge fund on this difficult question, they may be the means of doing incalculable good, not only to their own people, but to the great body of labouring men throughout the country. Let them rest assured that the labourer is to be benefitted solely by truth. No revolution in any country whatsoever can ever make two and two anything but four. If the working men are wronged, then let them demonstrate how the treatment they receive violates the laws of right, and depend upon it there are enough people wishing right to prevail, ultimately to put an end to the wrong. The process may seem a slow one, but there is no hastening it *by force*—conviction alone can work the change. Mr. MAYHEW himself believes that the working men of England are grossly wronged by capitalists. All production is according to the very first principles of political economy—a partnership between the man of money and the man of muscles, in which the monied man agrees to advance to the working man his share of the produce in the form of wages. Look at the labour question in whatever light we may, these are the very elements of it. It may offer some violence to the pride of the capitalist to be told that his labourers are partners in his business, but common sense and justice admit of no other view being taken of the transaction. That this fundamental contract is violated, and that the labourer does *not get his fair share of the produce at the present day, none can doubt*—the padlock, to quote a solitary instance, which is made for a halfpenny, is sold for a shilling. In place of the original compact a new law has been instituted, by which the *necessities* of the working man—instead of equity—are made to determine the value of his labour. This is what is called the law of supply and demand, which taking no heed of the result (that is to say, whether the value of the materials on which the workman has exercised his skill has been doubled or increased even a hundredfold by the operation), says, that the proportion of the wealth which is to come to the labourer is to be regulated by no other principle than what the capitalist can induce or force him (by starvation or chicanery) to accept. Now this to Mr. MAYHEW appears to be the very reverse of justice, and contrary to the fundamental principles of the very science of which it is said to be a part. Unfortunately, however, the law of supply and demand has got to be recognised by the rulers of the land, and to be considered almost as a part of the commercial creed of the country—the last "new commandment," as it were—against which it is political blasphemy to raise one's voice. Until the injustice of this principle is exposed and made generally known, there is no hope for the labouring man; for a necessary corollary (and certainly a most convenient one to all employers) of the law of supply and demand is the dogma of free labour, which asserts that in any way to restrict the liberty of the capitalist to buy his labour in the cheapest market and sell it (of course) in the dearest, is to interfere with the "rights of commerce." This, however, would seem to perpetrate an even greater iniquity than the present wage-law—and that solely for the benefit of the capitalist—at *the expense, moreover, of both producer and consumer*, giving rise at once to underpaid workmen and overcharged purchasers—to cheap labour and dear commodities *for the mere aggrandissement of the middleman*. To buy labour at the cheapest possible rate, without any regard to the value of the produce, is to defraud the producer, and to sell it at the dearest possible rate (without any regard to the prime cost of the commodity), is to swindle the purchaser. Surely this was the principle of trade which guided the dealings of Ikey Solomons, [Sic] the Jew fence, and yet he was tried the Old Bailey and transported for putting it in practice. In the case of the receiver of stolen goods, the main iniquity consists in not paying a fair price for the labour of the article purchased; and indeed it is often this buying of articles far below their equitable value that constitutes the chief evidence as to the guilty knowledge of the receiver. If no restriction whatever is to be placed upon the dealings of capitalists, and they are to have full liberty to buy in the cheapest market—despite the principles of justice—then why in the name of common sense prosecute the receiver or the thief, when their whole crime consists in not paying a proper price for the labour of the commodities they obtain? Under these circumstances it behoves the great body of working men to protest loudly—but calmly and resolutely—against the iniquity of the law of supply and demand, and against the doctrine of free labour which seeks to make the remuneration of workmen depend on the greed of commercial men rather than the principles of justice. There are no men who can make this apparent better than the coal-whippers[7]—no men who have had greater experience of the atrocities that can be perpetrated under the *free labour* principle, and none who if they will but tell all they know, and all they have seen, and tell it dispassionately—appealing, to the consciences rather than the passions of their fellow-creatures—can do more to bring about that state of right and truth which all good men desire. This is the sole object MR. MAYHEW has in view—all he wishes is to make the public aware of the infamies that can be practised upon the labourer when the trader is allowed to use him as his own as his own brutalizing love of gain may dictate; he hopes by showing these things to induce some change in our social state (though at present he hardly knows *what* change) by which the workman may ensure *his fair share of the produce*. There are many means proposed to obtain this end. Protection, Chartism, Co-operative Societies, Socialism, Communism, and many other social and political panacea; but with these MR. MAYHEW has in his present vocation nothing to do, and he wishes it to be distinctly known and understood—without reservation or cavil—that he is in no way connected with any social or political party or sect whatever. MR. Mayhew is neither Chartist, Protectionist, Socialist, Communist, nor Co-operationist; but a mere collector of facts, endeavouring to discover the

several phenomena of labour with a view of arriving ultimately at the laws and circumstance affecting, and controlling the operation and rewards the labourer, as well as of showing the importance of the poor and the working classes as members of the State.

ANSWERS TO CORRESPONDENTS.
[No.10, 15 FEBRUARY 1851]

Edited out:
GINGER-BEER SELLER, B.P.M.

═══════════════

The following has been forwarded by the Rev. Robert Montgomery:[8]—

"61, Torrington-square, Thursday.

"My dear Sir,—The sacred cause of Christian philanthropy is vastly indebted to the noble efforts you are now making to enlighten the *polished* darkness in which the upper classes are veiled from a real and adequate acquaintance with the dismal realities of the poor man's life around them. *Personally*, I have to thank you for admonishing my own selfishness, and expanding my own sympathies, by your deeply-moving details in your LONDON LABOUR AND POOR. It is not likely that you have ever heard of, much less read my last volume, 'GOD AND MAN'. Nor do I refer to it as having intellectual claims on your attention. But there is *one essay* in it which; I believe in point of subject stands ALONE in our literature. It is entitled

---

[7] See Note 5. Coal whippers' gangs were paid by publican contractors at night after they had consumed a large amount of their pay on the publican's own inferior produce.

---

[8] Robert Montgomery, 1807-1855, Anglican religious poet, author of *Satan* 1830, his then quite famous poem, *God and Man*, 1850 and *Christiania*, 1851. See Lord Macaulay, *Critical and Historical Essays Contributed to the Edinburgh Review*, Longman, Green, Reader and Dyer, 1870, pp.122-34, "Mr Robert Montgomery's poems". "The writer evidently means to caution us against the practice of puffers, a class of people who have more than once talked the public into the most absurd errors, but who surely never played a more curious or a more difficult trick than when they passed Mr Robert Montgomery off upon the world as a great poet." (p.123)

'The benefits THE POOR *confer on the rich*'—the reverse side of the question as generally discussed. Of this, I say, I beg you to accept the enclosed extract: do me the favour TO READ IT: and, if it can be of the remotest use to your sublime cause, it will gladden the heart of, my dear Sir, yours faithfully,

"ROBERT MONTGOMERY.

"N.B.—This is a *public* letter and at your discretion can be used. Is it *possible* to get some of these people to hear the *Word of God?* if so, pray command my labours."

From J.C.(M.D.) the following has been received:—

"In Dr. Carpenter's 'Prize Essay on Intoxicating Liquors'[9] he has quoted some statements from the 'Inquiries by the Commissioner of the *Morning Chronicle*' (see Appendix A. and B.) which, so far as I can make out, seem to imply that a man may carry up as many as sixty tons of coals on his back, from a ship's hold sixteen feet deep in the course of a day. 'I have *backed* as many as sixty tons in a day since I took the pledge.' 'Many teetotallers have backed coals out of the hold, and I have heard them say over and over again that they did this work with more comfort and ease than they had when they drank intoxicating drinks. Coal-basking is the hardest work that it is possible for a man to do. Going up a ladder sixteen feet high, with 238 lbs. weight upon a man's back, is sufficient to kill any one.' May I beg you will have the kindness to say in the notices to correspondents in 'London Labour,' &c. whether I am right in my conjecture. It has been supposed that the work performed by the South American miners of carrying up loads of 200 lbs., from a depth of eighty yards, twelve times a day, was about the greatest amount of labour a man could undergo; but this would far surpass it. My object is to investigate the amount of muscular power which a man is capable of exercising, and I trust you will excuse the liberty I have

[9] William Benjamin Carpenter, *On the Use and Abuse of Alcoholic Liquors in Health and Disease*, Prize Essay, Gilpin, John Churchill, 1850.

taken of thus encroaching upon time which is so much and so usefully occupied." Speaking from memory, the passages above quoted are correctly given. There was, however, together with the weight carried, a statement as to the aggregate height to which the substances were lifted in the courses of the day's labour, which J.C. must be well aware is an important element in the calculation. The copies of the *Chronicle* in which the Letters on the London Coal-whippers were originally printed not being at hand it is impossible to refer J.C. to the precise date of their appearance; but Mr. MAYHEW believes it was at the beginning of last year. [MCS, Vol. 2, Letter XIX to XXI, 21-28 Dec 1849, pp.150-218] The impression left on Mr. MAYHEW's mind by the investigation was that stimulating drinks were *in no way necessary* for the performance of the severest labour. Mr. MAYHEW was the more particular in his inquiries upon this subject, because he knew there existed a deeply-rooted conviction in the minds of the industrious classes that hard work could be performed only with the assistance of some kind of fermented liquor, and the result of the investigation most assuredly was that such a belief was in no way founded upon truth. Mr. MAYHEW (being no teetotaller) investigated the subject purely as a question intimately connected with the welfare of the working classes, and without reference to any preconceived opinion whatsoever. As Mr. MAYHEW takes great interest in the subject to which J.C. is directing his attention he would be happy at all times to afford him any information within his power, and be equally glad to be made acquainted with the results at which J.C. may arrive. When it is remembered that to the *muscles* of men we owe so many of the comforts and necessaries of our lives surely the subject of muscular energy, irritability and durative power must rank among the most important of studies, and the more so because the physical causes of crime, vagabondism, industry and a host of other virtues and vices, which must be *in some measure* due to the bodily conformation of the individuals, have been hitherto wholly unexplored by *impartial* scientific men. The phrenologists alone have looked into the subject; but unfortunately they are theorists with a disposition to warp rather than discover facts. Ethnologists have done little or nothing towards increasing our knowledge of the physical conformation of the predatory and vagabond races of the world. Nor have the revelations of Drs. Marshall Hall[10] and Carpenter, concerning the automatic, consensual and voluntary actions of men been as yet attempted to be applied to the enigmas of moral or social philosophy. Dr. Hall's theory of fatigue appears to throw a flood of light on the causes of industrial and idle habits. When *will* the physician be considered as necessary a functionary in our gaols and unions as the clergyman? for when he is, we may hope for some more useful knowledge than we are at present vouchsafed, concerning the causes and treatment of criminals and paupers. At present our prison reports, and our goal and poor-house discipline are as unphilosophic as the "wise-saws" of our old nurses.

"I have noticed in the seventh Number of your Journal," writes a lady without a name, "a statement that 'lavender', in common with other flowers, is sometimes sold for 'immoral purposes.' With the curiosity so natural to a daughter of Eve, I feel very inquisitive to know what purpose or purposes, it can be 'immorally' applied to? Flowers have always been associated in my mind with ideas of rural happiness and as emblems of purity and simplicity, and therefore your announcement has startled me very much, leaving me after all my cogitations in a labyrinth of doubt and conjecture. If you will have the courtesy to solve this query for me, in one of your future Numbers you will confer a great favour."— [The subject is not exactly feminine—but the immoral purposes are the same as those for the sale of flowers in the streets; by young girls,

---

[10] Marshall Hall, *Medical Essays on the Effect of Intestinal Irritations...On Some Effect of the Loss of Blood, On Exhaustion and Sinking from Various Causes*, Nottingham and London, 1825.

frequently used as a cloak.]

The following petition has been handed to MR. MAYHEW by the poor half-witted and very persecuted harp-player, so well known in the streets of London; and as he can vouch for the worthiness of the petitioner, as well as his inability to obtain his living by labour, MR. MAYHEW gives publicity to it here in the hope of enlisting the sympathies of some of his readers in behalf of the poor musician.

"TO THE PUBLIC.

"Ladies and Gentlemen,—Your humble Partitionar as been obtaining a lively hood the last 4 years by playing an harp in the streets and is desirous of doing so but from the delapedated condition of my present instrument I only produce ridicule instead of a living Trusting you will be kind enough to *asist* me in getting another I beg to remain your humble Partitionar,

FOSTER."

"L.Wallington (Gray's-inn-terrace) 1s.; Mr. Briggs, 1s.; T. L. Is.; Jno. Ballantyne 1s; A friend 1s.; T.N. 4d.; J. Hughes 6d.; Mrs. Ganston 6d; Dubois 1s.; J. Ellis 6d.; Mrs. Bridges 6d.; Mrs Hosleham 1s. H.M. 5s."

Two pounds ten shillings will be sufficient to obtain such an instrument as is required. Subscriptions may be forwarded to Mr. JOHN HOWDEN. 69, Fleet-street.

W.R. (a farmer), of Bury St. Edmunds, writes to point out what he conceives to be "two trivial errors" concerning the relative quantities of nutritive matter contained in butcher's meat and fish. He says:—

"I think there are two fallacies in the argument used; for that solid matters differ in *nutrition* is evident, or else straw would be as nutritious as flesh." [Straw consists principally of silex, which is incapable of assimilation; but fish and meat are both proteinaceous compounds, and therefore capable, though in different degrees, of supplying the waste of the muscular tissues.] "They may also differ in *wholesomeness*, which is a great point" [the writer, however, does not tell us what he means by this same "*wholesomeness*"] "and even supposing the solid matter in flesh and fish equal in nutritious properties, there is an error in the estimation; for the 26 per cent. of solid matter in meat evidently contains one-third more nutritious matter than the 20 per cent. in fish; for, if otherwise, we might as well say that an infusion in water of 26 drops of laudanum, in a phial holding 100 drops, is only 3 per cent. [and a fraction] stronger than an infusion of 20 grains, which would plainly be incorrect."

[But, surely, according to Cocker,[11] it would be in no way right to assert that an infusion containing 26 parts of laudanum in 84 parts of water (which is the proportion given as regards the solid and aqueous parts of meat) is 5 per cent. and a fraction stronger than an infusion containing only 20 parts of laudanum in 80 parts of water. W.R's error lies in taking 100 parts of water in both cases, instead of the proportions here given.]

MR. MAYHEW is obliged to W.R. for pointing out the other error in calculating, in which he is perfectly right. The mistake shall be rectified at the earliest opportunity.

The following has been sent by a lady signing herself "FELIX FŒMINA"(lucky woman):—

"Respected Friend,—In that portion of thy very interesting work relating to the street-sellers of plants, &c., I have looked in vain for some notice respecting our branch of this trade, which, though, no doubt, very small and of recent introduction, is so elegant and attractive that it seems a pity it should be overlooked. I allude to the dealer in *ferns* in a growing state, bought for the purpose of planting, either in the famous 'Ward's cases,' or on rock-work, &c. in gardens. There is, or was lately, *at least* one man to be met with near the Bank, who sells these beautiful favourites of the botanist, or of the mere lover of Nature, with their roots fit for cultivation. I think I have heard of another in Cornhill, and there may be many more. I have been informed, long journeys, in search of ferns on their native rocks and mountains, are found to answer, in order to procure them for sale. Probably thou art already in possession of particulars, but thou couldst most likely obtain them, if needful, from Richard Dell, Cornchandler, Pimlico."

[It is, of course, impossible to give a particular account of *each article* sold in the streets. The rule adopted is to describe only such articles of which the sale is a special vocation, or means of living. Some of these may escape notice; but such as are omitted by mistake will be added in a Supplement at the conclusion of the Volume on the Street-folk.]

H.E., HYDE PARK-SQUARE, writes as follows:— "Sir,—In reading, the description you give of a 'Penny Gaff', [LLLP, Vol.1, p.40] you expatiate upon the obscenities contained in a song, which has for title. 'Pine-apple Rock'. Upon procuring a copy, and perusing the same, I cannot say I find the bundle of filth you describe. I enclose the song, and I trust you will agree with me that it is not half as objectionable as any nightly song at Evans's[12] and the Cyder Cellars."

[The indecency lay principally in the gestures of the singer. The performance has, however, been suppressed; but this is useless, without supplying some more healthy amusement. The same scenes are nightly enacted in different parts of the metropolis.]

[11] Edward Cocker's *Decimal Arithmetick* (1678), was the basic text of mathematics of the time.

[12] Evans's Late Joy, 3 King Street, Covent Garden, a famous Bohemian song-and-supper room opened in the 1840s.

ANSWERS TO CORRESPONDENTS.
[Nos.10-11[13,] 15 FEBRUARY 1851,
22 FEBRUARY 1851]

Edited out:

W.M.H.; F.F.; AN UNWORTHY PROTECTIONIST; R.;
L.L.; AN OBSERVER, WHITECHAPEL; H.W.H.; P.L.
MANCHESTER; M.F. LIVERPOOL; F.R.; L.A.P.; M.H.W.;
B.Y.R. SHEFFIELD; L.A.R. MARYLEBONE; B.B.
NEWCASTLE; L.O. NORTON FOLGATE; W.R.; P.S.R.
WESTMINSTER; A PARENT; L.L. GREENWICH; A
WESLEYAN; R.F.A.; H.G.; E.B.; ALMA MATER;
BLANDFORD; T.L., BATH; R., READING; LONG SONG
SELLERS; A.M.; J.M. AND J.W.

PETER.—The question seems entirely theological, and is not within the scope of this work.

A FISH FACTOR.—No further intelligence can be given of the precise derivation of the word "Bummaree". [LLLP, Vol. 1, p.67] In Mr. Knights "Cyclopaedia of Political, Constitutional, Statistical and Forensic Knowledge," (referred to by a Fish-factor), it is stated: "Bottomry, Bottomree, or Bummaree, is a term derived into the English maritime law from the Dutch or Low German. In Dutch, the term is Bomerie or Bodemery, and in German, Bodmerei. It is said to be originally derived from Boden or Bodem, which in Low German and Dutch formerly signified the bottom or keel of a ship; and according to a common process in language the part being applied to the whole, also denoted the ship itself. The expression *bottom* having been commonly used to signify a ship, previous to the 17th century." In this statement we have most probably the word. How it became possessed of its present signification at Billingsgate, seems never to have been ascertained.

QUESTOR—The following information—at this correspondent's request, and in acknowl-edgement of the trouble he has taken—is derived from the "Standard Library of Political Knowledge":—"The laws relating to vagrants continued substantially upon the footing of the statutes of 39 Eliz. and 7 Jac. I. for more than a century, until, in 1744, they were reconsidered and remodelled by the statute of 17 Geo. II., c. 5. This was the first legislative measure which distributed vagrants into the three classes of idle and disorderly persons, rogues and vagabonds, and incorrigible rogues. Although this statute is now wholly repealed, it continued in force nearly a century, until 1822, when a temporary Act., Stat. 3 Geo. IV., c. 40 passed, repealing all former laws, and re-enacting most of the provisions of the stat. 17 Geo. II., c. 5, with many additions and modifications. The provisions of the stat. 3 Geo. IV., c. 40 was, however, entirely superseded by the 5 Geo. IV c. 33, which now (1846) constitutes the law respecting vagrants. This Act was amended by the 1 Vic. c. 38 (1838). The third section of the statute Geo.IV. declares what persons are idle and disorderly persons, and may be committed to hard labour in the House of Correction for any time not exceeding one month."

ANSWERS TO CORRESPONDENTS.
[Nos.11-12, 22 FEBRUARY 1851,
1 MARCH 1851]

Edited out:
C.B.; F.B.B.; J.L.; TANCRED; C.R.M.

The following valuable communication has come to hand. It is given entire, to show the use of some such institution as was advocated in a previous Number:—

"Sir,—I take the liberty of addressing you on the subject of the Loan Fund, advised by you in your 'Labour and the Poor,' for the relief of our suffering brethren of the streets. It is not for me to *advise* you; but I think, sir, if you could combine a savings'-bank and sick-fund with it, you would add materially to its benefits. I

---

[13] The early numbers are not all well defined: this number and the following could have been published on the wrappers of both numbers, or either.

know, from my experience of my order, that such of us as can save money from our weekly earnings would far rather place it in the hands of our friends than in those of any Government—who, say many, 'would, in any period of political commotion probably make of our money arms to crush us.' Besides, we want the spirit of mutual assistance, which is but enlightened self-help, more largely among us; and would rather that our money went to help the struggling than be employed we know not how. In this building we in August last established a little sick-fund, and, as soon as we got a pound or two, talked of depositing it in a Government savings'-bank; but one or two of our members said, 'No—let us loan it out to such of our number as may require it.' We did so at 1£ at a time, payable in twenty-*one* weeks at 1s. per week, placing the profit in the sick fund. We soon found the applications for loans more numerous than we expected. To meet them, I proposed a savings' bank to receive deposits from 6d. upwards, bearing interest at 5 per cent. per annum as soon as they should reach 5s. Thus we shall receive 15 per cent. per annum for money lent, while we are paying 5 for that deposited; but, as the money is re-lent as fast as it comes in from the loans, the profits, in the course of twelve months, will be a great deal more; and as all will go to increase the sick-fund, relieve cases of sudden distress, or assist a poor member compelled by cessation of employ to leave us (as our rents are 4s., 5s., 6s., or 7s. weekly), every one is interested in the matter being a *bonâ fide* partner. The whole of our expenses, for box, lock, two keys, and books, have been under 4s., as our members have furnished them, charging only for materials. I would not trouble you, sir, but out of this matter perhaps you may pick some hint to assist your good intentions. I should feel very proud to see a savings'-bank formed for the working-classes, the stock of which would be loaned out to assist others not so fortunate; and if the ladies and gentlemen who correspond with you would guarantee the repayment of deposits, it would work well. I believe they would never be called upon for a shilling, and

you would make the assistance of the working-classes the work of their own order, bringing their two extremes together, and binding all in one bond of brotherhood. And if a rather higher rate of interest was required, and the profits of it passed into the sick-fund (after paying necessary expenses)—to which, if fixed at a low rate (ours is 2d. per week), many would gladly subscribe—it would do a great deal to make those who are improvident careful, and be a blessing to all who knew it. I am, Sir, faithfully, yours to command, B.B. Feb 19, 1851.

"P.S.—If in any of your future Numbers you intend to describe model-houses, which are now becoming a feature in London life, I will endeavour, if you please, to procure you correct information respecting this establishment from its commencement to the time of publication."

A communication has been received from the "Association for the Relief of the Poor of the City of London and parts adjacent, Office, 43, Bow-lane, Cheapside. Instituted, 1798," familiarly known as the "City Kitchen;" where, during the first season, as much as 2,614£ were expended in providing relief to near 20,000 poor. [MR. MAYHEW has no faith in soup. kitchens—they make life too easy.]

R.T. (of Edinburgh), makes the following suggestion, which shall be considered. It was in contemplation to give a Daguerreotype View of London, from the top of St. Paul's, as a frontispiece to the First Volume.[14] "In the course of perusing of your very interesting work LONDON LABOUR, &c., an idea has struck me which I think would enhance the value of it, and be of great service to many of your readers, more particularly the provincial ones which is to publish with your work a *Plan of London*; the cause of this suggestion is the repeated mention made of the various streets that are frequented by the street traders, also it might be the means, of increasing the sale,

[14] H. Mayhew used the idea in his 1856 *Great World of London* later published as the *Criminal World of London*, 1862. Reprinted by Augustus Kelley, 1968.

inasmuch as that parties intending to visit London at the Great Exhibition, would find the plan very useful; many I have no doubt will be curious enough to see some of the more noted street characters mentioned. I find that in a great measure the Edinburgh costers are subject to the same treatment as in London, all or nearly all the stands or stalls have been removed from the streets, and those using barrows are compelled to keep moving on. Yours. R.T. Edinburgh." [Will R.T. favour MR. MAYHEW with some further information about the Edinburgh street-sellers, if he have the means of obtaining it.]

A.S.E., of Redland, Bristol, makes the following correction of a quotation from Mr. M'Culloch; where there are so many facts to collect, of course it is impossible to prevent the occurrence of such errors in the hurry of a first publication. "Sir, in page 129, last sentence, you state that. Mr. M'Culloch estimates the average consumption of butter, in London, at 6,250,000 lbs. per annum, or 5 oz., weekly, each individual.' There must be a mistake either in Mr. M'Culloch or your quotation, as this would make the population of London, only 384,615. If we assume the annual consumption correct, and the population 2,000,000, we should have the weekly individual consumption not quite 1 oz. If we assume the weekly consumption of each individual to be 5 ozs., and the population to be 2,000,000 the annual total of con-sumption would be 32,500,000 lbs. Which is correct? With due respect. A.J.E."

The following has been received from "C.P.:—Sir, seeing in your prospectus of LONDON LABOUR, that you intend giving an account of the London shopmen, and having been a shopman for some years at a linen-draper's, as I have now left the trade, I shall be happy to give you the results of my experience, on condition no names are mentioned in your periodical; should you think this worthy of attention, and hint the same in your correspondents' page, I will then put all down on paper I consider worth telling and forward it to you; or if you prefer it, I will call on you

and, 'put you up' to some of the most amusing 'tricks of trade'." [MR. MAYHEW will be glad to receive the promised communication. The London shopmen will be treated of at the earliest opportunity. The distribution of wealth and consequently the distributors, may be said to be almost as important as the production and producers of it. Strictly speaking, the street-sellers now treated of belong to the class of distributors.]

J.W., of James-street, Gray's-inn-road, a bricklayer's labourer, sends a long and valuable communication touching the condition and earnings of the workmen in his trade. Among other things, he states that, a great many of the constant hands have been reduced from 3s. and 3s. 6d. per day to 2s. 8d., *since the repeal of the Corn Laws*. Mr. MAYHEW will be happy to hear again from J.W. should he have any fresh facts to communicate.

ANSWERS TO CORRESPONDENTS.
[No.14, 15 MARCH 1851[15]]

F.B.B., of Alfred-street. Bedford-square, sends a letter in answer to certain observations printed among the "Notices to Correspond-ents" in Number 10. It is impossible to give the entire document, but the following extracts are sufficient to show the spirit and arguments of the writer. Mr. MAYHEW's comments are given between brackets.

"Sir,—Allow me to say that I think your observations on labour and capital, in No.10 of 'London Labour,' very erroneous and mischievous, and calculated to mislead the working classes. I may observe, by the way, that I am no capitalist or employer of labour. You

[15] Dates were added on the covers of *LLLP* from that date.

assert that 'the working men of England are grossly wronged by capitalists;' and 'that the labourer does not get his fair share of the produce at the present day,' you add, 'none can doubt.' Now I beg to say that I, in common with many thousand others, very much 'doubt', nay distinctly 'deny,' the truth of your assertion. Political economists consider that the wages of the labourer are his share of the produce;" [the halfpenny out of the shilling padlock] "and they believe this share is necessarily regulated by the law of supply and demand." [A share is a portion regulated by equity, and not by a scramble.] "If wages are not to be thus regulated, I desire to know by what other standard can they be regulated? To talk of 'conscience' and 'justice', is to use vague terms of no definite meaning."(!) "The dictates of 'conscience' depend upon organization and education; what one man's conscience teaches, another man's denies." [Does truth depend on the same circumstances? To what organizations and in what schools does 2+2=5? So of moral truth.] "There is no definite and invariable standard of right." [So that Rush and Greenacre were condemned to death for not conforming to the fashion of the time.] "The same is true of 'justice.' The law of supply and demand is evidently a law of nature" [though justice and right are not], "and to interfere with it would introduce endless confusion and mischief. Would you compel a capitalist to give a certain amount of wages, irrespective of all risks and losses, and the profits which he calculates necessary to repay him for capital, knowledge, and superintendence? Surely this would be gross injustice, if it were practicable! [The returns of the capitalist then are to be regulated by the principle of justice, while the remuneration of the working man is to be left to a scramble, or the law of supply and demand. What Mr. Mayhew desires is, that the amount coming to both parties should be regulated by the eternal principles of equity (if F.B.B. can understand such things)—the same as all partnerships are. If the labourer and capitalist are not partners, then, of course the equitable principle does not hold; but as this partnership is the fundamental axiom of political economy, why surely the principle which is used to determine the 'rights' (the word is quoted, in obedience to the prejudices of F.B.B.) of partners should be applied to settle what is due to the labourer as well as the capitalist.] "You and others, who declaim on this subject, never consider the population question—the overcrowding of the labour market. This, I am convinced is the chief source of our social evils. The fault of low wages is not in the capitalists, but in the labourers, who overcrowd the labour market, and compete with each other. If the working classes have no prudence, no self-denial, they ought surely to bear the consequences of their deficiency in this respect—not the capitalist. If they will recklessly increase the population of their own class, they must take the natural consequences in the lowering of wages. Other classes practise self-denial in this respect" [the highest personage in the realm, for instance;[16] but capitalists never are family men, of course.] "It might be hoped, that if the working classes were duly informed on the subject, and were better educated, and this may be expected from national education, they would at length learn wisdom and prudence; which will never be the case, so long as they are put upon a false scent, and are taught, by unreflecting sentimentalists, that they are entirely blameless, and that all the fault and wrong is with the capitalist and the Government. It is very easy and very cheap benevolence to indulge in vague generalities and high-sounding declamation about 'conscience' and 'justice'—'injustice,' 'wrong' and 'oppression;' but not so easy to prove where the 'wrong' and 'injustice.'" [Because, according to F.B.B., wrong and injustice are mere conventional phantasms—things of organization and education.] "From the style of your writing, you appear to belong to the class of impulsive

---

[16] Queen Victoria, although only thirty-one, already had six children: Victoria-Adelaide (1840), Albert Edward (1841), Alice (1843), Albert (1844), Helena (1846), Arthur (1850).

sentimentalists (see *Edinburgh Review,* on 'English Socialism'), who are too apt to suffer their feelings to overbear their reason and judgment—a more dangerous class to take up any 'cause' I cannot conceive, or one more likely to do injury to those whose interests they advocate"

[Excepting *those,* be it observed, who allow their reason and judgment to overpower their feelings, a class of which it may be added the Devil himself is the apt and sublime archetype. Mr. MAYHEW has printed the above letter—abuse and all—because he thinks it may be taken as a fair sample of the present fashionable economical creed—a creed which does not hesitate to tell us that "justice," "right," and "conscience" are matters of "organization" and "education," mere whimsies of the stomach, or bugbears of the nerves or dogmata of the schools; for the propounders of such doctrines, being unable to perceive that conscience is the exercise of the judgment on moral propositions, and justice the perception of moral equality or equity, are likewise unable to perceive that to deny the existence of the conscience is to deny that there is any such faculty as judgment in man, while to make equity and other moral truths mere conventions is to reduce the most fundamental truths of all, viz., those which depend on a perception of equality, to matters of pure fashion. The population question, in which F.B.B. goes "the whole hog," like Stuart Mill—declaring that there is no hope for the workmen of this country until they imitate the Catholic priests and register vows in heaven of perpetual celibacy—is one of which Mr. MAYHEW purposes exposing the fallacy in its due place. Suffice it, for the present, that he believes the superabundance of labourers in this kingdom to be due to the creation of 600,000,000 of steam men (which is the estimated power of the aggregate machinery of England) within the last hundred years—a fact of which economists and populationists never condescend to take the least notice—though where the difference can be between a steam engine performing all the functions of the labourer, and oftentimes of the artizan, and a human machine doing simply what the thing of brass and iron does—it is beyond commonsense to discover. The entire number of human operatives in England and Wales are not more than 4,000,000—the steam operatives are at the least 150 time as many or 600,000,000—and when it is remembered that these competing steam labourers are things that can work night and day without any sense of fatigue—without cravings or desires—without children to feed and educate, or wives to support or clothe—it surely must be evident to all at what fearful odds the mere creature of flesh and blood—of stomach brain and (though F.B.B. and his school object, still it must be added,) *heart*—must enter the field against them. And yet, knowing the enormous rate at which the steam population has been increasing in this country during the last century—at the rate of no less than 6,000,000 of steam labourers per annum—Mr. Stuart Mill and others, when writing about remedies for low wages, do not hesitate to tell us that there is no hope for the working man until he is taught to restrain his passions—stigmatizing all who object to their "preventives" and "checks" as sentimentalists, who suffer impulse and feeling to overbear reason and judgment. Verily, as Coleridge declared, the heart often reasons much sounder and clearer than the head. Moreover, the extraordinary anomaly with these writers is, that while crying out loudly for the non-increase of human labourers, they say not one word against the propagation of the steam ones; for, with a lop-sidedness peculiar to such logicians, they attribute almost every evil in the land to the fact of there being 4,000,000 workmen to supply nearly 20,000,000 of individuals with food, clothing, shelter, warmth, light, and, indeed, every necessary and luxury that human nature can either demand or desire—declaring that one-fifth of the population are far too many to create the wealth required for the sustenance and enjoyment of the whole, and a good part of the world besides; and that, consequently, the labour market of the country is overstocked to such a degree that distress and want must be the necessary portion of a considerable number; but (mark the absurdity) never even so much as hinting the while that the 600,000,000 of steam rival operatives which have been created within the last century have in any way tended to induce the overstocking of the said labour market, nor venturing to propose that *capitalists* should be taught to restrain *their* passions (for wealth) and made to refrain from annually bringing so many steam labourers into existence. That there are too many steam-engines and mechanical labourers is proved by the repeated gluts in the Manchester and other markets—such gluts being admitted on all hands to be the necessary consequences of over-production. Manchester manufacturers, however, while they admit the over-production, attribute the glut rather to under-consumption, saying that it is impossible there can be too much calico till every man and woman in the kingdom has a superabundance of under-clothing. But how is it possible for working men and women to avail themselves of the superabundance of materials for shirts, shifts, and petticoats, when the only thing they have to give in exchange for such articles is their labour? and of this, by the invention of machinery, the division of labour, and the large system of production, we are daily depriving them—or in others seeking how to produce more wealth with fewer labourers. When the economy of labour is the ruling principle of the science of manufacture, how can we wonder at the superabundance of labourers? Or, knowing these things, how can we, without laughing in our sleeve the while, seek to prove that such superabundance of labourers is due solely to the unrestrained sensuality of the working classes? With 600,000,000 of steam men to help to do the work of the nation, no wonder that a considerable portion of the 4,000,000 of human creatures can get little or no work to do! But we are told steam-engines create work for the human machines. There must be, it is said, some man or child to tend them; whereas human machines are pure social incumbrances, causing no addition whatsoever to the aggregate demand for labour. Every fresh pair of feet that come into the world do not create a demand for an extra pair of shoes—nor each new back want clothing—nor another head require additional shelter—nor another stomach additional food to be produced. Certainly not. The steam man is the greatest of national blessings—our fellow-man the greatest of national curses.

But in order that the natural additions to the aggregate demand for labour, created by each new workman who is brought into existence, should have free play, it is necessary that there be a corresponding demand for the workman's own labour. If he be not employed, of course he cannot employ others to make his shoes—his coats, grow his bread, or build his house; for if deprived of work by his steam competitor, then he must go barefoot, barebacked, empty-bellied, and houseless,—the fate of thousands in this country, as witness the handloom-weavers, the sawyers, &c. Even to reduce the workman's wages, is to decrease the aggregate amount of work to be done in the kingdom. The national income, which is estimated at 300,000,000£ sterling per annum, may be said to consist of three equal parts: 100,000,000£ going to replace capital, 100,000,000£ being the gross amount of profits accruing to the capitalists; and 100,000,000£ the gross amount of wages received by the labourers. The latter, or wage fund, constitutes the great purchasing fund of the country, for the whole of this is (with the most trifling exceptions) consumed; whereas the profit fund is mainly (perhaps more than half) saved with a view of increasing the capital of the capitalists. Hence, to decrease the wage fund is consequently to decrease the purchasing fund of the community. F.B.B. should not venture to write on subjects to which he has evidently paid but little attention, and to which he can contribute no new idea. This magpie mania for mere chattering is one of the worst signs of the times. Mr. MAYHEW must decline replying to all similar communications for the future.

The following letter has been received from

"An Employer," in answer to some statements made among the Notices to Correspondents in a recent Number of this Work. It is printed here in full, because it is desirable that the arguments against any proposed measure should at all times be patiently attended to:—

"Sir,—In the correspondence published in No. 9 of LONDON LABOUR AND LONDON POOR, you notice a proposed Act of Parliament intended to prohibit the stoppage of any part of a workman's wages under any pretence whatever, and proceed to enumerate some instances in which you state the 'system' produces injustice; I am not prepared to deny injustice is done to the Workpeople in the cases you mention, but were the 'system' carried out as proposed, the Master Manufacturers would in some cases, at least, be the victims of injustice. I allude more especially to the Owners of stocking-frames in the Midland Counties, to prevent the payment of rent for which would be the object of such an Act as you mention, and is, I presume, the intention of the 'Universal Anti-Truck Society,' over which your correspondent, Mr. Briggs presides.

"You are probably aware, Sir, that in the generality of cases the Manufacturers of hosiery goods in the Midland Counties are the owners of numbers of stocking-frames, which are let, in some cases, to middle hands, in others directly to the workman, at certain fixed rents, in most instances to be worked at the house of the hirer, for the benefit of the Manufacturer, he of course supplying the material, and paying the wages of the workman, less the rent of the frame.

"The effect of the Bill proposed by your correspondent will be to prevent the Manufacturer, who has been at considerable expense in constructing the machines, from receiving the fair return of his outlay; in other words, it will compel him to supply tools to the workman at his own expense, which may or may not be used for his benefit.

"The injustice of this will be obvious, but it will be still more so in cases, and I believe there are many where 'frames' are held by trustees of deceased Manufacturers, as so much ordinary property, for the benefit of their widows or children, who rely perhaps solely for their maintenance upon the rents obtained for the use—they not being in any other manner connected with trade. In those cases whole families would be deprived of the means of maintaining themselves in their proper station in society by the operation of the Act.

"Without entering into the question of the right of any legislature to interfere in contracts between master and workman, or the expediency of its so doing, I merely wish to draw your attention to the above circumstances, to show the great danger that persons, however well-intentioned, though unacquainted with the minutiae of the questions they wish to legislate upon, may incur, and the great injustice they may do by endeavouring to pass such Acts as the one proposed, without first fully and calmly hearing both sides of the question, and from the habit of forming general conclusions hastily from particular circumstances.

"I am, Sir, your obedient servant.
"AN EMPLOYER."

Mr. Mayhew not yet having had occasion personally to investigate the condition of the "stockingers," and knowing nothing of the system of "frame rents" but by common report, he considered it best to forward the Employer's letter to Mr. Briggs (the President of the Universal Anti-Truck Association), so that he, who had devoted much time and attention specially to the study of the circumstances of the case, might deny or admit the truth or justice of the several statements above given. Subjoined is Mr. Briggs' reply: -

"28, Iron Gate, Derby, 14th February, 1851.

"Dear Sir,—As regards labour and work, why should there be any difference between the 'printer,' the 'weaver,' or the 'stocking-maker?' They have each and all to get their living by labour, and they each and all are employed in machinery belonging to the employer. The stocking-frame is not worth more than from 5£ to 10£, while the printing-press is worth from 30£ to 100£; yet, because a printer employs a man to work at his press, at so much a day, or so much per token, who ever heard that the printer charges the workman a rent for the press, and deducts it from his wages? The 'Employer,' at Loughborough, knows very well where is the trick—in plain English, the robbery. If it be *idem per idem*, one and the same thing, why does the 'Employer' want to make stoppages at all? Why not give his workman so much less per dozen, and pay him for every dozen he makes? The 'Employer's' reason is obvious,—because, if he did so, he could not, when he had no work, in slack times, to give the man, get paid for his unemployed frames out of his workman's future earnings in the brisk season. The 'Employer's' object is, to keep the man under his thumb, and always ground down and beggared.

"'Employer' first says, that if you prevent the manufacturer from stopping the rent from the workman's wages, you hinder him from receiving the fair return of his outlay. Now, this is untrue; nor is there a word of sense in the assertion. If an employer lays out money in machinery, what has the value of that to do with the workman's wages? If he cannot pay the man for his labour, he ought not to employ the man. The object of the universal anti-truck law is, that he should not nurse up his property with the man's labour.

"He secondly says, that it will compel the employer to supply tools to the workman at his own expense. This is again as untrue as absurd. The Act will prevent an employer from stopping the rent of tools from his man's wages; it will not prevent his finding a man tools, if he likes. He is not, and will not then, be bound to find him tools or machinery, unless he choose; but if any employer will find his workman tools or machinery, then the Act declares simply, he shall pay the man for his labour. What has the poor man to do with his master's property? It is nothing but employment he wants, and nothing but labour has he to give. If a man cannot get work without tools, there are plenty of men to lend them to him, or to set him up with them, independent of his master; but if his master will not employ him, unless he can stop the rent for them out of his wages, it prevents workmen getting employment and wages for their labour.

"I know hundreds of poor men now, with frames and tools of their own, that cannot get employment unless they will take frames of their master, and submit to have a fixed rent stopped from their uncertain wages, whether they earn as much or not.

"It is a monstrous untruth to say, that the 'Act preventing employers from stopping from their workmen's wages a rent for the frame,' can deprive the owners of frames, or their widows and families, of the means of maintenance. Owners of frames have nothing to do with employers, nor will the Act have anything to do with one man letting a frame to another, if he does not employ him. That rent is got by law. The Act is simply to prevent employers stopping such rent from wages. The Act will better the widow's property, as, if employers cannot stop rent from wages, it will give better scope to her to let it. The Loughborough 'Employer' might as well say, because a master cannot stop from the wages of his workman the rent of a house which he lives in, and of which the master is the landlord, it would injure the rent of houses—on the contrary, it would not only better that property, but would leave the workman free to rent a house where he liked, instead of his employment being dependent on his consenting to take a house of his employer, and have the rent stopped from his wages. The stoppage system is the ruin of all labour; it must be put an end to.

"I send you my short account of the laws relating to working men and their wages, with a *verbatim* copy of the present Anti-Truck Act; you will please notice it as you like. Nothing short of the principle of universal anti-truck can ever better the condition of the working man. This must be enacted into a positive law. It is after the most mature reflection and consideration in my mind thus:

"That the entire amount of the wages, the earnings of labour, shall be actually and positively paid in the current coin of the realm, without any deduction or stoppage of any kind whatever.

"I am, dear Sir,
"Your respectfully,
"Jeremiah Briggs."

[The above reply appears to Mr. Mayhew fully to controvert every one of the assertions of the "Employer." The system of stoppages is so crying an injustice of the present time, that, acting upon the law as given in Mr. Brigg's valuable treatise on the enactments concerning the wages of working men, Mr. Mayhew has made up his mind to try the question in London, by bringing either Messrs. Nicol, Messrs. Moses, Hyams, or their "sweaters" to account for their iniquities before some metropolitan police magistrate. It is high time that some one took the bull by the horns, and since public opinion has made but little impression on the worthies above named, it will be advisable to see whether fine or imprisonment will have any terrors for them. At least, if by their chicanery they are able at present to keep clear of the law (which Mr. Briggs' excellent pamphlet—a work indispensable to all Trade Societies, and which, indeed, should be possessed by every one who wishes to see justice done to those to whom we owe so many comforts), the very publicity given to the proceedings, and the glaring iniquity of the dealings of these employers, will force upon all parties the necessity of some such alteration of the law as Mr. Briggs and the Universal Anti-Truck Association desire. Mr. Mayhew would suggest that in the proposed Act a clause be inserted forbidding the payment of wages in public-houses. This is as great an evil as the direct stoppage of wages. In the case of the lumpers, the men are tricked three nights a week into the tap-room of their employer, and there induced (not forced) to guzzle away that which should be devoted to the maintenance of their wives and children. Indeed, the villanous tricks practised by dishonest employers upon working men are beyond number, and cry aloud for instant redress. The Government have promised to bring in a Bill this Session to remedy the evils of the ballast-heavers; and Sir George Grey[17] assured Mr. Mayhew some months back they would give their support to

---

[17] Sir George Grey (1799-1882), Home Secretary in Russell's first cabinet (1846-1852).

any measure that bid fair to put a stop to all similar wrongs practised on working men. With but a dozen earnest workers in this direction, it is incalculable the good that might be done.

J.N., of Bermondsey-street is informed that the first volume of LONDON LABOUR will be complete about July; the price, bound in cloth, will be about 6s. or 7s. In the present position of the undertaking it is impossible to state the exact price. It is Mr. MAYHEW'S intention to make the volume devoted to the Street-folk as full and perfect in its detail as possible. He also hopes to be able to give a comparative view of the state of the Street-folk in other large towns.

ANSWERS TO CORRESPONDENTS.
[No.15, 27 MARCH 1851]

A gentleman who forwards some valuable information concerning benefit clubs, writes as follows on the subject of the wages of bricklayers' labourers:

"Seeing that a communication has been received from J.W., a bricklayer's labourer, in which, amongst other things, he says, that the wages of his class have been reduced from 3s. and 3s. 6d. to 2s. 8d. since the repeal of the corn laws, I beg totally to deny that such is the case, and I do not wish you simply to put statement against statement, but if you think it worth your while, I think I can produce you the time-books of my father from thirty to forty years past, to prove that the rate of wages has been the same for that period, that is, 17s. per week in summer, and 16s. in winter, or 2s. 8d. and 2s. 10d. per day; and my memory serves to remind me, that of all the branches of the building trade the wages of the bricklayers' labourer have been the most stationary, and never have we been asked for more, except at the time of the greatest activity in railroads, when occasionally 3s. per day might be asked by men who, from their past employment or superior strength, would more properly come under the denomination of navvies. Should you require any information which it may be in my power to give you, I shall feel happy in doing so."

Mr. MAYHEW is obliged for the above counter-statement, of whose truth there can be no doubt, as regards the firm to which the writer belongs. The original statement of J.W., the labourer, may however be true likewise. He might have been one of the men of "superior strength," who at the time of the "greatest activity in railroads," it is admitted received 3s. per diem, and who now get only 2s. 8d. The real difference between the two assertions appears to be, not as to the *fact* of the reduction, for this the last writer admits while seeking to disprove it, but as to its cause. The master bricklayer refers the decrease, or rather the increase, from 2s. 8d. to 3s. during the period of greatest activity in railroads, to the demand for labourers of "superior strength" at that time; whereas J.W. attributes the decrease in his wages since then to the cheapening of provisions. If the wages of bricklayers' labourers stood at 3s. a day during the "railway mania" only, and ceased when that ceased, then of course the master is right in his inference; but if the diminution was not made until the reduction in the price of food occurred, and that was the cause assigned by J.W.'s master at the time of making it, then it would appear that the labourer is correct in his statement. That such a diminution of wages has already commenced in many trades, owing to the cheapness of provisions, Mr. MAYHEW knows from his own personal investigations. During his inquiry into the condition of the labourers at the timber docks, [MCS, Vol. 5, pp. 46-61, Letter LVIII, 27 June 1850] he found that the wages of the men there had all been lowered. This was stated at the time in the account furnished by him to the *Chronicle*; but though the fact of the reduction was printed, every line

referring to the cause of it was withheld from the public by the Editor (Mr. MAYHEW has the proofs now in his possession), for that journal being inveterately free-trade in its principles, of course would not allow any fact to appear in its columns which went to show that the minimum, or natural value of all labour, like the minimum or natural value of every other thing, was regulated by the cost of its production; and that, when the supply exceeded the demand, the same natural value was necessarily the point to which the price ultimately descended. But the *Chronicle* had been long theorizing in the contrary direction, and, consequently, could not be expected—even in an "impartial" inquiry—to stultify itself by publishing facts in opposition to its own preconceived opinions. It had asserted that wages in no way depended on the price of food, and it would, therefore, never have done for so impartial a journal to have been the means of *proving* that they did. Had the operatives, however, been steam-engines, instead of mere human machines, the economical school to which that journal belongs would have been the first to have declared that any reduction in the cost of producing the power (as, for instance, in the decrease of the price of coals to one-half their value), would necessarily, if the market were overstocked, be followed by a proportionate reduction in the sum charged, in the price of the goods, for the power employed in their manufacture. To all who will or can think without prejudice on the subject, it will be evident that as there are necessarily three kinds of value appertaining to all commodities—to wit, a natural value regulated by the cost of production—a market value, regulated by the relation of the supply to the demand—and a money value, regulated by the currency—so must labour partake of all these three characteristics; and, consequently, as the natural value or cost of production is that to which the market value of all things must necessarily descend whenever the market is glutted, it holds that to reduce the cost of production in articles of which there is a superabundance, is to reduce their market value in an equal ratio. This is the A B C of political economy, and those who say otherwise,

ANSWERS TO CORRESPONDENTS

either do not know the alphabet of that science, or have some interest in perverting it. Now that the labour market in this country is glutted, there cannot be a doubt, hence the market value of such labour has a tendency to sink to its natural value or cost of production. The cost of the production of human labour is precisely the same as the cost of the production of steam labour—viz., the market value of the substances required to produce it—together with the expense of the wear and tear of the machine, and interest for the capital sunk in it. Reduce any one of these items, and the labour can and will (provided, as we said before, there be a glut of the article) be correspondingly cheapened. What coals are to the engine, food is to the man—the source of power; what the wear and tear is to the thing of brass and iron, so is sickness and accident to the creature of flesh and blood; and what the capital sunk in its *con*struction is to the machine, so is the time and money expended in *in*struction to the workman. For each and all of these an equivalent should be given as the lowest compensation to the producer, and, in the case of the steam-engine, such an equivalent is generally yielded to the capitalist (for if not, he withdraws his capital and leaves off producing); but in the case of the human engine, when wages are driven down to their ultimatum—as in hand-loom weaving, shirt-making, slop work, ballast heaving, making of soldiers' clothing, fancy cabinet-work, and the like—there is seldom any allowance made to the labourer for the wear and tear of the machinery of his frame; nor do his wages include any return for the capital and labour sunk in learning his business. The consequence is that the burden of the wear and tear of the human machine in the time of sickness or accident, is thrown upon the parish, who are left to remedy it as best they can and will. Moreover, as the manufacturer in the price he receives for the labour of his engine *in* work, is paid for the interest of his capital when *out of* work, even so should the wages of the employed labourer be sufficient to keep him when unemployed; for otherwise the rate-payers will have to make up in charity to him, what his employer should

have given him as a right. Cheap food *should* be the greatest of all blessings to the poor; but so long as the labour-market is overstocked, and wages are regulated by the principle of supply and demand, it is utterly impossible that a diminution in the price of provisions should not, sooner or later, be followed by a corresponding diminution in the price of labour. Wages, in such a condition of the labour-market, must necessarily tend towards the lowest possible subsistence point; and whatever may be the money value of the smallest quantity of food sufficient to support life, such will be the wages of the people in those trades where there is a superabundance of labourers. That this should not be, Mr. MAYHEW is most ready to admit; nor could it occur, if the remuneration of the workman depended, as it should in equity, upon the increased value such his labour gives to the materials upon which it is exercised. As was before stated, the proportion that the operative contributes towards the ultimate value of the produce, should be the determining principle of his amount of recompense. For instance, it is stated by M. de Villefosse, that in France the labour exercised upon 1£ worth of bar iron, in the manufacture of polished steel sword-handles, increases its value to 972£, or very nearly a thousand-fold.[18] The sum actually paid in wages to the workmen engaged in the production of these articles, M. Villefosse does not state; but supposing it to amount to 500£, surely no one would assert that in such a case justice was done to the labourer; for why, in the name of equity, should the capitalist receive as *much* as 500£ for supplying 1£ worth of material, and the labourer receive *as little* as 500£, when he, by his skill alone, makes the 1£ worth nearly 1,000£? Nor would it be any justification to the capitalist to say, that many indigent men, having no material upon which to exercise their skill, would gladly have accepted the same, or even a smaller sum. The production is essentially a partnership or joint stock association, to

[18] Monsieur de Villefosse, *Des Métaux en France. Rapport Fait au Jury Central de L'Exposition des Produits de L'Industrie Française de L'Année 1827.*

111

which the man of money contributes 1£, and the man of skill nearly 1,000£; and these proportions alone should determine the relative amount of remuneration coming to each. The capitalist should undoubtedly receive a fair recompense for the use and risk of the material, which is as necessary to the result as even the labour itself; and this, together with a proper reward for all other services he may render to the work, should be expressed in the estimation of his share of the produce. But that he should be allowed, because he contributes a *portion*, to take advantage of the workman's necessities, and grasp nearly the *whole* of the produce, is as monstrous as it is contrary to the fundamental principles of political economy. If the padlock which in our own country is made for a halfpenny and sold for a shilling, is honestly worth that sum in the market, then it is plain, according to the principles of equity, the *workman* making it is defrauded—not receiving his fair share of the produce; and if a halfpenny be sufficient for the making of it, then it is equally plain, judged by the same standard, that the *purchaser* is defrauded—being called upon to pay more than a fair return for the capital and labour invested in the commodity. Let us, however, once admit the law of supply and demand as the guiding commercial principle, and, despite all equity, we must allow the transaction to be perfectly fair, saying that the manufacturer merely carried out the glorious policy of the enlightened commerce of the present time—buying in the cheapest market and selling in the dearest. It is true, he underpaid the producer, and overcharged the consumer, while he enriched himself at their joint expense; but this, we are assured by our modern sages, is necessary for the good of the community,—a sentiment so extremely *liberal*, that, as "there is nothing like a good cry," the political propounders of it had better throw up their caps, and shout at once, "Success to Swindling."

Mr. MAYHEW in saying thus much is anxious not to be misunderstood. He wishes capital to have every just reward and stimulus for its use. That the accumulator of labour should have his fair share of the produce to which the labour he has accumulated is so necessary an auxiliary, that he should be recompensed for the risk of his property, and that he should be paid for his superintendence of the manufacture—common honesty and common sense demand. But that the capitalist should be at liberty to pay for the labour he employs *without any regard to the increased value that such labour may give to the articles on which it is exercised,* appears to MR. MAYHEW to be one of the crying iniquities of the present day. If a publisher were to give a needy author 10£ for writing a book, and that book were afterwards to produce a thousand clear profit, surely not even the most rabid "economist" would dream of maintaining that the transaction was a fair one; and if it be unfair it is so simply because the publisher took advantage of the author's poverty, and gave him a sum which bore no proportion to the ultimate value of his work.[19] And herein lies the great injustice of the principle of supply and demand. It trades upon the workman's necessities, and pays him at a rate which has no relation to the increased value that he by his labour has given to the materials upon which he has operated, yielding him, instead of his fair share of the produce, barely sufficient to cover the cost of his subsistence.

The "equitable" wage-principle here advocated in contradistinction to that of the "law of supply and demand," is not entirely unknown in commerce. The mode of working the mines in Cornwall, by what are called "tribute," or payment for raising and dressing the ore by means of a certain part of its value when rendered merchantable, and which, as Mr. Babbage tells us in his "Economy of Manufactures," is found to produce "such admirable effects,"—the payment of the crew in whaling-ships—the profits arising from fishing with nets on the south coast of England—the "fourth penny" among the Irish weavers—are all instances of the equitable mode of payment or "tribute" rendered to working men. The establishment of M. Leclaire, the

---

[19] This is exactly what happened. See J.A. Sutherland, *Victorian Novelists and Publishers*, University of Chicago Press, 1976, pp. 42-100.

French house painter, is also well-known to be conducted on a similar plan, and perhaps to be the most just and practical illustration of the principle that is at present in existence—the capitalist being paid a fair interest for the use of his money, a return for his risk, and a salary for his superintendance; while the workmen (who receive a certain weekly wage) are allowed to participate with himself in the profits. The introduction of this "tribute" system into factories has been ably advocated by Mr. Babbage, who sums up its advantages in the following terms:— (1) Every person engaged in the business would have a direct interest in its prosperity. (2) Every person would have an immediate interest in preventing waste or mismanagement. (3) The talents of all would be directed to its improvement in every part. (4) None but workmen of high character and qualifications would be admitted into such establishments. (5) When any circumstance produced a glut in the market, more skill would be directed in diminishing the cost of production. (6) All real or imaginary causes for combinations of workmen against their employers would be totally removed.

The tribute, or equitable wage-principle, it is evident, is merely a mode of carrying out that *partnership* in the produce which the fundamental axioms of political economy acknowledge. In all production the capitalist supplies the past labour (accumulated in the form of materials, &c.), and the workmen the present labour. The union of the two constitute the produce, which, therefore, it is plain *the two should share in the proportion which they contribute towards the result.*

A correspondent, dating from the Athenæum Club, sends the subjoined epistle: "Sir,—In your Prospectus, it is mentioned that the class of unfortunates—Street-walkers—are to be written about; and I hope that, in some of the many true tales which you must have heard, you will point out for publication those that bear upon the cruel treatment which the frail fair one expects, and generally receives, from those who ought to be her best friends. On more than one occasion, I *know* that the frowns of the father, the upbraidings of the mother, the sisters' taunts and jeers, and the sulkiness of the brothers, have

arrested all idea, all hope of returning to home; and this ought surely not to be. As a class, they are more 'sinned against than sinning;' and many would give their right hand to be rescued from a life of sin and shame. I think you can do much good in arousing families by *true* details, how wrong they are in stopping the least advance of these poor girls; and I hope that when you come to that portion of your valuable and original history, that you will use your powerful pen in their behalf; and although you may not have open thanks, still many will be grateful to you privately. If not giving you too much trouble, I should like to know whether you have received this note, and if your views coincide with my ideas. I am, Sir, yours very faithfully, PITY."

[MR. MAYHEW has no time at present to write an essay on prostitution, even if he were inclined to do so, nor to inquire into the matter. The subject *will* form part of the present Work, though when it will be entered upon it is impossible now to say. MR. MAYHEW (speaking before investigation) has no doubt that *many* of the "unfortunates" are driven to lives of vice and crime by the harshness of parents and relations; but that the greater part of the prostitution of this country is so induced, he is in no way prepared to admit. However, when he comes in due order to this branch of his subject, he will endeavour to ascertain the several causes (for these appear to be many, and all widely different), and also to arrive at an estimate of the relative influence of each. The prostitution of this country is a matter that has been wholly neglected. The curious work on the prostitution of France has no counterpart in England.[20] MR. MAYHEW hopes to be able to fill up the hiatus—at least, no pain shall be spared on his part.

P.Q.R., FINSBURY.—The betting of the coster-boy, as described in a former number, and alluded to by P.Q.R., [LLLP, Vol. 1, p. 16], is illegal and punishable according to the present state of the

---

[20] Alexandre Parent-Duchâtelet, *De la Prostitution dans la Ville de Paris*, Baillière, 1836 and following editions. See Alain Corbin, *Les Filles de Noce*, op. cit., pp. 13-34 and his introduction to Parent-Duchâtelet's edited text, *La Prostitution à Paris au XIXème Siècle*, Le Seuil, 1981.

law. By 5 Geo. IV., c. 83, indeed, persons betting &c., in any street, or public and open place, are liable to summary punishment as rogues and vagabonds. In all probability the information sought by P.Q.R. will be found in the most reliable form in the Report of the Evidence taken before Select Committees in 1844. The inquiry was not limited to gaming in London.

L.C.H.—A lady has been kind enough to address a communication to MR. MAYHEW, of which the following is the principal portion: "On reading of your proposed Loan Society, it occurred to me that you might not have heard of the Provident Society at Manchester, which has been found to work there extremely well, not only by encouraging small savings, but especially by bringing the middle classes in contact with the poor, upon friendly, not almsgiving terms. The whole town is divided into districts; one, two, or more ladies undertaking each as far as their present number of visitors will go. The secretary first explores the neighbourhood, making a list of the houses where he thinks it is desirable the ladies should go, and leaving at each a paper to explain the objects of the society. These he of course makes them understand, and the visitor follows him about a week after. If they wish to enter it, she leaves a card, on which is to be put down what they can spare for the week; entering the sum also in her own book at the same time. They can at any time withdraw their money, an order for the sum being given by the visitor from her cheque-book; but if taken again within three months after being deposited, they do not receive the bounty upon it, which is a penny for every shilling. It seems to me that something of this kind might be attempted in London, perhaps in connection with your loan society. The effect of the visiting in Manchester has been most marked, in softening the manners of the people, and in discovering and alleviating many cases of distress, besides the direct object of encouraging provident habits. The secretary going first to explore the neighbourhood, would be in London more necessary even than in Manchester. Ladies, however anxious to do their duty to their poorer neighbours, are afraid to venture out of the most frequented thoroughfares, knowing nothing of the inhabitants of the back streets. This society both obviates this difficulty, and another of almost equal importance, by giving a definite object for the visit, without which it might seem intrusive." The secretary of this society, it is stated, is Mr. Taylor, Faulkner-street, Manchester.[21]

F.F.—The names of persons giving information or statements for the purposes of this work, *are never revealed, for any purpose, without the parties' concurrence.*

ANSWERS TO CORRESPONDENTS.
[No.16, 29 MARCH 1851]

Edited out:
G.B.

═══════════════

W. sends a long complimentary epistle requesting to be informed what are the remedies for low wages. To understand this we must first comprehend the circumstances by which wages are at present regulated. "Wages," says Mr. Mill—the best "economical" authority perhaps on the subject—"depend upon the demand and supply of labour; or, as is often expressed on the proportion between population and capital,"—the term population here meaning, as he tells us, "the number only of the labouring class, or rather of those who work for hire," and the term capital referring solely to that which comes under the denomination of "circulating capital—and not even the whole of that, but the part which is expended in the direct purchase of labour." In plain English, we are informed this means, "the more money there is offered for labour, and the fewer labourer there are to ask for it, the

---

[21] On philanthropy in Manchester see, Joan Mottram, "The Life and Work of John Roberton (1797-1876) of Manchester, Obstetrician and Social Reformer", M.Sc., UMIST, 1986.

greater will be the share of each"—"which of course," adds another gentleman, quoting the passage, "is self-evident." But is this partition of the wage-fund amongst the labourers quite as self-evident as is asserted? Let us see. Suppose the number of labourers belonging to a particular trade to be 1,000; that there is just enough work to keep them all fully employed; and that the wage-fund, or gross sum annually "expended in the direct purchase of their labour" amounts to 50,000£; in such a case it is manifest each of the labourers would receive 50£ per annum, or say 1£ per week. Then suppose the number of labourers to be doubled, or increased to 2,000, while the quantity of work remains the same, or sufficient to employ only half the number—in this case would the wage fund be shared among the whole of the 2,000 labourers, and each receive 10s. a week for working half-time, according to the statement which is said to be "self-evident?" Or rather, is it not far more self-evident the real result would be, that the labourers being twice too many, the wages would be reduced to one-half, and that, consequently, 1,000 of the men would be unemployed and get nothing at all, while the other 1,000 would get only 25,000£ or 10s. a week each for the same amount of work as before, while the remaining 25,000£ would, provided the market were *limited*, and the price of the commodities remained the *same* to the public, go to increase the profits of their employers; so that instead of the wage-fund being necessarily shared among the workmen, we see that in the same proportion as the supply of workmen increases beyond the demand for their work, so may the wage-fund be shared between the labourers and their employers—that is to say, the workmen in a given trade becoming half as many again as are required to do the work, and wages consequently being reduced one-half, the other half of the wage-fund *may be* apportioned among the capitalists. A reduction of price, it should be borne in mind cannot, *in many cases*, be followed by an increased of demand. What cheapness could possibly make the public require a greater quantity of hearses? Again; if the price of doll's-eyes were reduced one-half, could there be more eyes to get rid of than the demand for dolls allowed? So the demand for sawyers' work must be regulated by the demand for carpenters' work; and the demand for carpenters' work by the demand for builders' work. In such cases the market is necessarily *limited*, and *then* cheapness can benefit only the employer or the public *at the expense of the working man*.

Let us now see whether wages do *really* depend upon the number of the labouring class, and the amount expended in the direct purchase of their labour, or, in other words "upon the proportion between population and capital." The fallacy here lies in taking no notice of the *duration of the daily labour*, nor of the *rate of labouring*, both of which are manifestly as essential elements of the subject as even the *number of labourers* themselves. For let us suppose the operatives in a given trade be twice too many to do the work required to be done—on the assumption, of course, that each labours twelve hours per diem—(for it is only by assuming *some term* of labour that we can reason on the matter at all); then let the hours of labour be reduced to six, and it is manifest that instead of one-half of the operatives being out of work, the whole of them would be fully employed. Or let us suppose the number of operatives to be just sufficient to do the work required to be done (provided each labours only twelve hours a day), and let the hours of labour be increased to eighteen, then it is *really* self-evident that there will be one-third too many labourers and that only two-thirds of the trade will be fully employed. As it is with the duration of the daily labour, so it is with the rate of labouring. If there be just sufficient work to keep the whole of the operatives belonging to a given trade fully occupied, on the assumption that they each labour at a particular rate or, in other words, get through so much work in a certain space of time, then let anything occur to induce or compel the men generally to double their rate of labouring, and so get through twice the quantity of work in the same space of time, it is manifest there will be full employment for only half the men, while the other half will have no work at all to do. Hence we see that wages depend, not only upon the proportion between the number of labourers and amount of money expended in the direct purchase of their labour, but also on—matters equally important for the right understanding of the subject, but as yet wholly omitted from all "economical" consideration—the duration of the daily labour as well as on the rate of labouring; and, consequently, that anything which tends to *increase* either the number of labourers—the duration of their labour—or the rate of labouring, tends in precisely the same proportion not only to *decrease* the amount of money coming to the operatives, but (provided the prices to consumers remain the same) likewise to *increase* the amount of profit accruing to their employers. *The Messrs. Nicol, of Regent-street, are said to have amassed 80,000£ each, in a few years, simply by reducing the wages of the 1,000 workmen they employ to one-third below that of the "honourable" trade.*

Let us now proceed to ascertain what are the circumstances that tend to affect the wages of operatives in the several modes above mentioned.

I. The circumstances which tend to increase the number of labourers in a trade appear to be as follows: (1) The labourers increase in a measure according to the ordinary rate of the population—trades generally descending from father to son. (2) They increase according to the demand for labour. (3) According to the number of apprentices taken, and consequently according to the number of "little masters" in the trade. (4) According to the demand for children's labour.

II. The circumstances tending to extend the hours of labour are (1) The "domestic system," or working at home—as enabling a man to labour as early or as late as he pleases. (2) Piece work—as giving the labourer a direct interest in increasing his amount of labour. (3) Time-work—or work required against a particular period. (4) Reduction of wages—as nec-

essitating a greater quantity of labour in order to obtain the same amount of income.

III. The circumstances inducing a quicker rate of working are (1) Piece-work—for the same reason as that given above. (2) Reduction of wages—as inducing "scamped-work." (3) The "strapping system"—as in the joiners' trade where men are required to get through a certain amount of work in a given time. (4) Increased supervision—as causing increased exertion. (5) Division of labour—as creating increased facility.

This contradiction to the theories of economists Mr. MAYHEW, on investigation, found to be due simply to a large number of the workmen having passed, since 1831, from the state of journeymen into that of little masters; and so not only toiling longer hours all the week, and Sunday too, as well as labouring at a far more rapid rate for themselves than they had been in the habit of doing for others, but, forcing the market with the goods they were obliged to sell as fast as made, whether there was a demand for them or not, and thus reducing the prices generally throughout the trade. The same facts and reason were found to hold good in the turners' trade, which had also decreased in "hands" and increased in work, while wages had fallen—and that simply through the over-work and consequent cutting down of prices by the little masters.

But, besides the above circumstances affecting wages, there are others equally important, and which must be ascertained before any effective remedy for low wages can be devised. The matters spoken of as yet relate chiefly to the labourers—to the supply of the labour—as well as to the quantity of work *done* by the operatives. They in no way concern the *demand* for such labour—or, in other words, the quantity of work *to be done*. This, it is evident, is quite as essential a point to be evolved as any other; for to *decrease* the demand for labour is, of course, the same as to *increase* the supply; reduce the quantity of work to be done, and it is tantamount to lengthening the hours of labour or quickening the rate of working; in either case, the same number of labourers must be thrown out of employment. Let us, therefore, see now what regulates the quantity of work to be done.

That the wages do not depend, as "economists" would have us believe, *solely* upon the supply of labourers and the demand for their labour—that is to say, upon the number of workmen to do the work required to be done—is *proved by experience;* for the "hands" belonging to the cabinet trade decreased, between the years 1831 and 1841, no less than 15 per cent.; and though the quantity of work during that period increased considerably, wages were, nevertheless, in some instances, as much as 400 per cent. higher in 1831; so that here was *more* work to be done with fewer hands to do it, and yet *less* wages for the doing of it!

The circumstances tending to decrease the amount of work, or demand for labour, are (1) Increase of the price of the commodities to consumers. (2) Decrease of the purchasing fund, or amount annually expended upon such commodities. (3) Panics—as inducing an indisposition on the part of the public to expend money in the purchase of goods. (4) Decrease of the amount of capital—and so allowing a less sum to be expended in the purchase of labour. (5) Decrease of the quantity of materials to be made up; as failure of the cotton-crop, &c. (6) Over-production—as requiring no further labour until the stock; accumulated has been consumed. (7) Machinery—as superseding manual labour, and so lessening the quantity of work for the labourers. (8) The seasons—as preventing the performance of certain kinds of labour at particular periods of the year. (9) Fashion—as superseding the demand for certain commodities.

Hence we perceive that anything which tends to *increase* the number of workers—to lengthen the hours of work—to quicken the rate of working—or to *decrease* the quantity of work, must necessarily, so long as the remuneration of the labourer continues to be regulated by the law of supply and demand, be followed by a *decrease* of wages; and, *vice versâ,* anything which tends to *decrease* the labourers—to shorten the hours of labour—to retard the rate of labouring—or to *increase* the quantity of work, must necessarily be accompanied by an *increase* of pay to the labourer.

The above law, however, it must be distinctly understood, holds good *only so long as the price of the commodities remains the same to the public;* for if that price be reduced in the same proportion as wages are reduced, then it is clear that the public, and not the employer, is benefited—but *at the expense of the working man.* For the same reason, machinery and the division of labour, which enable a greater quantity of commodities to be produced with the same or a less quantity of labour, tend in some cases to increase the demand for labour by cheapening the cost of production and so lowering the price, and consequently increasing the demand for the commodities. But this is a result, it should be borne in mind, that can be attained only in connection with the production of those commodities, *the demand for which is infinitely extensible* (as, for instance, with the several articles of cotton manufacture); for where the market is necessarily *limited,* and the demand regulated by some concomitant circumstance— (as, for instance, in the sawing of wood, where the quantity of sawyers' work depends, as was before stated, on the quantity of carpenters' and joiners' work, or in the threshing of corn, where the quantity of threshers' work depends on the quantity of corn grown; so that the increase of the one cannot take place without the previous increase of the other)—it is manifest, that under these circumstances, either to quicken the rate of working by the division of labour, or to reduce the amount of labour by machinery, *is to deprive a number of labourers of employment, and to lessen the wages of the remainder.* In such cases, the cheapness is likewise attained at the expense of the working man—that is to say, the capitalists are enriched and the labourers pauperised by it; for it admits almost of demonstration that cheapness, brought about by lessening the reward for labour, can never benefit any other portion of the community than the monied classes; since a given quantity of money will, of course, when prices are lowered, exchange for a greater quantity of commodities; but that the *labourer can be in any way benefited by a lowering of prices, when this same lowering has been affected solely by a reduction of the price of his own labour, is an absurdity of the most glaring description.* The only legitimate mode of cheapness to a community is that which is attained by increased facilities of production applied to the manufacture of those commodities the demand for which is *infinitely extensible.* If in such cases a labourer, by improved methods of manufacture, can be made to produce a greater quantity of commodities in a given time, with the same amount of labour on his part, and for that labour he receives the same amount of remuneration, then, of course, all parties will be benefited—the capitalist class and the working class—both then being able to obtain a greater quantity of commodities for the same quantity of money.

There is still another circumstance affecting the labourer's reward; viz., the mode of *distributing* the returns for the produce. But this, together with the usual means adopted to reduce wages, and the remedies for the same, will be considered in the next Number.

MR. MAYHEW, however, wishes it to be distinctly understood, that he in no way pledges himself to the principles here asserted from time to time. It should be remembered he is collecting facts, and merely avails himself of the *waste* pages of this periodical as a means of recording the opinions which are forced upon him in the course of his investigations (such opinions being at all times carefully excluded from the work itself). He reserves to himself therefore (as person unconnected with party), the right of changing or modifying his sentiments as often as a more enlarged series of facts, may present new views to his mind. It is in this light that he wishes his speculations to be received—for speculations they are, though, perhaps based upon a greater number of phenomena than any economist has as yet personally obtained. For the present he can only declare his determination to follow the facts, whithersoever they may lead (for he has no object but the truth), and if he be open to the charge of generalising, before he has made

himself acquainted with all the particulars, he at least has a greater right to do so than any economist of the present day—seeing that he is perhaps the first who has sought to evolve the truths of the Labour Question by personal investigation. As yet political economy has been a purely armchair science—gentlemen who troubled their heads about the matter have done *no more than* trouble their heads; they have sat beside a snug sea-coal fire and tried to excogitate, or think out the several matters affecting the working classes—even as Adam Smith, the great founder of the science retired for twelve years to an obscure village in Scotland to dream upon the laws concerning production and the producers. And yet it is upon the cobweb philosophy thus spun out that the whole of the legislation of the present day is made to depend!

MR. MAYHEW will at all times be glad to listen patiently to any *new* ideas, though he must object to disgorging of the old ones, in opposition to the sentiments he here propounds; he will also be pleased to receive any additional facts from working men, whose greater experience may cause them to detect omissions and errors in the enumeration of circumstances given here or hereafter. A desire for the public good precludes party bigotry.

A SUBSCRIBER says: "I am sorry you should have disfigured your hitherto interesting publication by such vile prints as 'Illustrations of Street Art.'" The prints were a necessary part of the subject treated of. How is it possible to impress upon the hundreds and thousands who never see such things any notion of the character of the "art" furnished to the poor? Surely no written description could have conveyed so vivid an image of it to the reader's mind. MR. MAYHEW perfectly agrees with his subscriber that the prints in question are vile, and the villainy of them was the sole reason of their being given. It is necessary that the public should have *some* idea as to the means at present in force among the humbler classes, for what Mr. Burnet has aptly called "the education of the eye." How can we expect people to have a sense of or reverence for, the beautiful, when such barbarisms form their daily mental food? MR. MAYHEW thinks the aesthetics of the poor a subject fraught with the greatest interest.

MR. MAYHEW prints the following bill, and as he can vouch for the worthiness of one of the sufferers, he will be happy to receive subscriptions in their behalf:—"Calamitous fire! To the humane public. The particular attention of the benevolent is called to a distressing case of two industrious individuals, William Prince and Thomas Wicks, who have lost the whole of their little property, amassed during years of toil, in a few hours, by an accidental fire, which broke out on the morning of February the 28th, on the premises of Mr. Mathews, builder, 2½, Cleveland-street, Fitzroy-square. A few friends of the above trust that no further appeal need be made to the public, than by stating, that by this occurrence two deserving families have been rendered quite homeless and destitute. Through the exertions of W. Prince and his wife, they were the means of saving four lives and preventing an immense sacrifice of property."

H.G. is labouring under a mistake. No ridicule was intended, and if she have been pained, the writer is grieved. Her second note has never come to hand.

The following needs but little comment:—"I have been a regular subscriber to, and advertisement for, your excellent work, LONDON LABOUR AND THE LONDON POOR, ever since its first appearance. I take great interest in it, and have quoted it from pulpit and platform with effect. Though I know little of London, I know something of the dangerous classes included in your comprehensive "Encyclopaedia of struggling humanity." I have had thirteen years' experience as a clergyman, and have seen something of the lodging-houses, and the 'dodges' of various 'lurks;' and though I have never witnessed anything so bad as what you describe, I have not unfrequently had a pretty fair sample submitted to my observation. As a clergyman working in a poor district of a large manufacturing town, and having all the worst lodging-houses of the place

in my walk, I beg to thank you cordially for the manner in which you have drawn public attention to these rallying points of disease and crime. I hope that as you proceed, many of our good easy citizens will begin to feel that the worst elements are at work in the substratum of society, and that if we are to escape a moral volcano, something must be done. My object however, is not merely to thank you, but to ask if you think your printer could so arrange his paper, as to admit of the 'Answers to Correspondents' being bound up with the work, without spoiling the uniformity of it by the necessity at present imposed, of binding up advertisements at the same time. I take as much pleasure in reading these answers as many other parts of the work, not only because they show the effect of your publication on the public mind, but because they contain a vast amount of your own common sense which to me is very valuable." [MR. MAYHEW is afraid that the work cannot be arranged as the gentleman desires. He will however, for the future, endeavour to insert the greater part of the correspondence in the two last pages, so that those who please may bind them up with their Numbers.]

ANSWERS TO CORRESPONDENTS.
[No.17, 5 APRIL 1851]

The Rev. J.B.W. favours us with the subjoined curious etymology, from an equally curious source:—"Your readers being by this time familiar with the term 'patter,' may be glad to know its etymology, which I have just met with. To 'patter' is to say 'Paternosters,' in which sense the word is used by Tyndall, one of the exiles of Queen Mary's time. For this information I am indebted to no less grave an authority than the Rev. Dr. Pusey.—(Letter to Bishop of London, p.78, ed. 3.)"[22]

MR. MAYHEW has to acknowledge the receipt of a cheque from P.P. for 1£, to be dispensed as a loan in equal proportions to the "reduced gentlewoman," and the "reduced tradesman," mentioned at p.250; also 15s. in postage-stamps, from the Rev. J.S., to be applied as follows:—5s. for poor Foster, the harper; 5s. for the "reduced tradesman;" and 5s. for the "reduced gentlewoman,"—the two latter sums to be offered by way of loan—the money when repaid to be lent to any similar applicant. The above-mentioned sums have been handed to Mr. Howden, who will see that the wishes of the gentlemen are duly carried out.

The following should have been answered in the last number:—"Sir,—Can you be so obliging as to inform me if I could obtain a living by tinselling pictures; if so, how and where am I to sell them? I am employed during the day, but that does not bring me in a sufficiency to make a living; so I want to do something in the evening on my own account (tinselling pictures, for instance.) so that I may be able to obtain a respectable and comfortable living. I hope you will pardon me for the liberty I have taken in addressing this to you; I should not have done so, had I not known your kind and liberal feelings towards the industrious. I remain, Sir, &c.—HENRY." [MR. MAYHEW is unacquainted with the practical part of the profession to which the writer refers. He would, however, object on principle to be connected in any way with what is known in "Political Economy" as an "aid to wages." He has, in the course of his inquiries, seen so many injurious effects proceeding from the subsistence of artizans being eked out by other employments, that he could not conscientiously give any advice on such a matter. If the wages of the present occupation of "Henry" are below subsistence point, then the best thing he can do is—if it be at all possible—to move into some other better-paid trade. But to seek to gain a competence by means of uniting another occupation with his present one, is only to

[22] E.B. Pusey, *Letter to the Bishop of London*, J.H. Parker, 3rd edition, 1851. E.B. Pusey was one of the main promoters of the Tractarian movement in Oxford which promoted Anglo-Catholic rituals and a theological reconciliation with the Roman Catholics.

enable employers still further to reduce his earnings. The prostitution which needle-women, in many cases, are forced to resort to as an "aid to wages," is one of the causes of sempstresses being so badly paid. As before stated, the minimum value of labour is the smallest amount that the labourers can subsist upon. Those, therefore, who add prostitution to needlework as a means of living, can afford to undersell those who do not, and conse-quently become the means of ultimately reducing the more virtuous to the level of their own degradation.]

JUVENIS, of Camberwell, requests to be informed, "if it is intended to issue binding at a low price (as in most cheap publications), on the completion of the work?" [Most likely some arrangement will be entered into with a bookbinder, to supply covers at a fixed rate.]

C.B., of Portland Town, says:—"Being a subscriber to your useful work, LONDON LABOUR, I take it to the shop to read, for I am a journeyman tailor. The is a passage at page 89, that some of my shopmates find great fault with, and don't believe you are stating correct, when you say that cocoa nuts are generally spelt 'coker.' They wish to know in what work of M'Culloch's they are spelt as such, and how long they have been entered as such at the Custom House; for they cannot find them spelt so in any work they have seen. You will please to answer this on the wrapper of LONDON LABOUR, and you will much oblige me, as I defend you as well as I am able." [The orthography is "coker" in M'Culloch's "Com-mercial Dictionary;" and they are certainly so written at the Customs, and by all fruit brokers. Mr. Keeling (of the firm of Keeling and Hunt) was the first gentleman who made MR. MAYHEW acquainted with the commercial distinction.]

W.A., of Tower-street, says:—"At the foot of the first column of page 218 of LONDON LABOUR (No.11), a paragraph appears which is utterly incomprehensible to me, and I should feel extremely obliged if you would afford me an explanation of its meaning in your next Number. Your informant states that: 'From the hasty glance he has taken at the patterers, any well-constructed mind may deduce the following inference: *because* a great amount of intelligence sometimes consists with a great want of principle that no education, or mis-education, leaves man like a reed floating on the stream of time,' &c. Now, I want to know what is *the* inference any well constructed mind may deduce? If you will favour me with a word in explanation in your next, I shall feel more indebted to you than ever." [The meaning of the sentence is, that an utter want of education, as well as a bad education, leaves man without directive power. The passage is certainly misty.]

R.A., asks where the colours that the shops use in painting the scenes and characters in small theatres are to be had—"their colours," he says, "being so much clearer than the cakes one can buy in the shops?" Can any correspondent supply the information, MR. MAYHEW is profoundly ignorant of the subject.

A.E.L., of Shepherds Bush, says, "Pray give me an answer whether you do not think socialism is the remedy for all the misery of the working man?" MR. MAYHEW is not in a position at present to reply to the above question. He has merely a "book-knowledge" of the subject as yet, and to answer before investigation would be as injudicious as unjust. At some future time he purposes inquiring specially into the matter, and then he will not hesitate to publish the result of his inquiries. Concerning the other matter referred to in A.E.L.'s letter, it being not the most agreeable subject to have to touch upon, MR. MAYHEW must be excused making a reply. In such a case, the supply must necessarily be regulated by the demand.

A literary gentleman forwards the following observations—"It appears from your notice to correspondents that your illustrations of the conditions of LONDON LABOUR provoke various comments. May I venture to say how deeply interested I am in you revelations? In compiling an appendix sometime back to a Prize Essay on the working classes of Great Britain, I found your letters in the *Morning Chronicle* of invaluable service, and believe your present publication will be the means of great good to the classes you so ably befriend. *Is there anything to be done by men like myself* of humble literary pursuit in alleviation of those evils. Would any movement, do you think, for the promotion of co-operative labour among the manufacturing poor, which the advocacy of the press might promote, tend in any measure to meet the wants of the case? I am sometimes troubled lest the frightful exposures of suffering and class wrong, should fail to give birth to commensurate effects for the cure of the evil. The conviction is growing among thinking men that capital has innumerable crimes to answer for, and that in the continuance of such a policy of competition as we have seen in modern times, there is no ultimate hope for the workman; but the vaguest ideas are afloat as to the true remedy. Public opinion waits to be taught and guided, and many men who have something to do with its formation, want to receive their cue from some master, who like yourself have made this subject in its million aspects a familiar thing. The artizans themselves are trying to solve the problem; but if the secret lies in the wild form of socialism we see in 'Co-operation Associations,' it is pity that their encouragement is left to a little band of comparatively obscure and feeble men." MR. MAYHEW has already given the only answer he can at present give the above question. He is not in a position to speak fairly upon the subject, and therefore must decline speaking at all.

AN EDINBURGH STREET-SELLER, who adopts the signature of "Mac," proffers information as to the street life of that city. He sends the following letter:

"I have been a constant purchaser of your valuable publication of LONDON LABOUR since its commencement, and to its truthfulness as regards 'travellers,' I can bear witness. Unfortunately for myself, I have travelled different parts of England, &c., in various occupations, and have seen 'every move on the board,' and been well acquainted with men who well knew both Captain M—and Nicholas A—; and their exploits as mentioned by you are perfectly true, and many others I could tell, with which, I dare say, you are also acquainted. For upwards of three years past I have been a resident here, endeavouring to obtain a honest livelihood in various ways of street-trading (as I am not capable of doing bodily labour), and in a great measure, I may say, I have succeeded, having placed myself in a state of comparative comfort; but still the 'moral brand' of being on the streets is a 'sticking-plaster.' The reason of my writing to you is, my having noticed an answer to 'R.T.,' requesting information as to the Edinburgh street-sellers, and not knowing whether he can or will supply you with any, I have taken the liberty of volunteering any information in my power. A complete crusade is declared against all street-sellers here: they are not even safe when moving along, even if they have only a tray hanging in front of them, for *if they only stop to sell a single halfpennyworth, they are liable to be summoned, and ultimately fined or imprisoned.* Cases in point I have known, and can give the names of the parties. Baillie Dick, one of the sitting magistrates, used the following words to a poor lad, who was summoned for standing in one of the markets with a board hanging in front of him, selling sweet-stuff— (the same lad had often been convicted of theft, but at length had determined to get a living honestly, and is still rigidly adhering to his resolution)—'We will let you go this time, but if ever you are brought here again for the same offence,' (looking at the 'offender' as if he were guilty of a most heinous crime), 'you will be fined and imprisoned.' Now, sir, was not that enough to make that lad return to his former vicious courses? The patterers, or 'speech-criers,' as they are called here, are the only ones the police have not interfered with; but this street-trade is, I believe, also intended to be stopped—at all events, there is a talk about it. A great reformation has taken place here with these men within these two years; the majority of them are teetotallers, or act up to the same principle, and it is said by many that the Edinburgh criers are the most respectable they ever saw. This small outline will of course be of little or no service to you, but any information you may wish for, I shall be happy to oblige you with, if it lays in my power. Of course I do not wish to be known in the matter, as the opinions of many of the street-sellers here are much against you (but the most of them are very ignorant and bigoted), and if it were known amongst them that any party was giving any account of them, he would be sure of a 'ferricadouzer,' or 'mugging,' as we call it. I however send my name and residence in confidence, and you can either drop a line by post, stating what information you require (which mode, if agreeable to you, I should prefer), or answer at your convenience in your answers to correspondents."

MR. MAYHEW will communicate with "Mac" by letter. He is much obliged for his offer.

MR. MAYHEW prints the following letter from a showman of his acquaintance—a struggling, hard-working man:

"Pardon me for taking so great a liberty as to write to you. Sir, you are publishing a work in weekly numbers called LONDON LABOUR AND LONDON POOR; you took a memoir of my life a short time ago for that work. My life was a street-showman, from an early age having a crippled arm, and no other means of getting a living. I am still the same as I described to you, and a showman, but for the want of the sum of 1£ 10s. I am living a miserable and starving life. The loan of the required sum would be the means of saving me from entering a work-house, which I do not desire to do if I can live honest by perseverance and industry. I have parted with all things I had to make money of, to bring forth, if possible, a novel and pleasing exhibition, being models made of glass and stone-work, representing large buildings of British and foreign views; also a mechanical representation of a cataract, or mountain torrent, with real water; but for the want of the required sum, I am completely at a loss. If I could get a person to be a friend to me in my present circumstances, I would give the sum of 5s. for the loan of the above-mentioned sum, and pay it up by instalments at 2s. per week, and give a security for the same, or leave the value of it as a security. If you doubt what is stated by me in the few lines written to you, you can come yourself and inquire into my character, or send a trust-worthy person to do the same. You can see, by instituting an inquiry, that there is no imposition."

Should any reader feel inclined to lend the amount above-named, MR. MAYHEW will see that proper security is given for the repayment of the money. Of course MR. MAYHEW could be no party to the premium of 5s. for the loan of 30s. The exhibition is at least a harmless one, and the man being crippled in his right arm, has not the power of working for his living—a circumstance which drives many hundreds to the streets.

G.P., of Manor-place, Edinburgh sends the "Reports of the Edinburgh Lodging-house Association" with the following observations— "I do so to show you that the houses are equally bad with those you describe in London, and what progress has been made here in model dwelling-houses. There is also an association for building model lodging-houses, which has already commenced operations, and it is likely to prove a very profitable investment for the shareholders as well as being the means of conferring comfortable houses on the working-class. Your Edinburgh correspondent is right as to the removal of the stalls from the streets—*it has been productive of great injury in every respect to the class of stall-keepers, who were totally dependent on that for their living*. Should you wish any information about lodging-houses, charitable societies, street-sellers or poor in Edinburgh, or any of the towns in Scotland, I shall be glad to give you what I know, and also endeavour to obtain from other sources." MR. MAYHEW wishes to give at the conclusion of this account of the London Street Folk, a brief account of the numbers and earnings of the several classes of Street Folk in all the large towns throughout the kingdom, and will feel obliged to G.P. for any well-authenticated information. The classification of the London Street Folk will do for all towns. G.P. quotes the following passage from a work now in course of issue, and entitled "An Inquiry into Destitution, Prostitution, and Crime in Edinburgh"—as a proof of the evils caused by removing the street-sellers from their pitches in that city: "In this house, we found a family who had previously earned a scanty and precarious subsistence by keeping a barrow—as a sort of stall—on the street, in which they hawked whatever might be in season at the time,—fruit, fish, or confectionery, as the case might be. Now, however, thanks to the wisdom of our civic rulers, if they venture with their barrow on the public streets, fines and imprisonment are their certain fate. We cannot, for the life of us, conceive what has tempted the head of our police to proceed as he has done in his late system of, what we will venture to call, *ejectments;* for really we cannot find a word that appears to us more appropriate. It is possible enough that the absence of these stalls may make the streets look better and cleaner; but will it tend to the general cleanliness and morality of the city at large? In our opinion, quite the reverse; for what must be of necessity the effect of depriving some 200 families of the means of making a miserably poor, but still honest living, especially when this was with them emphatically their last resource; for surely it will never be maintained that the class by whom stalls were kept, had other resources to fall back upon? No, no: it was their last effort from utter hopeless destitution. It has been forcibly removed, and what can be, nay, what are the results? Here we have a poor woman, with two daughters of from thirteen to sixteen years of age, and a son somewhat younger. Day after day have they parted, piecemeal, with their furniture—their clothes go next—and now, when all is gone, think you their honesty can survive? Is it not ten thousand probabilities to one, that the girls, even while we write, have swelled the mighty and polluting flood of prostitution, and the boy added one more to the already but too numerous body of thieves and vagabonds in our metropolis. Nor is this any solitary case—it is the result naturally to be anticipated from such a procedure—it is the rule, and the exceptions are, we are perfectly satisfied, 'few and far between.' Now, who are the gainers by the late change? Not the poor creatures themselves, for they have lost their all—not the city, for increased poor rates, and increased destitution, and increased crime constitute but a sorry gain. Is the appearance of the streets, then, all we have to show as a set-off against such an amount of suffering? Truly, we do not wonder at a magistrate refusing to enforce the enactments of the City Police Bill; nay, we are only surprised that there are men to be found out of Bedlam who could find it in their heart to give effect to such an atrocious blunder—to call it by its very mildest name."

MR. MAYHEW is most happy to give publicity to the following letter. The institution which is the subject of it seems likely to prove a great benefit to all parties.

"Sir—As one much interested in your benevolent exertions, to bring to light the destitute condition of such numbers of our people, will you allow me to draw your attention and that of your readers to on institution which, I cannot but think, if more widely known, might help to save some from the humiliating want which presses so heavily on their spirits. Some time since an institution was established in Fitzroy-square, designed to provide a superior class of nurses for the sick, its title being, 'The Training Institution for Nurses, for Hospitals, Families, and the Poor.' The plan of the institution known as 'St. John's House', and therefore bearing on its front a manifestation of its principles, is to receive as probationers young women who, after a certain term of training sufficient to qualify them to become nurses, are then enrolled as such, and sent forth to discharge their self-denying but charitable office.[23] It should also be observed, that the institution is founded in connection with the Church of England,—that its services are constantly maintained in the house, and that all the inmates are expected to avail themselves of its ordinances. Now, sir, as one desirous of appreciating the opportunities of bringing to

light cases of female distress, with which the service to which you have devoted yourself must furnish you, it has stuck me that the institution to which I have referred might present a fair field for the employment of many who are now pining away under labour and difficulties. The needlewomen, for example (for it is such that I have particularly in my eye), many of them, as they are found to be reduced in circumstances,—those who have known brighter days, but are now suffering what is worse than poverty, viz., all the bitterness which invade it from cold hands and unsympathizing hearts. And then again, the workers for those establishments where it is only by slaving day and night that anything like the means of subsistence can be obtained. These, and such as these, have been in my view in addressing you this letter; and feeling interested, as I do, in the success of the Nurses' Institution, it has occurred to me, that if publicity could be given to the existence of this establishment amongst the numerous class by whom, as personally interested in your statements, they must be read, it might lead to the settlement in an efficient and, at the same time, useful mode of livelihood, of some whose present circumstances would render it a most desirable change. There need be no care for the morrow where everything is provided free of charge, with the addition of a fixed annual payment: whilst, if there is a willing heart, surely few things can tend more to recompense for the past, than the opportunity of becoming useful to the suffering, sympathy with whom so many of the classes to which I am referring must have learnt by personal experience. Can you, then, find room amongst your notices to correspondents for these few lines? I could have written more, but that I would not intrude further on your space. If they should attract the notice of any one who would be glad to avail themselves of uniting such a service and provision as I have referred to, as I hope may be the case, they can learn further particulars by applying at St. John's House, Fitzroy-square, I am &c. — M."

[23] See R. Few, *A History of St. John's House*, 1884, and Ann Summers, *Angels and Citizens, British Women as Military Nurses*, Routledge & Kegan Paul, 1988, p. 20. "Probationers" and "nurses" received wages while "sisters" were patrons paying supporting fees.

ANSWERS TO CORRESPONDENTS.
[No.18, 12 APRIL 1851]

Edited out:
F.C.; D.; L.H.K.; COMFRATER; OLIVE LEAF; C.

In the Notice to Correspondents accompanying Number 16, Mr. Mayhew in reply to a letter from one of his readers, proceeded to specify the several circumstances regulating wages which in the course of his inquiry among the London operatives had fallen under his notice. Four distinct kinds of circumstances were then enumerated, viz.:—1. The number of labourers; 2. The hours of labour; 3. The rate of labouring; 4. The quantity of work; and under each of these heads a large variety of particulars were shown to be comprised.

In Political Economy wages are made to depend solely upon the proportion between population and capital; that is to say, between the number of labourers and the amount of capital expended in the direct purchase of their labour. But it is very evident, since wages are but remuneration for labour, that the quantity of labour exacted for a certain amount of wages is an essential element of the subject. Among economists, however, all idea of work is discarded from the question, though it must be manifest even to childish comprehension, that wages remaining the same and work being doubled the remuneration for labour must be decreased one-half: hence it is impossible to come to a right understanding of the matter without allowing the quantity of labour to enter into the proposition. According to the inconsistencies of political economy, if the tailors respectively received one year thirty shillings for making two coats, and the next year only the same amount for making double that number, the remuneration for their labour would remain unaltered. But, surely, to increase the quantity of labour, while the "amount expended in the direct purchase of that labour" remains the same, is—according to Cocker—to decrease the wages in precisely the same proportion. To extend the quantum of work is plainly tantamount to augmenting the number of workers; for the wage-fund, or gross sum expended upon such work remaining unchanged, it follows that the individual remuneration for a given amount of labour must be identical in both cases.

The quantity of work, however, has, so to speak, a double or reverse action upon wages, and this is most essential to be borne in mind. According to the law of supply and demand, when work increases (without a corresponding increase in the number of labourers), and the demand for labour consequently increases, while the supply continues the same, wages must rise; but this is true only so long as the capital of the trade, or fund out of which the labourers are paid, admits of being augmented. The amount of the Wage-Fund must of course determine the amount given in exchange for the labour. If this fund be small, wages must necessarily be low; and if large, high wages will be the consequence. It is true, that in the several trades any increased demand for labour is *usually* followed by a rise of wages, because the capital of any one trade admits of being augmented by advances from the capital of others. But though this is true of any *one* trade, it is by no means, and, indeed, cannot possibly be true of *all* trades. For the gross Wage-Fund of the country not admitting of sudden extension, but being regulated by the sum saved or set aside out of the national income of the past year for the purposes of production during the present, it is impossible that this fund can be extended according as the amount of work or demand for labourers grows greater; hence it follows, that though in any *one* trade an increased demand for labour at a particular time may be attended with an increase of wages, this cannot be the case in *all*, and that, on the contrary, a greater amount of work throughout the nation must necessitate a decreased amount of remuneration for it; that is to say, there will be greater quantity of work to do for the same (or, as we shall see presently, even less) pay, which, of course, is equivalent to the same quantum of labour for less wages.

Thus, during the railway mania, the pay of "labourers" was increased, not because the capital, or gross savings of the country had suddenly been augmented, but because a considerable sum at that time was withdrawn from other trades and invested in railroads. Consequently it appears that wages—so far from depending (as economists would have us believe) upon merely the supply and demand for labour, or, as others term it, the proportion between population and capital—are regulated rather by five distinct circumstances, every one of which exerts, according as it is either increased or decreased, a like increasing or decreasing influence upon the amount of remuneration coming to the labourers individually. These five circumstances are—

I. The numbers of labourers.

II. The hours of labour.

III. The rate of labouring.

IV. The quantity of work.

V. The amount of the Wage-Fund, or gross sum expended upon the purchase of the labour.

The next point for consideration therefore becomes, what regulates the amount of the Wage-Fund? This is the most important question of all, as this constitutes not only the standard by which the exchangeable market value of the labour is estimated, but also the stock out of which it is remunerated; for though, so long as this stock remains unchanged in amount, wages will increase whenever the number of labourers, the hours of labour, the rate of labouring, or the quantity of work, are decreased, still, the other circumstances being unaltered, it follows that wages must depend upon the extent of the fund out of which they are paid; that is to say, if the Wage-Fund be doubled, then a given quantity of labour will exchange for twice the former quantity of wealth, and consequently that wages must rise as that fund becomes greater, and fall as it is diminished in amount. Hence, to ascertain what determines the extent of the Wage-Fund is a most essential point.

The extent of the Wage-Fund appears to depend, as before stated, in a great measure, upon the amount of capital, or sum set aside for production, in this or in any other country. But since the elements of production are of three distinct kinds, viz., (1) Labour, (2) Instruments (as tools machines, shops, &c.), and (3) Materials, it follows that the wealth set aside for the purpose of production must be divisible into *three* distinct funds or sources, from which each of such elements can be supplied. There must be a Subsistence Fund for the maintenance of the labourers—a Sinking Fund for the purpose of providing tools, machines, buildings, &c., and a Material Fund, out of which the substances upon which the labour is to be exerted may be procured. Now these three parts constitute the whole of the capital or stock set aside for future production. The sole office of capital is to provide such funds, and that only is capital which contributes to one or other of them—or rather, such is productive capital (of distributive capital, or that employed in distribution, and its influence on wages, I purpose speaking by-and-by). It is a question of arithmetic, therefore, that the increase of any one of the three parts must (if the whole remain the same) be followed by proportionate decrease in the others; that is to say, if any of the funds set aside for the purpose of providing some one of the elements of production be augmented, such augmentation can only take place at the expense of either of the remaining funds. Now it is evident that the material fund, or that part of the national income saved with a view of providing the materials on which the labourer is to operate regulates the aggregate quantity of work to be done throughout the country, and that, if a greater quantity of materials are obtained, there must necessarily be a greater quantity of work to do. But a greater quantity of materials *can only* be obtained by an increase of the Material Fund, at the expense of either the Sinking or the Subsistence Fund, or both; but since the sinking fund, or that portion of capital which is annually sunk in tools, machines, factories, &c. is, in this country, manifestly being *increased,* rather than *decreased*, every year, it follows that the augmentation of the Material Fund can only be brought about by a corresponding diminution in the Wage-Fund, or sum devoted to the subsistence of the labourers; and that, consequently, any increase in the national quantity of work must necessarily be attended by a like decrease in the aggregate amount of remuneration received for it by the workers; or in other words the wage law is—*the more work there is to do, the less the workpeople will get for it*. This is a matter that admits of demonstration, and yet one which no political economist has as yet either discovered or, having discovered, thought fit to make known. But political economy is the science of money-making. Let me, however, so as to impress this necessary decrease of wages, as consequent on the increase of materials, the more strongly on the minds of working-men, and those who really wish them well—let me put the question arithmetically, thus:—Say that the sum annually expended on material in this country equals 50,000,000£ sterling, and that the Wage-Fund, or sum paid for operating on those materials, equals 100,000,000£ sterling; in that case, it is clear that, for making up every one pound's worth of stuff, the labourers will receive two pounds. Then let us suppose the sum expended on materials to be doubled, or to equal 100,000,000£, in this case it is evident there would be twice as much work to be done, and since the Material Fund could only have been doubled by decreasing the Wage-Fund to one-half, the sum consequently coming to the labourers would be reduced to 50,000,000£, or, in other words, there would be not only twice as much work to do, but half as little again to receive for it, for the labourers would get only 10s. instead of 2£ for every pound's worth of materials made up by them. Hence wages would be four times less than they were. Still further to exemplify the principle, let us now suppose the Material Fund to be increased to 125,000,000£, and the Wage-Fund consequently to be decreased to 25,000,000£; then it is manifest that the quantity of work will be increased one-fifth more, while wages must decline again one-half; so that there will be twice and a half more material to be made up than at first, and only one-fourth the amount of wages to receive for so doing; or, in other words, the workman will be paid ten times less wages for the same quantity of labour. But it may be said that, twice and a half more mate-

rials being made up, commodities must be twice and a half more abundant, and therefore twice and a half cheaper; consequently, every shilling the workman receives will exchange for twice and a half as much as formerly, or be to that amount increased in value. But since the labourer receives ten times less, it is clear that, notwithstanding the increased value of money, he must be four times poorer by the alteration. The effect of the change, however, upon the moneyed classes and the capitalists in general is precisely the reverse. Every pound of their money is thus made twice and a half more valuable, that is to say, it will exchange for that extra quantity of commodities, while the employers' profits, depending upon the gross amount of capital devoted to the purposes of production, will be in no way reduced. It is of no consequence how the 150,000,000£ are apportioned; for whether five-sixths be spent upon materials and only the sixth upon wages, they get the same aggregate amount of profit as they would even if one-third only were devoted to materials and the remaining two-thirds to the subsistence of the labourers. The gross capital being the same in both cases, viz., 150,000,000£, it is self-evident the gross profits would also be the same. It may, however, be further urged that if profits are the same in either case, there is no reason why the employer should impoverish the labourer by expending the greater portion of his capital upon materials. The answer is, that though the gross profit fund of the country would be in no way extended, and the employers as a body, therefore, would be in no way benefited by so doing, still many of what are called enterprising tradesmen would individually be large gainers thereby—for, spending a greater quantity on materials, and, consequently, obtaining a larger amount of produce, those who were the first to make the alteration would be enabled to undersell the rest, and, consequently, to force their trade to a greater extent. Now that this increase of the quantity of materials to be made up, and consequent decrease in the remuneration for the labour employed upon them, is one of the great evils of the day, and one of the main causes why the operatives are daily becoming more and more overworked and underpaid, all my invest-igations go to prove. The cheapness which Political Economists cry up as such a boon to the Poor Man is here plainly shown to be a gain only to the Rich; such Cheapness is produced solely at the Operative's expense; that is to say, by making him do more work for less pay, I have before alluded to the Messrs. Nicoll, who, having reduced the wages of the 1000 workmen in their employ to one-third below the amount paid by the "honourable" part of the tailoring trade, or from 36s. to 24s. a week for the best hands, have been enabled to force their trade to an enormous extent, and to amass 160,000£ in a very few years. This is the effect of cheapness upon the employer: let us now see what effect it has upon the employed. The following are two instances (printed in the Morning Chronicle) of overwork and underpay taken from different trades.

A waistcoat hand, whom Mr. Mayhew visited during his investigations into the state of the tailoring trade in December, 1849, narrated the following facts.

"The effect that the continual reduction has had upon my earnings is this—before the year 1844 I could live comfortably and keep my wife and children (I had five in family) by my own labour. My wife then attended to her domestic and family duties, but since that time, owing to the reduction in prices, she has been compelled to resort to her needle as well as myself for her living." (On the table lay a bundle of crape and bombazine ready to be made up into a dress.) "I cannot afford now to let her remain idle— that is, if I wish to live, and keep my children out of the streets, and pay my way. She makes dresses. I never would teach her to make waistcoats, because I knew the introduction of female hands had been the ruin of my trade. *With the labour or myself and wife now I can earn 32s. a week, and 6 years ago I could make my 36s. by my own labour alone.* If I had a daughter I should be obliged to make her work as well, and then probably *with the labour of the three of us we could make up at the week's end as much money as up to 1844 I could get by my own single hands.*"

Here is the statement of a worker at the "fancy cabinet" trade (a trade, by the by, in which the number of hands have decreased, work increased, and yet wages fallen to an enormous extent):—

"The most of us has got large families. We put the children to work as soon as we can. My little girl began about six, but about eight or nine is the usual age. '*Oh, poor little things,' said the wife, 'they are obliged to begin the very minute they can use their fingers at all.*' The greater part of the cabinet makers of the East End have from five to six in family, and they are generally all at work for them. The small masters mostly marry when they are turned of twenty. You see our trade's coming to such a pass, that unless a man has children to help him he can't live at all. '*I've worked more than a month together,*' continued the wife, '*and the longest night's rest I've had has been an hour and a quarter; aye, and I've been up three nights a week besides.* I've had my children lying ill, and been obliged to wait on them into the bargain. You see, we couldn't live if it wasn't for the labour of our children, though it makes 'em— poor little things!—old people long afore they are growed up.

"'Why, I stood at this bench,' the wife went on, 'with my child, only ten years of age, from four o'clock on Friday morning till ten minutes past seven in the evening, without a bit to eat or drink. I never sat down a minute from the time I began till I finished my work and then I went out to sell what I had done. I walked all the way from here (Shoreditch) down to the Lowther Arcade, to get rid of the articles.' *Here she burst into a violent flood of tears, saying, 'Oh, Sir! it is hard to be obliged to labour from morning till night as we do, all of us, little ones and all, and yet not able to live by it either.'*"

MR. Mayhew has been favoured with the following from Messrs. Keeling and Hunt, Gentlemen to whom he is indebted for much valuable information:—

"Monument Yard, London, 7th April, 1851
"Sir,—Your correspondent, C.B., of Portland Town, has properly questioned the accuracy of the word "*Coker,*" as applied to nuts sold under the generally known title of 'Cocoa,' the proper derivation being '*Cocos nucifera,*' one of the palm tribe and a native of India, first imported

in 1690. From the researches we have made, we can only infer the word '*Coker*' is a corruption, or, more properly speaking, a Custom-house licence, to create a distinction in the mode of levying the duty on this description of fruit, and the kernels of a nut which is the produce of a different description of tree, and the decoction of which is used so generally for the purpose of beverage; for the term '*coker*' we find, upon reference to the Customs Acts of Parliament, was classified many years back by Mr. Hume, the then Chairman of the Board of Customs, and has been retained accordingly.

"The correct word is '*Cacao*,' '*Coco*,' from whence the English adaptation '*cocoa*,' is decidedly correct; but the word '*Coker*' and other anomalies are retained in order to discriminate between the duties levied upon articles bearing similar names, but different in use—in a similar way to *Prunes* (the French for Plums), which pay 7s. per cwt. duty, and Plums, commonly called French Plums, which pay 20s. per cwt.—'*Coker*' nuts, commonly called '*Cocoa*,' are now free of duty; while Cocoa in husks and shells pay one penny per pound duty.

"Will you afford us this opportunity to bear testimony to the general good character and valuable assistance we derive from the 'Costermongers' engaged in the sale of our description of produce, and who have only to be treated kindly to render them as useful and as grateful a body of men as can be encouraged.

"We are, Sir,
"Your obedient servants
"KEELING AND HUNT."

ANSWERS TO CORRESPONDENTS.
[No.19, 19 APRIL 1851]

In the last Number of this work Mr. Mayhew, in prosecution of his inquiry into the circumstances regulating Wages, proceeded to set forth the conditions which determined the amount of the Wage-Fund, or stock, out of which the labourers are paid. Productive Capital, or that portion of accumulated labour which is devoted to the purposes of production (in contradistinction to Distributive Capital, or the portion devoted to the distribution of the commodities produced), we have seen to consist of three distinct elements or funds— viz., the Material-Fund, or stock devoted to the supply of material; the Sinking-Fund, or that devoted to the construction of tools, machines, factories, and other instruments of labour; and the Subsistence-Fund, or that devoted to the maintenance of the labourers. We have also seen that the Material-Fund regulates the gross quantity of work to be done, and the Wage-Fund the gross amount of remuneration to be received for such work; and, since the Material-Fund can only be increased at the expense of the Wage-Fund, that if a larger proportion of the Capital of the country be devoted to the purchase of a greater quantity of materials, there must necessarily be more work to be done, and less wages to receive for it. Facts, moreover, were cited to show that this increase of work and decrease of wages was going on in many of the trades of the present day, and that it constituted one of the main evils of our social economy.

But if the Material-Fund is so intimately connected with the Wage-Fund that the increase of the former must necessarily be followed by a corresponding decrease of the latter, in what way does an alteration in the quantity of Capital apportioned to the Sinking-Fund affect the amount devoted to the subsistence of the Labourers? That is the next point to be ascertained. To understand this, we must keep steadily in mind the fact that Productive Capital is wealth set aside for the purposes of future production, and that such Capital is necessarily of two distinct kinds, viz., that which is consumed after being once used, and which consequently requires to be continually reproduced, as materials and food; and that which is more permanent, admitting of being used more than once, and whose reproduction therefore is spread over a series of years, as tools, machines, factories, &c. The alkali and tallow which constitute the "materials" out of which soap is manufactured are, it has been truly said, destroyed after one application to the purpose for which the soap is made; and if there was not a fresh supply of such substances produced year after year, it is evident that the national stock of that commodity must ultimately come to an end; and in the same manner the quartern loaves which the agricultural labourer consumes during his work are, by that very work, reproduced; and thus the supply is kept up, so that we see that Capital invested in the subsistence of labourers, as well as in the materials upon which the labour is exercised, is continually being replaced, and that if it were otherwise, the country must necessarily be impoverished to precisely the amount which we consumed without being reproduced.

Now it is the peculiar quality of Capital sunk in instrumental labour, that is to say, in the construction of tools, machines, factories, &c., that it is not *immediately* reproductive, but requires a series of years before the advantages gained by the new instruments are sufficient to make good the amount of wealth consumed in their construction. The wealth sunk in a large factory is years before it is repaid, even as a steam-engine does not return the cost of its production for some considerable time. No one commodity alone pays for the construction of the tools used in its manufacture, but the expense of such tools is spread over as many commodities as they are capable of producing. The plough, the harrow, the horses, the waggons, the barn, the threshing machine, do not depend for their remuneration on a *single* harvest, but on a series; even as the loom is not paid for out of the first piece of cloth woven, but out of the thousand and odd that it is capable of weaving. There is scarcely any form of labour to which the returns may be said to be immediate, with the exception of that of the hunter and fisherman, and almost every different kind of work differs in the period required for its remuneration. The wealth expended in the construction of a canal or a railroad is a long time before it can possibly be returned, whereas the food required to sustain the savage during his search after the spontaneous products of the earth must be made good almost immediately. The barbarian can hardly afford to wait a day for his remuneration, whereas the civilized man is often engaged in operations that require perhaps a century or more to be fully compensated. Now it is an essential quality of all production that every commodity must be paid for before it can possibly be produced. Nature gives no credit. We cannot obtain the least particle of wealth from her, without first expending a certain amount of wealth in procuring it. If it be merely the act of gathering wild fruit, the operation requires the destruction of a certain quantity of muscular tissue, without which no act can be performed, or in other words, so much strength accumulated in the limbs of the agent, by means of the food previously consumed, must be expended in the operation, and this, unless recompensed, must sooner or later end in that physical bankruptcy which we term starvation. But though Nature gives no credit, Man, as we have seen, is obliged to credit Nature to a large amount; and it is the long credit often given in the form of sunk capital, that is the cause of so much distress to those who have nothing but their labour to live upon. We have before seen that according as one or other of the elements or funds essential to production is increased, the rest must be correspondingly decreased; that is to say, if an undue proportion of the Capital, or gross stock set aside for future production, be devoted to the purchase of materials, and besides this a considerable sum be sunk in the construction of tools, machines, or buildings, there can only be a small amount left for the subsistence or wages of the producers; for it is a mere question of arithmetic, that, assuming the entire productive fund to equal 9, if $3\frac{1}{2}$ represent the amount devoted to one element, and 4 that apportioned to another, there can be but $1\frac{1}{2}$ left for the third. We have already seen the operation of an undue increase of the Material-Fund upon the Wage-Fund, and it is here evident that the increase of the Sinking-Fund must be attended with precisely the same effect. Let us suppose, for the sake of argument, that the productive capital of the kingdom equals 300,000,000£ sterling, and that one-third of this is sunk in machines and factories, while the other two thirds are devoted to the supply of materials and the subsistence of the workpeople; then it is evident, since Capital invested in the instruments of labour is not immediately reproductive, but requires a certain term of years before the wealth expended is returned, that the next year the Productive Fund of the country must be diminished one-third (minus, say, a tenth—on the assumption that the sunk Capital will be replaced in ten years) below that of the previous year—or, in other words, that the country must be nearly one third poorer—the Productive Fund being thus equal to 200,000,000£ instead of 300,000,000£ sterling as before.

Then let us suppose that the next year the same proportion (one-third) of the Productive Fund is sunk in the same (immediately) unproductive manner—that is to say that 70,000,000£ more are invested in machines and factories, and the remaining 140,000,000£ (instead of 200,000,000£) devoted to materials and wages; in which case it is evident that the community, instead of being one-third, must now be (within a fraction) one-half, poorer than in the first instance. Assuming further, that the Productive Fund is thus reduced to 150,000,000£ in round numbers (allowing 10 per cent. per annum for the return on the Sunk Capital), and that the same process of sinking one-third again goes on, it is evident that at the end of the next year the Productive Fund of the country must have decreased two-thirds, or from 300,000,000£ to 100,000,000£, while the particular funds out of which the materials and food of the labourers are to be supplied must have decreased one-half. And assuming, for the mere sake of argument, that the Material and the Wage-Fund continued equal all this time, it is manifest that each of these funds must have declined one-half also,

and, consequently, that the gross income of the labourers must be one-half less than it was three years previously. With the capitalists, however, the case will be very different—for since the aggregate amount of profits upon Capital depends solely upon the gross amount of Capital employed, without any regard to the mode in which it is partitioned among the several funds or elements of production, it follows that, though the labourers get one-half less, the gains of their employers will be in no way diminished; but rather by the increase of commodities the value of every pound sterling of their Capital will be considerably increased.

The enrichment of the Capitalist class and impoverishment of the working class, by the investment of the national savings in machinery and the several instruments of production, that is here advanced, is by no means a singular opinion, but is maintained by some of the more enlightened of the Political Economists. The following passage may be cited in corroboration of the conclusion (if corroboration be needed, to establish that which is a question of mere figures, viz., that $3^{1}/_{2} + 4 + 1^{1}/_{2} = 9$, even as $3 + 3 + 3 = 9$). Mr. Ricardo (the author of the "Theory of Rent") tells us, in his article on "Machinery," he had once thought "that the labouring class would, equally with the other classes, participate in the advantage, from the general cheapness of commodities arising from the use of machinery."[24] He had since become convinced, however, "that the substitution of machinery for human labour is often very injurious to the interests of the class of labourers. *My mistake*," he says, "*arose from the supposition, that whenever the net income of a society increased, its gross income would also increase. I now, however, see reasons to be satisfied that the one fund from which landlords and capitalists derive their revenue may increase, while the other—that upon which the labouring class mainly depends—may diminish; and therefore it follows, if I am right, that the same cause which may*

---

[24] See M. Berg, *The Machinery Question and the Making of Political Economy*, Cambridge University Press, 1980, pp. 72-3.

increase the net revenue of the country may at the same time render the population redundant, and deteriorate the condition of the labourer." Amongst other deductions from his views he enumerates the position, "3rdly, that the opinion entertained by the labouring class, that the employment of machinery is frequently detrimental to their interest, is not founded on prejudice and error, but is conformable to the correct principles of political economy". Mr. Stewart Mill, too, is somewhat of the same opinion. *"I cannot assent to the argument,"* he says, at p.116 [*Principles of Political Economy*], *"which is relied on by most of those who contend that machinery can never be injurious to the labouring class*—namely, that by cheapening production it creates such an increase demand for the commodity as enables ere long a greater number of persons to find employment in producing it; the fact though, too broadly stated, is no doubt often true. The copyists, who were thrown out of employment by the invention of printing, were, doubtless, soon outnumbered by the compositors and pressmen who took their place: and the number of labouring persons now occupied in the cotton manufacture is many times greater than were so occupied previously to the inventions of Hargreaves and Arkwright, which shows that, besides the enormous fixed capital now embarked in the manufacture, it also employs a far greater circulating capital than at any former time. *"But if this capital,"* continues Mr. Mill, *"was drawn from other employments; if the funds which took the place of the capital sunk in costly machinery were supplied—not by an additional saving consequent on the improvement—but by drafts on the general capital of the community, what better are the labouring classes for the mere transfer?* In what manner is the loss they sustained by the conversion of circulating into fixed capital made up to them by a mere shifting of part of the remainder of the circulating capital from its old employments to a new one. *"All attempts,"* he adds, *"to make out that the labouring classes, as a body, cannot suffer by the introduction of machinery or by the sinking of capital in permanent improvements are, I conceive, necessarily fallacious."*

Those, therefore, who tell us that it is a settled point in Political Economy that machinery tends to benefit the labourer as well as the capitalist, are either ignorant of the writings of the most eminent and thoughtful of the economists on the subject, or else it must be evident they have some intention to deceive. Since, then, it is admitted that the increase of the Sunk Capital of a country must necessarily be attended with a corresponding decrease in its Circulating Capital—that it to say, that the wealth devoted to the construction of tools, machines, factories, &c., must necessarily diminish the sum set aside for the supply of materials and the subsistence of the labourers; let us now take a cursory glance at the quantity of Capital that has been invested in the instruments of labour within a comparatively recent period. In one manufacturing town, we are told, there are 200 factories, and that each of these establishments requires an outlay of 100,000£ (see Dodd's Textile Manufactures[25]); hence the Capital sunk in Manchester alone, within little more than the last half century, amounts to no less than 20,000,000£ of money. But, according to the latest report of the Factory Inspectors, the gross number of such establishments throughout the country amounts to 4330; and calculating the same amount to have been sunk in each of these, we have the enormous sum of 433,000,000£ thus expended, which is at the rate of 50,000,000£ of money sunk every year since about 1760, or 100,000,000£ per annum (a third of the national income), dating from the commencement of the present century. But that is not all: if to this we add 300,000,000£ sunk in turnpike-roads, canals, and railways (not to speak of mines), we shall then see good reason for that gradual impoverishment of the labouring classes and enrichment of their employers, which is the marked feature of the present age.

But though the most enlightened of the economists have been able to perceive that

---

[25] G. Dodd, *The Textile Manufactures of Great Britain*, Knight's Library, 1844.

ANSWERS TO CORRESPONDENTS

according as the fixed Capital of the country is increased, its Circulating Capital must be necessarily and correspondingly decreased, none, that I am aware of, has yet drawn attention to the fact that this Circulating Capital consists of two distinct and conflicting elements, viz., the Material-Fund and the Wage-Fund; and that according as either of these is extended, so must the other be proportionately diminished—a proposition more important to the labouring classes than perhaps any one yet propounded in Political Economy, and one which not only intimately concerns the welfare of the working man, but affords the sole explanation of the growing tendency to overwork and underpay; and which moreover helps us to perceive how it is possible (in direct opposition to the boasted law of supply and demand) for there to be more work to do and less wages to receive for it—as for instance in the Cabinet Makers' trade— where, since 1831, the hands have declined 33 per cent., the work increased enormously, and yet where wages 20 years ago were 400 per cent. better than they are now.

Still the great evil remains to be pointed out. The depreciation of labour is not so much due to the isolated agency of each of the above-mentioned causes, *but to the combined operation of the two*. If within the last century we have invested upwards of 400,000,000£ of Capital in the construction of machines and factories— the very construction of these instruments requires that they should be kept continually in action, for every moment that they are unoccupied the Capital invested in them is lying idle; hence, as Mr. Mill tells us, in quoting from Mr. Babbage, "the only profitable mode of employing machines is to keep them working through the twenty-four hours." The consequence is that they must necessitate a vast increase in the quantity of materials, and so give rise to an equally vast decrease of the remuneration of the workpeople. If, therefore, these machines be employed night and day in making up materials, they must also be employed night and day in reducing the subsistence of the Labourers. Now, another gentleman, in estimating the difference between the produce by hand and by machinery, assures us, "that in a Cotton factory with a steam-engine of 100 horse power, there are 50,000 spindles, which are superintended by about 750 persons. The quantity of yarn produced by this mechanism in a day, would extend 62,500 miles in length—being as much as would require the labour of 200,000 persons with the common spinning wheel. We believe," adds the Gentleman with an air of triumph, that betrays an utter want of thought on the social bearings of the question, "there are now upwards of 2,000 such cotton-mills, giving motion to at least 20,000,000 of spindles, and the whole consequently doing the work of 400,000,000 of persons, if estimated by the power of hand labour."

But if these 20,000,000 and odd spindles are perpetually doing the work of 400,000,000 individuals, of course they must require to be supplied with 400,000,000 times as much materials as each of these individuals could work up; and, consequently, it is plain that the Material-Fund must, by the introduction of such an enormous power of machinery into one trade alone, be increased as much as the Sinking-Fund, out of which the machines were provided; and that the Subsistence-Fund, therefore, must be decreased in a double proportion—that is to say, the investment of a large portion of the productive Capital of the country in machines and factories, necessitates the apportionment of an equally large amount to obtain an increased quantity of materials. Hence, it is a matter of demonstration, that there must necessarily be a proportionately smaller sum left for the maintenance of the workpeople. The quantity of raw material imported for the cotton factories in 1849 was 654,000,000 lbs.; in 1839 it was 387,000,000 lbs.; and in 1815 only 100,000,000 lbs. The quantity of foreign wool used in the woollen manufacture in 1847 was 82,000,000 lbs., and in 1840 only 49,000,000 lbs. The quantity of raw silk imported for the manufactures of this country in 1847 was 5,000,000 lbs.; in 1841, only 4,000,000 lbs. This enormous increase in the quantity of materials used in but three of our manufactures, may enable us to form some idea as to the portion of Capital annually now devoted to the Material-Fund, for the entire manufactures of this country: while the 700,000,000£ of money before specified as sunk within a comparatively recent period in the machines, factories, and facilities for transit, will likewise afford us the means of making a guess as to the portion of the gross Capital annually invested in the increase of the instruments of labour as well as the appliances for the distribution of the products of that labour. Now, putting these items together, it surely does not require a superabundance of brains to be able to perceive how, after supplying both such funds, the amount left for the subsistence of the labourers must be comparatively trifling. And here lies the sole explanation why there is yearly growing in this kingdom a *greater quantity of work to be done, and a less amount of remuneration to receive for it*; for the vast increase of machinery not only requires a vast increase of materials, in order to be kept continually working (night and day, we have heard is the only economical mode of employing it), but a like extensive augmentation of the means of distribution, or carriage, and diffusion, all of which circumstances not only give the labourers more to do, but yield them (from the extra amounts of Capital required to be thus expended) less wages for the additional labour. And since the profits of employers as was before stated, and the interest upon the Capital, depend upon the gross amount of the Productive-Fund (no matter whether sunk in machinery, expended in materials, or laid out in labour), it follows that the increase of the Material and Sinking-Funds at the expenses of the Wage-Fund can in no way tend to decrease the gains of the Capitalists, but will rather—owing to the extra quantity of commodities produced with the same amount of Capital—give an additional value to their money, and so enrich them almost in the same proportions as it beggars the workpeople.

In the next Number Mr. Mayhew will proceed to examine the conditions of the Distributive-Fund (or amount of Capital devoted to the purpose of distributing the commodities produced), with a view of discovering how *that* Fund influences the Wage-Fund.

The following sums have been received for the Crippled Street-seller of Nutmeg-graters, and have been handed to Mr. Howden, who will see the money profitably applied:—Mr. P. (Temple), half a sovereign; and the subjoined sums in Postage Stamps: B.W., 3s.; E.H., 1s.; a Purchaser from the First, 2s. 6d.; E.J.S., 5s.; a sympathiser, 5s.

Thirty shillings from Mr. P. (Temple), to be offered by way of loan to the Street-showman whose letter appeared in No.17.

THE CRIPPLED STREET-SELLER OF NUTMEG-GRATERS has forwarded the subjoined:—

"Sir,

"I feel grateful for your Exertions in my behalf. I have received the sum of £2 1s. 0d. from the publisher, 69, fleet street. I am gazed at in the street with astonishment; and observations made within my hearing with respect to the Exact likeness of the portrait. I have purchased with the money so kindly forwarded to me a few articles of furniture and a little stock, and I have taken a room in the Boro' Road, there not being sufficient room at my present Lodging.

"I am, Sir, with respect,

"Your Humble Servant,

"C—A—"

It is a rule with Mr. Mayhew not to reveal the addresses of his informants. If W.E.C. wishes to make any communications to the person mentioned in his letter, a note sent to the office, 16, Upper Wellington street shall be forwarded to him. W.E.C. will see that to choose to do other than this would be a breach of faith on Mr. Mayhew's part. This answer will apply to all other applications for addresses.

Mr. Mayhew begs to state, once more that he cannot become the dispenser of alms to any person. He therefore, wishes it to be distinctly understood that all monies forwarded to him for the relief of any poor street-seller are considered by him as loans, to be repaid by trimestrial instalments, and which when returned may be again advanced to others equally deserving. For the assurance of ladies and gentlemen forwarding money, a letter will be sent to them, informing them of the amounts having been applied as requested, as well as communicating to them the rate at which it is promised to be returned. The letter will also state that the donor can always withdraw as many of the instalments as might be in hand. Mr. Howden will be glad to show his arrangements on the subject to any one calling at North Wellington-street. It is necessary that in money matters of so peculiar a nature, the transactions should be beyond the shadow of a suspicion.

W.S.B. is utterly incomprehensible; nor does the writer of the passage alluded to mean anything of what was before stated. What W.S.B. means that the writer meant, it is impossible to divine.

H.W.M.W. who writes from Basingstoke, is thanked for the information touching the country stalls, as well as for the statements as to the difficulty of obtaining copies of "London Labour" in the Agricultural districts.

ANSWERS TO CORRESPONDENTS.
[No.20, 26 APRIL 1851]

Edited out:
E.C.R.; F.C.; TEMPUS FUGIT; A.B.C.; A LADY; A GENTLEMAN.

We are now in a position to see the falsity of the Wage-Law as enunciated by Political Economists. This law according to Mr. Stewart Mill, the latest authority on the subject, is as follows: "Wages depend upon the demand and supply of labour, *or*, as it is often expressed, on the proportion between population and capital"—limiting the term population so the labouring class, and capital to that which is expended in the direct purchase of labour.

In the first place this proposition confounds things essentially distinct; under the impression that they are one and the same. The demand for labour is here—with an eminent want of discrimination—jumbled up

with the capital or stock set aside for the remuneration of the labourer: this is manifest from the use of the particle "*or*," showing as it does that the terms of population and capital are considered to be merely different modes of expression for what are believed to be the same conditions—the demand and supply of labour. "Wages depend," says the writer (book ii., chap. 11), "on the demand and supply of labour, OR, *as it is often expressed*, on the proportion between population and capital." Now that the *demand* for labour is a condition essentially distinct from the *capital* expended in the direct purchase of that labour, has been already shown. The one represents the *work*, and the other *pay*. The demand for labour is regulated by the quantity of work to be done; that is to say, the by the aggregate amount of materials to be operated upon: whereas the *capital* to be expended in the direct purchase of the labour represents the aggregate amount of *remuneration* to be paid for such operations; and that these are not only diverse, but positively OPPOSITE elements of the Wage-Law, was demonstrated in No.18 of this periodical. The Material-Fund and the Subsistence-Fund, which Political Economists believe to be identical, were then proved to be so essentially distinct, that precisely in the same proportion as the former increased the latter is diminished—causing more work and less pay. That wages cannot be said to depend solely on the demand and supply of labour is self-evident, because wages are simply remuneration for labour; and the proposition thus stated includes no mention of the fund out of which out of which the labourers are remunerated, and the gross amount of which must necessarily be one of the conditions determining the amount of wages. Nor can wages, on the other hand, be said to depend solely on the number of labourers and the amount of the capital expended in the direct purchase of their labour, for this form of the economical proposition takes no notice of the quantity of labour to be done, or amount of materials to be operated upon for a given amount of capital.

Hence we see the prodigious short-comings and jumblings of Political Economy, the dogmas of which are enunciated with the same confidence as if they were matters of Revelation, constituting as it were the Bible of Selfishness—the Gospel preached by Mammon, giving unto us the last new commandment, "*Do your neighbour as your neighbour would do you*,"—in contradistinction to that higher code of kindness and charity which Edinburgh Reviewers and Manchester Men do not hesitate now to rank as morbid sentimentalism.

For the last two weeks public attention has been here drawn to the circumstances regulating the amount of the Wage-Fund. It has been shown that the Wage-Fund is a necessary element of the Productive-Fund, or gross amount of Capital set aside for the purpose of future production; it has been shown moreover that the circumstances which, from the very constitution of things, are requisite for production are three, viz. (1) Labour; (2) Instruments, as tools, machines, or workshops; and (3) Materials; and it has been further shown that these three circumstances require the gross Productive-Fund of the country to be divided into three other funds, that is to say, into—

I. THE MATERIAL-FUND, or that portion of capital devoted to obtaining the substances upon which the labour is to be exerted

II. THE SINKING-FUND, or that portion of capital devoted to the construction of tools, machines, and factories or workshops.

III. THE WAGE-FUND, or that portion of the capital devoted to the Subsistence of the Labourers.

These three funds being altogether exactly equal to the entire PRODUCTIVE-FUND, or gross amount of Capital set aside, out of the past produce, for the purpose of future production.

Hence it follows (as a mere matter of arithmetic) that the increase of Wages depends upon either the increase of the total Productive-Fund, or the decrease of those particular portions of it which constitute the Material or Sinking Funds; and *vice versâ*, the decrease of Wages depends upon either the decrease of the whole or the increase of the other parts. We have likewise seen that the increase of the Sinking-Fund, or investment of a large amount of Capital in machines or factories, naturally reduces (from the very necessity of keeping such machines, &c., in continual employment and so preventing the Capital sunk in them from lying idle) the increase of the Material-Fund; that is to say, a greater portion of the gross Productive-Fund must be expended upon materials, and consequently there must be a smaller portion left for the subsistence of the Labourers. Nor is this all: the very necessity of keeping the increased quantity of machinery in continual action, and so operating upon a larger amount of materials, gives rise, at almost regular intervals, to an over production of commodities; for the Subsistence-Fund of the Labourers being decreased, of course the Purchasing-Fund of the community is correspondingly diminished, and hence periodically arise those commercial crises or social anomalies in which a superabundance of wealth co-exists with a superabundance of poverty—when the manufactures of the country are brought to a stand-still because, from the increase of the Material-Fund and decrease of the Wage-Fund, we have made up more commodities than the great mass of the people have the means of purchasing, and thus produced, at one and the same time, more and more clothing, and more and more nakedness—too many shoes, and too many bare feet—too many shirts and too many shirtless.

But these are only a portion of the evils resulting from an undue increase of the Sinking and Material-Funds. The expenditure of a larger amount of Capital upon machinery not only necessitates an increase of expenditure upon Materials, and consequently the production of a greater quantity of commodities, but this greater quantity of commodities necessitates, in its turn, an equally-extended means of distribution: more warehouses must be built—the facilities of transit must be increased, while a greater number of persons must be employed in selling, and the "premises" of the sellers must be "enlarged." We have seen that the increase or decrease of the Wage-Fund, depends indirectly upon the augmentation or dimi-nution of the Productive-Fund; but what regulates the Productive-Fund? what circumstances determine the amount of the gross Capital set aside, or saved out of the past produce, for the purpose of future production? The Productive-Fund, say Political Economists, is limited by two things:—

(1.) The amount from which the saving is effected.

(2.) The strength of the dispositions which prompt such saving.

The amount from which the saving can be made is, according to Economists, the *surplus* of the aggregate produce which remains after sullying the necessities of life to all concerned in production—including such as are engaged in replacing materials as well as keeping the sunk capital in repair. This surplus constitutes, we are told, the gross Profit-Fund of the country, or that portion of the national income which is left after paying the total cost of production. But according to this reasoning the entire income of the country must be made solely of the Productive and Profit-Funds; whereas it is clear that the Distributive-Fund, or that portion of wealth annually expended upon the conveyance and exchange of commodities belongs neither to Production nor to Profit, and that the Capital set aside for the purpose of distributing the wealth when produced is a totally distinct kind of Capital from that devoted to the production of it. A railway does not add one single commodity to the riches of the country—it merely increases the facility of exchanging the produce of one district for that of another. Nevertheless, railways and railway-engines, ships, docks, warehouses and shops, must surely be considered as Capital. According to Political Economy, however, they cannot be *Capital*,

because, though part of the national savings, they are not saved with a view to future *production*; nor can they be Profit because they form no part of the Surplus which remains after replacing materials, repairing the instruments, and maintaining the labourers employed in producing the wealth of the community.

But the expenses of distribution must be paid out of the Profit-Fund; hence we see that the Distributive-Fund not only does not add, in any way, to the gross produce of the community, but serves rather to decrease the national profits, and so to diminish the stock out of which the Productive-Fund alone can be increased. The Distributive-Fund, therefore, limits both the Productive and the Profit-Fund; that is to say, the entire national income is composed of three elements—the Productive-Fund, the Distributive-Fund, and the Profit-Fund; these three parts being exactly equal to the whole, and the increase of any one of them necessitating a corresponding decrease in either or both of the others. The national income is said to be 300,000,000£; assuming therefore, that the three funds are respectively equal, it follows that 100,000,000£ will be devoted to Production, and 100,000,000£ to the Distribution of the Produce, thus making the National Capital amount to 200,000,000£; while the remaining 100,000,000£ will constitute the Profits on that Capital. If, however, the cost of Distribution be increased from 100,000,000£ to 150,000,000£, then it follows either that the Productive and Profit- Funds must be both reduced to 75,000,000£ each, or that the Productive-Fund must be reduced to 50,000,000£, while the Profit-Fund and the gross amount of Capital remain the same. The latter is by far the more probable result of the two; for since the strength of the desire to save depends in a great measure on the amount of Profit or reward for such saving, it follows that to decrease the Profit-Fund would be to diminish the disposition to set aside a portion of the present product with a view to future production and future gains, and consequently to reduce in a like ratio the gross savings or

Capital of the community. Supposing, therefore, that the savings remain the same, viz. 200,000,000£, it is manifest that, if a larger proportion of those savings be devoted to the distribution of commodities, there must necessarily be a correspondingly smaller amount expended upon their production. But since the gross Profit continues unaltered, and this Profit depends upon the quantity of commodities produced over and above those spent in production, it is demonstrable that the Material-Fund can be in no way reduced. It follows, therefore, that the Wage-Fund alone must bear the burden of the diminution, and that *by just so much as the cost of distribution is increased must the remuneration of the producers be decreased*. Hence we see that not only does the augmentation of the Material-Fund give rise at once to a reduction of the Wage-Fund, as well as to an increase of the cost of Distribution; but *vice versâ*, an increase of the cost of Distribution necessitates not only an augmentation of the Material-Fund, but a reduction of the Wage-Fund. Anything there-fore which tends to increase the amount of Capital expended upon Distribution tends, in a like ratio, to decrease the amount of remuneration coming to the producers; while, for precisely the same reason as Capital sunk in the instruments of production requires a greater amount of materials to be made up (in order that the Capital so sunk may never be idle), so does the Capital sunk in the appliance of distribution (as ships and docks, railways and railway engines, canals and boats, turnpike-roads and carriages, warehouses and shops,) demand the transport and sale of an increased quantity of commodities. Conse-quently a greater number of such commodities must be produced, and, therefore, not only a larger amount of materials must be made up, but, being made up, must necessarily be attended with the same result—namely, *a decrease in the amount of remuneration coming to the labourer.* If in the tailoring trade, for instance, a double proportion of the Capital is expended upon cloth, of course there must be twice the number of clothes to be made up, and half the amount of wages to receive for so doing; again, in the textile manufactures, if double the proportion of the capital be expended upon machines, twice the quantity of raw materials must be operated upon in order to keep those machines continually employed.

But it may be said that the production of an increased quantity of materials requires an increased quantity of labour; and that therefore to increase the Material-Fund or amount of Capital expended upon the substances to be operated upon, is to increase the Wage-Fund, or amount of Capital expended on the operatives. Let us see, however, whether such be the fact. To expend a larger proportion of the Capital belonging to the tailoring or shoemaking trades upon cloth or leather, is clearly to reduce the Wage-Funds of those trades in precisely the same proportion, and so to make more work and less pay. Thus it is manifest the tailors and shoemakers cannot but be doubly injured by such an arrangement; but it will be asked are not the woollen manufacturers and tanners proportionately benefited? No! they are not; and for precisely the same reason: to produce a greater quantity of cloth and leather, a greater proportion of the Capital of those trades must be expended upon wool and hides, and a less proportion consequently be left for the subsistence of the workmen. Nor can the producers of wool and hides be benefited; and likewise for the same reason. The production of a greater quantity of commodities requires the consumption of a greater quantity of materials, while a greater quantity of materials necessitates a less quantum of subsistence accruing to the labourers. The Capital of every trade is regulated by the amount of wealth saved out of the *past* produce, and it is impossible to increase the gross capital till the *future* produce is obtained. The *present* Capital must be limited by the *past* savings; and though it be impossible to increase the whole, still the holders of the supplies can augment any one part and diminish another at pleasure by the process of exchange.

To render this portion of the subject more

clear, let us suppose that one-half of the entire corn produced be set aside for the production of the next year's crop; then the corn so set aside will represent the grain-capital of the growers, and this grain-capital, of course, will constitute the fund out of which, not only the seed, but the food of the labourers employed in sowing, rearing, and gathering the future crop, must be supplied. If, therefore, half of the corn so set aside were to be used as seed, there would be still half left for the labourers to live upon. But the holders of the accumulated stock of grain can do with it as they please; they may put any portion of it they think fit into the ground for the purpose of fructification, while the labourers must live as they can upon the remainder; for no more than what is left over and above the portion used as seed can they possibly get to subsist upon. Let us suppose, therefore, that two-thirds of the corn set aside for future production are used as seed, then it follows that the labourers will have only one-third, instead of one-half, left for their subsistence. But the quantity of seed regulates the quantity of work, while the quantity of food determines the amount of the labourer's remuneration; hence, it is manifest, that in the latter case the labourers will have more work to do and less to receive for it; and since the Capitalists' profits depend on the difference between the quantity of corn set aside for future production, and the quantity reproduced, it follows that the more grain there is used as seed, the greater must be the produce, and, therefore, the greater the Capitalists' gains. Now, if for seed in agriculture we substitute materials in manufacture, and if we convert the term Produce into Commodities, we shall readily and clearly perceive that if a greater proportion of the Capital of the country be devoted to materials, there necessarily must be a less proportion to be paid as remuneration to the work-people—in a word more work and less pay—greater profits and smaller wages, will be the inevitable result.

But if, in the tailoring and shoemaking trade, a double proportion of Capital is expended upon cloth and leather, and twice the number of garments and shoes produced (at half the wages), it follows that there must be a considerable increase in the appliances for distributing the extra quantity of goods; there must not only be a greater number of shops, but increased means of conveyance—a greater number of porters, carriages, or ships, must be employed; for if the amount of Capital expended upon materials is so great that more commodities are produced than are required in the immediate neighbourhood of their production, it follows that the market for such commodities must be extended; while, in order to do this, there must be greater facilities for transporting the increased produce to distant parts. Now that this augmentation of the cost of production, both in the appliances of transit and in the means of sale, has been going on most rapidly of late years, no one, with his eyes open, can doubt. Within our own time shops have been changed into palaces; we have seen "extensive alterations" go on everywhere, and "premises" continually "enlarged," until retail "establishments" have swallowed up house after house, and eventually overrun entire streets. We have seen the number of assistants behind the counters of such establishments increase from units to hundreds—we have seen the main thoroughfares of our cities become daily more and more impervious, from the dense throng of wagons, and vans, and carts, and stages, and trucks, laden with goods—we have seen docks after docks, with their giant storehouses, built round our coasts—St Katherine's, Birkenhead, Great Grimsby—for the better transport and housing of our increasing materials and productions—we have seen our mercantile marine swell and swell, as our produce has grown greater, until we can almost bridge the Atlantic over with our ships—we have seen, moreover, the country scored in every direction with iron railroads, along which monster trains of goods are daily whirled from one end of the kingdom to the other. These changes have all been wrought in our own time, while the majority of our canals and our turnpike roads date scarcely beyond our fathers' time. The Capital sunk of late years in the appliances of distribution must have been enormous; if we reckon docks, ships, canals, railways, warehouses, shops, and carriages, it cannot have been less than five hundred millions since the commencement of the present century; and when we remember that this vast sum has not only been sunk in *unproductive* instruments, but that the interest at least on the capital must every year be made good out of the national produce, we can readily understand how, in the words of Ricardo, "the one fund from which landlords and capitalists derive their revenue may increase, while the other—that upon which the labouring-class mainly depend—may diminish." If, out of the gross Capital or savings of the country, a greater proportion be devoted to the purposes of distribution, of course a correspondingly smaller amount only can be devoted to production; and hence, by just as much as the distributors are enriched, to precisely the same amount must the producers be impoverished. Nor is this all. This vast amount of wealth being sunk in the mere *interchange* of commodities, it follows that, in order to promote such interchange, and thus prevent the Capital from lying idle, trade is forced in every way, and every kind of expedient put in practice, so as to dispose of a great quantity of commodities, and thus enhance the aggregate amount of profits. Prices are cut down to the very quick—Capital is lavished, either on advertisements, circulars, or the decoration of premises—gas-lights, plate-glass, and architectural embellishments, are used as snares to catch customers— "tremendous failures," "awful sacrifices," "bankrupt-stocks," mock "auctions," "selling off," pretended "fires" and "custom-house seizures," and a thousand other tricks, are resorted to, merely to push off an extra number of commodities; while the extra number of commodities so pushed off necessitates of course the manufacture of a greater quantity of materials. Hence there is not only a larger proportion of capital expended upon materials in the production of these commodities, but a greater amount of the national savings is afterwards consumed in disposing of them when produced; so that the Distributive-Fund being thus increased, the Productive-Fund is correspondingly diminished, while the Wage-Fund, which is an integrant part of the latter, suffers a double reduction; that is to say, it is reduced, first, by the increase of the particular fund devoted to the supply of materials, and secondly, by the decrease of the general fund set aside for the purposes of production.

A gentleman has made the following calculation in connection with this subject. "There are," he says, "two thousand five hundred master-tailors in London, whose function is the distribution and superintendance of the work done by others. As Mr. Mill has said of distributors generally, their work might be done by *one-tenth* of the present number under an organized system of trade, so that two thousand two hundred and fifty of these middle-men tailors are useless burdens on the industry of the men. The money now paid to these two thousand two hundred and fifty middle-men, is for their rent, say at 50£ a year each, 112,500£; their superintendence, say at 100£ a year each, 225,000£; and their profit, say at 100£ a year each, 250,000£— making a total of 562,500£."

This sum, if shared equally among the 21,000 working tailors in London, would give to every one of them very nearly 27£ a year in addition to his present wages. "But," continues the gentleman, suppose the like process to go on throughout the Kingdom, and our million, middle-men, distributors, or traders with their at least 200£ a year each, reduced to a hundred thousand individuals, and the 180,000,000£, now uselessly spent on them saved to the producers and consumers at large." Then it follows that every one of the four million of the working classes would have 45£ per annum added to their present incomes. These are startling statements; but they are not cited here with a thorough belief in their truth, for it is impossible to say—devoid, as we are, of all facts upon the subject—whether Mr. Mill's assumption that, under an organised system of trade, the work of distribution might be done with one-tenth the present number of distributors, be correct. The hypothesis is quoted merely to impress the reader with a conviction that the

Wage-Fund is indirectly limited by the Distributive-Fund; that the gross Capital, or saving of the country, consists of two portions, the one devoted to the purposes of production, and the other to distribution; and that according as the Distributive-Fund is increased, so must the Productive-Fund be decreased; while, according as the Productive Fund is decreased, so must the Wage-Fund be proportionably diminished.

Next week we will see how the *Profit*-Fund influences the Wage-Fund.

ANSWERS TO CORRESPONDENTS.
[No.21, 3 MAY 1851]

Edited out:
W.M.B.; S.E.K.; E.F.R.P.

⎯⎯⎯⎯⎯⎯⎯⎯

"It becomes interesting," says Mr. Babbage in the fourth edition of his "Economy of Machinery and Manufactures"[26] (p.163), "to trace the various proportions in which *the material* and *the labour* unite to constitute the value of many of the productions of the arts."

But if the arguments advanced by Mr. Mayhew, in these pages within the last few weeks, be correct, it becomes something more than "*interesting*" to do this,—it is absolutely *essential to the welfare* of the workman that the relation between the *labour* and *material* be known; for if wages are *inversely* proportional to the sum expended on the substances upon which the labour is exerted, *the relative values of the materials and the work will tell us immediately the arts in which the operative is comparatively well or ill paid.*

But important as the knowledge of this subject is, not only to the workman, but to society in general, scarcely any attempts have been made to collect facts bearing upon the point, and the following table, as to the comparative price of labour and of raw

⎯⎯⎯⎯⎯

[26] C. Babbage, *On the Economy of Machinery and Manufactures*: Charles Knight, London, 1832.

materials entering into certain French manufactures, which has been ascertained with great care by M. de Villefosse, in his "Statistical Researches upon the Metals of France," is extracted from Mr. Babbage's book, in the hope of inducing working-men to do the same thing for English products—each dealing with his own particular handicraft—so that we may really have some accurate data concerning this most *vital* question; for every working-man will be able to perceive, immediately he devotes his mind to the subject, that the relation between the materials and the labour expresses precisely the difference between the amount of capital expended *out of* his trade, and the amount coming to himself and his fellow-operatives.

M. de Villefosse, in the subjoined table, however, does not give the sum paid to the workman, but merely the selling price of the manufactured commodity; nor does he tell us whether that selling price be the wholesale or the retail charge. This is unfortunate, because, according as it is one or the other, so will the cost of distribution and the gross profit be increased or diminished; but as it is we are left to *infer* from the selling price the sum paid to the labourer. Still, deficient as the table is, it is better than none, and is here inserted as a nest egg, in the hope of obtaining, by means of the imperfect article, others more full of life and intelligence from working-men themselves. Those operatives who may favour Mr. Mayhew with any such information, need not trouble themselves to reduce the respective amounts paid for labour and materials, into the proportions below given. They should, however, be most particular in describing the *quality* of the materials and giving only their wholesale price; they should also add the wholesale price of the manufactured article as expressing the more uniform value, and affix to the retail price the character of the shop (whether 1st class, 2nd, or 3rd,) whereat it is so charged. It will be better in all instances to give, if possible, the sum paid for materials by the employer, as well as the sum received by him for the manufactured article, adding at the same time a note so as to show whether the employer engages society or non-society hands; and if the latter, whether he may be fairly ranked as belonging to the second or third class of employers (always considering those who pay "society" wages as of the first class). It is to be hoped that, in order to prevent the possibility of cavil, workmen sending such information will in all cases of doubt give the benefit of it to the employer; for it is much better that the case should be under rather than over stated. All that it will be necessary for working-men to detail will be (1) the sum paid to them for the making of a particular article, (2) the wholesale cost of the materials entering into that article, and (3) the wholesale (and, if possible, retail) price of such article when finished. If several workmen be employed upon the different parts of any one article, then the wages paid for each and every of such parts should be stated, together with the price of the materials for the whole. And if the workmen are paid by the day rather than the piece, then the wholesale price of the materials that one can operate upon in the course of a given time, the wages he would earn in that time, and the wholesale value of those materials, after being so operated upon by him, should be one and all accurately set down. It the working-men will but continue to assist Mr. Mayhew in his undertaking, he hopes before long to collect such an overwhelming mass of facts as *must* cause justice to be done to them.

In France the quantity of raw material which can be purchased for 1£, when manufactured into

	£.	s.	d.
Silk goods ....is worth 2		7	$4^3/4$
Broad cloth and woollens.................2		3	0
Hemp and Cables.............................3		12	$9^1/4$
Linen comprising thread laces 5		0	0
Cotton goods 2		8	$9^1/2$
Sheets or pipes of moderate dimensions...1		5	0
White lead...2		12	0
Ordinary printing characters 4		18	0
The smallest type.............................28		6	0
Copper sheeting................................1		5	$2^1/4$

	£.	s.	d.
Household utensils 4		15	$4^3/4$
Common brass pins tinned...............2		6	$9^1/2$
Rolled into plates covered with 20th silver 3		11	$2^1/4$
Woven into metallic cloth, each square inch of which contains 10,000 meshes...............52		4	7
Leaves for silvering glass ....became 1		14	7
Household utensils 1		17	0
Vermilion of average quality 1		16	$2^3/4$
White oxide of arsenic......................1		16	7
Sulphuret (orpiment) 4		5	$2^1/4$
Household utensils 2		0	0
Machinery...4		0	0
Ornamental, as buckles, &c 45		0	0
Bracelets, fixtures, buttons, &c.....147		0	0
Agricultural instruments...................3		11	$4^3/4$
Barrels, musket................................9		2	0
Barrels of double-barrel guns, twisted and damasked..................233		1	7
Blades of penknives.......................657		2	$9^1/2$
—razor, cast steel 53		11	$1^3/4$
sabre, for cavalry, infantry, artillery, &c...............................16		1	$4^3/4$
—of table knives 35		14	0
Buckles of polished steel, used as jewellery 896		13	$2^1/2$
Clothiers' pins...................................8		0	7
Door-latches and bolts 8		10	0
Files, common...................................2		11	0
—flat, cast steel 20		8	$9^1/2$
Horse-shoes 2		11	0
Iron, small slit, for nails 1		2	0
Metallic cloth, iron wire, No.80......96		14	$2^1/4$
Needles of various sizes 70		17	0
Reeds for weaving 3–4ths calico................................21		17	$4^3/4$
Saws (frame) of steel........................5		2	$4^3/4$
—for wood 14		5	7
Scissars, finest kind 446		18	$9^1/2$
Steel, cast 4		5	7
—cast in sheets.................................6		5	0
—cemented 2		8	$2^1/4$
—natural...1		8	$4^3/4$
Sword-handles, polished steel 972		16	$4^3/4$
Tinned iron 2		0	0
Wire, iron 10		14	$2^1/4$

The present price (1832) of lead in England

(adds Mr. Babbage) is 13£ per ton, and the worth of 1£ of it manufactured into

Milled sheet lead............becomes £1 1 7

The present price of cake copper is 84£ per ton, and the worth of 1£ of it manufactured into

Sheet copper.................becomes £1 2 2¹/₄

The above table enables us to see at a glance the relative sums expended upon materials and labour in different handicrafts. In the case of "polished steel sword handles," for instance, we perceive that for every 1£ laid out in steel, not less than 971£ 16s. 4³/₄d. goes to the workman; whereas in the case of milled sheet-lead the workman gets only 1s. 7d. for operating upon the same amount of materials. In the first instance, therefore the labourer receives very nearly 999£ out of every thousand composing the Capital of the trade; whereas in the latter instance he gets only 1£ in every 12£, or but little more than 80£ out of 1000£.

The following table expresses the only facts that Mr. Mayhew has been able as yet to obtain respecting the relative quantity of materials made up, and the prices paid to the operative for so doing, in a given trade in England. It will be seen from the subjected exposition, that whereas the materials in the cotton trade increased upwards of sixfold between the years 1815 and 1844—the quantities imported in those years being respectively 100,000,000lbs. and 640,000,000lbs.—the prices paid for weaving decreased very nearly threefold, or from 3s. to 1s. 1¹/₂d. Hence it is evident one of four things must have ensued, either (1) a greater proportion of the Capital employed in the trade must have been expended on materials, and a correspondingly less proportion have accrued to the workmen; or (2) the gross sum paid for materials remaining the same (the price of cotton having fallen sixfold) the operatives, if not increased in number, must have had more than six times more work to do for nearly three times less wages; or (3) the operatives must have increased threefold (while the gross amount of the Wage-Fund remained the same), and so

Years.	Weight of Cotton Wool Imported.	Prices paid for weaving a piece of 72¹/₃ Calico.		Years.	Weight of Cotton Wool Imported.	Prices paid for weaving a piece of 72¹/₃ Calico.	
	lbs.	s.	d.		lbs.	s.	d.
1790	22,640,000			1829	222,767,411	1	4
1800	30,640,000			1830	263,661,452	1	4
1815	100,709,146	3	0	1831	288,674,853	1	4
1816	95,280,965	2	6	1832	286,832,525	1	4
1817	126,303,689	2	6	1833	303,656,837	1	4
1818	178,745,577	2	6	1834	326,875,425	1	4
1819	151,153,154	2	0	1835	363,702,963	1	4
1820	151,672,655	2	0	1836	406,959,057	1	4
1821	132,536,620	1	8	1837	407,286,783	1	4
1822	142,837,628	1	8	1838	507,850,577	1	3
1823	191,402,503	1	8	1839	389,396,559	1	3
1824	149,380,122	1	8	1840	592,488,010	1	3
1825	228,005,291	1	8	1841	487,992,355	1	2¹/₂
1826	177,607,401	1	6	1842	531,750,086	1	1¹/₂
1827	272,448,909	1	6	1843	673,193,116	1	1¹/₄
1828	227,760,642	1	4	1844	646,111,304	1	1¹/₂

have had each twice as much work to do for three times less pay; or else (4) the Wage-Fund must have been doubled, while the operatives increased six times in number, and so got *each* three times less pay for the same amount of work.

The facts of the subject appear to be that the hands increased 120 per cent., while the price of cotton fell upwards of 600 per cent. The total number of hands employed in manufacturing in 1801 was 1,877,107; while in 1841 it had risen to 2,251,927: and the price of cotton in 1814 was 2s. 6d., whereas in 1844 it had fallen to $4^3/4$d.

TEMPUS FUGIT writes from Bristol as follows:—

"My dear Sir,—I should feel obliged by your informing me whether you intend making any distinction between each Volume of your Work ("London Labour and the London Poor"), or whether parties can have them bound as they please."—Subscribers can have them bound as they please.

Mr. MAYHEW prints the following entire, because it shows how erroneous a view some persons may take as to the object of his labours.

"Sir,—I cannot deduce from your "London Labour" what is the ultimate object intended by you—the good of the street seller or his injury.

"The exposé of the tricks of their trade in the several numbers already issued will surely injure far more than enhance the profits derived by the poor individuals seeking an existence by the sale of various articles in the streets of the metropolis.

"Since the appearance of the number of your work referring to the sale of oranges, I have heard parties exclaim, when the orange-seller has offered his or her fruit for sale, 'Oh no! they've been biled;' and with various other articles doubtless the same thing occurs.

"The real cause of persons purchasing articles in the thoroughfares or environs of London is the hope of obtaining them much cheaper than by patronising the tradesmen, who certainly has his rent, together with many other expenses, to cover before making a profit; but if your publication benefits *him* (as I

fear it may do), is it not to the injury of a very industrious hardworking class, who probably would be in the workhouse if not in the streets earning their 'half profits?'

"The deep distress and misery which many have to undergo, and which has been faithfully described by you may have done some good, as they have been relieved by contributions from the charitable and well-disposed; but this I fear would be found to be the exception, not the rule.

"Excuse me, therefore, when I say, that in my humble opinion your work tends to the injury rather than the welfare of the Street-Poor.

"Your obedient Servant,
"G.N."

Mr. Mayhew's aim in the investigations that he is now making into the condition and earnings of the several classes of society is simply to *come at the truth* respecting them. It is impossible to benefit any class or any individual by falsity. If there are customs and practices among the street-sellers that are unjust, the mere fact of making them known will put the public on their guard against them, and so bring them to an end. It is the dishonest portion of the street-folk who injure the more honest members of that body. "How is it possible for us," said a costermonger, "to be just and fair in all our dealings, when, by using slangs, any of our people can sell twice as cheap as those who carry fair weights and measures, and get all their custom away from them." There are many of the street-sellers who mean well enough, but who are compelled to *compete* with the tricks of the unprincipled. Then again, the lurkers and sham street-sellers lead the public to look upon the street trade generally as a cloak for beggary, and an encouragement to idleness. The exposure of the lurkers' tricks will be sure to render them abortive, and *then*, and then only, they will be abandoned.

Moreover, Mr. Mayhew has no desire to depict the street-sellers other than as they really are. Were he to canonize the whole race of costermongers, and to paint the patterers as angels, what good could possibly come of such sickly sentimentalism? It is high time that the truth concerning all classes should be known, so that what is right among us may be cherished, and what is wrong put an end to as soon as possible. This was and is the sole object of the beginning and continuing the inquiries concerning "Labour and the Poor."

OMICRON is thanked—a list of the Errata will be published at the conclusion of each volume. Any blunders that may be detected—and such things are inevitable where so much is to be done in so short a time—should be made known, so that they may be corrected in due time.

E.C.R. makes the following offer:—

"Sir,—I have felt much interested in some of the cases mentioned in your valuable work, 'London Labour and London Poor,' and beg to ask you whether you could undertake to distribute to such persons as you consider worthy of help, a few small articles which they might dispose of in their usual way. If so, I propose to send you a small lot of Cheap Fancy Articles, which I would leave to your discretion to divide into such portions as you think would be best likely to suit the persons for whose relief they are intended; so that they might, by the disposal of the gift, be put in possession of stock-money. Some articles I could send might be rather superior to those generally sold, but that would be no objection, I conceive, but probably an advantage, in selling them. An early answer will oblige. I enclose my card, but do not wish my name made public."

To *give* goods is the same as *giving* money, and Mr. Mayhew objects, he repeats, to gifts of all kinds. The best way of serving any man is to teach him to trust to himself—and certainly not to others—for a living: the more one does to inspire a person with faith in his own powers, the greater the benefit that we confer upon him. Mr. Mayhew desires that every man in the kingdom should be able to live in comfort on the fruits of his labour—and most certainly not on the labour of other people. These who cannot labour, we, who can, are bound in charity, and indeed justice, to assist; but those who *can* labour we injure rather than benefit by helping them to live without labouring. All, it seems, that we should do to the able-bodied who are in want is to put them in the way of working for what they want. To do other than

this is to destroy a man's self-reliance; and this is perhaps the greatest injury that can be inflicted on the poor, being often the main cause of their poverty. If the goods are to be advanced as loans of stock to needy street-sellers who have been forced to live upon their stock-money, no objection can be raised; for the same plan has been found to succeed among the Jews most admirably.

The subjoined is from the landlord of the Low Lodging Houses spoken of in a former Number. It is printed here entire, so that if wrong has been done, reparation may be made:—

"Sir,—As the Landlord of the Houses referred to in page 317, I would beg to call your attention to the remarks of your Correspondent. I am there described as being 'a member of a strict Baptist Church, living in great splendour,' &c. [LLLP, Vol.1, p.317-18] Now, I am not a member of that community, never have been, nor in fact, am I a member of any Dissenting Body; as to my living in great splendour, &c., I can assure you, from statements which I have enclosed, that my average profits do not exceed 2£, 10s. a week. I am also reported as paying my Deputies 1¹/₂d. a day: now this is correct, in one instance; but as the House does not average more than 3s. a week, I think it sufficient; if the returns increase, his pay increases; to another I pay 9s. 4d. a week, and find him all the requisites; the whole of the others are rented at so much a week, allowing the party who rents them a comfortable income. The Deputies are reported as dealing in Stolen Goods, and taking in couples for short periods, to increase their incomes. Now, this must be made in ignorance; and all I can say is, that if they do so, it is quite unknown to me; and I judge that I am correct in this remark from my knowledge of their character and general conduct. They are charged with harbouring the worst class of characters, and such as I have repeatedly told them I would not allow; I have no need thus to caution them, from there being such persons in the Houses, but as the poor are of such a migrating nature, continually changing their Lodgings and almost next to an impossibility to know all their characters and occupations, I endeavour as much as possible to enforce this on them, as well as the admission of Stolen Goods into the Houses, which would be followed with instant dismissal, but which I have never had occasion to carry out.

"But let me ask, who is to provide for these unfortunate persons? Are they to be left to the Streets, because we have no Model Lodging Houses that will meet their case? Have you not, in your valuable work, shown that there are thousands who are wanderers and unprovided for, who know not in the morning that they will earn enough to pay for their Lodging; let them apply to the Model Lodging Houses now in existence: their abject condition and the price (a week in advance), would soon settle the question: we do not want Model Lodging Houses for the mechanic and the artisan; we want Model Lodging Houses for the ragged, shoeless, shirtless, unwashed, hungry, and destitute of our streets. We want a Model Lodging House that shall provide for the separation and classification of the sexes; where can a poor man and his wife find a refuge, but in the Common Lodging House? There now appears to be a movement in the right way; but these Models must be, as your correspondent wisely remarks, conducted on a different footing: the poor must find and feel that they have liberty in these Model Lodging House; till the difficulty has been met and grappled with, and other accommodation supplied, Common Lodging Houses as necessary evils will exist; when that period comes, I shall be happy to relinquish mine for a more honourable occupation.

I cannot conclude without observing, that, from my knowledge of many of the characters described in your work, your statements are unfortunately too correct. If I can afford you any further information on the subject of Lodging Houses, I shall be most happy. Trusting you will do me the favour of correcting the mistakes referred to by inserting a part or the whole of this in your answer to correspondents,

"I remain, sir,

"Yours very respectfully,

"L.H.R."

Mr. Mayhew regrets exceedingly, that any of his correspondents should have led him into error, as they appear to have done in this instance; for he has no reason to doubt the truth of the counter-statements contained in the preceding communication. Touching the advantages of the Model Lodging Houses referred to at the close of the above epistle, Mr. Mayhew, speaking before investigation, and merely drawing his conclusions from facts communicated to him concerning the conduct of those establishments, must confess he has not much hope of any direct good accruing from them. He believes, however, that they will ultimately give rise to some better devised and more liberal plan for the improvement of the low lodging-houses of the metropolis. To put the poor in the leading-strings of lords and ladies, appears to Mr. Mayhew to be almost as ill-advised as to leave them in the hands of mere mercenaries. There is after all but one way to help the Poor, that is to teach the Poor to help themselves; and so long as committees of noblemen have the conduct of their household affairs, so long as my Lord This or That is left to say at what time they shall go to bed and when they shall get up, there can be no main improvement in their condition. The Curfew Bell, even though instituted by the most zealous benevolence, is still as irksome as that enjoined by the most arrogant despotism. As was before said, the Poor *are* poor generally from a want of self-reliance; any system therefore (however well intentioned) which deprives them of all voice in the management of their own affairs, can but tend to increase their helplessness and poverty, and to keep them the same perpetual slaves of circumstances.

It is but right that the following should be given entire. It will be seen that it goes to contradict the account recently printed as to the condition of the Model Lodging House in Drury Lane. It will be observed, however, that in the letter above given from the landlord of the Lodging House in Thrawl Street, the writer asserts that from his own experience he can corroborate the greater part of the statements made in "London Labour" concerning the Low

Lodging houses of London. Nevertheless partial errors may doubtlessly have been committed, and perhaps the description of the Charles Street Lodging House may be included among the mis-statements—at least such would appear to be the fact, from the subjoined document. The correspondent alluded to gave his impression of the condition of that establishment, but the majority of the inmates seem to entertain very different opinions from himself on the subject:—

"Model Lodging House,

"2, Charles Street, Drury Lane.

"Sir,—

"We, the undersigned inmates of the above Model Lodging House, collectively beg to be allowed to disburden ourselves of the undue odium heaped upon us so mercilessly in the invidious aspersions of your correspondent last week. [LLLP, Vol.1, p.317] If the mis-statement of your informant is not refuted, the public will naturally infer that the common habits of the Lodgers present a scene of savage life, and that the interior displays the constant aspect of a perfect Babel; being, as erroneously asserted, 'the scene of dirt and disorder, with noise confusion, and intemperance abounding from morning till night.'

"Though there is no separate Reading Room, yet we have a small library, composed of books (presented by members of the Society, by whom the house was established) which, though not engaging the taste of all, is at times resorted to.

"The books most in request being Chamber's Information and Tracts. Besides this, however, we have a list of Periodicals subscribed for by the *Lodgers*—these are eagerly and attentively read as they appear. The character of these works will, we think, sufficiently speak in our defence for whilst occupied in their perusal, which happens at all spare intervals of leisure, the time so spent must prove the untruth of the alleged disorder, &c.

"The following is a list of weekly Publications taken in, viz:—

"London Labour—from the first.

"Household Words.

"Tomlins's Help to Self-Educators.

"The Builder.[27]

"Mechanics' Magazine.

"Knight's Cycopaedia of the Industry of all "Nations.[28]

"Expositor.

"Chambers's Journal.

"The People's and Howitt's Journal.

"Family Herald.

"London Journal.

"Weekly Dispatch.

"With these few remarks we leave this statement in your hands for candid inquiry, which if resorted to will assuredly reverse the unfavourable impression your strictures are calculated to produce on the public mind.

"We remain

"Your constant Readers,

"J. Johnson.	Thos. Passmore.
"W.R. Robinson.	J.E. Aubrey.

"Lodgers resident between three and four years.

"A. Kates	Wm. Smith.
"John Smith.	H. Powell.
"Fredk.Harcourt.	Jas. Taylor.

"Lodgers resident between two and three years.

"Joseph Yates.	E. Wolstenholme.
"George Hunt.	W. Hind.

"Lodgers resident between one and two years.

"F. Smith.	Thomas Trotman.
"J. Green.	J. Lush.

[27] See Ruth Richardson, "Notorious Abominations: Architecture and the Public Health in *The Builder*, 1843-1883", in W.F. Bynum, S. Lock, R. Porter, *Medical Journals and Medical Knowledge*, Routledge, 1992, pp. 90-108, and the contemporary social reform book by the editor of *The Builder*, George Godwin, *Town Swamps and Social Bridges* (1859), reprinted Leicester University Press 1972, which followed *London Shadows: A Glance at the Home of the Thousands* (1854). *The Builder* was a very lively professional and political journal.

[28] See Scott Bennett, "Revolutions in Thought: Serial Publication and the Mass Market for Reading", in J. Shattock and M. Wolff, *The Victorian Periodical Press: Sounding and Sampling*, Leicester University Press, 1982, pp. 225-57.

"Lodgers resident between six and twelve months.

"The above list of names might have been considerably extended had it been requisite."

Since the above was forwarded, a letter bearing the signatures of the first two persons named in the above list, has been received, stating that there is "not a single scintilla of truth" in the information furnished me respecting the Model Lodging House in Charles Street, Drury Lane, and adding that the doors of that particular Model "are never even nominally closed till midnight, and never rigorously at that hour."

ANSWERS TO CORRESPONDENTS.
[No.22, 10 MAY 1851]

Edited out:
J.S. HUDDERSFIELD; NEWCASTLE-UPON-TYNE; C.J.R.; E.D.; C.M.

Before proceeding to the consideration of the relation between Wages and Profits there are a few points which require further elucidation, in order to impress them firmly on the mind.

We are told in Political Economy that the remuneration of labourers is regulated by the demand and supply of labour, *or* by the proportion between the circulating capital and the number of labourers. These two determining circumstances, which are thought to be one and the same, are essentially distinct; for the demand for labour, or quantity of work to be done, is very different from the amount of circulating capital, or gross sum set aside for the remuneration of the labour: and by themselves they are incomplete, each omitting an essential condition; for the law of demand and supply, *per se*, takes no notice of the amount of remuneration coming to each labourer, but merely expresses the relation between the quantity of work to be done and the number of hands to do it, while the law of population and capital (as it is called) leaves out

all mention of the quantity of work to be done for a given amount of pay, expressing solely the relation between the labourers and the gross sum devoted to their remuneration.

But the Wage-Law of the Economists is not only untrue theoretically but practically. In the London Cabinet Trade, for instance, the demand for labour increased considerably from 1831 up to the present time (200 miles of houses having been built in the Metropolis within that period), while the supply of labourers decreased during the same time no less than 33 per cent., and yet the wages were in 1831 as much as 400 per cent. better than at present. The Cotton Trade, again, may be cited as an instance of the insufficiency of the above law. The materials used in that trade we have seen increased between 1814 and 1844 from 100,000,000 lbs. to 646,000,000 lbs., that is to say, the demand for labour increased very nearly 650 per cent.; while on the other hand the number of labourers engaged in manufacture in 1801 was 1,877,107, whereas in 1841 it was 4,129,034, or, in other words, the supply of labour had increased only 120 per cent. within that time; and yet Wages in 1814 were nearly 300 per cent. better than in 1844 – the prices paid for Weaving being 3s. at the former period, and 1s. 1^1/2d. at the latter. If the law of supply and demand were true, and wages rose in proportion as the quantity of work to be done increased, and the number of hands to do it decreased, *the weavers should have received in 1844 not less than 5s. for the same quantity of labour as they, got 1s. for in 1814; whereas the fact is, they were paid in 1844 only 1s. 1^1/2d. for that for which in 1814 they had 3s.*

But the Wage-Law as evolved by the Economists is not only untrue as regards the demand and supply of labour being the sole circumstances regulating the amount of remuneration for a given amount of work, but it is equally false when looked at in another aspect; for it is just as incorrect to say that the reward of labour depends upon the proportion between the number of labourers and the amount of circulating capital. The facts of the Cabinet Trade are sufficient to assure us that the decrease of wages was in no way due to a corresponding decrease in the amount of circulating capital employed in that trade; nor could it be ascribed to an increase in the number of operatives among whom the capital to be shared, for, as we have seen, the hands decreased during the fall of wages no less than 33 per cent., so that the decline could not be owing to an increase of labourers. Nor was it owing to a decrease in the amount of circulating capital, because, as the work increased considerably during the period, it is evident that a larger proportion of such circulating capital must have been expended on the materials used in the trade, so that while the Wage-Fund was considerably diminished, the Material-Fund on the other hand must have been considerably augmented, and hence the gross amount of circulating capital must have remained very nearly the same. The alteration of the relation between these two Funds, however, would naturally induce a greater quantity of cabinet work, and a *less* sum to receive for it, so that while the number of pounds sterling spent on materials was largely increased, it is clear that the amount received for making up every one pound's worth of such materials must have proportionately decreased, and consequently that *wages would have fallen even while the amount of circulating capital remained the same, and the number of labourers was lessened.*

But let us, for the sake of a greater clearness, put the question arithmetically. Let us say that at a given period the number of operative Cabinet Makers was 10,000—that the amount of the entire circulating capital employed in the business was 2,000,000£, and that of this the sum of 1,000,000£ was expended in the purchase of wood and other materials for the trade, while the remaining 1,000,000£ was devoted to the payment of the operatives engaged in fashioning the wood, &c., into furniture. In this case it is plain that the operatives would have received 1£ for every 1£ worth of materials made up by them. But now let us suppose, while the circulating Capital of the Trade and the price of materials remained the same, that the portion of the capital expended on materials was increased to 1,600,000£; then, of course there could have been but 400,000£ left for the workmen, and they consequently would have received only 5s. (instead of 1£) for every 1£ worth of materials made up by them. Hence it is a matter of demonstration, that though the gross amount of the circulating capital remained precisely the same, the wages paid for a given amount of labour must have fallen 75 per cent., or, in other words, the remuneration of the labourer must have been 400 per cent. better at the former than at the latter period. Nor could the number of labourers have influenced the result further than as regulating the average quantity of work, and the gross annual income accruing to each. In the first instance it is clear that, assuming the work to have been equally distributed, and the number of workmen to have been 10,000, while the sum spent on materials amounted to 1,000,000£, each of those workmen must have had in the course of the year 100£ worth of materials to make up, and have received the same sum for his labour. In the second instance, however, the number of hands in the trade having decreased 33 per cent.—that is to say, having fallen from 10,000 to 6666, while the amount devoted to the purchase of materials increased 60 per cent., or from 1,000,000£ to 1,600,000£, it is evident that every one of the workmen must then have had very nearly 250£ worth of materials to make up, and have received only about 60£ for so doing; that is to say, each would have been required to do more than twice as much work for little more than half the pay. And such appears to have been the real fact of the case.

The Wage-Law has two distinct forms: 1st, the *particular* amount of remuneration for a particular amount of work is *inversely* proportional to the quantity of circulating capital expended in the purchase of materials. 2nd, the *aggregate* amount of remuneration or annual income of each labourer is inversely proportional; (a) to the number of labourers, the hours of labour, or the rate of labouring; and (b) to the relative amount of the Material-Fund.

The following table expresses the various operations of the Wage-Law, resulting from the increment of any one or all of the three elements—the Material-Fund, the Wage-Fund, or the number of Labourers, either with or without the increase of the circulating Capital. The National Income is reckoned by McCulloch and others at 300,000,000£ of which 100,000,000£ is said to represent the Amount of profits, 100,000,000£ the amounts expended on materials, and 100,000,000£ the amount paid to the labourers; hence the circulating Capital of the country would appear to be about 200,000,000£. The total number of the working classes would seem to be, according to the returns of the last census, about 4,000,000. The first column below represents the gross Wage-Fund of the country expressed in millions of pounds sterling; the second column the gross Material-Fund; the third the number of working-men; the fourth the average income of each of the operatives; the fifth the average number of pounds' worth of materials made up by each of such operatives; and the sixth the amount of wages paid for making up every one pound's worth of material.

I. THE CIRCULATING CAPITAL REMAINS THE SAME.

1. The amount of the Wage-Fund in Millions.	2. The amount of the Material-Fund in Millions.	3. The number of Labourers in Millions.	4. The average amount of Income obtained by each Labourer.	5. The average quantity of work done by each Labourer expressed in pounds sterling.	6. The Pay given for making up £1 worth of Materials.
1 { A £100	£100	4	£25 0 0	£25 0 0	£1
Increase of Labourers $\frac{1}{2}$.					
B £100	£100	6	£16 13 4	£16 13 4	£1
Increase of Materials $\frac{1}{2}$.					
2 { A £50	£150	4	£12 10 0	£37 10 0	6s. 8d.
Increase of Materials and Labourers $\frac{1}{2}$ *each.*					
B £50	£150	6	£8 6 8	£25 0 0	6s. 8d.
Increase of Wages.					
3 { A £150	£50	4	£37 10 0	£12 10 0	£3
Increase of Wages and Labourers.					
B £150	£50	6	£25 0 0	£8 6 8	£3

II THE CIRCULATING CAPITAL IS INCREASED $\frac{1}{4}$.

Increase of Material $\frac{1}{2}$*.					
1 { a £100	£150	4	£25 0 0	£37 10 0	13s. 4d.
Increase of Material and Labourers $\frac{1}{2}$ *each.*					
b £100	£150	6	£16 13 4	£25 0 0	13s. 4d.
Increase of Wages $\frac{1}{2}$.					
2 { a £150	£100	4	£37 10 0	£25 0 0	£1 10s.
Increase of Wages and Labourers $\frac{1}{2}$ *each.*					
b £150	£100	6	£25 0 0	£16 13 4	£1 10s.
Increase of Materials and Wages $\frac{1}{2}$.					
3 { a £125	£125	4	£31 5 0	£31 5 0	£1
Increase of Materials, Wages and Labourers $\frac{1}{2}$ *each.*					
b £125	£125	5	£25 0 0	£25 0 0	£1

* N.B.—A decrease in the price of Materials is the same as an increase in the amount of the Material-Fund.

Now, referring to the above table, we perceive two different operations of the same law: the first of which has relation solely to the *pay* given for making up a certain amount of materials; and the second to the average amount of *income* obtained by each labourer;

and directly contrary to the law of supply and demand, or that of population and capital, it may be now seen that *the number of labourer in no way influences the* PAY *of the labourers*, but solely the average *income* of each; that is to say, it affects nothing but the share of the Wage-Fund accruing to the labourers respectively. The reader is requested to pay particular attention to this point, for if the law, as here expressed for the first time, be correct, it follows that our legislation is conducted on entirely false principles, and that all the popular theories and remedies respecting low wages are based on groundless assumptions, as an increase in the number of labourers cannot reduce wages—such a result being producible only by an increase of the sum spent on Materials.

Concerning the amount of *Pay* coming to the Labourer for a definite amount of work, we have the following canons:—

Capital remaining the same.

If the Material-Fund be increased one-half, the Pay will be decreased two-thirds. (See A 2, in above Table.)

If the Wage-Fund be increased one-half, the Pay will be increased threefold. (See A 3.)

If the number of Labourers be increased one-half, the Pay will remain the same. (See B 1.)

Capital increased one-fourth.

If the Material-Fund be increased, one-half the Pay will be decreased one-third. (See a 1.)

If the Wage-Fund be increased one-half, the Pay will be increased one-half also. (See a 2.)

If the Material-Fund and the Wage-Fund be both increased one-fourth, the Pay will remain the same. (See a 3.)

If the Material and the Wage-Fund and the number of Labourers be severally increased one-fourth, the Pay will still remain the same. (See b 3.)

Concerning the average amount of Income obtained by each labourer, the results are materially different.

Capital remaining the same.

If solely the number of labourers be increased one-half, the income of each will be decreased one-third, while there will be one-third less work for each to do. (See B 1.)

If the Material-Fund and the number of Labourers be respectively increased one-half, the income of each will be decreased two-thirds, while there will be the same quantity of work for each to do. (See B 2.)

If the Wage-Fund and the number of Labourers be respectively increased, one-half the income of each will be the same, while there will be two-thirds less work for each to do. (See B 3.)

Capital being increased one-fourth.

If the Material-Fund and the number of Labourers be respectively increased, one-half the income of each will be decreased one-third, while there will be the same amount of work for each to do. (See b 1.)

If the Wage-Fund and the number of Labourers be respectively increased one-half, the income of each will be the same, while there will be one-third less work for each to do. (See b 2.)

If the Material and the Wage-Fund and the number of Labourers be respectively increased one-fourth, both the income and the amount of work accruing to each will remain the same. (See b 3.)

Or, to reduce the above laws to a formula, we may say let C represent the Circulating Capital; M, the Material-Fund; W, the Wage-Fund; L, the number of Labourers; I, the average Income obtained by each labourer; Q, the average quantity of work performed by each; and P, the Pay for making up a certain amount of materials: then we have the following results:—

(1) $C - M = W$.

(2) $C - W = M$.

(3) $\dfrac{C - W}{L} = Q$.

(4) $\dfrac{C - M}{L} = I$.

(5) $\dfrac{C - M}{L} \div \dfrac{C - W}{L} = P$.

It will be now seen that the Wage-Law of Supply and Demand takes notice only of that peculiar form of it expressed in No. 3, while the law of Population and Capital recognises only the phase set forth in No. 4; but these, it is evident, relate solely to the average income and the average quantity of work done by each labourer—they do not in any way refer to the amount of pay accruing for a definite amount of work, nor can this possibly be arrived at by either of them alone. That which concerns the pay, however, is, after all, the principal Wage-Law, expressing, as it does, the relation between the remuneration and the work, that is to say, the quantity of money received in exchange for a definite quantity of labour, which is all that is meant by the term Wages.

To tell us what will be the amount of the average income of each labourer, without telling us how much work he will be required to do for such income—and this is all that the Economical law of Population and Capital can be said to achieve—is to give us no knowledge on the subject of wages; while to inform us, on the other hand, that the quantity of work to be done, and the Number of labourers to do it, regulates the wages accruing to each, is *to beg the whole question*, seeing that it makes no reference to the Wage-Fund out of

which the labourers are to be paid: as the former dogma ignored the *work*, so does the latter the *pay*. And yet these are the laws by which, according to the dicta of such men as the Editor of the "Economist" and the Manchester School, as well as those most shallow and most ignorant pretenders—the Free-trade gentry—tell us that the welfare of the working classes must for ever be regulated.

To reduce the subject, however, down to the level of the intellects of these people, let us put the following case:—Let us assume that the gross grain produce of this country is 100,000,000 quarters, and that one-half of this quantity is consumed, while the other half is set aside for future production; and that of this again, one-half is used as seed for the next years crop, and the other half as food for the labourers engaged in sowing, rearing, and reaping it; let us assume, moreover, that there is an unlimited supply of land, and that the increase on the seed is always twenty-fold, while the quantity devoted to feeding the labourers is never augmented—then we have the following expression:—

	Gross amount of the Produce of the previous year in Millions of Quarters.	Quantity consumed in Millions of Quarters.	Gross quantity set aside for future production.	Quantity devoted to the feeding of the Labourers.	Quantity used as seed for Future Crop.	Gross Quantity produced.
1st year.....	100	50	50	25	25	500
2nd ,, ...	500	250	250	25	225	4,500
3rd ,, ...	4,500	2,250	2,250	25	2,225	44,500
4th ,, ...	44,500	22,250	22,250	25	22,225	444,500
5th ,, ...	444,500	222,250	222,250	25	222,225	4,444,500

By this table it is evident that the profits of those who hold the capital may increase at a most enormous rate, even while the amount devoted to the labourers remains precisely the same, and while their work increases in almost an equal ratio with the profits of their employers. According to the above exposition, we perceive, that in five years the net income of the profit-mongers would hare increased nearly five thousand-fold, or from 50 million quarters to 222,250 million quarters; while the work (which of course would be regulated by

the quantity set aside as materials for the future produce) rose nearly ten thousand-fold, or from 25 to 222,225. The sole objection to such a state of things being possible, lies in the productive power of the labourers. In ordinary circumstances, of course, the same number of workmen could not be made to do such immensely different quantities of work; but it is evident that any increase in their productive powers must necessarily be attended by a corresponding increase in the profits of the capitalists, for since profits are but the surplus which remains after replacing materials and paying for the keep of the labourers, it follows that the greater the quantity of materials that can be operated upon by a given amount of labour, the greater will be the produce, and consequently, the greater the profits. Hence it is plain, that what is called the economy of labour, or the production of an equal amount of wealth with a smaller number of labourers, or a larger amount of wealth with the same hands, is *the greatest possible good to the employer, and the greatest possible evil to the employed;* for the products are *directly* proportional to the materials, while the wages are *inversely* proportional to them. Any process therefore which tends to economize labour, tends at the same time to increase the proportion of capital expended on materials, and thus to decrease the sum accruing to the labourer; so that, unless the market can be widened to the same extent as the labour has been economized, the labourers must necessarily be injured precisely as much as the profit-mongers must be benefited by the change.

Hence it becomes highly important in an inquiry like the present to ascertain the several means by which labour can be so economized—or, in other words, how a greater quantity of commodities can be obtained for the same quantity of labour.

There are, strictly speaking, but two modes of arriving at such a result: the first is by making the men work longer time, and the second by causing them to get through more work in the same space of time. Under each of these modes of economizing labour are included several distinct means of obtaining the same end.

I. We may economize labour by making the men work longer time either by

1. *Increasing the hours of labour.*
2. *Increasing the days of labour,* and so making the men work on Sundays.
3. *Increasing the seasons of labour* and so making the men work at times when the business would naturally be slack.

II. We may economize labour by making the men get through more work in the same space of time, either by

1. *Causing the men to work quicker,* which may be effected in several ways, as (a) by increasing their interest in their work, as by piece-work; (b) by reducing their wages, and so making them strive to do more work in order to get the same amount of money; (c) by attaching some premium to the greatest quantity of work done by a number of men, or some penalty to the least, as in what is called "the Strapping system," where men are set to race against each other, the slowest being dismissed; and "the Bonus system," where those who do the greatest quantity of work in a given time are encouraged with some reward for their extra exertions; (d) by requiring a certain quantity of work to be executed within a certain time, as in task work; (e) by dividing the work into a number of distinct parts, and so increasing the facility of the workmen, as in the division of labour.

2. *By omitting certain details from the work,* as in "scamped work," in which either less care is devoted to the finishing, fitting, or joining of various parts of the work, or else some of these parts are entirely omitted. The Messrs. Nicolls' head workman told Mr. Mayhew that his employers having reduced his wages one-third, he put two stitches into his work instead of three.

3. *By increasing the facilities for receiving and returning the work,* as by arrangement for shortening the distance to be travelled in large factories, and by the intervention of middle-men in the "domestic system" of manufacture.

4. *By the invention of tools and machinery* for expediting in the several industrial processes, as a plough which will enable a man to turn up ten times the quantity of land in the same space of time as he could dig over with a spade; or a lathe which will turn a banister rail in ten minutes, and a thousand-fold truer and better than could be done by a file and chisel in a day; or by a "mule jenny," by which one person spins as much yarn as 300 individuals could by hand.

5. *By abridging or improving some of the processes of labour,* as the hot blast for the smelting of iron, and the chemical methods of tanning, &c., &c.

The above appear to exhaust the several means of economizing labour, or, in other words, of enabling the same number of hands to operate upon a greater quantity of materials. And we are now in a position to see how the Wage-Fund is regulated by the Profit-Fund; this will be set forth in the next Number.

ANSWERS TO CORRESPONDENTS.
[No. 23, 17 MAY 1851]

Edited out:
C.O.U.P.; A BELGRAVIAN; W.C.

———————

OLIVE LEAF suggests that a portrait of the Editor of "London Labour" should form the frontispiece of Vol. I. This is impossible at present.

Another letter from the same gentleman says:—

"I am indebted to you for the address of the Poor Poet. I have by this evening's post forwarded a donation of 1£ 10s. expressing a wish that it might be employed as stock money in purchasing some saleable articles which his son could dispose of, and which, under the Divine Blessing, might enable him to get a better living.

"Could you oblige me by stating in your next what time you are likely to treat of the subject of Apprentices and Journeymen?"

Mr. MAYHEW purposes giving the results of his inquiries in the state of the working classes immediately the excitement of the Great Exhibition has lulled a little.

G.R.L. makes the following benevolent suggestions:—

"You mentioned in one of the late Nos. of 'London Labour and the Poor' the injury inflicted on the eyes of the tailors who make soldiers' coats, in the bright scarlet colours of

the cloth. [LLLP, Vol.1, p.340] There can be no doubt this is the case, as any one may convince himself who will look for a short time at a scarlet shawl or other article in a good light. But would it not be an alleviation of this injury if these tailors, when at work, would wear spectacles of *flat* glass, and of such a *colour* as, combining with the scarlet, would produce a dark or neutral tint? The colours on the enclosed card will serve to illustrate my meaning. Such spectacles, needing no grinding, might be made very cheap; and though I well know how difficult it would be to most of these poor men to raise a single shilling, yet whatever sacrifices they might make for that object would soon be repaid by the increased quantity of work they would do, setting aside the saving of their eyes. I make the suggestion, and shall be very happy if it prove of any value.

"The colours on the enclosed card are very smeary, because laid on too thick and very unskilfully, but they will show my meaning."

The best tint for the glasses would be green, as being the "complimentary" colour to red. The suggestion, though excellent, as offering a simple remedy for the evil, is rendered valueless by the fact that *a workman wearing spectacles in a workshop is instantly dismissed.*

H.H. writes:—

"The 'Times' says, 'The only political chloroform under which British industry is suffering just now is full employment, with abundance of bread, and meat, and drink and other necessaries of life.'

"Might I ask, in three words, whether this is true of *slopworkers* and *needlewomen* generally, taking those classes as the types of labour-suffering?"

The *Times* and other free-trade journals of course have an interest in making the working people appear as well to do as possible. As a sample of the peculiar "arguments" by which the welfare of the operative class has been attempted to be demonstrated, we may cite that which endeavours to prove, by the increase of the excise returns, that workmen must be better off because they can afford to spend more money on spirituous liquors. Now it has been long known to statisticians that such a circumstance is due to a precisely opposite cause. "It is fact worth notice," said a statistical journal, entitled "Facts and Figures," published in 1841, "as illustrative of the *tendency of the times of pressure to increase spirit drinking*, that whilst under the privations of last year (1840) the poorer classes paid 2,628,286£ tax for spirits, in 1836, a year of the greatest prosperity, the tax on British spirits amounted only to 2,390,188£. So *true is it that to impoverish is to demoralize*."

A Friend sends the subjoined derivation:—

"As you say you have been unable to find the etymology of HABERDASHER, [LLLP, Vol. 1, p.35] I inclose you the following from an old dictionary, published 1698.

"Haberdasher (q. Habcidas?) Ge. *Have you that?* or Avoir d'acheter, F. *Having to buy*; or Kooperdaseer, D., *a merchant of toys or small wares.*"

The latter is doubtlessly the true root of the English word.

The subjoined requires no comment, seeing that it speaks well enough for itself and other too:

"National Philanthropic Association,[29]

"40, Leicester Square, April 29th, 1851.

"Dear Sir,—Allow me to suggest, in aid of your most laudable endeavours in favour of the Poor, that much good may be done to the STREET-SELLERS, whose condition you are so well describing, and whose interests you are so ably advocating, if you will give a hint in the *proper quarter*, that such persons (under due restriction, and under the observance of the Police) may be safely—nay, advantageously—permitted to vend their little wares within the inclosure of Hyde Park during the approaching Exhibition. Their exclusion is *without reason*

and *without justice*; and they now congregate in the approaches, so as to have already become a positive nuisance to the Inhabitants. What must they be before the end of May?

"A paved Court leading from near the principal (I think it is called the *Victoria*) entrance to Knightsbridge, is so crowded by stalls, &c. as to be absolutely impassable. Why not let them wander over the Park, to enliven it by their invitations to buy, by their varied cries, and by the exhibition of their Engravings, Coloured Prints, Trinkets, Ginger-Pop, Lemonade, Oranges and other Fruits? Such permission would add to the picturesqueness of the scene and assimilate it to the celebrated Fairs and Festivals of the Continent; the *coup d'oeil* would rival the attractions of Kensington Fair (which I am glad to see announced for the entertainment of the Public at large), nay, it would be the best of all foils for the Crystal Palace itself.

"As I have stated, there is neither reason nor justice in the exclusion of these Bees from the Hive of Industry. Let the Police, therefore, admit all Vendors of Articles proper to be sold, who are clean in their persons, and somewhat decent in their attire, excluding gamblers and mendicants of every sort; honest and legitimate employment will thus be afforded to about three or four thousand persons, who, with their families, must otherwise remain in a state of semi-starvation, or become burdensome to their respective Parishes.

"I am,
"Dear Sir,
"With the warmest esteem and respect,
"Yours very truly,
"C. MACKENZIE, Sec."

"H. Mayhew, Esq.,
"16, Upper Wellington Street."

If the case were properly stated to the Prince, there is little doubt that the necessary permission (under certain restrictions) might be obtained. Mr. Mayhew would be happy to co-operate with any persons towards such an object.

One of the Master Tailors alluded to in No.19, as refusing the Blind Needle-Sellers admission to their workshops, states his reasons

---

[29] Not to be confused with the Charles and Helen Bosanquet's later organisation. The National Philanthropic Association was directed and served by C. Cochrane. See J. Winter, *The Teeming of the Streets of London*, Routledge, 1993, pp. 120-35.

for so doing. [Allen & co. Bond Street, LLLP, Vol. 1, p. 341] He says:—

"In reading one of your able Pamphlets, entitled 'London Labour,' I was surprised and grieved to see my name mentioned in a way anything but creditable; and knowing your wish to do justice to everybody, I take this opportunity of addressing these few lines to say that I feel satisfied, if you had made yourself acquainted with my side of the story, you would not have mentioned my name in the way you have. My workmen are as much opposed to people coming in and hindering them from working as I am; and if you were to see the dirty filthy scamps that endeavour to come into the workshops, you would wonder how I *could* admit them. Most of them come from the Dials, and have been observed by my workmen covered with Vermin, begging of the workmen under the pretence of selling needles, &c., and they afterwards get drunk with the money. They have also sent their wives and daughters, when they know very well that they have liberties taken with them. One of my workmen was telling me, that a women named —— —— used to come round, and he has seen the men carry her round the workshop with her clothes over her head. I considered that I was encouraging such things by allowing these people to come in. You will perhaps say—but why not allow only one or two? I answer, if you permit one you cannot stop any, for when once it is known they are permitted, they are always in and out under a pretence or another. It is a well-known thing, that the men generally send for Beer when these people come in, which encourages drunkenness, profligate habits, &c., instead of their keeping their money to take home for their wives and families, which they do now. Am I to consider one or two poor needle-sellers, or fifty or sixty workmen, to say nothing of my own property, which I was continually losing till I adopted this plan? and last, though not least, the nuisance of these people bringing Vermin into the rooms where my Customers' Clothes are being made. If any deserving man wishes to sell needles or anything else, they can always see my men at

the Beershop or House of Call. And in conclusion, I have but to remark, that everything ought to be done by a principle; mine is to conduct my business with comfort to all around me, and I flatter myself that my workmen (some of whom have been in our employ upwards of 30 years) are as respectable as any in their trade, and the pride of their employers. Hoping you will reconsider this, and do me justice in your next number,

"I remain, Sir,

"Your very humble servant,

"WALTER DANL. ALLEN,

"For ALLEN and Co."

The reasons above given must be considered to be sufficiently cogent if true. Perhaps the facts may have been observed in one or two instances, and have been inferred to be so in all. If every blind needleseller, or indeed the majority were covered with vermin, then how culpable must be those master tailors who admit such people into their establishments. The blind man whom I saw was scrupulously clean.

The POOR POET [LLLP, Vol. 1, p. 279] thus rhythmically acknowledges the receipt of the money sent for him:—

To H. MAYHEW, ESQ.

To the Labouring Classes
I know you are Kind,
And a Friend and Defender
In you They did find,—
For you've sought the Cot
Of the Wretched and Poor,
Where Merit sits shrouded
In silence obscure,
Oh would But the wealthy
Tread Those steps of thine,
What vice Might Be crushed—
And what Virtue Might Shine.
The sixteen Shillings you sent
Our Wants did decrease,
To pray for your Welfare
I shall never cease,
Your kind Benefaction
I did not abuse,
From Your Bedridden Servant,
The Brazier,
JOHN HUGHES.

My Thanks are Sincere,
They are honest and true,
May Heaven Shower Blessings;
On Squire
                    MAYHEW.

WC., a Brighton Correspondent, writes thus:—"I have been an attentive peruser of your valuable work, 'London Labour,' &c., and it has occurred to me that if you could publish the whole of your correspondence (*except* private), in the form of an appendix, at the end of each set, it would be an improvement, as otherwise it (the correspondence) would be all lost."

The evil, Mr. Mayhew fears, is a necessary one at present. In the next volume, perhaps, some alteration may be thought of. How the defect can be remedied, it is difficult to say. The Observations on Wages Mr. Mayhew purposes republishing in a book form when complete.

C.O.P. (of Macclesfield) says:—"*Pedlars.*—The following description of this class occurs in the 90th Canon of the Irish Church, A.D. 1634: 'Also they (the Church-wardens) shall see that none of those *light wanderers in markets and pelting sellers, which carry about and sell pins, points, and other small trifles, whom they call Pedlars*, set out their wares to sale, either in the Church yard, or near the Church, all that time; *i.e.* of Divine Service."

"*Qu.—Unde derivatur Pedlar?*"

"Thank you for your political œconomy. I have now lived nearly ten years in this large manufacturing town, and what you state respecting material, produce, and wages, exactly corresponds with my experience. I should say that there are ten times the amount of raw material and machinery here that there were twelve years ago,—yet the wages of the workpeople have been *steadily going down*. I am nothing of a Political œconomist, but I can judge of facts. If you want any Statistics, I think I can get them easily, as our operatives are a most intelligent race here."

Touching the Statistics, Mr. Mayhew would be especially grateful for them. They are the only guides we have in politico-economic reasoning. Will Mr. P. see No. 21, and collect a few facts after the manner there mentioned?

The derivation of Pedlar is said by lexicographers to be *peddling sellers*—other refer it to the Latin *pede*, from their travelling on foot; the passage above cited, however, would seem to connect the term "pedlar" with "pelting sellers." But then what is a "pelting" seller?

A LADY observes, with reference to the subject of harmless amusement for the Poor, that in a "*Country* parish, a Magic Lantern on a large scale, with dissolving views, and all kinds of changeable and amusing slides, has been found to answer, and prove an inexhaustible fund of amusement. The poor people," she adds, "delight in *pictures*, and the various transformations always meet with the same applause; the more so as, from the great variety, all are not shown on the same night. It occupies their minds too to puzzle out what the transformations or views mean, and then there is the laugh, &c. It may be unfit for Mr. Mayhew's purpose, but she thinks the fact worth mentioning."

The following requires no comment:—
"Sir,
"Seeing in your periodical an account of street Ballad-singing, I have ventured to pen a few remarks relative thereto. I have often stood to listen to the rude music of those ditties, and it struck me they were not disagreeable, and, being a student of music, I committed to memory the tunes and wrote them on paper; if your correspondents, therefore, should feel desirous of obtaining the music (of any street ballad) they can by communicating with me.
            I am, Sir,
                  "Yours truly,
                        "W.J. Barrett.
"No.2. Scot-street, North-street, Whitechapel-road."

The annexed epistle is printed not only as *a literary curiosity*, but also as an illustration of the character and language of a most peculiar class.
"Dear Friend,
"Excuse the liberty, since i saw you last i have not earned a (thickun) we have had such a (Dowry of Parny) that it completely (stumpted) or (Coopered) Drory the (Bossmans Patter) therefore i am (broke up) and not having

another friend but you i wish to know if you would lend me the price of 2 Gross of (Tops, Dies, or Croaks) which is 7 shillings of the above mentioned worthy and Sarah Chesham the (Essex Burick) for the Poisining job. they are both to be (Topped) at Spring-field (Sturabon) on Tuesday next. i hope you will oblige me if you can for it will be the means of putting a (Quid or a James) in my (Clye) I will call at your (Carser) on Sunday evening next for an answer, for i want to (Speel on the Drum) as soon as possible. hoping you and the family are quite (All Square)

"I Remain Your Obedient Servant

EXPLANATION OF THE ABOVE CANT.

Thickun ....means a Crown piece
Dowry of Parny..............a Lot of rain also water
Stumpted or...................Spoiled or no use
  Coopered
Bossman.........................a Farmer
Patter.............................a Trial
Broke Up ....No stock or the means
......................................to get it
Tops, Dies, or Croaks....An Execution
Burick ....A Woman
Sturaban.........................A Prison
Quid or James...............A Sovereign
Clye ....A Pocket
Carser............................A Gentleman's house
Speel on the Drum........going in the country
All Square......................All right, all well.

"You can put this in your work if you think proper.

"Yours Truly, &c. &c.
"____ ____."

The Manchester Bolt Makers send the following.

"Sir,

"I have been requested by a number of my fellow-tradesmen (bolt makers) to write to you, and get if possible your opinion upon the following question:—Is it possible to form a Loan Society in connection with the present Bolt-makers' Trade society?

"We feel our present weak and powerless state, partly through a want of union among our members, and not being able to compete against our employers' capital.

"As a means of strengthening our position we thought of a Loan Society (our tradesmen do borrow of others), but will it be secure? Can we lend to a shareholder, and recover the money? We could put our money into the Bank, but for the sake of the interest given, it is no use to put it there. If the above is untenable, can you throw out a suggestion that you think will be of any service?

"On behalf of my shopmates
"I remain,
"Yours respectfully,
"____ ____."

To prevent mistakes, and to avoid speaking on a subject that Mr. Mayhew knows nothing about, the above inquiry was referred to a legal gentleman who takes great interest in the welfare of the working-classes. His answer is as follows:—

"I do not see anything to prevent the Boltmakers' Trade Society from forming the proposed Loan Society among themselves, and recovering money from a shareholder. The scheme of the Friendly Societies, upon which the Loan Society is founded, is that of vesting all the property [legally] in a trustee or treasurer which precludes all quibbles as to partnership."

Legally, then, there appears to be no difficulty nor does there seem to be any economical objection to the proposed scheme. But Mr. Mayhew, when he comes to treat of the remedies for low wages, will enter more fully into this part of the subject.

ANSWERS TO CORRESPONDENTS.
[No.24, 24 MAY 1851]

Edited out:
EMILY C.; E.L.; M.H.

The Cases for binding Vol.I. of "London Labour" are now ready, and may be had of all persons supplying the periodical.

The following is printed in the hopes of convincing the sceptical.

"My Dear Madam,

"I have seen the poor Poet whose story Mr. Mayhew has told, in his great work on the lives of the poor. It was a grief to me to find, from the opinion of one of the first surgeons in London, who, to oblige me, visited him, that he is *incurable*. I had hoped that care and science might help him, but find that opiates are the only source of relief he can look for upon this earth. These my friend has supplied him with, for he found no respite to his agony in the paltry remedy upon which for five weary months he has depended to preserve him from 'going mad,' as he said. I have not felt myself at liberty to reveal the fact that I am acquainted with him, and that he is the original of that simple, touching, *truthful*, artistic picture found in No. 14 of 'London Labour.' What I read there, I saw in his room, and how much more, that a bungler would have caught at to work up into something that the world would pronounce exaggerated. As it is, there are people who presume to say this of some of Mr. Mayhew's tales, such classes as the ignorant, and even the good, who are ready to believe what they *hope*, namely that they are overdrawn. To these, *if I had permission*, I would gladly speak, in justice towards a great power and a truthful accuracy which *I* never doubted, and of which it is almost a presumption in me to speak. I need only add the last words the poor poet spoke to me, "If Heaven had sent you to me a little sooner, I might have been saved." Perhaps not, but he shall not be utterly neglected, even though his case is hopeless.

"I am,

"My Dear Madam,

"Yours very truly,

"F.C."

The poor harp-player has sent the subjoined:—

"B. Foster returns his most sincere thankes to the Gentlemen that have been so kind to assist him with a harp, and begs to inform them that he goes out to evening parties for 5s.

"No. 46, Eagle-Street, Red Lion-square."

"W.E.C. presents her compliments to Mr. MAYHEW, and would be pleased (if it occasion no breach of confidence between Mr. Mayhew and his informants) to know whether the blind man whose portrait is engraved in the 'London Labour,' and with whose person W.E.C. is familiar, is the same man as he who gives so interesting an account of the loss of his dogs, in the same number of that publication."—Yes.

The funds entrusted to Mr. MAYHEW being all lent out, the following letter is printed in the hopes of inducing some gentleman or lady to make the required advance:—

"Sir,—I am exceedingly sorry to trespass upon your valuable time, but knowing the great interest you take in the poor, I make no further apology. My name may probably be familiar to you as the author of a small work recently published, entitled 'Our Labouring classes," &c., &c., for which you kindly subscribed; and though this work may contain nothing new, yet it will at least be an evidence that I am also actuated by a desire to do good to those around me. I am not, sir, a street-seller at present, but how soon I may be obliged to adopt that mode of life I cannot tell, as I have a wife and four young children to keep, and not upon an average above 9s. per week to keep them with. I however manage to keep clear of debt, and I am therefore thankful. But to the purpose of this letter—I have, sir, a brother-in-law, who has been for years idly wandering about the country and living in low lodging-houses, I fear no better than a vagrant. He is now, however, desirous of honourably earning his living, and as he has been living with us for a few weeks past, I sent him out last Saturday night with a barrow of old books (I am a bookseller), promising him a small commission on what was sold. The beginning was encouraging, as out of bad and small stock 6s. 1d. was taken. From this the rent of the barrow (6d.) had to be deducted. I believe therefore that a living might be obtained for him, and myself also find considerable advantage if I had a barrow of my own and a little stock to send him out every day. If, therefore, sir, you could by any means lend me, or obtain for me the loan of 2£ *i.e.*, 1£ 10s. for the barrow and 10s. for the stock, for a short time, I will faithfully return the same at about 1s. per week, with moderate interest. I can give you satisfactory references for myself, and no doubt obtain security. I will take the responsibility on myself, so there will be no risk from my brother-in-law, and it will save him from at least the workhouse. I have resided more than two years at my present address.—I am sir your obedient servant,

S.C."

The annexed is from the CRIPPLED NUTMEG-GRATER SELLER. It requires no comment:—

"24 Bond-street,
"June 2, 1851.

"MR. MAYHEW.

"Sir,—I cannot express my gratitude to you in this letter, for while writing I am so different in my feelings to what I was before I saw you, that I am inwardly quite another being. Had I been like others, I should have had no difficulty in expressing perhaps what to them would have been but ordinary gratitude, but to you and those who, through you, have so altered my condition, I can but give you my blessings and my thanks; and at the same time let you know what I have done with the money sent for my benefit. I have bought a good suit of new clothes, furniture for my home, a donkey and cart, and am getting in a stock of goods, to leave off going about the streets as I did before you saw me.

"I am having some bills printed, and shall go round London in the General Line. I have written to the Superintendent of the L division for leave to have a stand of goods in Lambeth-walk on each Saturday night, having obtained the permission of two shopkeepers (Mr. Hall and Mr. Page) to do so. Returning my most sincere thanks to you and those who have so kindly assisted me, and also to Mrs. Mayhew for her very great kindness to me,

"I am,
"Your very obedient humble
"& afflicted Servant,
"CHARLES ALLOWAY."

"Sir,
"In looking over the number of your journals, as I cannot personally thank these who have assisted me, I beg most humbly to acknowledge the following subscriptions from

	£.	s.	d.
D.	0	4	0
M.P.	0	10	0
B.W.	0	3	0
E.H.	0	1	0
A Comforter	0	1	0
A Purchaser from the first.	0	2	6
E.J.S.	0	5	0
A Sympathizer	0	5	0
Two Ladies, Lymington	0	5	0
3 Sympathizers.	0	4	0
R—, Liverpool	0	5	0
P.P.	1	0	0
Miss L.C.F.	0	10	0
C.E.	0	5	0
F.W.	0	2	0
E.F.R.P.	0	5	0
S.E.K., Pevensey	1	10	0
Newcastle-upon-Tyne	0	3	0
St. John's Gate	0	10	6
Some Servants in Eaton-square.	0	1	8
C.O.U.P., Macclesfield	0	7	6
J.H.	0	10	0
A Belgravian	0	10	0
W.L.H.	0	5	0
A Lady left at 69, Fleet-street	0	5	0
By Mr. How (collected)	2	1	0
A Gentleman	0	7	0

This last subscription was given to me yesterday, for which I am truly grateful, and wish you to know that I have received it."

ANSWERS TO CORRESPONDENTS.
[No.28, 21 JUNE 1851]

The following is one of many similar inquiries:—

"DEAR SIR,—Might I trespass so far upon your valuable time as to ask you to oblige me with the address of some poor sempstresses or milliners who are known to you through the medium of your laborious and most praiseworthy investigations on behalf of the poor? Mrs. B. is anxious, as far as lies in her power, to employ some and induce her friends to do so, instead of proceeding to the shops. With many apologies for troubling you,

"Believe me, dear sir, yours very sincerely,
"C.J.B."

Mr. Mayhew objects, on principle, to comply with any such request as the above. The best way of serving the members of such trades as are underpaid is to encourage those shopkeepers only who are known to pay good prices for their work. The names of these it is Mr. Mayhew's intention to publish in his future inquiries, under the sanction of the several trade societies, so that those gentlemen or ladies who really wish to benefit the workpeople may have it in their power so to do. Were the public aware of the evils of the small master system, (or the chamber-master, or garret-master, or jobbing-master systems, as they are sometimes called,) that is to say, of converting workpeople into petty-traders seeking and obtaining employment on their own account, such applications as the present would seldom or never be made. The small master can only compete with the large by employing cheap labour or labouring himself underprice. The advantages that the large master derives from the extent of his capital, the small master can only seek to counterbalance by the use of inferior materials and workmanship. As society is at present constituted, the capitalist and the labourer are two distinct individuals. And the union of the two functions in separate persons is generally a great evil. The only mode in which the combination of the functions of capital and labour can be carried out so as to be able to compete with the large employers is by association; that is to say, by the aggregation of a number of small capitals possessed by working-men into one large "joint stock," so as to produce a sufficiently extensive capital to compete with the large masters. By these means, and perhaps by these means only, can operatives obtain *direct* employment for their labour without injury to their trades. That

middlemen, whether in the form of employers or distributors, are great evils, there cannot be the least question; but assuredly it is a much greater evil to revert to the primitive economic principles, and employ the labourer directly, for the loss of time in seeking a market for that labour, and the precariousness of employment necessarily connected with such a mode of work, must entail a larger proportion of misery, as indeed may be seen in those trades where the system of small masters—that is to say, of the direct employment of journeymen—has been introduced. Until some system of association or co-operation can be successfully carried out among operatives, it is better that people who wish well to the working-classes should give their work to those employers who are known to mean and do well to their journeymen. The names of such parties Mr. Mayhew will, so far as his knowledge goes, always be happy to supply. The names of journeymen, on the other hand, he must beg to withhold, especially as he has reason to believe that they are often requested with a view of getting work done at cheaper rate than the ordinary prices of the trade.

W.H. of Manchester says:—
"Sir,
"I am sorry to find that you take the Feargus O'Connor[30] view of the machinery question, and seem to think we should be better off were it all destroyed; now suppose you had the power to 'smash' all the machinery in England to-night, I should like to know what the factory hands in this district would do for their wages *next* Saturday.

"I cannot see by your 'explanations' you have altered the fact, that 'wages are regulated by the law of supply and demand:' when there are two masters to one man, wages will be high, when there are two men to one master, they will be low."

"___"

The gentleman is under a mistake. Mr.

---

[30] Feargus O'Connor (1794-1855), Chartist leader, editor of the *Northern Star*, pronounced insane in 1852.

Mayhew does not object to machinery in the abstract. To be able to produce a greater quantity of commodities with an equal quantity of labour, *should be* the greatest possible benefit to the producers; machinery, therefore, which enables us to attain such an end, *ought to be* the greatest blessing. As it is, however, it enables society to do its work with fewer hands, and so transforms those labourers who would willingly work for their living into either paupers or criminals. People who take the opposite view, that is to say, that machinery increases the demand for labour, have to prove how it is that, since machinery has been invented, crime and pauperism have increased at so fearful a pace. The machinery advocates have also to account for the fact that, since the establishment of the London Saw Mills, no less than 2000 workmen have been thrown out of employ. Admitting that the number of operatives in the cotton districts themselves have been increased, it still remains to be shown whether there are more hands employed in the spinning of cotton in Great Britain now than formerly. One hundred years ago the wife of almost every labourer throughout the kingdom followed this occupation, and at present there is not one so engaged. More cotton may be spun by steam, but are there more spinners? But, even though there *were* more spinners, and machinery, in this particular instance, had increased the employment—because the market for cotton is infinitely extensible—there can be no question that, in the case of sawing by steam, it has pauperized a large proportion of the sawyers, and that simply because the market for sawn wood cannot be extended.

That wages are *not* regulated by supply and demand, the reduced payment for work in the London Cabinet Trade, where the hands have declined and the work increased, is *indisputable evidence*. Those who say wages *are* determined by the above law must show how the facts of this trade can be so explained. From 1831 to 1841 the number of journeymen Cabinet-makers in London declined 33 per cent. Work during the same period increased considerably, 200 miles of streets having been built, and, nevertheless, in 1831 wages were 400 per cent. better than in 1841. *Verbum sap.*: a word to the *wise*.

The following is from Guernsey:—

"Sir,

"In perusing your charming book on the 'London Poor,' for which allow me, as a clergyman of the Church of England, to thank you most sincerely, I perceived you somewhat hesitated to give a derivation for 'haberdasher.' Would you allow me to derive it from 'Girbzn' (haben), 'to have,' and 'Yüssur' (Tücher), 'clothes.'

"'Ich habe Tücher,' 'I have clothes'—*i.e.*, 'Haberdasher'.

"By the by, 'Patter' is twice used by Sir Walter Scott, in 'Ivanhoe,' and 'Bride of Lammermoor.'

"Ever, sir, yours,
"NEMO."

"P.S.—Possibly 'Haberdashers' may have been the first retail sellers of 'Saxony cloths,' whence the German derivation."

The above etymology is ingenious, but, it is feared, incorrect—at least, proof is wanted. There are but two modes of derivation—the *historic* and the *dialectic*. Historic derivation traces the origin of words *within* the language itself. In this form of etymology the signification of the word is altered, but the mode of writing remains the same. In dialectic derivation, however, the origin of the word is traced outside the language, and the *mode of writing the word is changed* (according to certain canons) *while the signification remains the same*. The rules for the changes of consonants in dialectic derivation, have been laid down by Grimm, those for the changes of vowels by Bopp; and etymology is mere childish guesswork, unless made to conform to these laws.

The derivation of "Duffer" as well as "Haberdasher" are as yet unproven. The word "Pedlar" is derived from the German *Bettler*, and the Dutch *Bedelaar*, signifying a beggar. This is proved not only by the changes of letters (for the Saxon P equals the German B), but by the German Bettel-Merck (literally beggar's merchandise), signifying Pedlar's-wares, trifles, &c.

G.P. writes as follows:—

"Sir,

"Being a subscriber to your valuable "London Labour," I have taken the liberty of addressing these few lines to you, in order that I may obtain your advice on going to Australia. I have relations there that strongly recommend me to come out. I have not the means of procuring the sum required by the Emigration Commissioners. I am a cabinet-maker by trade, and can turn my hand to the carpentering, or make myself useful in anything connected with the wood line. I can be well recommended for ability from some of the best shops where I have worked, also for sobriety and honesty—if that be any good to a man. I am willing to work my passage over, or sign articles to any master for a term, as long as I can get to Australia. I am a married man and have got two children. I have sent two letters to Lord Ashley, but he has never taken any notice of them. Since then a gentleman has told me Lord Ashley never did any good, but where it was made *public*. I offered my services to him to go as assistant to a schoolmaster, as I heard he was sending out children from the ragged schools. Nothing, sir, would give me greater delight than to be placed in any position where my little abilities would be of service to my fellow creatures. Do you think if I was to advertise in the *Times* newspaper it would be any good, offering myself to an employer to go with him? I am out of work at present, therefore I am unable to do anything where money is wanted to procure my passage. You see, sir, I wish to get out of my misery as soon as possible. It is an old saying, "stare poverty in the face and it will turn its back on you;" but I've found it at times stick closer to me than a brother, though I am not so bad off as many I read of. My home is comfortable, but I often think when I read your book what a tale of poverty I could tell on my first coming to London; there are so many cases like my own—but perseverance has put me a little better footing.

"Sir, whatever you should suggest would be my best plan to act on I will do it."

The best way of assisting the writer of the above is to print his letter. Some readers may perhaps have it in their power to obtain a passage for the poor fellow. That it is but prudent for a journeyman cabinet-maker to wish to quit a country where the remuneration for his labour is annually becoming worse, surely none can doubt; and were gentlefolks as intimately acquainted with the miseries and privations suffered by the cabinet-makers of London as the writer of these words, they would consider it but their duty to help to free the men from their present wretchedness. Mr. Mayhew will, of course, satisfy himself that the writer of the above letter is worthy of assistance, before extending him any aid that those who may have it in their power to help him may feel inclined to grant.

⁎ The Loan Fund account is deferred till next week for want of space. The document is as interesting as it is curious, proving beyond doubt the honesty of the poor.

ANSWERS TO CORRESPONDENTS.
[No.29, 28 JUNE 1851]

Edited out: F.C.

A Subscriber at Gateshead makes the following inquiry:—

"Sir,

"Will you oblige by informing me what will be the probable duration of the issue of 'London Labour and the London Poor,' as the time it will be in finishing is of some importance, and I have a particular reason for asking, and one which will materially, in all probability contribute to the sale of your exceedingly useful work. You will much oblige by giving an answer in the last number of your ensuing part, although I know it is perhaps not usual, but I have no doubt you will be kind enough to do so in this instance.

"I am, with best wishes,

"Yours &c.,

"Beauclerc."

It is impossible to return a definite answer;

but it is believed some years—probably five or six.

The following requires no comment, as no conclusions were drawn from the fact:—

"Sir,

"Having myself been a journeyman, and now being an employer, I feel great interest in the wage question now being discussed on the covers of your excellent work on 'London Labour and the London Poor.' In the Number for March 22, the establishment of M. Leclaire it referred to as an example of the 'Equitable Wage Principle.' As soon as I read this, it occurred to me, that I had seen it stated that M. Leclaire had either become bankrupt, or that his establishment was broken up, but I could not at first recollect where I had seen the statement; but upon reflection and reference, I found it so stated in the 'Art-Union Journal' for July, 1848, p. 213, near the bottom of the middle column, to which I beg respectfully to refer you. There is also another article on the Wage Question at p. 182 of the same volume.

"Yours respectfully,

"R.H."

The following account [opposite] of the moneys entrusted to MR. MAYHEW, to dispense for the benefit of the poor, as well of the manner in which the trust has been fulfilled, is presented to the readers of this periodical with considerable satisfaction; since it demonstrate what MR. MAYHEW has so often endeavoured to enforce—that the industrious poor of this country are as essentially honest as they are truthful, and especially to those whom they believe to sympathise with and to be anxious to relieve their sufferings. Of all people they have the keenest sense of and most lasting gratitude for benefits received—though this is but natural, seeing that the feelings and sentiments with them exist in all their native simplicity; and they are not sufficiently educated to indulge in the artifices and simulations of polite society. "When the terrible infliction of insanity," says Dr. Conolly, in his work "On the Construction and Government of Lunatic Asylum", p. 118, "falls upon the rich, it finds them more prepared to exhibit all its most varied and agitated aspects, and *perhaps less open to consolation from sympathy or kind attention than the poor; their intellectual faculties are more developed than those of the class living by manual labour, and their affections are less open to simple expressions.*"[31] Two years' close association with what are called the "lowest classes" has proved the justice of these remarks; for it has been invariably found by MR. MAYHEW that "those who have seen better days" constitute the worst class of the poor. The experience of the *Morning Chronicle*, where £800 was dispensed, went to show that the least faith of all was to be placed in the "broken-down gentlefolks;" though they were the class that generally obtained the most sympathy. The comparative unworthiness of this class might, however, have been inferred *à priori*, seeing that, though originally possessed of

FOOTNOTES TO TABLE OPPOSITE

a At present three weeks in arrears on account of ill-health.

b Nine weeks in arrears.

c Mr. Mayhew has known this person for some time, and the loan was granted to enable the man to obtain an honest livelihood by selling pictures; he is now in the country trading with the above capital and it is believed leading a new life.

d Keeps up her repayments with regularity.

e Repaid the whole as promised—the loan was of great service.

f Pays punctually and is doing well.

g Has only made one repayment, now six weeks in arrear.

h To be repaid in quarterly payments, none due yet.

i Promised to repay 1s. per week; there are eight weeks due and no repayment made.

j Pays regularly.

k Ditto ditto.

l Three weeks in arrear.

m Pays regularly and it much benefited by the loan.

n Pays regularly.

o To be repaid in monthly instalments, the first not due yet.

p Pays regularly.

q Nothing due yet.

r Ditto ditto.

s Ditto ditto.

31 Dr Conolly, *On the Construction and Government of Lunatic Asylum and Hospitals for the Insane*, John Churchill, 1847.

	Dr.	£ s. d.		Cr.	£ s. d.	£ s. d.	Dr. £ s. d.
1851.	To Cash Received of		1851.	*By Gifts to*			Repayments on Account of Loans
Feb. 8	L.C.F.	0 10 0		Poor Harpist' a harp	2 10 0		
	G.P.	1 0 0		Agnes M & J.W.,			
15	G.W.M	0 5 0		two poor needle-			
22	E.B.	0 5 0		women	0 5 0		
March 1	C.B.	0 3 0		Poor Blind Tailor	0 7 0		
8	W.F.P.	0 2 6		Poor Poet	0 16 0		
15	Kilvarlock	0 5 0		Blind Tape Seller	0 8 0		
22	G.B.	0 2 6		Crippled Seller of			
29	F.P.	1 0 0		Nutmeg-Graters	0 4 0	4 10 0	
	Rev. J.S.	0 15 0					
	Stranger	0 2 6		*By Loans to*			
	An Old Harpist . . .	0 5 0		[a] Reduced Tradesman . . .	1 5 0		. . . . 0 8 0
April 5	Cantab.	0 0 6		[b] Costermonger	1 0 0		. . . . 0 2 0
	C.A.	0 5 0		[c] Burglar	0 7 6		
	C.B.	0 11 0		[d] Toy seller	0 5 0		. . . . 0 2 6
	E.F.R.P.	0 5 0		[e] Tailor	0 10 0		. . . . 0 10 6
	P.P.	1 0 0		[f] Showman	1 15 0		. . . . 0 6 0
	Comforter	0 5 0		[g] "Flower girl"	0 10 0		. . . . 0 0 6
	Parkins	0 10 0		[h] Reduced Gentle-			
	A purchaser	0 2 6		woman	1 0 0		
8	B.W.	0 3 0		[i] Nutmeg-Grater			
	E.H.	0 1 0		Seller	9 17 0		
	D.	0 4 0		[j] Blind Tailor	1 2 6		. . . . 0 3 0
	E.J.S.	0 5 0		[k] Street Stationer	0 10 0		. . . . 0 2 0
	Sympathiser	0 5 0		[l] Chairmender	0 5 0		. . . . 0 1 0
	O.E.W.	0 5 0		[m] Street Pen-seller	0 15 0		. . . . 0 3 0
	F.W.	0 2 6		[n] Charwoman	0 10 0		. . . . 0 3 0
15	L.C.F., 2nd sub-			[o] Street Rhubarb-			
	scription	0 10 0		seller	1 10 0		
	E.F.R.P., 2nd sub-			[p] Servant for clothes			
	scription	0 15 0		to obtain a place	0 10 0		. . . . 0 1 6
	B.F.B.	1 10 0		[q] Dealer in Sausage			
16	Rev. Mr. B.	1 0 0		Skins	2 0 0		
19	A.B.C.	0 5 0		[r] Profile Cutter	0 5 0		
	M.C.	0 1 0		[s] Street Milliner	0 10 0	24 7 0	
	Two Ladies (Lea-						2 3 0
	ington)	0 5 0		To expenses:			
	Three sympathisers	0 4 0		Books for Accounts		0 10 0	
	R.J.	0 5 0					
	J.	0 2 0				29 7 0	
	"No more, &c." . . .	0 1 0					
22	E.S.M.A.	0 5 0					
	M.M.	2 0 0					
23	A.B.C., 2nd sub-						
	scription	0 10 0					
24	S.E.K.	1 0 0					
	W.M.B.	0 5 0					
29	Mrs. D. (Doncaster)	1 0 0					
30	Newcastle-on-Tyne.	0 3 0					
May 1	W.C.	0 10 6					
2	C.O.M.	0 7 6					
6	J.S.	1 0 0					
	T.L.	0 8 0					
7	J.H.	0 10 0					
10	A Belgravian	0 5 0					
13	Some servants						
	in Euston-square.	0 1 6					
	C.	0 5 0					
	Rev. J.E.	1 10 0					
	H.	0 10 0					
	A Wellwisher	0 3 6					
	Rev. J.R.	0 2 6					
	W.L.M.	0 5 0					
	E.L.	0 2 6					
	Emily C.	0 3 0					
	F.	2 0 0					
	M.H.	0 5 0					
	. . . .	27 10 0					
	To repayments						
	as above	2 3 0		Balance		0 6 0	
		29 13 0				29 13 0	

friends who could assist them, they had, by their continued want of energy, or prudence, or principle, exhausted the patience and benevolence of their own kindred. The present account shows that £27 10s. have been received, £4 10s. of which have been dispensed as gifts, and £24 10s. advanced as loans to 19 people, to be repaid in small instalments, with interest, at the rate of £5 per cent. per annum. Of the 19 borrowers, it will be seen that only 4 are defaulters; a proportion so small, that when the precariousness of the pursuits of the people are taken into consideration, as well as the slight legal hold there can be upon persons whose lodgings are almost necessarily changed every few weeks, the honesty of the poor street-folk—beset with temptations as they are—must appear to strangers almost marvellous.

The books and vouchers of the above accounts lie at the office, for the inspection of any persons who may be interested in the matter. MR. MAYHEW would take it as a favour if some gentleman would audit them.

ANSWERS TO CORRESPONDENTS.
[No.30, 5 JULY 1851]

W.H., of Manchester, sends the following reply to the remarks on machinery printed among the Notices to Correspondents in No. 28.

"Sir,—Though I am not convinced, I am much obliged for 'a word to the wise,' in the last number of your excellent work, and as I presume we both wish to arrive at the truth, I will take the liberty of making a remark or two on your notice of my letter.

"You state that when machinery is introduced into a business it at once throws a greater or smaller number of hands out of work, who immediately become either paupers or criminals, which I deny; for I find that in the year 1811, the proportion per head on the total population expended for the relief of the poor was 13s. 1d., whilst in the year 1841 it was only 6s. 2d. per head." [This is no argument, for, owing to the alteration effected by the New Poor Law, in 1834, the expenditure was in two years reduced from 6,000,000£. to 4,000,000£. In 1840, however, the ratio of the paupers, under the amended administration, to the gross population was 7.7 per cent.; in 1848 it was 10.8, and the increase was regular.] I have not the criminal statistics for the same period at hand," continues W. H., "but I have no doubt they exhibit a similar falling off." [In 1811 the number of criminals in England and Wales was 1 in every 1883 of the population; in 1848 it was 1 in 570, an increase amounting to no less than 468 per cent.]

"As for the displacement of labour by machinery, I will give you an extract from a little work in my possession: 'If the case of the handloom weavers be adduced as an example of the permanent displacement of labour by machinery, and if it be contended that it is the natural result of machinery to diminish employment in other trades, we must necessarily infer that wherever machinery has been largely introduced into any trade, the number of persons supported by it must have been diminished. We should infer that the agricultural population of this country must have been rapidly increasing, while the population engaged in those branches of manufacture in which steam power is used, must have been falling off or increasing less rapidly.

"'The correctness of such an inference may be estimated by the following facts. Between 1801 and 1841, Manchester increased in population from 90,399 to 296,183, or 227·5 per cent.; Liverpool, 231·5 per cent.; Leeds, 185·6 per cent.; Bradford, 440·5 per cent.; Bolton, 185·7 per cent., and so on.'" [But these statistics tell us only the numbers of those who have taken to spinning, &c., in the manufacturing districts; they do not show us the per contra side, viz.: *how many wives and daughters ceased spinning at home in the agricultural and other districts.*] "'Let us now compare these places with those agricultural countries in which machinery has exercised the least influence, and let us see if the absence of machinery has been equally favourable to the support of a growing population. In the same period, 1801 to 1841, Devon increased 55·3 per cent.; Somerset, 59 per cent.; Norfolk, 50·9 per cent.; Lincoln, 73·5 per cent.;

Essex, 52 per cent.; and Suffolk, 49·5 per cent. The average increase of these six agricultural counties did not exceed 50 per cent. in 40 years; while, setting aside the extraordinary increase exhibited in the towns already enumerated, the population of six manufacturing countries, viz. Lancaster, Middlesex, York (West Riding), Stafford, Chester, and Durham, *including all the agriculturists*, increased 112·5 per cent.'

"I hope, sir, these facts will set at rest your fears that England is going to pauperism and ruin in consequence of her immense productive power; and, for my part, I do not see how you can like machinery 'in the abstract' and not in any other shape. You appear to believe that machinery has been a curse to us instead of a blessing, and think it had been better had the steam-engine and the power-loom never been invented.

"I should like to know why 'the market for cotton is infinitely extensible,' and 'the market for sawn wood cannot be extended?' I can assure you that here, at least, the market for sawn-wood *has* extended considerably within the last ten years." [See below.]

"You will find that the general market rate of wages depends upon the ratio which the capital applied to the employment of labour bears to the number of labourers. If that ratio be great, the competition of capitalists must raise wages; if small, the competition of labourers amongst each other for employment must reduce them." [Did W.H. ever hear of the "relief in aid of wages" which was so general under the old Poor Laws? If so, will he show how the reduction of wages which was the necessary result of such a system is explicable by the canon of supply and demand for labour. Given the same quantity of work to be done and the same number of hands to do it, and yet—supply and demand remaining the same—*wages fall*.]

"I must apologize for the length of my letter, but I venture to hope that you will be able to find room for it in an early number of your work.

"Believe me,
"Yours respectfully,
"W.H."

The above letter is printed entire, so that the arguments advanced may have their full sway. To estimate the validity of these proofs attention must be drawn once more to the distinction so often pointed out in this periodical between those productions for which the market is *infinitely (or largely) extensible* and those for which the market is *necessarily limited*, and then we shall be in a position to understand how machinery can be applied beneficially (to the workmen) *only in the former case*. It is because W.H. is unable to apprehend this difference that he finds so much difficulty in discriminating between the use and abuse of machinery. But seeing that the most acute of the economists are in the same muddle, we can hardly wonder that W.H., who talks of supply and demand with true economical glibness, should be as confused on the subject as the gentlemen from whom he derives his ideas. That the supply of those commodities which serve to gratify *universal* wants and desires (such as articles of food, clothing, &c.) admits of almost indefinite increase, there cannot be the least question. Anything, therefore, which tends to decrease the cost of their production can but serve to extend the market for them, and so to give additional employment to the operatives engaged in their manufacture. If the diminution of the cost of production be brought about by a diminution of the labour, that is to say, by causing the workman (by means of machinery or some new tool) to produce a greater quantity of the commodities with the same amount of exertion, then the cheapening of the cost of production in connection with such commodities is a benefit both to producer and consumer, giving to the operative increased employment without decrease of pay, as well as the power of purchasing a greater quantity of necessaries at a less price. But if the cost of production be cheapened by making the workman do a greater quantity of work (without any mechanical aid whatever), and so causing him to give a greater amount of exertion for the same pay, or an equal amount for less pay, then the operatives are injured by the cheapness as much as the public and the moneymongers are benefited by it, *at their expense.* It is idle in such cases to say that diminution of the cost of production causes increased employment—since the pretended advantage merely amounts to the very questionable benefit, that *the working men have a greater quantity of work to do for the same wages.*

Such are the two opposite results of cheapness in connection with those commodities for which the market is *infinitely or largely extensible.* The one, cheapness, is as beneficial as the other is injurious to the working classes; and the cause of the difference should be continually borne in mind, viz., that *in the first case the workman is enabled to produce a greater quantity of goods with the same amount of labour; whereas, in the second, he is forced to produce a greater quantity by working both harder and longer.*

But if the introduction of mechanical aid is a benefit to the labourer in connection with those articles of which the supply admits of being *indefinitely increased,* it is far different with *those other articles for which the market is necessarily limited.* That there *are* such articles, and large classes of such articles too, it is highly important that we should bear in mind. De Quincey, in his "Logic of Political Economy," p. 231, has put this point so clearly and unmistakably, that it will be better to quote his words than run the risk of obscuring what he has rendered so distinct. "There are many articles," says he, "for which the market *is absolutely limited by a preexisting system to which those articles are attached as subordinate parts or members.* How could we force the dials and faces of time-pieces, by artificial cheapness, to sell more plentiful,—than the minor works or movements of such time-pieces? Could the sale of wine-vaults be increased without increasing the sale of wine? Or the tools of shipwrights find an enlarged market, whilst shipbuilding was stationary?* * * Offer to a town of 3000 inhabitants a stock of hearses, no cheapness will tempt that town into buying more than one." It is the same with all class productions. Publish "Fearn on Contingent Remainders" in penny numbers, and how many extra copies would be sold? Is it possible, by cheapening the cost of production, to get rid

of more barristers' wigs than there are barristers, or to sell of dolls' eyes more than double the number of dolls? To use the words of De Quincey, "the articles are past counting which are so interorganized with other articles" that *no diminution in their price can possibly give rise to an extension of their sale.*

Now the market for such articles being *necessarily limited,* and the quantity required consequently *definite,* it follows that, in such cases, the application of machinery causing that quantity to be produced with a less amount of labour—or, what is the same thing, a smaller number of labourers—must necessarily have the effect of throwing out of employment a number of workmen, *precisely proportional to the amount of labour saved.*

W.H. will now be in a position to comprehend how the sawing of wood by machinery has been as great an injury to the sawyers as the spinning of cotton by steam has been a benefit to the cotton spinners. The market for cotton goods is infinitely extensible; hence to cheapen the cost of production by enabling the workmen to produce a greater quantity with less labour, is to cause a greater supply to be required. Sawn wood, however, is one of those articles of which the supply does not admit of indefinite increase; the quantity annually required being necessarily limited by the quantity of houses and carriages, ships, furniture, &c., to be constructed in the course of the year. To saw more wood annually than is needed for the new buildings, vehicles, and vessels every year, would be precisely the same as to produce more than twice as many dolls' eyes as there are dolls. Hence the application of machinery to the sawyers' trade can but have the effect of enabling a smaller number of hands to execute the *requisite* and *fixed* amount of work; while the superseded hands must either seek employment at other trades or become paupers or criminals. If they do not or cannot work for themselves, they must, of course, live on the labour of others in one or other of the above capacities. Can any one with a thimbleful of brains in his skull believe that the threshing of corn by steam can *increase the employment* of the threshers? Surely the quantity of corn to be threshed is *lim-*

ited by the quantity of corn produced; and if by steam-threshing one man can do the work of a dozen, then, of course, eleven out of every twelve of the threshers must be thrown out of work by it.

W.H. should give over reading *little* works in his possession, and study Ricardo for a month or two. That W.H. *wishes* to go right, is evident.

ANSWERS TO CORRESPONDENTS.
[No.31, 12 JULY 1851]

Edited out:
Ref To N. BAILEY, MINSHEW, DR. SRUSLER AND DIEDRICH KNICKERBOCKER & IMAGINATIVE METAPHOR-ICAL ETYMOLOGIES OF HABERDASHER, AND HOLBORN

The following is from one of the bestknown of the Street-Poets, of whose services Mr. Mayhew purposes availing himself when treating of the ballad-singers:—

"Trusting you will pardon the liberty I have taken in thus intruding on your valuable time and attention, I beg to say that some time since a person connected with your establishment called on me, and at the same time stated that probably I should hear from you, and I should have esteemed it a great pleasure to have had that favour granted me. Respecting your work of the 'London Labour,' &c., I have, sir, been connected with the street-labour 35 years, and, since 1818, written most publications, doggrels, &c., beginning with the last years of George the Third, the life of Thistlewood, Thurtell, Probert, Fauntleroy, &c., &c.; the Ascension of George the Fourth, the Life and Death of Queen Caroline, and continually up to this moment for London, Birmingham, Liverpool, Manchester, Norwich, Exeter, Plymouth, and for travellers in different parts of the country, so that I am acquainted, having been a street-labourer 35 years, with the greatest part of the street and country fraternity. Most of those who deal in writing-paper, trinkets, &c., have risen from ballad singing. The old ditties published

for 30 years past are still in my memory, and might have proved useful to the work before the public; and if not too late, will now answer the same purpose. I have read and admire your work, as I consider it most useful information. If I can be of any service to you in giving any necessary intelligence required for the work before the public I shall be most happy, and consider it a great pleasure to render all the assistance in my power for the completion of your valuable work. During the past winter I had some poetry to get ready for Mr.—, and Mr.—, Fetter-lane, and gave them every satisfaction. Some years since I wrote the history of the river Thames from Sheerness to Hampton-court in verse, for a party; and I believe there is no one that has had any conversations with you respecting the street-sellers better able to give a fair, full, and satisfactory account of the same than myself. Should you, kind sir, feel disposed to grant me an interview, I will be ready at any moment it may be convenient to you to meet you. And as I am on the eve of removing from my present abode on account of the property being sold— the sooner the *better,* however—I would be thankful if you will be pleased to drop me a line in answer to this, let the consequence be what it may. Many of the verses of Queen Caroline, and up to the present day of most others, I can rectify. The lives of Corder, Greenacre, Good, &c., &c., were my simple production. Not wishing to intrude any longer on your notice, and fearing my long letter may tire you, the writing and legibility being not of the best description, I will for the present conclude,

"And remain,
"Your most obedient humble servant,"
"——."

The following etymological speculations or guesses are printed with a view to excite attention to the subject.

Gray's Inn, 23rd June, 1851.

"Sir,—As the word 'Haberdasher' seems still to puzzle the heads of the learned, I beg leave to add my mite of authority and speculation with reference to it. I propose first to begin on classic ground, from which so many popular expressions have sprung, for the origin of the word, and, failing here, to search for it in the best sources at my command...

[The Greek and Saxon long etymologies have been edited out.]

"Ash states the derivation of the word Haberdasher to be uncertain, and describes him as a dealer in small wares. Johnson, Sheridan, and Walker describe him, in addition, as a pedlar.

"In Shakspere's 'Taming of the Shrew,' Katherine, in speaking of the cap which the Haberdasher brings" [in one old dictionary I find Haberdasher defined as "a seller of caps"], says 'Gentlewomen wear such caps as these;' this was before the Sumptuary Laws, and speaks highly of the Haberdasher's wares. It is true that in Shakspere's 'Henry VIII.,' the porter's man says that among the crowd trying to get into the palace yard, 'there was a Haberdasher's wife of small wit that railed upon me till her pink'd parringer fell off her head from kindling such a combustion in the state'; but he adds, 'forty trunchoneers' (equal, it is presumed, to as many policemen) 'drew to her succour,' thereby showing that she was a person of some consequence, and probably employed upon some of the court pageantry." [But *query* as to the consequence and the court pageantry.]

"But, to descend a step in dignity, I find in the German and English Dictionary of Baily, Fahrenkrüger, the following derivation, which, if founded upon any authority, settles the question: 'Haberdasher (von *berdash* ein chemaligen Halstuchart)', Anglice, 'derived from *berdash*, a kind of neckerchief formerly worn;' so that, according to these lexicographers, Haberdasher meant a seller of berdashers. When we consider the aspirated 'a,' so natural to the Cockney, and call to mind the fact that Piccadilly got its name from something similar, the derivation is not to be despised. [The "position" (on dialectic philology) is not that of Mr. Mayhew, but the discovery of Grimm, and is now adopted by all philologists.]

.... I am afraid that I have mystified it more than ever.

"The word '*Bunmmaree*,' the derivation of which you state to be unknown, has excited my curiosity, and I subjoin what I can glean respecting it:—

"In the French Dictionary of 'Napoléon Landais,' I find the word '*Beaumaris* (prononcez Bô-ma-rie), gros poisson, espèce de squale;' and the definition of 'squale' is '(du Latin *squalus*, fait dans le même sens de *squalere*, être sale, crasseux, raboteux) genre de poissons cartilagineux. C'est dans ce genre, auquel appartiennent *les requins*, ou *chiens de͏̈ mer*, que se trouvent les plus gros poissons connus.' Most probably the 'scylium' or dog-fish of the British coast, which is of the shark tribe; hence the term 'Bummaree' may have been a term of reproach, equivalent to a 'shark,' or greedy man—the middlemen generally have been obnoxious to such epithets.

"Again, the word '*marée*', in French, signifies sea-fish generally; hence the name in question may come from the cry '*Beau-marée*,' 'prime sea-fish!' As the fisheries were formerly almost entirely in the hands of foreigners, this derivation seems not improbable. The term sea-fish, as distinguished from fresh-water fish, was more common formerly than now, inland places seldom seeing sea-fish; the cry, therefore, might have marked this distinction. Lucullus, who was a great gourmand, had lakes of salt-water for his sea-fish at his villa in Tusculum.

"I do not know whether Beaumaris, in the island of Anglesea, is pronounced Bô-ma-rie, if so, it might have something to do with the name 'Bummaree.'

"I must apologize for the length of this communication; but you will readily understand that one accustomed to follow facts as a matter of business, is apt to be led into a similar train when pursuing anything by way of amusement.

"Yours faithfully,
"WORTENKRÄMER."[32]

The suggestions above given are exceedingly ingenious, but unfortunately *unproven* in all

---

[32] This name is a pun on the German words *Wort* and *Krämer* meaning trader of words, or even haberdasher of words.

cases. As was before stated, if the word be derived from *without* the language, then the foreign root must bear precisely the same signification as the English word, but be spelt differently. Unless this can be adduced, or *proof* be given for the corruption of the original meaning, etymology is about as rational as the derivation of *Gherkin* from *King Jeremiah*. Cognate languages are to etymology what comparative anatomy is to natural history.

The first derivation of *Bunmaree* is very clever and almost satisfactory. What is a *berdash*?

ANSWERS TO CORRESPONDENTS.
[No.32, 19 JULY 1851]

Edited out:
L.J., F.C. & S.C.; LYMINGTON.

———————

The subjoined is printed entire because it is thought right to append a few words in answer to it:—

"Sir,—I consider that the perusal of your interesting papers on the London Poor will have an injurious effect on the minds of your readers if they do not endeavour to relieve the mass of wretchedness which they so vividly delineate. Many who object to giving money to casual beggars have no other channel through which to relieve distress. As this is my own case, may I trouble you to receive the inclosed 1£ for the use of any deserving person, or to be added to the Loan Fund. I believe this to be far the best way of giving money to the poor, and I am not at all surprised at the honesty with which such borrowed sums are repaid. I believe this to be the uniform experience of all who have tried this method of helping the poor. Few individuals have either the time or the ability for doing it themselves. But I have often wished that such loan societies, either local or parochial, could be formed. The capital, I think, should be subscribed and lent out without interest.

"Yours,
"S.D."

Mr. Mayhew differs, he regrets to say, with S.D. on the subject of interest. To allow the poor the use of money at less than the fair market value is to bestow alms upon them to precisely the extent of the deficient interest. The loans are advanced with the view of putting an end to the enormous usury that the humbler classes are obliged to pay by those who are too ready to trade on their necessities, and *certainly not with the view of teaching the poor that interest for money is wrong.* Mr. Mayhew is aware that this doctrine is held by many, but the arguments adduced in favour of it have always seemed to him to be inconclusive. Interest is literally rent paid for the use of money, that is to say, it is a share of the proceeds given for the use of the capital which, it should be remembered, contributes as much to the product as even the labourer himself. Let us not, in our wish to have justice done to the workman, forget what is due to the capitalist, who supplies the materials, tools, and subsistence, without which the cleverest operative would not only have no work to do, but no strength to do it even if he had the work. If by means of a loan of 100£, either in money or materials, I am enabled to produce, or obtain, something which I can exchange for 200£, surely the person helping me to such a result should receive a *portion* of the proceeds. Both justice and gratitude would prompt to such an act. Interest has been well defined to be the reward for saving or abstinence; if there were no reward there would be no saving, and consequently no capital; while, without capital, there could be no work. Mr. Mayhew wishes the poor to have the power of obtaining money at the same (but not a lower) rate than the rich. *At present it is precisely the reverse, for, though it is illegal to take more than 5 per cent. of a landlord, a pawnbroker is entitled, by Act of Parliament, to demand at the least 20 per cent. of the poor.* "I made a calculation," says Mr. Chadwick in his report on the poor of London and Berkshire, "as to the interest paid for their trifling loans at the pawn-shops, and found it to be as follows:

	Per cent.		Per cent.
A loan of 3d., if redeemed the same day, pays interest at the rate of .	5200	if in a week,	866
„ 4d. „ „	3900	„ „	650
„ 6d. „ ;.	2600	„ „	433
„ 9d. „ „	1733	„ „	288
„ 1s. „ „	1300	„ „	216

These are the iniquities that cry aloud for some remedy; and it is with a view to their abatement that the Loan Fund has been instituted.

W.H. retorts in the following strain concerning the remarks on his second letter printed in last week's Number:—

"Sir,—I am much obliged to you for the insertion of my last letter, and as I do not think you have adduced anything new in your answer to it, I must leave those to judge between us who take any interest in the matter.

"The *little* work from which I extracted is the 'Standard Library Cyclopaedia,' in four volumes, and contains hundreds of extracts from Ricardo, Mill, and other eminent writers on political economy." [This disjointed and inconsecutive reading is the great vice of the age; producing in the world as much chattering, on matters of which the talkers have no comprehension as there is in the parrot-room at the Zoological Gardens.] "I would recommend the work to your notice; possibly the study of it might remove some of your very gloomy ideas on the machinery question. I will observe, in conclusion, that I am sorry you should have thought it necessary to be severe in your remarks on my letter, for questions of this nature stand a much better chance of being properly discussed when treated of in a temperate manner."

Mr. Mayhew, intended nothing personal nor offensive to W.H. in the remarks appended to his letter of last week. If he have wounded the feelings of a gentleman whom he is satisfied *wishes* to go the right way, Mr. Mayhew regrets that he was not more guarded in his expressions. He is too happy at all times to attend to ideas in opposition to his own. All Mr. Mayhew requests is, that gentlemen with a taste for desultory reading will not occupy his time by repeating to him, for the thousandth time, the old opinions touching "supply and demand," and "machinery increasing employment," and such like dogmata. Any new fact or opinion he will be always ready to give every consideration to, but the continual disgorging of the *assumptions* of political economy, which Mr. Mayhew has found to be in no way borne out by facts, requires the patience of a quaker to tolerate. That these assumptions should be true is beyond the bounds of probability, for it is well known that Adam Smith, the founder of the *pseudo* science, when about to develop the laws of capital and labour, retired to an obscure Scotch village, and there sat thinking about them in his arm chair for fifteen years. As well might we suppose a person capable of excogitating in a back parlour the laws of Chemistry, or Natural History, or any other of those systematic aggregation of facts which we term sciences. That the canon of supply and demand for labour does not regulate wages has been, it was thought, proved over and over again in this periodical; but, as some may still have faith in the dogma, it is requested that those believing will endeavour to explain by means of it the following facts.

1st. How came the relief in aid of wages under the old poor-law to reduce the remuneration of labour?

2nd. How was it that the number of London cabinet-makers, having declined 33 per cent. from 1831 to 1841, and work having increased considerably during that period, wages, notwithstanding, were 400 per cent. better at the former period?

3rd. The gross weight of the cotton imported into England in 1800 was 30,650,000lbs., and in 1840, it was 592,500,000lbs., or in 40 years it had increased nearly twenty-fold. In 1800 the number of hands engaged in manufacture was 1,877,000, and in 1840 the number was upwards of 2,250,000; so that while the quantity of labour, to be done, or what is the same thing, the quantity of materials to be manufactured had increased nearly 2000 per cent., the number of labourers, or operative manufacturers, had increased only 20 per cent.

Hence it is evident that, according to the law of supply and demand, there being twenty times as much work to be done, and only one-fifth more labourers to do it, wages should have been one hundred times better in 1800 than they were in 1840; and yet the price paid for weaving a piece of calico (which may be cited as a type of the value of labour) in the cotton districts was in 1800 between 3s. and 4s., and in 1840 only 1s. 3d.; so that while the demand for labour had increased twenty times, and the supply of it only one-fifth, wages, instead of being one hundred times higher, were three times lower.—Or, taking W.H.'s increase of the total population of Manchester from 1800 to 1840 (viz. 200 and odd per cent.) as the increase of the cotton spinners and weavers, the facts would stand thus:—while the demand for labour increased 2000 per cent., and the supply of labourers only 200 per cent., wages, instead of rising ten times higher, fell more than half as low again.—Will the Editor of the *Economist* oblige Mr. MAYHEW by cracking these three economical nuts for him?

The following, from a medical gentleman, requires no comment:—

"Sir,—Allow me respectfully to add my own testimony to the correctness of your statements. In the course of professional duties I have paid much attention to the physiological characteristics of the lower classes, and am happy, most happy, that they have at length found a chronicler so truthful as yourself. There are good parts even in the worst pictures—there are pleasant sunbeams close beside dark shadows; and the generous fortitude, the unflinching integrity, which is frequently met with in the dismal alleys of London, stand out strongly in contrast to prevalent notions and bigoted opinions. The lean and gaunt inhabitants of rooms, where dirt usurps the place of light, may be vicious or uncouth, but they are so from *habit,* and their transgressions are often half redeemed by traces of a more exalted nature. Better it is that we should know all the misdeeds of a life, than that one, perhaps the only one, good action be passed over in silence.

"Your aim is great; your task of no ordinary difficulty; but it will form, when completed, a monument of individual research, rarely equalled, never surpassed! where the statesmen may ponder ere he legislates, and the metaphysical mind may glean a solution to some of the problematical causes of human error. To me your efforts are of exceeding interest; not only from their intrinsic merit, but from the immense fund of statistics you adduce. And this is a point upon which no correspondent has yet done you justice. It is pleasurable likewise to observe that the higher classes are making themselves acquainted with the condition of their degraded brethren; and that your eloquent advocacy is leading to a better understanding between the patrician and plebeian.

"Permit me to express a hope that no sense of delicacy may prevent the publication of this letter. It is the humble tribute of one who is a personal stranger."

W.W. says:—

"Have you considered the Law of Marriage in connection with prostitution? I think it lies at the bottom of it; and in case it should not have occurred to you, I have taken the liberty of suggesting it for your consideration.

"I do not think that much can be added to what Milton wrote upon the subject,[33] but as your papers will be so popular, and treat the subject so practically, it will be a good opportunity for making the public acquainted with the reasons which may be urged for a Law of Divorce more liberal than the present one, if we may be said to have one at all. I hope you will excuse my troubling you with this, but as I have not been able to think the subject out, I shall be very glad to see it done."

The subject will be attended to in its proper place and time.

---

[33] John Milton, *The Doctrine and Discipline of Divorce*, London, 1643.

ANSWERS TO CORRESPONDENTS.
[No.33, 26 JULY 1851]

Edited out:
EMILY C.; MRS G.N.; A LADY; VERAX.

━━━━━━━━━━

The subjoined is philological, and evidently from a gentleman conversant with the historic mode of derivation.

"Although your work is hardly the place to admit of a philological discussion, even on its covers, yet to correct error is always essential. Your ingenious correspondent 'Wortenkrämer' has fallen into a mistake, which is not unfrequent with those who take sounds as the basis of etymological enquiry. His derivation of *Holborn* is of this character: the real meaning of the word is shown in old *maps*, deeds, &c., where it is written 'Old Bourne' i.e., Old Brook, Bourne being an old Saxon term of that meaning (see Cole's Dictionary), and in the termination of many of our ancient towns, of which *Sherbourn* will answer for an example. Perhaps the signification of the word as a boundary might arise from streams being so often so used. The 'Old Bourne' was a stream which ran into the Fleet River.

"I am Sir,

"Yours respectfully,

"J.G.W."

Correspondent Wortenkrämer had but little philological knowledge; that is to say, of the *science* of language. His letter was printed for its suggestivity rather than its etymological correctness.

The following is from a Veterinary Surgeon, and is printed here as an act of justice. The information on the subject in question was derived from the Parliamentary Report on the subject. Mr. Mayhew can vouch for the integrity of the writer of the subjoined:—

"16, Spring Street, July 16, 1851.

"You have unintentionally been drawn into doing injustice to an honourable gentleman. I mean Mr. Bishop, the gun-maker of New Bond-street in your observation on THE FORMER STREET SELLERS, 'FINDERS', STEALERS, AND RESTORERS OF DOGS. [LLLP, Vol 2., pp. 48-50]

I will not repeat the remarks you made on Mr. Bishop's character, but will content myself with this assertion, that from the beginning to end they are erroneous. The dog has not throughout the metropolis a firmer friend than Mr. Bishop, who alone got the DOG BILL introduced into Parliament, and himself paid every farthing of carrying that measure.

"That Mr. Bishop may know some men with whom he, nor I, would like to be seen abroad with, is very probable, he being the disinterested medium of getting back one-half or more of the pets lost in London. This office he performs from pure love of the brute; and how he is mixed up with the people with whom he is obliged to treat his BILL will amply testify.

"Trusting to your sense of justice for the insertion of this letter,

"I remain yours &c.

E.M."[34]

The Crippled Street-Seller of Nutmeg-Graters writes as follows:—

"24 Bond Street, Boro'-road.

"Sir,—Notwithstanding all my exertions to forward myself in the general line of dealing, I have been unfortunate. I purchased a donkey with the view of hawking hardware through the country, but had scarcely provided the necessaries when my donkey took ill, and broke out all over sores, and is now useless either for work or for sale: this circumstance, together with keeping a boy and doing no business within the last month, has entirely deprived me of money and considerably lessened my stock. A friend of mine having a little pony intended for sale, would be glad to give me the preference, and take my donkey in barter, could I but pay the difference; he thinks he can cure the donkey and make him answer his business. Unless I dispose of him in this

---

[34] On Victorians and their pets and animals, particularly the protection of animals, see: H. Ritvo, *The Animal Estate*, Penguin, 1987, pp. 125-66.

manner, I have no chance of selling him, unless at an enormous sacrifice. To complete my trouble I gave an order for a little cart, for which I paid 30s. in advance; the man moved away and I have no clue to finding him or recovering my money. I have sufficient stock to go on with, but too heavy for a boy to wheel about with me as well. Sir, I have told you something respecting my father-in-law; he is since dead and willed all his property to his granddaughters. I expected he would repent in his last moments, and in pity leave me something, but such was not the case, and those who now hold the property are equally heartless. I would wish that these lines may meet their eyes; they may do from shame what they ought to do from generosity. Sir, what money I have received through the medium of your work I have laid out to what I believed the best advantage; but misfortune will sometimes happen to those more capable of conducting a business than me.

"Sir, my best respects to you and Mrs. Mayhew, and my hope to your welfare,

"C. ALLOWAY."

The Nutmeg-Grater Seller has already received upwards of 9£, and it would be unjust to others to solicit any further aid on his behalf. The letter is printed in the hopes of shaming his relations into doing their duty to one whom Providence, for some inscrutable purpose, has almost deprived of the means of assisting himself.

ANSWERS TO CORRESPONDENTS.
[No.34, 2 AUGUST 1851]

Edited out:
B.L.

E. will feel obliged by Mr. Mayhew stating how he estimates the number of hands engaged in the cotton manufacture in the years 1800-1840, as stated in his numbers of the "London Poor," No.32 and July 19. Are the numbers given those only employed in spinning and weaving, or what others are included, and from what source is the information collected?

The facts were taken (if Mr. Mayhew remembers correctly) from Messrs. Banfield and Weld's very useful "Statistical Companion" —the one for last year (a work of which W.H. and R.H., and R.B.B., and all others who speak without a knowledge of facts would do well to possess themselves). Not having the book at hand, however, Mr. Mayhew is unable to speak definitely on the subject. The weight of cotton imported was derived from Mr. Salt's "Facts and Figures," or "Statistics and Calculations," where a table is given for a series of years. The wages paid at the different periods were copied from the "Statistical Companion." Should E. not be able to find the facts as indicated, Mr. Mayhew will be happy to refer specially to the returns for him.

R.H. (the right initials surely should be J.W.) commits a rash attempt, at the imminent risk of his "molars," to crack "the three economical nuts" presented to the Manchester Schoolboys in No. 32 of this periodical; but makes the same wry faces over them as the French toy nutcrackers assume when engaged in a similar act. They are evidently too hard for him. And yet it is very plain the gentleman has cut his *wise*-teeth, from the fact of his dropping the nuts immediately he found that they were more than he could get through. He accordingly, with exquisite cunning, tries to open an entirely new subject for discussion, as witness his hand.

"London, 21 July, 1851.

"Sir,—In your answers to correspondents, I notice that you are very much addicted to the habit of throwing out insinuations, both against the policy of Free Trade, and the motives of those who advocate it. Now, sir, may I ask you to state, in an early number, How Free Trade interferes with the Rate of Wages, or the Law of Supply and Demand, as you assert it does?

"Is the Free-Trade policy any other than that of declaring that the revenue of a country should be solely raised from property?

"Surely, the only just system of taxation is that founded on a Property and Equitable Income Tax combined, and, as you must be quite certain, that is the only object aimed at by those whom you sneeringly call "Manchester School," &c., &c., &c. How can you reconcile you inuendos against us with the assertion that you are labouring for the good of the poor? Certain I am, nothing will benefit the poor as a body so much as the adoption of a just system of taxation; and that those who, like yourself, sneer at the efforts of Free Traders or Economists are only apparently the benefactors, but truly the oppressors of the working classes.

"To pass to another subject, allow me to call to your notice some curious statements made by you in your answers to correspondents. *Ex. Gr.*—'In the case of the receiver of stolen goods, the *main iniquity* consists in not paying a fair price for the labour of the article purchased.'

"Now, sir, *the main*, nay, *the only* iniquity, consists in purchasing an article not honestly procured, and is as great whether the receiver gives ¹/₄d. for an article worth 100£., or 100£. for an article worth ¹/₄d.

"'A railway *does not add* one single commodity to the riches of a country, it merely increases the facility of exchanging the produce of one district for that of another.' Indeed, suppose a town so distant from another, that fish caught rots on the seashore for want of a market, if a railway finds a ready sale for it some 300 or 400 miles off, is not that *pro tanto* an increase in production, not a mere extension of the facility of exchanging commodities. You must be aware that 20 years past, milk, fish, and fruit, were daily spoiled for want of a speedy conveyance to a market.

"Will you give something more than mere assertions that crime has increased in a larger ratio to population since Free Trade has been partially introduced. Give us a correct comparison of crime in two or three periods say 1600, 1700, 1750, 1800, 1850, showing how much of the apparent increase beyond the ratio of increase of population is owing to a *greater efficiency* in detection (amounting, I should say

at a mere guess, to more than 50 per cent. of our whole crime)? How much to the number of new offenses created by our various police and railway acts, and these points alone, truly estimated would, I believe, make all candid persons say that your assertion was not founded on correct data.

"In conclusion, allow me, in the face of your three nuts to crack, to ask you, Do not the poor of this country consume more food per head, and have more comforts than they did 50 years past? I answer, Yes.—Your obedient Servant, R.H., a constant reader and subscriber from the first."

The above letter really bristles with so many points, that one is as undecided as a dog with a hedgehog where first to lay hold of it. However, the good old proverb tells us—

"If you gently touch a nettle,
Lo! It stings you for your pains,
But grasp it like a man of mettle,
And it soft as silk remains."

Applying, therefore, the same rule to R.H.'s effusion, it may be said that Mr. Mayhew never as yet asserted that Free Trade interfered with the Rate of Wages or the Law of Supply and Demand; but as R.H. requests to be informed how Free Trade does interfere with the remuneration for Labour, Mr. Mayhew (though by the bye, he is far from ambitious of becoming teacher to the Manchester School) will just, as a lesson to the Cotton Academy, append the following facts collected by him during his inquiry into the condition of the labourers at the Timber Docks at the time of his engagement on the *Morning Chronicle*, the parts printed in italics being all studiously withheld from the public by the Editor of that *Free-Trade* Journal!

"*I don't know what is the cause of the reduction of the wages*," said a "rafter," "*but the men thinks it is generally owing to the cheapness of provisions. They say what's the use of provisions being cheap if they lowers our wages.*

"The men are dissatisfied," observed a deal porter. "*They say they would sooner have it as it was, because they say, if provisions comes up again, they won't get no higher price for their labour. The* wages of the casual dock labourer have been reduced a great deal more than those of the constant men. Three months ago they had 18s. a week, and now the highest wages paid to the casual labourers is 15s. a week. *This again the men say is all owing to the cheapness of provisions.*

"We now have," said another of the labourers "4s. 4d. a day of from eight till four (o'clock), and 5s.6d. a day from six to six: it used to be, till four months back I think, 4s. 10d. and 6s. 4d. *I haven't heard any particular reason for this lowering. Bread's cheap people says; but if bread fell 3d. a loaf below what it is, our wages would fall 3¹/₄d. to keep up with it."* The above are extracts from the copy supplied by Mr. Mayhew to the *Morning Chronicle* on the subject of the labourers at the Timber Docks (Letter LVIII.). The parts printed in italics, and all others of a similar character, referring the reduction in wages to the cheapness of provisions (even down to a single line), were excised by the Free-Trade Editor.

Now surely R.H. must allow that in this instance at least Free Trade *has* interfered with the rate of wages; and, if he would but take the trouble to inquire, he might find that a similar "interference" has taken place in many other trades—as for example the Market Gardeners. Mr. Mayhew mentions only these two instances, because he is acquainted with the facts above stated from his own investigations. Indeed, as has been before asserted in this periodical, if the price of coals be reduced, competition will of course cause steam-engines to work cheaper; and surely, by a parity of reasoning, if the price of bread be decreased, the same cause will have the same effect on the human engine. In the trades where the wages of the workmen are, from their superior skill, at "monopoly" price of course, the price of food will have little or no effect upon them; but wherever labour is at its minimum value, the market price will be regulated by the *cost of production* that is to say by the cost of the food, which gives the labourer the power to labour. (R.H. should have a quiet day's study of Stuart Mill's chapter on "Value.")

"Is the Free-Trade Policy," asks R.H., "any other than that of declaring that the Revenue of a country should be solely raised from Property?" Free Trade, Mr. Mayhew replies, is assuredly *the liberty to search the world for the cheapest possible labour*. Its effect on the revenue is a secondary consideration. The imposts on foreign commodities were neither instituted nor maintained as a source of income to the government, but simply as a means of protection to the home producer. This R.H. knows as well as Mr. Mayhew; and most assuredly Free Trade was neither advocated nor carried as an improved mode of collecting the revenue, but as a means of extending the market for our manufactures. Mr. Mayhew must confess that, viewed as a working man's question, the weight of the arguments appears to him to lean towards the side of Protection; and that, viewed as a capitalist's or trader's question, the facts are in favour of Free Trade. To the monied classes, of course, it is the greatest good to get two commodities for the same amount of money as they got one for formerly. To the working man, however, Free Trade, that is to say *unlimited licence to* the trader, is far from being a blessing. Of course if wages are regulated by a natural law like Demand and Supply, it would be as insane to attempt to interfere with the rate of remuneration for labour by any pretended *"protective"* edicts, as it would be to regulate the rising and setting of the sun by Act of Parliament. Mr. Mayhew is most ready to allow that under such circumstances the only two modes of benefiting the working classes would be either by increasing the "Wage Fund," or decreasing the number among whom it is to be shared. But if the rate of wages is—as Mr. Mayhew believes all the facts of the labour question go to prove—in a great measure arbitrary and dependent mainly on the will of the Capitalist—then it would appear that some kind of restrictive laws is required for the protection of the working man against the greed of the trader. If the price of labour be regulated by supply and demand, why do free traders object so lustily to all trade societies, that is to say to all combinations of working men, designed to uphold the rate of wages. Surely if the remuneration for labour be governed by a natural law, then it is utterly beyond the power of a body of operatives to interfere with them; if, however, the real rate of wages consists of as little as the master can force the men to accept, or as much as the men can force the master to give—according to whichever is the stronger—then it would seem better that some steps should be taken to stay this continual war of class against class, and to prevent the one wronging the other.

"The only just system of Taxation," says R.H., "is that founded on a Property and Equitable Income Tax." As a source of revenue this is most readily admitted; but it should be remembered that until all taxes on commodities are abolished, those which consist of certain imposts, instituted with the view of preventing the untaxed foreigner from underselling the heavily-taxed native in the labour market of this country, are among the last of such taxes that should have been repealed. It is useless to say that food and provisions generally are cheapened by these means, because facts have proved that as fast as food is cheapened so will the lowest grades of labour be; and so long as there are excise duties, of which the working classes contribute the greater portion, there should likewise be custom duties, so as to make the foreign labourer, who is brought into competition with the English, pay his quota to the burdens of the country.

Let us put a case: there are three kinds of taxes on commodities, viz., taxes on articles produced within the country, taxes on articles imported into it, and taxes on articles conveyed from place to place, or sold in certain privileged parts of it. The first are excise duties, the second custom duties, and the third tolls and market dues. Now let us suppose that a certain gentleman—a free-trade enthusiast—who objected to every kind of impost on commodities, was to go to the Duke of Bedford and persuade him that all market-tolls were very pernicious things, falling as they did entirely on the consumer—that cheap fruit was

the greatest possible blessing—and that instead of his forcing all who imported their commodities into Covent Garden to pay a toll before they were allowed to sell, it would be far more enlightened, and highly beneficial to the fruit consumers, if his Grace were to abolish every one of the tolls, and allow all fruit brought into the market to be sold without paying any market due whatever. Well, suppose the Duke became a convert to the new commercial principles, and proceeded to abolish the market dues on fruit brought into Covent Garden, *but still to continue the high rents and taxes on those who lived in the market itself.* Of course the dwellers in the market, heavily rented and rated and taxed as they were, would soon begin to find out that those who paid no toll whatever could undersell them, and that the whole of their business was rapidly passing into the hands of their more favoured competitors. In such a predicament, doubtlessly, those who were suffering from the heavy imposts on their industry would go to the Duke, tell him that it was impossible for them to compete with their untaxed neighbours, and beg that their burdens should be removed; whereupon the Duke would of course reply that his revenue must be collected and the expense of the market paid somehow—that cheap fruit was a great blessing—and that they could not possibly be badly off when fruit and vegetables were so much lower in price. Surely all the world but those who were interested in the matter would be able to see the injustice of such a line of policy! And yet enlarge Covent Garden Market into the Labour Market of this Kingdom and it is precisely what we have done to those who live in the market itself, and have heavy rent, rates, and taxes to pay in support of it. According to the most moderate calculation the working classes pay nearly one half of the revenue of the country; they pay nearly the whole of the Malt Duty, which is in round numbers 5,000,000£; the same with the Spirit Duty, which is 4,350,000£; the Tobacco Duty, amounting to 4,250,000 £; the Sugar Duty, 4,500,000£; and the Duty on Tea, which is

5,330,000£; making altogether 23,430,000£, out of about 50,000,000£.

The other points touched upon by R.H. hardly require any special notice. Concerning the *ethical* point, R.H. is unable to perceive *the iniquity* of not giving a just price for the making of an article. To give an *unjust* price is not *equity*, and therefore in-equity, or *in-iquity*, if there be any meaning in words. But, says R.H., the *main* and *only* iniquity in receiving stolen goods consists in *purchasing* what is not *honestly* obtained. The law declares the purchaser in such cases is as bad as the thief—*particeps criminis*. R.H., the Free-Trader, however, says not but why is what the "receiver" purchases *dishonestly* obtained? Simply because it has never been produced by the party selling, nor a due consideration given by him for it. In the matter of the railway R.H. confounds *exchange* with *production*; while, concerning the criminal tables demanded by him, he seems to be utterly unaware that the science of statistics is of comparatively modern origin, and that there are no data for making the collation he desires. But, even if there were such facts extant, could not R.H. make the comparison as well as Mr. Mayhew; though, to be sure, economists, from Adam Smith down to R.H., have shown the same aversion to collect facts as mad dogs have to touch water. It is so much easier to ensconce themselves in some snug corner and there remain all day, like big-bottomed spiders, spinning cobweb theories amid heaps of *rubbish*. If R.H. turns to "Porter's Progress of the Nation," p. 642, he will find that the number of persons committed as criminal offenders were, in 1805, only 4,605; whereas, in 1848, there were 30,349, an increase of 482 per cent., or even deducting 50 per cent. (*as R.H. desires*) for greater efficiency in detection, of 432 per cent. in 43 years! whilst the population during the same period increased only 79 per cent. (see p. 654, same work). It is but right, Mr. Mayhew should add, that *previous* to his inquiries he believed in Supply and Demand, and Free-Trade, as religiously as R.H. himself does. Let R.H. go through the same course of education, and, as a honest man, he will assuredly arrive at the same result.

G.H. says—

"You have promised an account of the Drapers, which has not yet appeared; I should feel obliged by your informing me when it is likely you will touch on them."

The Drapers, according to the Division laid down in the prospectus of this work, belong to the class of Distributors—including first sailors, bargemen, coachmen, carriers, porters, and all who are engaged in the conveyance of goods; and secondly, clerks, warehousemen, shopmen, and all who are engaged in the sale of them.

The subject of the Drapers' Assistants is a large one, and one which Mr. Mayhew is most anxious to investigate; for the trade is peculiar, being one in which competition and "puffing" and "pushing" are carried perhaps to the greatest extent, and consequently one from which a vast deal may be learnt. It is, moreover, one in which the health and mental improvement of the assistants are sacrificed greatly to the greed of the employers—owing to the tendency of the "cutting-shops" to keep open half through the night, so that no possible chance of custom may be lost.

ANSWERS TO CORRESPONDENTS.
[No.36, 16 AUGUST 1851]

Edited out:
PARVUS; J.R.R.; A.B.C.; ANNIE.; A QUERY ON "THE FISH" AND UNDERWATER BREATHING.

Due Notice will be given of the republication of the required numbers, which are now being reprinted.

The following, is inserted here with the view of directing attention to the subject:—

"Sir,

"As I read in your Notices to Correspondents, in answer to my inquiry, that it is your intention to submit the Laws of Marriage and Divorce to an investigation, I will suggest for your consideration a few thoughts which occur to me on the subject. If you insert these in your correspondence I hope to send more.

"Marriage is a civil and religious institution; persons who marry enter into a contract with another, and also with the Deity, by which they are bound to the observance of certain duties; the contract made with another person the civil power can enforce, but not so the religious one; it is therefore advisable that legislatures should treat marriage wholly as a civil contract.

"By eliminating the religious element from marriage, as far as the civil power is concerned, and allowing each person's conscience to determine the nature of the duty it imposes on them, the civil power is enabled without obstruction to resume its ordinary duty of protecting the person and property of individuals without infringing on their rights.

"A contract is a thing so well understood that had it not been for the successful attempt of the Roman Catholic church to make marriage a sacrament over the whole of Europe for some centuries, which most Protestant countries have not generally considered it to be, we should now in England be in the enjoyment of a domestic liberty the absence of which is the cause of more crime, misery, and destitution than can be conceived.

"Yours obediently, W.W."

Mr. Mayhew abstains for the present from making any comments on the above opinions.

A.B. sends another *conjecture* to the term Haberdasher:—

"Sir,

"You have referred to Baily, Johnson, Sheridan, and Walker on this word, will you allow me to present what a more modern lexicographer says about it. I give you the entire passage. The author's first quotation is from Chaucer's 'prologue.'

"Yours, A.B."

"Haberdasher—Minshew, from Ger. *Habdt*, haberdashery, *ihr das*, i.e., Have you that? or from the Fr. *Avoir d'acheter*, i.e. to have to buy. Skinner, whom Lye transcribes, runs far away. Gerenius—from the Ger. *Habe*, goods or wares—and *tauschen*, to exchange, as if a haberdasher were an exchanger of wares. Mr. Thomson con-structs a German compound, *haabvertauscher*, of *haab*, goods, wares—and *tauscher, ver-tauschier*, a dealer, an exchanger. The French *Avoir de pois* we formerly wrote *Haber de pois*, a similar corruption may have occurred in *Avoir d'acheter, haber d'achet, haberdash*."—Richardson's *New English Dictionary*.

Mr. Mayhew has but an indifferent opinion of Mr. Richardson as an etymologist. His Dictionary, however, is invaluable, for giving, in the copious examples cited as to the uses of the words by the earliest authors down to the present period, the chronology, as it were, of the changes that the several terms have gradually undergone in the language. Mr. Richardson also appears to have had some clear notions as to the historic mode of derivation, but as to the dialectic etymology through the medium of cognate language, he evidently had not the vaguest knowledge: indeed, the discoveries of Grimm and Bopp were not made known till Mr. Richardson had nearly completed his labours. Moreover, he was too intense an admirer of Horne Tooke to be able to add much to philological truth; for of all plausible creations of human ingenuity the "Diversions of Purley" looks perhaps the most like truth, and yet is the farthest from it. Horne Tooke was essentially a theorist; every fact was made to accord with his preconceived opinions, rather than his opinions made to accord with the facts. To give but one instance. It is well known that he conceived an idea that all prepositions and conjunctions were simply the imperative moods of verbs. As for example:—If (which is in Anglo-Saxon *gif*), he said, was the imperative mood of the Saxon verb *gifan*, to give, grant, and, consequently, that the meaning of the sentence, "If the law of Supply and Demand be true, then Protection for Labour is an absurdity," is, when literally translated, "*Give* or *grant* that the law of Supply and Demand be true, then Protection," &c. Following up the same ingenious course he pronounced "else" (which is in Anglo-Saxon *ales* and *als*), the imperative mood of the Saxon verb *alesan*, to let loose, to dismiss; so that when we say "We will do what is right, and nothing *else*," the literal meaning of words is, according to him, "We will do what is right, and dismiss that —— nothing."

Now, that this is *not* the literal meaning of the words, but a mere exercise of verbal ingenuity, the most superficial attention to dialectic derivation is sufficient to assure us; for, on turning to the Latin language, we find that the cognate term in that tongue for the Saxon *ales* was *alias* (otherwise), and this we immediately know to be derived not from *alesan*, to dismiss, but from *alius* another; so that the sentence really and truly means, "We will do what is right, *otherwise* nothing." Indeed, had Horne Tooke taken the trouble to trace the Saxon prototype, *gif* of the English *if* up to the particle in the parent Gothic tongue, according to the *historic* mode of derivation, he would have perceived that even the term upon whose apparent identity with the imperative of the verb *gifan*, to give, he founded his whole philological scheme—even this term, I say—had a very different origin from what he hastily assumed; and that really it was connected dialectically with the Latin *give*, and ultimately with a Hebrew verb meaning to choose, its fundamental signification being *"whether"* (like the cognate Hebrew particle), and which is evidently the sense of it in the sentence, "I know not *if* it be right or *if* it be wrong;" that is to say, "I know not *whether* it be right or *whether* it be wrong."

The term Haberdasher is still a mystery.

R.H. (the nutcracker) has gone surly. He has evidently, poor fellow, while trying to crack the nuts, *bitten his fingers*.

"In one portion of the lengthy—very lengthy—reply you have been pleased to make to my short letter, you say that I bristle at a great many points, but I am still as soft as silk; you rightly interpret my intention. I constantly notice that our opponents, Mr. Mayhew foremost amongst them, are accustomed to apply to us various appellations not used by ourselves, as 'Cotton academy,' 'Manchester school,' &c., &c., and which is applied by them in an invidious sense, as Socinian is applied to a Unitarian. Now I never allow these to be used without showing resentment; but I always do so in an inoffensive manner; whatever I say never rankles, and that is one great difference betwixt you and me. Your remarks on political opponents, persons as ardent in pursuit of truth as yourself, seem to me to have something in them destructive of character; *e.g.* 'exquisite cunning' is a term applied by you to me. I should say that a person of exquisite cunning was an exquisite rogue. I could pick out many more of the same sort.

"You say, 'R.H., surely the initials should be J.W.' I suppose by this remark you insinuate that I am J.W. writing under a different signature. There you are utterly mistaken; that practice I leave to authors who, writing for their bread, have no objection to take any side of a question, provided they are well paid for it.

"I see in the Quarterly Report of the Registrar-General just published a large increase of marriages and births; this fact is generally considered an indication of prosperity, but I suppose if I advance it as such you will say, 'It is a cobweb theory spun amidst heaps of rubbish,' therefore I shall only repeat the question I asked before, 'Do not the poor of this country consume more food and have more comforts than they did 50 years past?'

"Your obedient servant, R.H."

There are at the Zoological Gardens some small animals who are particularly spiteful whenever any one attempts to have a bit of fun with them while they are cracking their nuts, and we strongly suspect, from the viciousness of the above letter, that R.H. is one of the breed. Surely he must be the one "who had seen the world." However he is a very silly fellow; for assuredly we never meant, as the saying goes, to get the "monkey up" with him. But he *would* have a try to crack the hard things; and if he did find the nuts disagree with him (for they are very indigestible things, at best), why, he need not, because his bile has been stirred by them, so far forget himself as a gentleman as to utter things which, even if they were true, he would, in his lucid intervals, blush to repeat.

But R.H. has clearly passed the greater part of his life, dormouse-like, in cotton, so that he can hardly be supposed to be wide awake yet to the requirements of polite society. When he understands the meaning of cunning, and finds out that it signifies literally kenning, or knowing, his good sense will, we are sure, lead him to perceive that there was no intention to insinuate the least "roguishness" or dishonesty to him. No! no! we are thoroughly satisfied R.H. is. no knave; quite the reverse, we should say. He *will*, as Milton has it,

"Rush in where angels fear to tread;"
and at anything rational, poor man, *he* is utterly out of his element. If *he* had only to write for his bread, he would have to seek parish relief before the week was out. It is quite *plain* that he gets *his* living in some other way than by the exercise of *his* intellect—very probably by the labour of some other person's hands. However, all we *do* hope is that he will not allow anything we have let drop to disturb his *peace* (we had almost written *piece*) of mind, and that on no account whatever will he visitate us with a reply. We have already afflicted our readers with two epistles of his lively pen, and we can assure him we have no disposition, whatever his sins may be, to make him do penance in these sheets.

"Confess your faults" is a good round-hand copy, and we proceed to put the precept in practice.

An esteemed lady correspondent says—

"I fear the poor Nestie Man was ill-informed about the Kingfisher's nest. I, who have seen, nay assisted (with many a pang) at the taking of one, should say it is not a thing that could be taken in the hand and shown about, any more than a rat-hole. It was perhaps some other nest, therefore, that his informant pronounced a Kingfisher's. This bird cannot be said (I believe) to build a nest. In the sides of old gravel pits, near water, this bird will find, or perhaps even make holes that run for several feet parallel with the surface and about a foot and more below it. To take the nest in such a case you must dig down to it, guessing the probable ending of the excavation, and you will come upon seven or more very pale pink eggs, lying in a bed of small dry fish bones, of which

you may take up a handful. At least this is what we found, after watching a Kingfisher in and out of the hole many times.

ANSWERS TO CORRESPONDENTS.
[No.37, No.I "Those that will not Work", 23 AUGUST 1851, price 3d.]

THE Pages at the back of the Statistical Tables inserted in the present Number are left blank for the purposes of binding.

The following extracts from a speech recently delivered at a public meeting are here inserted, because Mr. Mayhew believes that they express very clearly and simply one of the great evils of the time—an over large machinery for the distribution of our products, and the puffing, pushing, and cheating necessarily arising therefrom. If the country be over populated, assuredly it is so with traders, rather than workers; and yet we never hear of schemes for shipping off some hundreds of them. That the distributor is a very useful element in the economy of every State there cannot be the least doubt, serving both consumer and producer; but an excess of such people is, perhaps, one of the greatest evils that can befall a nation. That there are most honourable men connected with trade Mr. Mayhew most readily admits, having in the course of his investigations met with many such, but that the majority are compelled—by the very excess of the class, and the consequent struggle to live—to resort to frauds, cheats, and chicanery that they in their consciences must despise, all experience goes to prove.

"Mr. Woodin said:—I shall endeavour to show the true position which the class to which I belong holds under competitive arrangements. As shopkeepers it is our province to distribute the productions of others—*we give no new intrinsic value to the articles that pass through our hands. We buy a stated quantity of goods for a given sum, and we sell a lesser quantity for the same sum—the difference is our profit, on which we live; the interests of the distributor and the consumer are therefore opposed to each other, because it is the interest of the consumer to get as much as possible for his money, and of the distributor to give as little as possible. Tradesmen are all well aware that their interests are opposed to that of their customers—they know very well that their only object in going into business is to get as much as they can for themselves, to give as little as possible to the producer for what they buy, and to take as much as they can from the consumer for what they sell, and the more they can take in this way, the nearer they are to their ultimatum—the realization of a fortune, and their retirement from business.* This is the real and only object of the whole class; but in order to obtain this object in the most speedy and certain manner, and at the same time to conceal it as much as possible from the public, they assume to be actuated by principles of the purest philanthropy—they enter into business for the sole purpose of benefiting the community; 'Pro bono publico' is their motto—their own interest is only a matter of secondary consideration. Thus the tradesmen pretends to one thing, and means to do and does do something very different. To ensure success it is necessary to be a good 'story-teller'. *It is an acknowledged fact, that the men making the greatest professions and the most noise are the most dishonest, and the greatest cheats in trade, but the most unfortunate feature in the case is, that the public generally give credence to those who make the boldest assertions.* As an illustration of this fact I would mention, that the parties who were lately fined, by government for adulteration, were, without exception, *making the greatest professions of the purity and cheapness of their articles, and of the fairness of their mode of doing business,* and I may add that they were doing the largest retail trades, and receiving more patronage from the public than others who were less noisy but

more honest; and the same view is borne out by the recent exposures in the *Lancet*[35]—all the parties exposed are doing the largest trades, and they all make the greatest professions of the purity of their goods and the uprightness of their dealings. *The object of these unscrupulous tradesmen is always to appear to be cheap; to maintain this appearance every article is adulterated that can be without being easily detected, and they are marked at such prices that their more honest rivals cannot compete with them.* They put ground rice with their white pepper; a composition called P.D., costing about one penny per lb., with their black pepper; chicory with their coffee; and potato flour with their sugar; tea comes to their hand ready adulterated with starch, gum, dirt, and paint. *Another trick resorted to, to gain an appearance of cheapness, is to sell some article which the public know the value of, at or below the cost price, and the public take it for granted that the person doing so is cheap in everything else.* Goods sold in this way are called 'leading articles.' Calico is a 'leading article' with the draper; he sells this at halfpenny a yard less than the cost; and this enables him to charge many shillings and often pounds more than the proper price for shawls and other articles that have no fixed standard of value. *The grocer makes sugar his principal leading article, because the public can pretty nearly tell its value; he therefore sells it a halfpenny a pound less than it cost him.* He thereby endeavours to lead purchasers to the conclusion that he is equally cheap in everything else—if he sells cheap sugar they think he must also sell cheap tea. This is called in the trade keeping a sugar trap to catch tea customers; but tea is a thing the public cannot so easily tell the value of, and in the sale of this article the grocer amply compensates himself for his losses in sugar. *By these and similar nefarious practices he attains his object; he gets a name for cheapness, gets plenty of patronage, and speedily makes a fortune."**** It must not be lost sight of that the distributor adds nothing to the wealth of the community, but subtracts from it; consequently there ought to be no more employed in that way than are sufficient to perform the duty efficiently. After due consideration, I am of opinion that one-tenth of the present persons so employed are suf-*

---

[35] See the reports of the "Analytical Sanitary Commission, Microscopal and Chemical Analysis of the Solid and Fluids Consumed by All Classes of the Public", for example in 1852, *The Lancet*, Vol. 1, pp. 132, 178, 200, 224, 294, 314, 340, 473-8, 525, 548, 595, on preserved provisions, beer, vinegar, pickles, spices.

ficient for that purpose; the other nine-tenths are mis-applying their labour, or at least their time, and the sooner that labour is directed to productive employment, the better it will be for themselves and for society."

Mr. Vansittart Neale[36] said:—"It had been calculated from the Post Office Directory for London and its suburbs in 1850, that the total number of retail tradesmen supplying certain goods was 4000, and estimating that each of them upon an average employed three persons besides himself, it would give a total of 16,000 engaged in the distribution of articles of grocery, or about one person to every eighty of the two millions and a half of all ages, which may be taken as the population of the district in question. This was a very much larger number than was needed for the purpose of distribution, and necessitated a keen competition among those engaged in it. When a tradesman with capital come into a new neighbourhood, and fitted up a shop with splendid plate glass front, ticketing all his articles at an apparently low price, and advertising them as the best and finest articles that could be sold, the consequences of such competition were perhaps to shut up twenty small shops; but in the course of the struggle fraudulent adulteration was carried on by all parties to a large extent."

18 Aug., 1851.

"Sir,

"I was employing a part of my leisure hours in collecting and arranging accounts of the earnings of persons engaged in the various branches of the manufacture of hats, both silk and stuff, but as you have requested me not to trouble you any more, in obedience to your wish I have ceased my labour; to show you, however, that I bear no malice, I enclose all I have ready.

"Your Obedient Servant,
"R.H."

---

[36] B. Colloms, *The Victorian Visionaries*, Constable, 1982, p. 92. Edward Vansittart Neale (1810-1892) was a prominent cooperationist Christian Socialist and shared the platform with Mayhew on at least one meeting of tailors (5 November 1850).

"Cunning may *literally* mean *kenning*, but is *never* used *now* in a good sense, it would be a poor excuse to make, after calling a person *inquisitive*, to say you meant *enquiring*; or, after using the term *impertinent*, to declare that you meant not keeping to the question: cunning is in the same class with the above two and many other words, which are never used by persons of education in their literal sense."

R.H.'s temper is better than his philology. One of the most elegant forms of literary art is the use of words in their literality; this was Sidney Smith's great charm.[37] The philological rule, unfortunately for R.H., is the very reverse of that which he enunciates. Words are never used in their literal, and always in their conventional acceptation by persons of *deficient education*—for the simple reason that it is impossible for the uneducated to know their radical signification. Those who have such knowledge feel an exquisite delight in discriminating between the correct and perverted sense.

No literary man knowing how to handle his tools would ever dream of using any one of the words cited by R.H. in any other than their literal acceptation—the context would show whether the conduct to which they were applied was an offence against good morals or not. Surely R.H. has heard the phase, "wrought with exquisite cunning," used even in common parlance. Does he fancy that this means wrought with roguery quite *recherché* (to use the French equivalent to exquisite), or with unusual skill—a work of the most expert *craft* or handicraft—not craft roguery, but craft in its true Old English sense of creation, production, from the Saxon verb creawian? It was precisely in this sense that Mr. Mayhew applied the words "exquisite cunning" to R.H. The terms themselves prove whence the phrase was borrowed, and exquisitely "knowing" was all that was intended to be implied—that is to say, R.H. endeavoured to meet the argument like

---

[37] Sydney Smith (1771-1845), religious author and pamphleteer, creator of the *Edinburgh Review*, complete works republished in 1850.

one *skilled* in the *art* of ratiocination, by *slily* proposing another.

Mr. Mayhew would not have condescended to have wasted so much valuable ink in explaining a matter that must have been patent to every scholar from the very beginning; but R.H. is clearly, from the tone of his last letter, too good a fellow to make an enemy of unintentionally. The Wage Table he sends is the best mode of argument after all.

⁎ Replies to several letters are postponed till the next number.

ANSWERS TO CORRESPONDENTS.
[No.38, 30 AUGUST 1851]

The subjoined is worthy of attention:—

"Sɪʀ,

"I venture to make a suggestion in reference to your work 'London Labour and the London Poor,' which I trust will not be taken amiss by you, for it proceeds from one who appreciates the purity of your motives, and admires your untiring zeal and laborious efforts in behalf of so large a portion of the neglected and suffering population of London.

"My suggestion refers to that portion of the work on the 'Prostitution of the Metropolis' shortly to appear in future numbers. Do you not think that it is likely to do *less harm* and *more good* if brought out in an entire volume, than in weekly numbers? Such a work is undoubtedly demanded. Nothing can be done to remedy an evil till the evil be fairly brought to light; but is there not danger lest the process of uncovering the evil, adopted by you, may *aggravate* instead of *diminish* its intensity? Will not the *cheapness* of a work, bearing a title unhappily so attractive to the young, the idle, the prurient, promote indeed its sale, increase the number of its readers, make it popular with the masses, but not thereby tend to the end designed by the author, *the reformation* of the present extensive system of evil?

"Such a work as you design, Sir, if brought out *in one volume*, would find a ready sale with such as are and ought to be really interested in the subject. The name and character of the author would at once attract the philanthropist, the statesman, the minister of religion, and all others whose callings and pursuits make such details necessary to be known. You need never fear a *loss* from the publication of the work in such a form. It would, indeed, present but little temptation to others, who might receive harm from its perusal, and its price would put it out of the reach of those to whom it might do most mischief—so far, the number of readers would be less, and its sale less extensive; but moderate gains, with the satisfaction of feeling that they were obtained without promoting evil, would (*you* of all men need not be reminded of this) be far more satisfactory than the richest revenue, clogged with but the faintest misgiving that it was gotten (partly) by increasing sin.

"Hoping you will excuse my freedom in thus addressing you, and believing you will take the hint in the same friendly spirit in which it is given,

"I remain, dear Sir,
"Your sincere Well-wisher,
"M. (a Curate of London)."

Mr. Mayhew regrets that he is unable to act upon the advice of his esteemed correspondent. To publish the account of the London Prostitutes complete in a volume would be, in Mr. Mayhew's opinion, to destroy a great part of the utility of such a work. Moreover, the price would render it available to those *only* who could afford to part with some 5s. or 6s. at once; whereas the great advantage of the "fascicular" mode of publication is, that it enables the poor to obtain expensive treatise by small instalments. But the London Curate sees great danger in the poor being *allowed* to read such books. Mr. Mayhew, however, takes a very different view; he believes that many young girls now go wrong *thoughtlessly*—that is to say, they are ignorant of the *necessary consequences* of unchastity. Many parents too, are either imprudently lax, or imprudently strict in the guardianship of their children, because they are unaware of the result of undue indulgence or undue rigour.

Mr. Mayhew hopes to be able to teach both parties the *ordained sequence of events* in these matters. The London Curate, of course, would not object to instructing the very humblest as to the laws of combustion or the causes of the seasons; and yet surely the natural order of the phenomena of vice is equally if not more important for the poor to know. No man thrusts his hand into the fire because he is *certain* it will burn him; render the sequences of moral events as apparently invariable, and there will be the same aversion to brave them, for the Great Lawgiver has most *benevolently* made them all ultimately terrible. The erring err sometimes from a want of faith, or sometimes for a want of knowledge respecting physical and moral causation. Give them this faith or this knowledge—let the future result be continually present to them—let the escapes from evil be demonstrated to be the accidents, and the sufferance from it the natural consequences of a deviation from virtue, and depend upon it the poor will be as prudent and guarded in their conduct as even the most respectable of us. This is the education that is *needed* more than all by the uninformed and the unthinking, and towards it Mr. Mayhew hopes to lend some little assistance. When "London Labour" is productive of misery the sooner the author converts his pen into "roast beef," as children say, by burning it, the better.

The following is printed here as one of many instances of the wrongs of the London Clerks, who are a most important body of London Labourers, numbering some thousands. Mr. Mayhew is most anxious to begin investigating their condition at the earliest possible period.

"An admirer of 'London Labour,' and a subscriber to most of the numbers, is desirous of knowing whether the *mass* of the poor *half-starved* legal and commercial clerks which are in this metropolis are to be set forth to the public eye—the writer thinks they ought; he is a clerk to a GENTLEMAN, who employs him about six hours per day in writing and as a messenger, at the *liberal salary* of 9s. per week. I am generally *fully employed*. I *know* that there

are very many in the city not paid much more than my pittance. I am a young man of good education and connections, but having been out of employment some time I eagerly snapped at the pittance I receive. My master is reputed to be *very rich*, and, I am sorry to add, very mean. You will scarcely believe that a security of 20£ was required before I entered my present service, but no one would be security for me, knowing the trifling pay I was to receive; he therefore waived that. In more prosperous times I have received good pay, from 1£ to 1£ 5s. per week. Both my parents are sick, my mother is *dying*, I believe, and out of my small salary I am compelled to aid them, for although their friends are able they are not willing, my father having been a very reckless man and a drunkard. They pay the rent and that is all, for they dislike him so much that they will not give to my mother for fear he should get a share. It is somewhat unchristian I must own, but his recklessness has been so great that I scarcely wonder at it. I should be glad to have employment in book keeping by single entry, &c. &c. after 4 P.M., if I could get it, for a trifle. I hope you will excuse this scrawl, but it is written in business hours in a great hurry. I perceive from your work that the most *ignorant* and *mindless* of the *lower classes* realize more than many who have received a good education and *possess ability*. Hoping you will forgive my intrusion and bad writing—

"I am, Sir,
"Your obedient Servant,
"W.D.M."

The writer of the above speaks but the truth in saying that the most ignorant and *mindless* of the humbler class earn more than he does. A *dustman, he will perceive, makes nearly double*, and many of the street-traders (the coal-sellers for instance) about four times as much as W.D.M. If W.D.M. wishes to become rich he must give over working for himself and *get to trade on the labour of others*. This is the great evil of our social system. By industry a man can scarcely keep himself from starving, whereas, by scheming and trading, he may ride in his carriage and become one of the "*respectable* classes."

The following is from a journeyman tailor—a gentleman long known and respected by Mr. Mayhew:—

"Dear Sir,

"Notwithstanding the many attempts to explain the meaning of the term 'haberdasher,' I observe that you say in your last number of 'Labour and the Poor,' that it is still a mystery. I don't know whether the following will throw any more light on the matter, but it struck me at the time as a still more curious application of the term than any that I have seen, so I transcribed it for you. It is from the 'Great Bible,' date April, 1540, in the British Museum, on vellum, presentation copy to Henry VIII., as is shown by the following inscription on the reverse of the fly leaf—'This Booke is presented unto your most excellent highnesse by youre loving, faithfull, and obedient subject and *daylye oratour,* Anthonye Marler of London, *haberdassher.*'

"In this case was the office, for such I presume it to be, of 'daylye Oratour' lay or clerical? if the former, what trade was Anthonye Marler? if the latter, how was it connected with the term 'haberdasher?'

"In an old dictionary, date 1701, I find three supposed derivations for it:—Habeidas, Greek, have you that? Avoir d'acheter, French, having to buy; or Kooper-daseer, Dutch, a dealer in small wares or toys, also a dealer in hats. In Boyer's French and English Dictionary, date 1747, it is used in the same manner, with the addition of 'mercer' being included under the term as at present.

"I remain, my dear Sir,
"Yours truly."
"——."

Will any clerical antiquary "enlighten our darkness" on this curious point? The "daylye Oratour" of course was a layman, but what was the haberdasher in those days? Mr. Mayhew has before stated that he considers the Dutch *Kooper-daseer* the most probable origin of the English haberdasher, for the consonantal changers are all in conformity with known laws,—$K=H$, and $p=b$, and s=sh; moreover the signification of "a dealer in small wares," is precisely that of the term haberdasher in the present day. Hence all the requirements for *dialectic* derivation are fulfilled; but what is *daseer*? Mr. Mayhew can find this part of the Dutch compound in no Dutch dictionary. Kooper is a dealer and the equivalent of our *chap*-man.

An Oxfordshire correspondent writes as follows:—

"Sir,

"As a constant reader of your publication 'London Labour,' I venture to address a few words to you. I am extremely interested in your work, and feel that the whole country is greatly indebted to you for your truth and honesty, and your manful advocacy of the labourer's welfare. It is, therefore, with no unfriendly spirit that I venture to criticise anything you put forth. I am not aware that any one can justly find fault with the body of the work, but I think it is occasionally otherwise with the fly sheets; to me, indeed, they are very interesting, and I should be very sorry if they were discontinued, but certainly they are your vulnerable part,—*e.g.,* in your number of Aug. 2nd you say that taxes were in the first instance simply protection, and not to furnish the exchequer. I think you will find it quite the reverse as a general statement, or at least as regards the history of this country: the two objects were always contemplated as joined together in early time.

"But it is not as regards such questions that I find fault with your fly sheets. Early in the work you intimated that you might see cause to modify your views and perhaps change them considerably. Now, I ask in all friendship whether, then, it is right to put forth views (I do not say statements) calculated to be drawn in with avidity by classes who have great reason for discontent, and who, be sure, will not abandon a theory which attempts to explain the source of their wrongs, in the same philosophical spirit in which you and I might modify our views upon further investigation.

"Is it morally right to offer yourself as a leader of the blind, when you confess you may find out after a time that you yourself did not see quite clearly?

"If I have not altogether mistaken your character you will, I am sure, pardon this freedom of speech.

"Having said my say, allow me now to furnish you with a little fact of the working of free trade in Oxfordshire.

"Turnip hoeing is reduced this year from *four* to *three* shillings an acre in consequence, it is avowed by farmers, of the cheapness of provisions."

Mr. Mayhew does consider it *morally* right to say *honestly* what he *thinks* upon all matters upon which his *opinion* is solicited. In so doing his usual practice is to cite a reason or determining cause for his judgement, so that others can receive his ideas for just what they are worth. Mr. Mayhew aspires to no leadership, nor even dictatorship, in social and political matters. He is a person who presumes to inquire and think for himself on such subjects, and he wishes others to do the same. In the early numbers he stated that he should appropriate the fly leaves of "London Labour" for the publication of certàin *speculations* on economical and other subjects, candidly warning the readers that the opinions there expressed were nothing but speculations, and reserving to himself the right of changing such opinions as often as he found *reason* to do so. Surely this is the very reverse of leadership or dictatorship, and it is in precisely the same spirit that Mr. Mayhew continues the publication of his sentiments from time to time. The passage referred to concerning the taxes is as follows:—
"The imposts on foreign commodities were neither instituted nor maintained as a source of income to the government, but simply as a means of protection to the home producer." Surely our Oxford friend will admit the truth of this statement as regards what were specially called "protective duties," and that it referred to nothing else is self-evident.

The following, from a clerical correspondent, requires no comment. It is printed here as a record of the fact:—

"SIR,

"It may perhaps afford some trifling illustration of the subject of 'Hot Cross Buns,' in your valuable work, to state that I well remember, when a boy about twelve years old (now *sixty* years ago), the distich you quote was set to music, and sung as a catch or glee; the several voices being so humorous and modulated as to produce a *comic* effect. Another of the same character began, 'The last dying speech and confession' another, 'Ah, how, Sophia,' but these words, being rapidly and humorously sung, caught the ear as 'A house o' fire, a house o' fire!' Such music was then much in fashion.

"I am, Sir,
"Yours most respectfully,
"R.W.N."

ANSWERS TO CORRESPONDENTS.
[No.39, No. II "Those that will not Work", 6 SEPTEMBER 1851, price 3d.]

Edited out:
THE REV. E.H.; IRVING; A GERMAN (CORRECTION OF MAYHEW'S ETYMOLOGY.)

====================

The following finds fault, under a mistaken idea, with the criminal statistics as given in No.37 of this work:[38]—

"Sir,

"Having completed, a fortnight ago, a work embracing the statistics of crime in England, Wales, Scotland, and Ireland, in reference to the social state of the population, and seeing your advertisement, I sent for No.37 of your publication, with which I was very much pleased—but in reference to the maps, if given at all with a view of being of service, they certainly ought to be correct.

"Let us examine Map 1, on the density of the population.

"You have computed the number of persons

---

[38] The maps and statistics which were later gathered at the end of the Vol. IV of the 1862 edition were originally distributed at the end of weekly issues, to be bound in the text with which they did not relate otherwise.

ANSWERS TO CORRESPONDENTS

to each statute acre whether it is capable of being cultivated or not; consequently it is no criterion to the means of employment afforded to a given population—you could not, for instance, compare Lincolnshire with North Wales or Cumberland—indeed, out of the 32,342,400 acres on which your table is computed in England, 3,256,400 acres of land are *incapable* of improvement, and ought to be deducted; and in Wales, out of the 4,752,000 acres, 1,105,000 acres are *incapable* of improvement, and the residue ought to be the foundation of the table in order truly to arrive at the density of the population to a given quantity of land—for if you give five men an acre of land in Norfolk, they might obtain their subsistence, but certainly not on the top of Snowden or Shap-Fells.

"Again, as to Map 2, in reference to crime.

"*Flintshire* is placed in the *black* book. It is a great pity you did not keep to the text '*each county* in England and *Wales*'—for Wales is lumped together. The average also is taken from England and Wales, while in truth all the *black part* is in England, therefore an average ought to have been taken for *England only,* or England and Wales *separately*. In that case Kent, Surrey, Suffolk, and Sussex would have been above the average. You cannot truly deal with England and Wales as *one*, without doing injustice to Wales, Scotland, and Ireland; to illustrate this take the year 1849, and we have those committed for trial, &c.:—

"In Ireland 1 in 194¾ of the population.

"In Scotland 1 in 601¼ ditto.

"In England and Wales 1 in 571¾ ditto.

"Thus, placing England as 1 in 571¾ instead of 1 in 556⅛ and placing Wales as 1 in 571¾ instead of 1 in 1070 of the population, the true gradation of crime would be thus:—

"In Ireland 1 in 194¾ of the population.

"In England 1 in 556⅛ ditto.

"In Scotland 1 in 601¼ ditto.

"In Wales 1 in 1070 ditto.

"My sole object in writing is to call your attention to these matters.

"I am, yours,

"W.B. Prichard, C.E., F.S.A."

The above objections are of two kinds—those which refer to the mode of estimating the density of the population, and those which refer to the mode of estimating the comparative criminality of the several counties.

As to the density of the population, Mr. Prichard urges that this should be calculated *not a*ccording to the entire area of the county, but according to merely that portion of it which is capable of cultivation. Now, with all deference to Mr. Prichard, the relative number of the population to a given quantity of arable land, or meadow land, has no connection whatever with the purposes for which the table was given, these being to arrive at definite notions as to the crowding of the people into a given space with the view of ascertaining whether the law be *generally* true that the greater the number of people congregated in a particular locality, the greater the crime. Of course the quantity of land capable of affording subsistence to the people must be less in the metropolis than in any other part of the kingdom—less even perhaps than "on the top of Snowdon or Shap-Fells," and yet surely Mr. Prichard would not cite the deficiency of cultivatable land in London as the cause why there are 24 criminals in every 10,000 of the metropolitan population and only 7 criminals in the same number of people in Cumberland. Some say the excess of criminality in the capital is due to the greater crowding of people; others that it is due to the greater temptation arising from the large amount of property existing there; others again that it is due to the greater poverty of the "lower orders" in that quarter. The object of the maps and tables is to put each of the criminal theories to the test of statistics. If it be true that the greater crime of London is due to the greater mass of people there congregated, then should those localities where the population is most dense have the greatest number of criminals. The tables and maps speak for themselves on this point.

As regards Map No. 2, Mr. Prichard errs in saying that Flintshire is placed in the black book; surely Flintshire is part of North Wales, and this he will see is left virgin white as indicative of its

189

relative purity. Then, with all a Welshman's pardonable love of country, Mr. Prichard urges that the criminal average should have been taken for England alone, saying that the whole of the black part is in England. This might have been gratifying to Mr. Prichard's nationality, but it is quite unusual and in no way necessary. Surely the honourable virtue of the Welsh is sufficiently evident. The Welsh counties would have been calculated separately, but the returns of the Registrar-General did not admit of this being done. Mr. Mayhew will be happy to give every attention to Mr. Prichard's book when published.[39]

Mr. Prichard, it will be seen, estimates the relative criminality of each county according to the *whole* of the population. This, with all deference, is a less simple method than the proportion to *a fixed quantity*. By Mr. Prichard's method the ratio is contrary to the numbers; that is to say, the intensity of the crime in North and South Wales is in the inverse proportion of 1370 to 1186, so that the district bearing the highest number has the fewest criminals, whereas, by finding the ratio to a constant quantity (say 1000 or 10,000 of the population in each county) we arrive at an immediate or less "roundabout" method of comparison: thus the relative criminality of North and South Wales is *directly* as 7 to 8 (of every 10,000 of the Welsh people). Mr. Prichard, moreover, appears to draw his conclusions from one year's returns only (1849). No averages can be depended upon under ten or five years at least.

If from an urn filled with different coloured balls, I draw only one ball, I can from that obtain no knowledge of the proportionate number of different coloured balls contained in the urn; but after a *series* of drawings, I shall be enabled to conclude (with more or less certainty, according to the extent of the series) the relative quantity of balls of each colour within the vessel.—*See Quetelet on Probabilities.*[40]

26th August, 1851.

"SIR,

"Seeing by last week's number of your most valuable work 'London Labour and the Poor,' that it 'was your intention of treating of a fourth class, viz., 'Those who need not work,' I should be much obliged by your informing me at what period of the work you intend entering on it; and also if it is your intention of giving portraits to illustrate the present subject of 'Those that will not work.' Hoping to have an answer, when convenient, in 'London Labour,'

"Your most obedient Servant,
"R.S.
("A reader from the first.")

Portraits of all the classes treated of will be given. It is impossible to say when those who *need not* work will be treated of, seeing that the Operatives and the Distributors have not been as yet entered upon. Mr. Mayhew hopes to pay his attention to all in good time, though really the subject he has undertaken is so vast that it becomes almost fearful to contemplate.

The following speaks for itself. It shows how the accursed cheap system is maintained, and how the wives of working-men are invariably used to degrade the value of labour for the production of slop goods of all kinds. Mr. Sidney Herbert[41] told us some eighteen months ago that the only remedy for the lowness of women's wages was to ship off our female-workers to the colonies. 20,000£ were subscribed for this purpose, some half-dozen ship-loads have been sent out—and yet it would appear from the subjoined that the remuneration for female-labour is not a farthing-piece the better: when *will* these Political Economists see their mistakes?

"SIR,

"I have read many of your details, and have felt shocked at the statement given of the

---

[39] W.B. Prichard author of a *Treatise on Harbours* (1844) does not seem to have published his study on crime.

[40] L.A.J. Quételet, *On Probabilities: Popular Instructions on the Calculation of Probabilities*, Beamish, 1839. (1st English edition.) S. M. Stigler, *The History of Statistics: The Measurement of Uncertainty Before 1900*, Harvard University Press, 1986, pp. 161-221.

[41] Sidney Herbert (1810-1861), Conservative MP South Wiltshire (1832-1860) Secretary at War, 1845-1846.

condition of many of the labouring population. You have done good service to humanity in exposing the tyranny and oppression of such employers as Moses, Hyams, &c., and I trust you will give the publicity of your pages to every case of extortion and defrauding of the poor. The following statement will show that in the 'lowest depth' of low wages there is 'a lower deep.' A Jew, or converted Jew Printer, trading not a hundred miles from the Farringdon-street end of Ludgate-hill, is now paying 1d. a thousand for cutting labels by scissars—formerly he paid 3d., then reduced it to 2d., and it is now at the sum I have named. He gives the work to the wives of the men in his employ, who dare not refuse to take it for fear he should discharge their husbands, and it must be sent in by a certain time. By working twelve hours a day, and entirely neglecting her household duties, a woman may earn 2s. 6d. a week, but she must work extremely hard to get that sum. This is the truth. I enclose my name and address, and dare the person (I will not outrage the term gentleman so much as to apply it to him) to deny what I have stated. Wishing you 'God speed' in your noble labours,

"I remain, Sir,

"Your obedient Servant,

"——."

The gentleman making the above statement forwards his name and address. Mr. Mayhew would be glad to hear from those who maintain that wages are regulated by the law of supply and demand, or those who believe that the price of food does not regulate the value of the lower grades of labour, how it is that in the agricultural districts a single man receives less wages than a married one? This question is put with the view of eliciting information on this most important subject. The facts that appear to be at variance with the Law of Supply and Demand have been stated in No. 32. They are briefly: (1) The depreciating effect of the relief in aid under the Old Poor-Law (2) The reduction of remuneration in the Cabinet-Makers' Trade, while work increased and hands decreased. (3) The increase of the quantity of work, and the decline of wages in

the cotton trade. (4) The upholding of the rate of wages by the trade societies. (5) The different wages paid to single and to married men in the agricultural districts. If wages are regulated by *natural law*, then, of course, the event recorded in the above letter is merely in *the regular order of things*;—but if wages are in a measure arbitrary, depending on the will of the capitalist save when controlled by trade societies, public opinion, and the like, then, of course, the Jew Printer, who pays 2s. 6d. for a week's labour, is as morally odious as the slop-fraternity in general. According to Political Economy, however, the Jew Printer is one of the great benefactors of society. Will R.H., or W.H., or the Editor of the Economist, oblige us with their opinions on this subject?

ANSWERS TO CORRESPONDENTS.
[No.40, 13 SEPTEMBER 1851]

The subjoined table of wages, which, if correct, is highly valuable, has been kindly furnished by R.H. Mr. Mayhew prints it here to preserve it, but he in no way pledges himself as to its accuracy. It is the production of a gentleman who is utterly unknown to him, and who gives no voucher for his respectability. The author is further a gentleman with a strong "economical" bias, and this alone Mr. Mayhew (without wishing to impute the least wilful perversion of the facts) is well aware will always give the mind a warp towards the interest of the employer, for Political Economy as it stands is super-eminently the science of trading.

The rate of remuneration for the working man, we are told, is to be tested simply by what may be termed a scramble—the law of supply and demand—without any regard to the subsistence of the labourers or the share they contribute towards the increased value of the materials on which they operate, though the rate of profits among traders, we are told, is to be determined by the cost of living. For instance, "in a small sea-port town," says Adam Smith, "a little grocer

WEEKLY WAGES OF STUFF HAT FINISHERS.

	1841 Lowest (s. d.)	1841 Highest (s. d.)	1841 Average (s. d.)	1842 Lowest	1842 Highest	1842 Average	1843 Lowest	1843 Highest	1843 Average	1844 Lowest	1844 Highest	1844 Average	1845 Lowest	1845 Highest	1845 Average	1846 Lowest	1846 Highest	1846 Average	1847 Lowest	1847 Highest	1847 Average	1848 Lowest	1848 Highest	1848 Average	1849 Lowest	1849 Highest	1849 Average	1850 Lowest	1850 Highest	1850 Average
J.P........n	7 3	60 0	31 6	6 4	56 7	32 2	14 0	57 0	33 4	3 0	60 3	33 2	9 3	44 11	27 5	9	57 8	33 4	10 4	59 7	33 8	15 7	56 0	28 9	13 9	47 0	30 4	5 8	63 2	38 8
J.H........n	17 4	88 0	38 10	10 10	59 7	41 6	13 8	35 0	28 0	7 4	60 5	32 9	13 6	76 3	36 6	7 0	56 0	27 4	12 2	65 4	37 5	6 7	56 0	28 6	13 8	48 0	30 1	1 13	65 4	38 8
J.W........s	2 4	72 2	34 4							4	52 8	28 11	9 0	31 8	17 5	11 11	65 11	32 1	14 2	32 7	21 10									
—S...h .....s	15 6	62 1	33 10				14 0	53 4	31 4	4 2	62 9	31 5							6 4	42 5	24 1									
—G.........g	1 2	56 0	37 4																											
—W.........s				7 0	64 6	38 0																								
J.W.P.......r				17 4	39 9	25 2																								
W.H.........n				15 4	34 7	22 10																								
J.C.........n				17 4	40 0	23 0																								
W.O....n																														
—H.......m																														
G.T.........r																														
C.J.........r																														
W.H.........d																														
Average			34 9			30 5			30 10			31 6			27 1			30 11			29 3			28 7			30 2			38 6

will make 40 or 50 per cent. upon a stock of a single hundred pounds, while a considerable wholesale merchant in the same place will scarce make 8 or 10 per cent. upon a stock of ten thousand. The trade of the grocer may be necessary for the conveniency of the inhabitants, and the narrowness of the market may not admit the employment of a larger capital in the business. *The man, however, must not only live by his trade, but live by it suitably to the qualifications it requires.* "A new Political Economy, one that will take *some little notice* of the claims of labour, doing justice as well to the workman as to the employer, stands foremost among the *desiderata*, or things wanted, in the present age. As the science now exists, Ikey Solomons, the Jew Fence, is the perfection of its principles. He buys in the cheapest market and sells in the dearest, and he is regulated in all his dealings *solely* by the principle of supply and demand. Were there more thieves and less receivers, of course he would give even less for the stolen goods than he does; and were there more receivers and fewer thieves, of course each receiver, by the principle of competition, would give more. Nor can the fence's exorbitant profits be quarrelled with "economically." They are, thus viewed, merely greater remuneration for greater risk, and *perfectly justifiable*. Has any economist, however, the courage to justify them, and say that the market should be thrown open, and free trade, *without any restrictions whatever,* allowed to the receivers of stolen goods? W.B.B., the economist, has told us, in these pages, that "justice" and "right" and "conscience" are mere conceits, having no foundation in nature—moral bogies, as it were, invented by old women to frighten the naughty, and surely after this Ikey, the economist, will be one of the forms of his hero-worship, at least if there be any worship in the gentleman at all. All this, however, but little concerns the Wage List of R.H., which, as was before said, is given here with a view to its preservation.[42]

The above statement of wages is, however, objectionable on other points besides those before raised, and as employers often deceive themselves, and the public too, respecting the earnings of their workmen, Mr. Mayhew will here append a short account as to how wage

192

statements should be made out *in fairness both to employer* and *employed*. Of course it is to the interest of employers to make it appear that their workmen earn as much as possible, and of working men to make out that their wages are as little as possible. There is a natural tendency to exceed the truth on both sides, and this tendency, even without wilfull dishonesty, will necessarily incline to exaggeration. For instance, an employer asserts that the wages of a working tailor are 36s. a week, and instantly the public conclude that the operatives in that trade have little to complain of. But in receiving this statement, we have first to inquire whether the operative earning this amouut of money belongs to the better or worse paid class of workmen, and if to the former, what are the wages of the latter, and what proproportion do the worse paid men bear to the better paid. But even suppose this done, it would still give us no accurate knowledge on the subject.

Wages are strictly remuneration for work done. Hence it is useless to tell us merely what the remuneration has been (for this is but the employer's side of the question); for a full and fair account, we should know how much labour has been given or exacted for the stated amount of pay (this is the working man's part of the subject). If the men are paid by the day they may, by extra supervision, be made to do double the amount of work usual in the trade (when their wages will be virtually reduced one-half). Such is the case in the strapping shops of the carpenters' trade. Or the men may be worked over hours, as by the "scurf employers" in the scavengers' trade. If, on the other hand, the men are paid by the piece, the price should be given as well as the ordinary rate of working; that is to say, the time that each piece occupies an *average* hand in making. A "quick hand" may work twice as fast as a slow one, and it would be unfair to cite this as the average earning of the several hands in the trade (though this was done to Mr. Mayhew by an army clothier respecting the "loopers"). It should also be stated whether the work is done at home or on the employer's premises. If on the employer's premises the ordinary hours of labour should be set forth, and if at home, or any work be taken home to finish in after hours, not only the same statement should be given, but mention should be made whether the workman employs any one else to assist him in. An employer, in contradiction to a statement made by Mr. Mayhew, that those who "loop" the soldiers' coats earn on an average 3s. 6d. a week, asserted that he was paying some of his hands as much as 15s. a week for the same work, and account books were proferred in proof of the correctness of the assertion. On inquiry it turned out that the 15s. had been received only by the quickest hands, who often took two coats home with them after their day's work, and employed "seconders" to finish the work for them, while the average wages of *all* the hands were proved by this employer's ledger to be less than Mr. Mayhew had declared.

But even after all this sifting, we shall have arrived only at the *nominal* wages of the workman, and these *nominal* wages are often merely a blind to the public and the trade, being widely different from the *virtual* wages, or sum really received by the operatives. The fashionable mode of proceeding among employers at present is not to reduce wages directly, but indirectly, by laying some extra charge upon the men—that is to say, to increase their burdens by a kind of *indirect* taxation as it were. Hence it behoves us to set forth most particularly in every trade what are the *deductions to the wages* said to be received.

Now these deductions Mr. Mayhew finds to be of several kinds. (1.) Fines or stoppage for positive or assumed misconduct. (2.) Rent charged for use of tools or implements of trade, as in the system of pence among the sawyers, and the frame rents among the stockingers. (3.) Cost of such appurtenances as the workman is made to find, as trimmings, in the cheap tailors' trade. (4.) Rent for gas. (5.) Rent for shop, occasionally introduced among piece workers as a fine for absence from work, on the plea that "the rent is going on all the same." (6.) Bonus paid to foreman in order to obtain work. (7.) Sum paid to middleman from whom the work is obtained. (8.) Stoppages for benefit or provident fund, to which the workman loses all claim in case of being discharged. This is not at all an unusual trick among employers. If, moreover, the work be done at home we must deduct all the necessary expenses in connection with it, which are thus forced on the workman. These are: (1.) Candles and firing, used expressedly for the work. (2.) Rent where the work is carried on in a distinct place. But these and the foregoing are only the more direct modes of reducing wages indirectly. The more indirect modes of lowering the remuneration for labour are: (1.) Reducing the quality of the provisions among those who board and lodge with their employers, as milliners, &c. (2.) Forcing or expecting the men to deal with the employer for their provisions, and charging them an undue price for the same. (3.) Forcing or expecting the men either to take lodgings of their employers which they do not use, or for which they are charged an undue price, or to rent houses of their employers on the same terms. (4.) Forcing or expecting the men to have their drink of their employer, and favouring those who expend the most of their earnings in this manner. (5.) Forcing the workpeople to find security for the work they take out, and thus to pay an undue price for their food or drink to those bakers, butchers, or publicans, who make a trade of "standing security" for the poorer workpeople. But the *aids to wages* are quite as necessary to be ascertained as even the *drawbacks*. These aids are of two kinds, according as they consist of either direct or indirect additions made to the earnings of the workmen. The Direct Additions to Wages consist of: (1.) Perquisites or gratuities obtained by the workmen from various sources. (2.) Tribute money, or a certain portion of the proceeds of the work, given to the workmen over and above their regular wages, as the fourth penny to certain weavers, &c. (3.) Profits derived by the workmen from the employment of other labourers to assist them, as sweaters, piece-masters, lumpers, and the like. (4.) Family workers, or those who avail themselves

of the assistance of the services of their wives and children in their work, as the Spitalfield weavers, the fancy cabinet makers, &c. The Indirect Additions to Wages, on the other hand, include all extraneous sources of income, or such gains as are not derived immediately from the work. These appear to be: (1.) Pensions. (2.) Allowances from Provident or Charitable Societies. (3.) Other work done in over time. (4.) Allotments of land. (5.) Parish relief. But even when all these additions and deductions are made, we arrive at, solely, the *occasional* wages of the workmen, and these afford us no means of estimating the absolute yearly income of the labourers. To ascertain this point, we must set forth the quantity of employment obtained by the operatives throughout the year, which is a matter of the highest importance in forming a just estimate of the condition of the labourers belonging to those callings especially which depend on the seasons, or on the fashion of the time. To frame a correct notion of the state of any class of work-people, we must not only cite the weekly earnings of the employed, but we must set forth the ratio of the employed to the unemployed; and if we show how much the constant hands get, at least in fairness we should exhibit how little falls to the share of the casual hands, and state the proportion that the one bears to the other. Again, it behoves us, if we would do justice to *both* employer and employed, to cite the duration of the season in those trades which are brisk and slack at various periods of the year, giving the difference between the earnings of the men in the busy and dull times; for most assuredly it would not be fair to quote the weekly gains of the hop-pickers for the few weeks of their employment, as an example of their ordinary wages, nor to set forth the earnings of the preference men at the docks (omitting all mention of the casual hands) as a type of the income of the dock labourers in general. Yet such are the ways in which statements of wages are generally made out by employers, who cite the nominal weekly wages of a few constantly-employed men as an example of the average *virtual* wages of the whole class, employed and unemployed, throughout the year, though they know as well as Mr. Mayhew does, that the two things are as different as *gross* and *net* profits. R.H. has certainly given the yearly nominal wages of a *few* hands in the hatters' trade; he forgets, however, to say whether they are fully or partially employed men, whether quick or slow hands, or, indeed, to qualify the statement in any way by such distinctive features, as would give an individual character to what might otherwise be mistaken for a general statement.

ANSWERS TO CORESPONDENTS.
[No.41, No.III, "Those that will not Work", 20 SEPTEMBER 1851, price 3d.]

The following curious document has come to hand. Mr. Mayhew will inquire into the facts and report accordingly.

"September 6th, 1851.

"Sir,

"In page 418 of your first volume, you speak of a meeting consisting of *thieves*.

"It has been agitated, time out of mind—Reform! Reform! Reform! has been posted in every hole and corner, for some political or great social purpose, and conceiving the idea that yours was a reform of the above class of outcasts, which has made me trouble you with these few lines; and also in bringing under your notice a case, which is worthy of your consideration, as well as every lover of his species, and of which I am afraid is not a solitary one.

"The case I am about to show is thus:—a young couple which are married, and both of which has led a dishonest life for many years, and both of which have refrained from those practices these twelve or fourteen months past; the husband has held a situation as a conductor of an omnibus. The proprietor, whose name is Bennett, and to whom he gave every satisfaction while in his employ, having to renew his

licence, it was refused him, although there was not a stain on his character, nor a complaint laid against him during the time he was a conductor; but it was refused him on account of his former life, and, having been convicted, he has been out of a situation this last four or five months. His master is willing to take him on again as soon as he regains his licence.

"Sir, could you tell me how a government can keep a man from getting an honest livelihood, or a nation can be justified in so allowing it, as it is done in their name, by those who represent them (or ought to). We are not all demigods, nor heroes in honesty, nor do I believe we all would go through the fiery ordeal of dying by starvation sooner than doing worse. If this young man of whom I speak can attain his end, he will become an honest man and a good member of society; such is my hopes, at any rate. All that is left now is a little of your valuable advice. 'Do good to all men' was the spring that moved me to this act, humble as it is, but still hoping to do more,

"I remain, yours, &c.,

"T—A—, *a constant reader.*"

Mr. MAYHEW has to acknowledge with thanks returns from the authorities of the under-mentioned places, in answer to the following queries:—

Number of prostitutes well-dressed living in brothels?

Number of prostitutes well-dressed walking the streets?

Number of prostitutes, low, infesting low neighbourhoods?

Number of brothels where prostitutes are kept?

Average number of prostitutes kept in each house of ill-fame where prostitutes resort?

Average number of prostitutes resorting to each?

Number of houses where prostitutes lodge?

Average number of prostitutes lodging in each?

The localities from which answers have been received are as follow:—

Metropolitan Police.

Dudley.
Dewsbury.
Reading.
Northampton.
Chesterfield.
Hertford.
Brecon.
Forebridge (near Stafford).
Newcastle (under Lyne).
Margate.
Bolton.
Dublin.
Canterbury.
Merthyr Tydvil.
Leicester.
Carlisle.
Belfast.
Wakefield.
Dorchester.
Huntingdon.
South Shields.
North Shields.
Warwick.
Halifax.
Manchester.
Borough of Lancaster.
Bath.
Leeds.
Glasgow.
Edinburgh.
Bristol.
Nottingham.
Liverpool.
Birmingham.
Plymouth.
Newcastle-on-Tyne.

Mr. Mayhew has also to acknowledge the receipt of Reports from the following Societies:—

Guardian Society for reclaiming females who have deviated from the paths of virtue.

British Ladies' Society for promotion of reformation of female prisoners.

British Penitent Female Refuge.

London Female Penitentiary.

Refuge for the Destitute.

Answers have likewise been received from several of the Metropolitan workhouses.

Returns have also been forwarded from some of the London hospitals.

The returns from the governments abroad, have not yet come to hand.

The following is sent to correct an error:—

"Sir,

"In your Answers to Correspondents in the 36th No. of 'London Labour,' &c., which has just reached me in Part 9, there is an error of the press, which renders the two first lines of my communication unintelligible. They should stand thus:—

"Haberdasher } *Minshew*, from Ger.
"Haberdashery } *Habt ihr das*, i.e., Have
you that, &c.

"In your estimate of the value of Richardson's Dictionary on account of the copious examples it contains from the earliest to the latest authors, and also of his notions as to the historic mode of Etymology, you concur in, I believe, the general opinion. I am aware the work has been censured as wholly deficient in what you term 'dialectic Etymology, through the medium of cognate languages.' But it is only fair to keep in mind that the author considered Researches into the Affinities of the Indo-Germanic tongues (the cognate languages, to which, I presume, you allude) to be the peculiar province of Comparative Philology, and quite out of place in an English dictionary. Thus, he observes of the display of Oriental reading made by Dr. Webster in his Preliminary Essays, 'that as introductory to a dictionary of the English language, it seems as appropriate and useful as a reference to the code of Gentoo laws to settle a question of English inheritance.' Whether right or wrong in this opinion, I do not discuss.

I am sufficiently national, notwithstanding my pride and joy in the Crystal Palace Exhibition, to wish the names of Sir Wm. Jones and John Horne Tooke not to be overlaid by those of Geisner and Bopp, great as they undoubtedly are.

"With respect to Horne Tooke, allow me to say, that I heartily subscribe to the following words of Lord Brougham, 'As everything that was done before' (the 'Diversions of Purley') 'was superseded by it, so nothing has been effected since, unless in pursuing its views and building upon its solid foundations.'—*Statesmen in the Time of George III., Second Series.*[42]

"I remain, yours, &c.
"A.B."

"What is meant," adds the same correspondent "by 'the Latin *give*' in the seventh line from the bottom of your second paragraph, col. 2?"

The word should have been *sive;* give was an error of the press. Surely Lord Brougham, great man as he is, is not the best possible authority to quote upon a matter of Saxon philology; but A.B., if he pushes his etymological researches little farther than Horne Tooke and Anglo-Saxon, will see that comparative philology is to the true understanding of languages, what comparative anatomy is to natural history. Without this all is vain conjecture, and the derivation of Gherkin from King Jeremiah, represents very truly the fanciful part of the science. Upon Horne Tooke's plan any derivation may be given, as witness his explanation of the origin of poltroon.

ANSWERS TO CORRESPONDENTS.
[No.42, 27 SEPTEMBER 1851]

Edited out:

R.H., D.W., B.H.G.D.; J.M.G. NORTHAMPTON; W.Y.Z; W.L.Y. WOOLWICH; J.T. LIVERPOOL; G.W.; A.B.C.

———

QUERY asks, If wages are not regulated by the law of Supply and Demand, on what *do* they depend? Wages depend, or *should* depend, upon the share of the produce justly accruing to the working man. Production is generally a joint affair; one party contributing the materials, tools, shelter, food, and superintendence necessary for the due performance of the

---

[42] Henry Peter Brougham (1778-1868), Lord Chancellor. The second series ran between 1839 and 1843.

work, and the other contributing the work itself. These are the two elements which make up the real value of every article produced, and common equity demands that each of the contributors should share in the result according to the proportion in which his contribution serves to increase the ultimate worth of the produce. The inquiry, therefore, into what regulates wages, resolves itself into a second inquiry, what regulates the share of the produce *justly* accruing to the working man. At present this is determined by a continual struggle between the two contributors as to how much the one can extort from the other, and how little the other can be starved into accepting. This is called the law of Supply and Demand, or the relation between population and capital, and is about as just a means of deciding what is essentially a point of simple equity, as a standing army is of settling the *rights* of nations. Neither numbers nor power have any connection whatever with a matter of abstract justice.

The many discontents prevailing among the labouring classes of this country arise mainly from the present mode of regulating wages. Socialism, chartism, communism are all necessary consequences of the infraction of the fundamental law of the true economy of national wealth, viz., that production is a partnership, and that the labourer is *therefore* entitled to a fair share of the produce. Give him this share, recognize his claim to *participate* in the wealth that he creates, and you not only stop all calls for grumbling, but you put an end to all new-fangled principles of society (for this is the foundation-stone of every "model city")— you make the interest of employer and employed one and the same; whereas now they are diametrically opposed, and so you destroy all that bitter enmity between classes which is ready at any moment at present to burst forth into physical fury. It wants but this fusion of interests to wed the two great clans of this country—the savers and the workers—into one united family.

But what regulates the share of the produce accruing to the workman? This, as was before stated, is determined by the additional value that the labour of the workman confers upon the materials supplied by the capitalist; the conferring of such additional value being the sole reason why the employer pays any wages at all to the labourer. It is no matter to the capitalist whether there be 10,000 or 100,000 labourers in the trade; he is determined in the price he pays for so much work by the price he will receive for it. Economists, however, deny that prices can in any way regulate wages.

Formerly the workmen of this country were all villeins—either "villeins in gross," performing the lowest household duties, or "villeins regardant," attached to the soil, and being specially engaged in agriculture. The services rendered by them were either arbitrary, that is to say, dependent on the mere will of their lord, which constituted a state of "pure villeinage"—or certain and defined, which constituted privileged villeinage, or "villein-socage;" but in either case the person and the property of the villein belonged entirely to the lord, for the labourers were *incapable of acquiring anything for themselves*.

We have put an end to the villeinage system of labour, thank God! but we have transferred the labourer from the tyranny of the noble to the greed of the trader, who, aware of the absence of all *legal* right on the part of the workmen to obtain any *share* (saving the barest subsistence) out of the wealth they produce, takes care to perpetuate the wrong that the labourers shall have no power to acquire anything for themselves.

After the villeinage system of labour came the hireling system, by which the compulsory villein of old was changed into the voluntary bondsman—the serf into the servant; the sole distinction being that for the sake of a small pittance over and above his subsistence (and often not that), the workman was made to part with all right to participate in the wealth he created, *for so long as he continued the servant of his master*. And this is the system which remains in force to the present day. The workmen of this country are all hirelings, selling their services for a little present subsistence, rather than being the just participators in the riches they produce. There are but two objections possible to the above line of argument: the one is that by the present arrangement under the law of Supply and Demand, the labourer *does* obtain his fair share of the produce; and the other, that the labourer has *no right* to any such share. The latter objection is, of course, a justification for pure villeinage, the wrong of which consisted mainly in depriving the labourer of the property he inherently possessed in his labour. The former objection is, however, of a different kind. It admits the right of the labourer to share in the wealth he creates, and asserts that by the law of Supply and Demand be obtains this share in as equitable manner as possible.

The reply to this, objection is first by the fact so often quoted here in illustration of the injustice done to the operative, viz., that the padlock which sells for a shilling the workman receives but a halfpenny for making, and this surely even the most unconscionable would not attempt to justify as a *fair* division of the proceeds between the capitalists, the distributors, and the producers.

A second answer to the same point is that the law of Supply and Demand cannot possibly be a *fair* method of testing the amount of the share of the produce accruing to the labourer; *seeing that it pays no regard to the value of such produce, but merely to the sum set aside by the employers for the remuneration of their work-people during the performance of the work*. By the law of Supply and Demand the workman's wages are made to depend solely upon the WAGE FUND, whereas they should, *in justice*, be regulated by the PRODUCE FUND, which are two very different things. The share of the Wage Fund accruing to each of the operatives depends simply on the number of workpeople among whom that Fund is to be divided, and pays no regard to the produce or value of the work; whereas it is here maintained that the operative should be remunerated in proportion to the amount of wealth which his labour contributes to the Produce Fund. This is the law of justice, the other the law of necessity.

The workman *creates* so much wealth; he, by the exercise of his skill, gives to one pound's worth of materials the value of two or three pounds; and, doing so, a certain proportion of the extra value belongs to him by the most cogent of all rights to individual possession— *the right of creation*. Deny this right, and you deny the very foundation of the rights of property. You may, by the communistic theory of society, dispute his title to participate in the wealth he creates; but, under the present system of things, it is *impossible* that you can do otherwise than admit it. "The property," says Adam Smith, "which every man has in his labour, as it is the *original foundation* of all other property, so it is the most sacred and inviolable. The patrimony of a poor man lies in the strength and dexterity of his hands."

Wages, then, depend upon the increased value that a workman, by the exercise of his skill, gives to the material on which he operates. The rate of remuneration for labour *should be* determined by the amount that the materials will sell for after being operated upon by the workman over and above their original cost and the ordinary rate of profit on the capital employed; and they certainly *should not* be regulated by what the employer can induce or compel the workman, through his necessities, to accept. The relation of the employer to the workman is that of a pawnbroker making an advance upon so much property deposited with him; and the employer, like the pawnbroker, is bound in justice to hand over to the workman the amount that the goods realize, when sold, over and above what he originally advanced upon them, and minus the ordinary rate of profit on the capital employed. And as the pawnbroker has no right to force the starving man to accept what he chooses (or the funds of his trade will allow him) to advance in full of all demands on the property when sold, so the employer should not have the power, because he advances the subsistence of the workman, to appropriate to himself the whole of the after proceeds of the labour. Who would say that the law of Supply and Demand would be a just means of regulating the amounts to be given by pawnbrokers to the poor, in exchange for their goods *(without regard to the ulterior proceeds of their sale)*? Does not the pawnbroker know that the poor hungry wretch is at his mercy, and will take whatever he can get? and what are the slop employers of the present day but labour pawnbrokers of the very worst kind, advancing what they please on the work, and over whom the poor workpeople have no control whatever?

The only true and equitable system of wages is the tribute system; or that which makes the remuneration of the workmen depend on the value of the produce of his labour, and which is opposed both to the hireling system, which pays no regard to the produce or just property of the labourer, and the villeinage system, which regards neither his property nor his liberty. As a villein, the workman is the *slave* of the capitalist; as a hireling, he is the *servant* of him, while as a tributer, he is his *partner,* having a common interest with him, and consequently being as anxious to promote his employers welfare as he is his own. As yet we have only reached the hireling system of wages; when the tribute system will be universally adopted throughout the land, of course, it is impossible to predicate; but until this is done the same poverty, the same discontent, the same class enmity, and the same danger to the community, must continue to exist as now prevails among us.

Mr. Mayhew has to acknowledge the receipt of E.B.'s communication. The valuable table of wages and expenditure which he forwards will be given in as early a number as possible. Will E.B., however, oblige Mr. Mayhew by stating whether he is a quick hand or not, and the usual hours of labour with him, both of which conditions he will perceive are necessary qualifications for an individual statement? Are there also any deductions to be made from the wages given? and have the prices paid for his labour remained the same through the series of years indicated?—if not, please name the difference.

ANSWERS TO CORRESPONDENTS.
[No.43, No.IV "Those that will not Work",
4 OCTOBER 1851, price 3d.]

In the last number of "Those that will not
work," a letter was printed from T. A., who
wrote on behalf of two thieves who were
inclined to lead an honest life, and one of
whom had been refused his licence as an
omnibus conductor, on account of his previous
career. Mr. Mayhew promised to institute
inquiries as to the facts of the case, and to
report thereon. He has accordingly placed
himself in communication with the
Commissioners of Police, from whom the
following reply has been received:—

"Metropolitan Police Office,
4, Whitehall Place,
24th Sept., 1851.

"SIR,

"I AM directed by Mr. Mayne to acknowledge
the receipt of your letter of the 22nd instant, and
to acquaint you in reply, that after repeated careful considerations of the circumstances of the
case of the party mentioned, he felt it his duty
not to grant him a licence as conductor of an omnibus, and that Mr. Mayne regretted he was
obliged to come to that conclusion; but he cannot enter into any statement of the grounds upon
which he acts in executing a very responsible, dis-
cretionary power.

"I am, Sir,
"Your most obedient Servant,
"C. YARDLEY,
"Chief Clerk."

By the above it will be seen that the
Commissioners assert themselves, in as delicate
a manner as possible, to have had sufficient
cause for the refusal of the licence; let us,
therefore, look calmly at the case. It may,
doubtlessly, be a great evil that those who have
adopted criminal courses as a means of
subsistence should, when they may be disposed
to reform, be denied by the government
authorities the means of earning an honest
livelihood. But suppose for a moment that the

police were to grant licences to men whom they
knew, and whom it is indeed acknowledged, to
be thieves, to act as omnibus conductors; that is
to say, to fill situations not only of great trust to
the omnibus proprietors, but of no little
temptation to the conductors themselves, as
well as involving a continued intercourse with
the public, and consequently requiring persons
of at least civil, sober and honest habits! What
would the public say if the police were to take
this privilege upon themselves, and, believing
in the tales of repentance urged by old
offenders, they were to elect persons of known
dishonesty to fill situations of considerable
temptation, and requiring no little command
over the temper and habits? T.A. forgets, in his
zeal for his friends, and his desire to see an
opportunity for reformation afforded to all
those who have led a dishonest life, the
peculiar nature of the duty confided to the
Police Commissioners. The police have a very
onerous and ungrateful office to perform, and
to those who have not had occasion to see them
other than in their public capacity, it may
appear that they sometimes carry out the
authority entrusted to them with undue
harshness but to others who, like Mr. Mayhew,
have had repeated occasions to seek from them
information on subjects connected with the
poor and the criminal classes, they are most
certainly a body of persons actuated by every
desire to benefit and improve the condition of
the people generally. Mr. Mayhew *knows* this
from his own experience, and indeed he is
most glad to be called upon to make this public
expression of his opinion on the matter. For
many months now he his been in frequent
communication with the heads of the police
force, receiving important information from
them, and, as a man wishing to do justice to all
parties, he must confess that they are a body
"more sinned against than sinning." That there
may occur among members of the force
repeated instances of a tyrannical use of the
power entrusted to them, Mr. Mayhew does not
attempt to deny, but assuredly these are the
exceptions; and, so far from their being in any
way countenanced by the Commissioners, he

knows that no persons regret or censure them so deeply as they do. People are apt to forget the benefits they owe to the vigilance of the police—the protectors by night and day of our persons, property, and liberties, from undue aggression; we should remember, when we lay our heads down on our pillows, to whom we owe the security of our slumbers.

Mr. Mayhew is well aware that the police appear to working men to be a force instituted by the rich against the poor, and created to maintain the laws, in their oppression of the humbler classes. That the duty of the police is to maintain the laws, there cannot be the least doubt. If we are to have any laws at all, there must be some force to see them executed; a lawless community is neither desirable, nor, thank Heaven! possible for any length of time. The error of the poor people generally lies in considering the harshness of some of our laws to be the harshness of those who execute them. The street-sellers are an instance of this mistake; they visit the errors of the street acts on the heads of the force which carries them out, and so get to regard the police as the great enemies of the people and themselves. And so T.A., thinking only of the injury done to the conductor who has been deprived of his licence on account of the dishonesty of his past career, and forgetting the duty the police owe to society in general, upbraids them with a tyrannical exercise of power. The Commissioners dare not make any such hazardous experiments as to delegate situations of trust to those who are known to them to be untrustworthy.

Suppose T.A.'s friends, after receiving their licence, were to lapse into their former malpractices; and let us say, for the sake of the argument, that they were to avail themselves of the situation of conductor to pass counterfeit money, and it then came out that the police, from benevolent motives, gave licences to known thieves—what would parliament and the press have to say on the subject? Or suppose the temptation of continually receiving large sums of money for the proprietor of the omnibus was to prove too strong for those who had once subsisted by thieving, what would their employer say to the police for licensing, and so tacitly vouching for the fitness of known bad characters to fill posts of trust?

But though the police, as government officers, cannot grant to persons of notoriously dishonest propensities the opportunity of leading a new life when they are so inclined, Mr. Mayhew, who stands in a different position with the public, will be happy to interest himself on behalf of the two persons mentioned in the letter of T.A., and if they can assure him of the sincerity of their desire to reform, he will do all he can to put them in the way of carrying out their resolves. Will T.A. communicate again with Mr. Mayhew on the subject?

The following is very valuable, as correcting a derivation given in this work. A.B., who objects to the use of nothing but Saxon in the etymology of the English language, will here see how important it is that all languages (as proceeding from one parent stock) should be consulted for the complete understanding of our own:—

" SIR,

"I have been a reader of your work upon 'London Labour and the London Poor,' from its commencement, and therefore take the liberty of correcting what appears to me a mistake in your number of this week, viz., your derivation of the word 'shoful.' It is, as you are perhaps aware, constantly in use among the Jews of the present day, and is, I should say, evidently derived from the Hebrew subs. שֵׁפֶל (shēphel), a *low* or debased estate, see Psalm cxxxvi. 23, 'in our *low estate;*' Ecc. x. 6, 'the rich sit in a *low place.*' Hence the Hebrew adjective שָׁפָל '*base*' (as in 2 Sam. vi. 22, '*base* in mine own sight;' Ezek., xxix. 15, '*basest* of the kingdoms,' &c., &c.); and the Chaldee שְׁפַל (shăphāl), as in Dan. iv. 17, 'and settest up over it the *basest* of men.' Qy.—May not our English word shuffle come from this?" [Mr. Mayhew thinks not.] "I hope you will excuse me troubling you with this suggestion, but some of your derivations have been so ingenious, that I thought an additional 'notion' might not be altogether unacceptable.

"I remain, Sir,

"Your obedient Servant,

"E.L."

The above is conclusive, and proves to us that nothing short of direct dialectic derivation is sufficient to satisfy the mind. All indirect and conjectural etymology (as derivation from supposed roots) is mere waste of learning. *Indirectly*, almost any etymology may be given, but *directly*, that is to say, by finding the exoteric term itself in some foreign language, differently spelt, but meaning the same thing, there can be no error. The subject of the slang or cant language of a country is most peculiar; and all countries seem to have a distinct criminal or mendicant phraseology; even the Hottentots have their "cuze-cat." The *"argot"* of the French, the *"roth-spræc"* of the Germans, &c., all seem to be formed on the same basis— partly metaphorical and partly by the introduction of such corrupted foreign terms as are likely to be unknown to the society amid which the slang-speakers exist. There are several Hebrew terms in our "cant language," obtained, it would appear, from the intercourse of the thieves with the Jew fences; many of the cant terms, again, are Sanscrit, got from the gypsies; many Latin, got by the beggars from the Catholic prayers before the Reformation; and many, again, Italian, got from the wandering musicians and others: indeed the showmen, of whom we shall have to treat shortly, have but lately introduced a number of Italian phrases into their cant language. The slang of this country, of which there are several varieties (Mr. Mayhew once was in company with a crossing sweeper, who could speak three distinct kinds of cant, and who was evidently not a little proud of his learning), is a most interesting subject, and one which will occupy us largely when we come to treat of the thieves and their ways. Some of the slang phrases, are merely old English terms, which have become obsolete through the caprices of fashion. For example, the slang phrase, "that is not the *cheese*," expressive of something not approved of, and which was supposed to have some fanciful reference to the caseous comestible, being occasionally Frenchified by the witlings

of the day into *"C'est ne pas le fromage,"* and occasionally paraphrased by them into "it is not the precise Stilton," was, or rather the *cheese* was, nothing more nor less than an old English term, meaning, *choice*. Chaucer says,—

"To chese (choose) whether she wold him marry or no."

And the Anglo-Saxon *cyst* (from *ceosan*, to choose) means not only *choice*, election, but what is or would be *chosen* for its excellence; hence, "it is not the *cheese*," signified, simply, it is not what I should *choose*. So again, "that's not the ticket," meant merely, that's not etiquette. Those who know the derivation of the word etiquette itself (having the same origin) will not hesitate to adopt this rendering, strained as it may appear to others. But the whole subject of "cant" is, to the philologist, replete with interest of the most profound character.

[Returns have been received from the following towns, in addition to those acknowledged in No. 41:— Bradford. Gloucester. Lewes (Sussex). Grimsby. Whitehaven. Buckingham. Lincoln. Falmouth. Peterborough.]

The following has been received, and is acknowledged with thanks:—

"Aigburth, Liverpool, 12th Sept., 1851.
"SIR,
"May I take the liberty of asking about what date you expect to commence your remarks on the state and conditions of prostitution, as I may be enabled to give you some information on the subject which you would not be likely to get at. If you will give me an answer in the next number of your periodical I will send you my name and address.

"Yours obediently,
"B.H.G.D."

Will B.H.G.D. be kind enough to communicate the nature of his information as soon as possible? There are several peculiarities in connection with prostitution in Liverpool that will require special notice. Of course all communications will be in the strictest confidence.

ANSWERS TO CORRESPONDENTS.
[No.44, 11 OCTOBER 1851)]

Edited out:
W.P.; T.L.L.; A.C.; W.T.S.; G.W.S; T.A.

A working man sends the following extraordinary illustration of the boasted principle that machinery increases employment, and so, by extending the demand for labour, raises the wages of the workman:—

"Sheffield, September 22, 1851.
"Sir,

"I beg to be excused in the freedom I take with your patience in the perusal of these few humble lines, but having been a constant and an attentive reader of your valuable work, 'London Labour and the London Poor,' I should like to hear the opinion of R.H. or J.H., of the Manchester school, on this question. I ask what is the cause of reduction in the price of railway-spring making? We well know that railways keep continually increasing, consequently the demand for those articles must be greater; and, on the other hand, it is perfectly well known that there are no more manufactories of them than there were a few years ago; but the supply is on the increase, and is now wanted to be made cheaper. Three or four years since there was no machinery; and since its introduction it has completely put away with the practice of forging the work. The price of forging railway-springs was 1s. 10d. per cwt., at which rate two good workmen would earn about 12s. per day; but now the same work that they used to get 12s. for is done by machinery at the cost of not more than 3s. or 3s. 6d. It seems most singularly strange to us where the profit goes to if the proprietors do not get it. So much for the forging. A strike has recently taken place to maintain the price of fitting railway-springs; and appeals to the public have been circulated through the town of Sheffield, of which I inclose one for your inspection, merely to show you and the public that the produce of the Cyclops Works (specimens of whose

manufactures occupy so large a space in the Great Exhibition) is procured from the working men with a great deal of tyranny by the rich capitalist. I beg a thousand pardons for intruding on your patience, and remain,

"Yours,
"A WORKING MAN."

The inclosed bill is as follows:—
"THE APPEAL OF THE RAILWAY SPRING MAKERS TO THE INHABITANTS OF SHEFFIELD AND THE PUBLIC GENERALLY.
"FELLOW TOWNSMEN,

"Our present condition and circumstances impel us to submit for your inspection the following facts, in the hope that they will excite that sympathy and a good feeling which we think we are deserving of, and which have often been displayed in cases similar to ours.

"We, of course, are a class of artizans who are placed in the unenviable plight of having to resist most unjustifiable aggressions on the part of certain capitalists, in the price of our labour. We are precisely in that condition when self-defence not only becomes a duty, but even a moral obligation. The facts we are about to state in support of the above assertion are simply these:—About four years ago the price of railway springs fitting and vicing were 5s. per hundred weight, this was the current price: but the following year a reduction was attempted at by one of our greatest employers, which eventually succeeded. The consequence of this was, the price of our labour was reduced from 5s. to 3s. 6d. per hundred weight. We submitted tamely to this reduction, as we wished, if possible, to preserve harmonious relations with our employers, and especially with two principal ones, with whom the present contention has arisen. But mark! the reduction which we assented to was not doomed to rest there, for it gave a stimulus to the rapacity of the two manufacturers aforesaid, for they shortly afterwards made a further attempt, which, if quietly submitted to, will take at least from 30 to 40 per cent. from the price we have previously been receiving; but this is not all: from the disposition which is manifested towards us, we have no guarantee when this cheapening process is to terminate. Since the time that we suffered our work to be lowered to 3s. 6d. per hundred weight, the grinders receive at the rate of 3d. per hundred weight out of it, and the benefit that we derive from their services in this respect does not exceed 6d. per man per week; and it is an important fact to state, that there are men belonging to us, who have worked for the two employers aforesaid, for scanty wages, and the same men, in consequence of having to perform their work with very bad materials, have been subjected to all the insults and tyranny that the cruelty and selfishness of man towards his fellow man can possibly devise. But perhaps it may be said, 'there is a numerous class of artizans in other trades who are working for very low wages, and therefore they are equally deserving of public sympathy.' If such remarks should be made, we shall here beg to state the following appalling facts relative to our trade. It is indisputably one of the most laborious description, and we almost venture to challenge the ingenuity of man to produce one of a more pernicious tendency, or one that has a more destructive influence on the human constitution than ours. We not only work in one of the hottest atmospheres, but we have to breathe a sulphurous and poisonous blast, arising from the material that we work with. Men of the most robust constitution scarcely attain the age of 50, and in no one instance can we find a man who has attained the age of 60. We can further state, as a positive fact, that scarcely any man can follow our trade for the space of a dozen or fourteen years, without being completely emaciated, and consequently unfit for labour.

"Fellow Townsmen, we will not trespass too much upon your patience by presenting to you large number of harrowing details, affecting our welfare. You will perceive by the above description, that we, as a class of artizans, are fairly entitled to some consideration; you will also perceive, that in consequence of our lives being so much embittered, and shortened, that we can put in a strong claim for living wages, as some compensation for the miseries we undergo, resulting from our employment. A little timely aid on your part will put a check to the insidious designs of two rapacious employers, who care nothing about moral obligations, justice, or humanity; who look upon the human machine as a means only of procuring for themselves the lion's share of the good things of this life, and who, in short, feel not half the tenderness towards human beings as they would towards inanimate machinery. The present struggle we have with them is a most important one; it is almost a case of life and death. When it is considered that our calling has contributed largely to the triumph of mechanical science, whereby stupendous machinery outstrips the celerity of the wind, or almost equals the rapidity of lightning, and whose beneficial influence is felt by all classes of the community; surely a combination of circumstances like these, entitles us to no small share of commiseration. Every dodge, no matter how mean and artful, has been tried by the two employers alluded to, to effect our downfall. They have tried to engage men from London and elsewhere to take our places, and as an inducement have offered them the same price as we are struggling to maintain, but they have signally failed in their object. They have also tried to effect their selfish designs by the means of articled apprentices, &c., but this, we have no doubt, will prove a decided failure. We have the proud satisfaction of stating that all our other employers are quite willing to give the prices which we consider it our duty to uphold, and we have still the greater satisfaction of knowing that our men are firm.

"Once more fellow Townsmen, we say a little timely aid on your part will very quickly terminate a struggle which is at war with humanity and justice, and be assured that you will have the pleasing satisfaction of rescuing one of the most useful class of artizans that the community can boast of from inevitable ruin.

"Yours, very respectfully,
"THE COMMITTEE OF RAILWAY
"SPRING MAKERS.

"The Committee will sit at the house of Mrs. Johnson, Railway Hotel, Wicker, at half-past

Seven o'clock every Saturday evening, and close at Ten, they will also sit every Monday evening at half-past Seven, and close at Ten, when the subscriptions in aid of our cause will be thankfully received and gratefully acknowledged."

"Sept. 18, 1851."

Mr. Mayhew has been informed upon unquestionable authority that, owing to the cheapness of provisions, a general reduction of wages is contemplated by the manufacturers throughout the country. Should this be the case, it will, at least, open the eyes of the people generally to the Manchester motives for carrying free trade. The benefit derived from the alteration of the corn-laws will then stand thus:—20,000,000 quarters of corn reduced from 50s. to 40s. per quarter = 10,000,000£. sterling gained by some class or other. By whom, is the question? Certainly *not* by the landlords, or farmers, or agricultural labourers; and if the wages of working men be generally decreased, in consequence of the cheapness of food, which was said would be such a benefit to them, it certainly cannot be alleged that the operatives will have ultimately gained one penny by the measure; and since neither artizans nor agriculturists will have benefited by the change, who must have pocketed the 10,000,000£. saved by it, but the very manufacturers and traders who advocated the alteration, and used the poor merely as a stalking-horse to cover their own dishonest ends. Of course, to capitalists cheapness is the greatest possible blessing—to cause a sovereign to exchange for twice the previous quantity of commodities is to double the income of each capitalist through the country; but since this very cheapness is now brought about by the cheapening of the labour upon which alone the working man has to live, that which is said by economist to be the greatest possible benefit to the *community,* is a gain only to the small portion of it termed the moneyed classes. Assuredly were it not for the trade societies, the country would have been destroyed by the greed of the capitalists long ago.

ANSWERS TO CORRESPONDENTS.
[No.45, No.V, "Those that will not Work", 18 OCTOBER 1851, price 3d.]

Edited out:
RETURNS FROM DOUGLAS, CAMBRIDGE; THE SUPERINTENDENT OF CAMBRIDGE POLICE; W.G. JUN. GLASGOW; H.B.T.T. (BIRMINGHAM)

The following is an offer of assistance for which Mr. Mayhew is much obliged, and of which he will avail himself when required.

"Wednesday Morning.

"My dear Sir,

"Whilst returning last night from Hackney, I happened to fall into conversation with the driver of the 'bus by which I travelled. Amongst other things, I asked him if the fraternity to which he belonged had as yet been honoured with a visit of inquiry from you. He told me *no*, but that he had heard of your benevolent labours, and that he should be most happy to give you any information that he could in reference to his calling; and that, if you wished it, he would gather together, to meet you at any place you might appoint, a number of drivers whom he evidently regarded as the cream of his profession,—to use his own words, "a set of gentlemanly, educated, intelligent men." He said, moreover, that he was very pleased to find that your researches would embrace his class, because the result of your investigation into its condition would enable the public to distinguish between the persons to whom he has referred, and those who by their misconduct, brought reproach on the whole guild. I, accordingly, asked him for his name, and said that I would forward it to you. It is—: he drives one of the *Clapton* omnibuses. You will find him a civil, pleasant fellow, with some good-humoured, old-fashioned prejudices against trains and their congeners, steam-boats. He says that he has never been on a railway, and has not intend to go on one, unless forced to do so by business; and he edified me with an account of a trip to Gravesend which he took some time ago, driving down thither in a pony-cart in two hours from Cornhill, and then quietly seating himself at the window of his inn to enjoy simultaneously his shrimps and porter and the chagrin—as they came up from the pier—of some friends who had started from London Bridge by boat, at the same time that he left Cornhill, and who were both astonished and mortified to discover that he had got first to the common goal. I trust you will pardon my intrusion: my only motive for obtruding this scrawl upon your notice was the hope that I might be able to save you a little trouble; a service which I think all your readers are bound to render you, when in their power, in return for the weekly treat with which you furnish us, and for which we look forward as longingly as the city clerk for his Sunday pine.

"X.Y.Z."

Mr. Mayhew in the *Morning Chronicle* treated of omnibus drivers and conductors, but very briefly and imperfectly. [MCS, Vol. 6, pp. 37-45, Letter LXXI, September 26, 1850] Before long he purposes dealing with the Transit question again, and then will be thankful for such information as the friend X. Y. Z. can give him.

The following extract is from a pamphlet forwarded to the office of this work, and entitled "A Lecture by William Tweedie,[43] on the subject of Total Abstinence from Intoxicating Beverages, a practical and efficient Remedy for Scarcity of Employment and Low Wages, lessening fierce competition, and relieving commercial depression:"—

"How far," inquires the lecturer, "will temperance principles add to the remuneration of the labourer, or increase the profitable labour to be performed? This can only be shown by an appeal to facts.

"First, I invite your attention to the following table, which shows the amount of labour employed in the production of several articles of manufacture, in daily consumption by the people. And here I would explain, that to enter fully into an examination of all the elements of production would be a tedious and unnecessary

[43] William Tweedie, prolific religious writer involved in the Papal aggression agitation, *The Truth of God Against the Papacy*, 1851.

task; inasmuch as both the preparation of raw material and retailers profit involve much the same amount of labour in the several articles enumerated. I have, therefore, fixed upon some raw material. I have taken the article when it comes into the hand of the manufacturer, as raw material; and, when it is manufactured, I have done with it. For instance, I take wool (when the manufacturer buys it) as raw material; I have done with it when it is cloth; consequently, I exclude the grower and the retail seller. It is the same with ale or beer. I consider the malt, hops, yeast, and fuel, all as raw material; I have done with them when the liquor leaves the brewery, and is sold to the retailer.

"TABLE I.

"Amount of Labour given in the production of—

	Value of the labour employed. £ s. d.	Value of goods. £ s. d.
Books, A	0 16 0	1 0 0
Silk, B	0 10 0	1 0 0
Blankets, C	0 10 0	1 0 0
Copper household pans, D	0 15 0	1 0 0
Tin „ „ D	0 9 0	1 0 0
Broad cloth and Woollen, D	0 11 0	1 0 0
	£3 11 0	£6 0 0

A Babbage's Economy of the Arts and Manufactures, pp. 205, 317.

B Howard and Co., silk manufacturers, Macclesfield.

C From an extensive firm in Witney.

D Babbage, 166. The average taken from present prices.

TABLE II.

"Amount of Labour given in the production of—

	Value of labour. £ s. d.	Value of goods. £ s. d.
Ale or beer *	0 10 6	6 0 0

* From an experiment on a small scale.

10½ bushels of malt, at 8s	£4 4 0
Hops	0 19 0
Fuel	0 2 0
Yeast	0 0 6
Brewery expenses	0 4 0
Labour	0 10 6
	£6 0 0

If carried out on a large scale the labour would be less. The articles in the first table are all taken from large manufactories.

"From this table it appears that a man who spends 6£ a year upon books, blankets, broad cloths, silks, and saucepans, gives employment for 20 days, at 3s. 6d. per day; while, by spending the same upon ale, beer, or stout, he can only give employment for three days at the same rate of wages. Take the facts in another way, and they show that 21 persons now in the habit of spending 2s. 4d. per week upon intoxicating drinks—that is a QUART of porter daily—could, by transferring that sum to the articles I have enumerated (and the like returns may be also procured for shoes, hats, and furniture), give employment for a whole year to a man at a guinea per week. Thus something can be done at once. There are few who take these drinks at all who do not spend on them 2s. 4d. a week; and they thus prevent, during the year, 17 days' remunerative labour being performed, at the rate of 3s. 6d. per day, or 21s. a week; and this labour would not only add to the happiness of the labourer, but it would add to the real wealth of the community, for it would give the people more clothes, more shoes, more furniture; and few will be found ready to deny that such things are needed. When, indeed, everybody has plenty of such articles, we shall no longer think that want of employment is the greatest curse of the community. Until that happy period arrives, each and all of us must do what we can to lessen this evil. We can do much with present and permanent advantage to ourselves. But the money spent upon intoxicating drinks not only robs the artizan of his field of labour—*the poor man's capital*—but it does more, it robs him of his food. These drinks are not made of sea-sand, of sea-water, or any such article, the absorption of which we would not much miss, but they are made of the best grain which England produces. The effect of this is twofold: it first impoverishes the people who buy the drink, and it impoverishes those who have thus to pay an extra price for the food they require."

Mr. Tweedie's arguments appear to be sound enough; indeed, the drinking customs are among the most pernicious habits of the poorer classes. The misfortune is, that many operatives positively look upon beer as necessary for the performance of hard labour; whereas it is a physiological fact, that the stimulus derived from the imbibition of fermented liquors is followed by a corresponding amount of depression, so that just as much as a man gains in energy at one time does he lose at another. The poor man's energy is his sole patrimony; so that to spend money upon stimulating beverages is not only to waste his hard earnings upon a brutalizing propensity, but to deprive himself of the power of getting more. This want of energy is a marked feature in every drunkard's character; the unshorn beard, the untidy home, the deferred work, are all proofs that the main evil of drink to working men lies in the destruction of those energies from which they derive their subsistence; and it is curious to note how many of the men who have fallen from a state of comparative competence to positive indigence, owe their degradation to the moral and physical apathy induced by the continued indulgence in stimulants. The teetotallers have done the State great service in making known the injurious effects of what they call "intoxicants;" and Mr. Mayhew, though not himself convinced of the necessity of *total* abstinence, will always be happy to aid the teetotallers in their endeavours to instruct the people on this point. Mr. Mayhew's inquiries among the coal-porters convinced him that it was possible for operatives to perform the severest labour on water. One pound of meat is, *staminally*, worth a hogshead of the best beer ever brewed, and what is better than all, the *stimulus* derived from it is *continuous*. Mr. Tweedie, who derives the argument above cited from what has been stated in this work concerning the apportionment of the circulating capital of the country into two funds, viz., that devoted to the purchase of materials, and that devoted to the payment of wages to the workpeople—the one rising as the other falls, and *vice versâ*—appears to have discovered another very cogent reason why the working classes should desist from beer drinking; for if it be really true that the labourer gets only 1s. 8d. out of every 20s. spent in the manufacture of beer, the remaining 18s. 4d. going for the purchase of materials; whereas, in the case of books and copper pans, he gets at least 15s. out of every 20s., and in silks, blankets, and broad cloth, not less than 10s. out of the same sum,—then it is clear, that working men should do all that lies in their power to discourage the consumption of an article which yields so little to the labourer and so much to the capitalist.

ANSWERS TO CORRESPONDENTS.
[No.46, 25 OCTOBER 1851]

Edited out:

T.L.L. (ETYMOLOGY OF 'DAYLYE ORATOUR').

R.H. sends the following qualification of his statement of wages concerning the stuff hat finishers.

"Remarks intended to have accompanied the table of wages of stuff hat finishers.

"The workpeople are all paid by the piece; the exceptions to this rule are rare, and are generally learners, who receive a stipulated but varying portion of their wages.

"The prices paid are as under:—

"Finishing stuff hats, 11d., 1s., 1s.2d. each, according to quality.

"Finishing plates (a coarse hat), 6d., 7d., 8d., 10d. each, according to quality.

"Finishing wool bonnets, 8d. each.

"Finishing stuff bonnets, 1s. each

"Finishing Naples hats, 5d., 6d., 10d. each, according to quality.

"Altering old bonnets, 6½d. each.

"Altering old hats, 8d., 10d., 1s. each, according to quality.

"These are London prices.

"It is seldom the case now that a workman is confined to the stuff hat finishing alone, the majority of finishers being both silk and stuff. The persons whose wages have been given you have been employed solely on beaver hats, and as that is a rarity, I thought it would be acceptable to you when you came to treat on the condition of the persons engaged in the manufacture of hats.

"When silk hats were first introduced the stuff men would not allow the masters to finish them in the same shop with beaver hats; but as the stuff trade declined they were glad enough not only to relax this rule but even to learn the trade themselves. There seems every probability (unless fashion, omnipotent in everything, intervenes) that beaver hats will cease to exist as a manufacture; they are certainly more comfortable to the head, but the impossibility of imparting a good or permanent colour to them is a sad drawback to their use; besides which, the beavers have so much decreased in America that it is doubtful if a sufficient quantity could be imported to supply the demand that would arise if they should ever again supersede the use of silk hats.

"In the finishing of stuff hats, a girl or woman is employed to pick out those coarse hairs that the clearing machine has failed to remove from the beaver. She is paid 1d., 1½d., 2d. per hat, according to quality, and this must be added to the prices given above, making 1s., 1s. 1½d. or 1s. 4d. per hat.

"In most cases the workpeople employ their own wives or daughters to pick for them, each finisher employing a different person, sometimes one picker working for two or more men. Under these circumstances there is not anything like full employment for them. Since 1846 the picker for the men in the table sent you has been paid by the employer. During 1846 her wages were as follows:—highest week 16s. 11d.; lowest week, 2s. 11d.; average throughout the year, 9s. 9d. per week, with about half employment. At present, the girl who picks in our shop fills up her time with trimming hats, and averages 10s. or 11s. per week.

"The wages given you are net wages; if you will multiply the average by 52, you will have the yearly wages.

"There are no deductions beyond these. The men employ a boy to run errands for them, and look to the fire; the practice is, for each man, in turn, to light and keep it up; this they find troublesome, and therefore get a lad to do it for them, but if they like to take their turn, and fetch their beer or dinner themselves, then they do not pay him.*[44] All tools are found by the employer; no rent is charged for standing room, or gas, or anything whatever; there are no fees to foremen; and the employer finds soap and towels for the men to wash with.

"In our place a fire is found for the men to cook their meals on.

"With the above wages an average workman, *fully* employed, could earn 50s. per week, say from 8 A.M. to 8 P.M."

The above is given without comment. R.H. sends also the earnings of silk hat finishers, and promises other statements of the earnings of men—all of which will be most acceptable; but he persists in withholding his name or address, saying, of course Mr. Mayhew will make inquiries into the truth of his statements, and that is all that is needed. Since the above was in type R.H. has forwarded several valuable averages of wages. They are of the greatest service, and Mr. Mayhew is much obliged for them.

The following letter has been received from the Director of the Anti-Truck Society at Derby. It treats of the stoppage of workmen's wages; so often touched upon here, that it requires no comment. Those who think well of the object, and feel inclined to forward it by their subscriptions, can send them to the address of the writer, 28, Iron Gate, Derby.

"THE LABOUR QUESTION.

"Dear Sir

"I regularly read your replies to the questions put to you by the political economists, and am satisfied therewith. QUERY asks, 'If wages are not regulated by the law of supply; and demand, on what *do* they depend?

now I myself say, they *should* depend on supply and demand, but *do* they? I say they do not, and I will tell you why. The *fraud* practised by the *manufacturer* on the LABOUR of the *working man* by *stopping* a part of his LABOUR is the awful cause of all the *working* man's present misery. LABOUR is an *element* of itself, to be paid for by itself, *unconnected* with the property and machinery of the EMPLOYER—the STOPPAGE *system* is the *fraud*; how can *wages* depend on supply and demand, if by a *fraud* of the EMPLOYER he stops any part of the WAGES? and what are *wages* but the *earnings* of LABOUR? Therefore what a man earns for *labour* is his wages; keep the word *labour* distinct, and distinctly understand that *wages* are the earnings of *labour*, and then let the employers answer you, how *labour* can depend upon supply and demand unless the *entire* amount of the *labour* is not paid for without any *stoppages*. There are two ways in which the employers defraud *labour*; one is the STOPPAGE SYSTEM, and the other is the TRUCK system.

"If a PRINTER *employs* a man to print for him *in his press*, he pays him for his *labour*; if a HOSIER *employs* a man to make stockings for him, *in his frame*, he STOPS the *labour* for the *rent* of the frame. This *fraud* of the *hosier* is a mixing up of the relation of *landlord* and *tenant* with the *employment* of a workman to a master; now one negatives the other; for if a master *employs* a man to work for him, *in his frame*, how can the workman have the frame to *his own use*, which he must do, if he is to pay a *rent* for it?—if not, there can be no *rent* at all.

"Wages are the *earnings* of LABOUR; keeping that in view, and never losing sight of it, nothing short of the UNIVERSAL ANTI-TRUCK LAW can save the working man from the *fraud* of the *employer*, or secure him the full reward of his LABOUR.

"This, and this only will remedy the destroying of man's *labour*; no one has so wisely gone into the question as you have: you see the right of the *labourer* to share in the production, and you will now see that it is a *fraud* only that prevents him doing so; it is the *fraud* of the master mixing up his own *machinery* with the

---

[44] Each man pays the lad about 1s. per week; sometimes there are more than one—at present, in our shop, there are four lads at 8 or 9 years, all children of the workmen, and they earn perhaps 2s. a week. [Mayhew's Footnote]

man's *labour,* and STOPPING from the labour a rent of the machinery, instead of keeping the *labour* distinct and paying for it, the *labour,* without any *stoppage:* can QUERY reply to this, or does he admit that the Universal Anti-Truck Law ought to be passed next session?

"It is absolutely necessary, then, I say, to pass the UNIVERSAL ANTI-TRUCK LAW, for the sake of the 'Existence of Life' to the working man; unless every workman is paid the ACTUAL EARNINGS of his labour, he can have nothing to live on; what it to become of the children and wife of a working man, if he is not to he paid what he *actually earns?* The employers only pay them *by the piece,* that is, the quantity they actually do; surely, then, that *actual* earning ought not to be STOPPED by reason of *fines* or frame *rent,* or *charges;* the working man simply asks to be paid for the *actual earnings* of his *labour;* such a request is just, holy, and right, and no one can stand in the way of it, without offending against the law of God and the interest of his country. Labour is an *element* of *itself,* to paid for *by itself,* unconnected with the *property* or *machinery* of the employer; what law can be so just, as that which secures to the working man his *actual earnings* without any deduction?

On the other side, I give you the UNIVERSAL ANTI-TRUCK LAW, the *first* clause of which is the principle thereof, viz:—

"That the ENTIRE *amount of all* WAGES, *the earnings* of LABOUR, *shall be actually and positively* PAID *in the current coin of the realm,* without any deduction or stoppage *of any* kind whatever.

"The *second* clause is the security that no employer shall offend against it; if he does he shall be punished in the County Court.

"The *third* clause declares that no employer shall mix up anything with *labour,* but shall simply pay for the *labour* when done and earned.

"The *fourth* clause is against set-off. The *fifth* against any trickery to avoid the law; and the *last* clause to show workmen that they shall not neglect their work; existing laws are very strong against neglecting work. I humbly and earnestly pray you will assist to pass this law; it will do more good for England than all the laws

besides; what is so natural and simple as the UNIVERSAL ANTI-TRUCK LAW, and why do employers want to evade it? The *system* of *stoppages* is deplorable, because of employers *stopping* their men's *actual* earnings. Wicked employers make a profit out of their men's wages that they may undersell their neighbours; this works the most frightful of evils—this is that baneful and pernicious evil, called *unlawful and unholy* COMPETITION.

"*Honest* EMPLOYERS are content with making a *profit* on their goods *after the labour is paid for;* but *unprincipled and wicked* EMPLOYERS try all they can to undersell their neighbours by getting *a profit out of their workman's wages,* by paying them in goods, so as to get *a double* profit; or, by stopping their wages for fines, or frame rent, and charges, so as to get their work done for little or nothing; no consideration whatever being had as to how the *workman* is to subsist, or what the state of starvation and misery the wife and children must be in. Nothing can cure this frightful evil, but the UNIVERSAL ANTI-TRUCK LAW, that the actual earnings of *labour* shall be paid for, without any *stoppage* whatever.

> "I am, Sir,
> "Your obedient Servant,
> "J. BRIGGS."

The following comes from the Correspondent who furnished the facts printed in No. 39 concerning a certain Jew printer of Farringdon-street. Certain parts are omitted touching the printer's past career, with which Mr. Mayhew has no desire to meddle.

"I have not yet done with the Jew printer of Ludgate-hill; I have waited patiently to see if he would offer any reply to the statement made in your Number of September 6th. I have taken care that your Journal should reach his hands. This person on the most trivial reasons discharges men on the instant, and when asked for the required usual notice, sneeringly replies, 'you may summons me;' his motto is (and he openly avows it), *'wages are too high and must be reduced,'* and for this end he employs a host of boys at 4s. and 5s. per week, and, whenever he can, substitutes their labour in the place of men's. These lads he treats most shamefully, making them, poor fellows, work night after night as *over time*, and then docking them if their fagged and overwrought bodies cannot do quite so much labour the next day.

"I am, Sir,
"Your obedient Servant,
"****"

"Boy labour or thief labour," said an enterprising shoe-factor to Mr. Mayhew, "it's all the same to me, so long as I can get my work done cheap." This boy and apprentice labour is the great curse of the printer's trade.

The two following letters; are touching the meaning of the term *"Daylye Oratour"* mentioned in the Notices to Correspondents attached to No. 38:—

MORPETH, OCT. 4, 1851.
"SIR,

"I think I can throw some light on the 'Office' of 'Daylye Oratour.' I believe that 'Anthoyne Master of London, haberdasher,' by so entitling himself, merely intended to intimate that he daily offered prayers for his Majesty's welfare. *Orare* means not only to speak or deliver an oration, but to entreat, to plead, to pray to the gods. Thence, of course, 'Oratory,' a place where prayer is wont to be made. But the question is, I think, set at rest by an expression which I remarked some time since in a MS. letter, of date early in the 17th century, which I regret I must quote from memory, as I have not now access to the papers. The context was to this effect: 'If God protract your life and grant you, &c., 'for which' the writer continued, 'I shall be to Him a ____ orator.' I leave a blank, for I am not certain what adjective was used; it might be 'constant' or 'daily.' But this use of the word, 'orator' fixes, I think, the meaning in your correspondent's quotation.

"I have had thought of addressing you about 'trampers' lodging-houses in the country towns but doubt whether what I could say would be of any value to you.

"I am, Sir,
"Truly and gratefully yours,
"W.T.S."

ANSWERS TO CORRESPONDENTS.
[No.47, No.VI "Those that will not Work",
1 NOVEMBER 1851, price 3d.]

"R— street, Glasgow.
"Sir,
"During a recent visit, about two months ago, to London, some things came under my observation, which I have thought I might send to you, as they may be of use in the course of your exposure of London prostitution. I give you real names and addresses, as a guarantee for the strict truthfulness of what I write.

"One Saturday evening I alighted at the Quadrant, Regent-street, from a Bayswater omnibus, about nine o'clock. I was immediately struck by the number of well-dressed young females loitering on the pavement of the Haymarket; two especially attracted my attention; both young, good-looking, and apparently intelligent; one—I can't say both—*rouged*. I watched them for a little, saw them laughingly address one or two gentlemen, and then I walked slowly close by to give them an opportunity of speaking to me: this they were not long in doing. I at once found they were French girls, speaking English imperfectly. They said to me, "we come from Paris, have been here about three months, and are going back soon." I urged them to give me their address, but they would not, pressing me to go with them to where they lived, which they said, "was quite at hand, and you will be gratified—have the pleasure immediately." Without heeding my refusal, they turned their faces towards the Quadrant and walked on at a pretty smart pace. I followed them a little behind; at last they stopped at No.—, U– J— street; one of them opened the door with a latch-key, and both entered, leaving it partially opened. I had gained my object, and without delay I walked off. Immediately after I saw them again on the pavement.

"The next day I dropped a parcel of tracts into the letter box of the house I saw them enter, and a day or two after I sent another package through the post.

"On the Monday afternoon I was walking on the north side of the Quadrant: on the balcony at the windows above M—, Milliner, No.—, I observed three ladies standing; one of them noticing that I had seen them, *beckoned to me with her finger.* The day after I sent *them*, too, a parcel of tracts.

"In Regent-street and Piccadilly I strolled about till after dusk. I think I counted *'apartments to let'* or *'furnished apartments'* put in windows and on doors, by dozens, which I had not observed by daylight. In windows of coffee rooms, &c., I found 'private apartments for ladies.' This appeared to my mind an ambiguous intimation, and admitting a perfectly honourable interpretation. I came, however, at length, to the window of the —*Coffee House,* Piccadilly, across the whole length of which, at the bottom, there was a gauze screen, through which the light from the gas shone faintly; I observed something *painted* on it, and, on looking more closely, I read, 'private apartments for ladies,' and on a line below, in letters not quite so large as those above, *'and, for private apartments, ladies.'*

"My mind was now fully interested in the investigation, and I resolved to go to the Casino in Great Windmill-street, thinking that I should gain a little more insight into the horrid system: nor was I mistaken; the first thing that met me was, as I went in; the charge of admission is nominally 1s., but some *ladies* who passed in immediately before me laid down only 6d. Having entered, I found a large hall, brilliantly lighted, with a band on an elevated platform at the further end. I expected that there would be a stage and *professional dancers;* in this I was wrong—the dancers were the visitors, who each, according to his fancy, joined in the dance, the young women with their bonnets and shawls on, the young men with their hats on, and topcoats and sticks, if they chanced to have them with them. The attitudes were anything but decent. While I was there—about 30 minutes—the place was not very crowded, though the visitors were evidently coming in greater numbers; and I understand that as the evening advances, the

attendance becomes very great.

"The young women had, for the most part, gentlemen along with them; there was, however, a considerable number without any *friend.* I was standing near to one of these, a young girl, *rouged,* when a young man came up and said to her, 'may I have the pleasure of paying, my addresses to you?' She, however, was at the moment joined by a gentleman whom she had evidently been expecting.

"I had for a short time previous been watching a girl whose whole appearance much interested me:—she was apparently under 20, not painted, tastefully and decorously dressed; she might be called beautiful, and there was an innocence about her looks which made me feel it strange indeed that she should be in such a place. She had stood alone for about a quarter of an hour; no one had spoken to her, she to no one. There was a liveliness in her eye, but a pensiveness at times crept over it. Poor thing, thought I, can I do anything to save you, *if you are fallen?* for had I met her anywhere else I should never have thought her fallen. I went to her and said, 'Have *you* no friend here?' She said 'No.' 'Do you expect any?' She replied, 'No, certainly, or he would have come along with me.' 'Will you go with me, then?' 'Where?' she asked. 'To my lodgings.' 'No,' she said, 'I cannot go to your lodgings.' I pressed her; she refused. 'Oh,' she said, 'we can find numbers of places in the neighbourhood; if you do not choose to pay for such accommodation, I cannot go with you.' I now requested that she would at least go out with me; she consented, and we left the Casino; I led her to my lodgings, which were at hand, but she would not go in; she said, 'No, I am not so hardened; I cannot go into respectable people's houses; You will get plenty of girls in the Argyll rooms, who will go anywhere with you, but *I* am not so bad yet.' I tried to persuade her, saying I would take all the responsibility; but she was firm, and at last said, 'Let me go back to the rooms, *my time is precious;* I cannot go with you.' I then asked her to walk with me a little, to which she agreed; we crossed to a quiet street and walked slowly down it. Now I told her why I had spoken to her and taken her away from the room; that it was for no improper purpose, but to see if I could not do her some little good. The conversation that followed I cannot detail; her history was this: she was the daughter of an officer, who after her mother's death had kept a mistress, under whose care she lived till the decease of her father. Immediately upon this event she was driven from the house; she went to an acquaintance's, a young woman, whom she accompanied the same evening to the theatre, the first time she had entered one: she was then under fifteen; she is now eighteen. They were spoken to by some officers who pressed them to have some wine in the refreshment room: she remembers going back to the theatre, *but no more*. Next morning she found herself in the barracks, in bed with one of the officers. She was now ruined, without a friend to whom she could go. She was kept by the officer while the regiment remained there. When it left she became the mistress of other officers in succession. At length she was induced to go to London, where for some time she lived in a *gay* house; till, going one evening about twelve months ago to the Casino, she met a young man, by whom she has been kept in lodgings since; she, however, with his knowledge, sees occasionally other gentlemen, as her *friend* cannot afford quite so much as will keep her. The house in which she lodges is kept by a woman, whose daughter is also *in keeping*.

"I have said I cannot detail my conversation with her—some of her expressions only can I give: 'Oh do not talk to me about serious things; I'm miserable enough already; my heart is often like to break when a smile is on my face; when sitting in my room alone, I am often like to go mad. I have had no Bible these four years—I could not read it and turn into that bed with a man in the evening. *I would do anything but starve to get out of this life; but what can I do?*' [Mr Mayhew has put these words in italics, to point attention to them.] 'If I ask for work, I can give no character. Who will trust me? Oh, don't speak to me of what I may become, I know it all; but I hope something will turn up to enable me to better my

condition. I was once a very good girl, never one Sabbath absent from the Wesleyan chapel.' [Query? while she was living under the same roof with her father's mistress!] 'I cannot swear and drink as others do; I am not yet so far gone.'

"I made an appointment to see her next day, having made up my mind to make an effort, before leaving London, to get her into an asylum, if she were willing to go. But instead of meeting me she left a note for me, from which I learnt that her *friend*, having heard of our interview, had persuaded her to go and stay with him at his own lodgings for a little, and that if I had anything to say to her she would call for any note I might leave; I did write, and left it along with some tracts. Since my return I have addressed a letter to her at her old lodgings, but have received no reply; if she had not returned to them it is not likely that such a landlady would make any efforts to have it sent to her. Her name was A— M— G—; her lodgings, No.—, J— street—, Waterloo-road. Her *friend* whom she called James, was the son of a solicitor, in whose counting-house he is occupied; more about him she would not tell me.

"The evening of the day on which I hoped to have done something for her rescue, I left for home, thoroughly sickened by what I had seen of London life, on its dark and gloomy side.

"I make no comment on these facts. It is a naked recital of what I saw, and I leave it to you to make any use or no use of them, as seems to you advisable.

"Before you close, will you be able, think you, to do or suggest, anything that will give good promise of abating, if not of extirpating, the frightful evil? I *almost* despair.

"This is written very hastily; you will, however, I think, be able to make it out.

"Yours respectfully,
"W.G., Jr."

The above account of the London adventures of a well-intentioned gentleman from the country are both interesting and instructive, and Mr. Mayhew is much obliged to the writer. They are instructive, as teaching us how ready the well-intentioned are at all times to magnify evils. Those who have paid attention to mental phenomena, know that it is the peculiar character of the feelings to distort, exaggerate, or highly colour, all objects upon which they are centred. W. G., jun., evidently came up to London from Glasgow, *prepared* to find the prostitution of the metropolis much greater than it really is, and hence his mistake as to the general character of the houses in Regent-street. To his inflamed imagination the whole of this locality seems to have appeared a colony of brothels and places of "accommodation." That there are in this street some few houses of an infamous character carrying on the worst possible trades, under the cloak of respectable businesses, Mr. Mayhew is fully aware, and purposes, when he comes to this part of the subject, to let the public see how the "*market*" for prostitutes is regularly supplied from such quarters. But that it is the practice of the inhabitants of Regent-street *generally*—or even anything but exceptionally—to put out at night cards of "APARTMENTS TO LET," with the view of announcing that their houses may be used for base purposes, is a stretch of morbid fancy that is in no way warranted by the truth. The fact is, W. G., jun., on passing up Regent-street in the daytime had been diverted by other matters, and consequently failed to notice many of the announcements which at night attracted his attention, awakened as it then was to the subject. The gentleman is equally wrong concerning the coffee house he mentions, and construes a harmless announcement into an immoral sign. Mr. Mayhew is also afraid that the distribution of tracts among the profligate is a pure waste of good wholesome paper and print. Could the well-intentioned distributors of such things hear what is said of them, and see what is done with the papers they leave, they would begin to perceive, perhaps, that the enormous sum of money thus expended every year might be far more profitably applied. Up to March, 1849, the Religious Tract Society had distributed 500,000,000 copies of its publications; but whether the beneficial results

have been in any way equal to these prodigious means, it is for those to say who believe in such a mode of "doing good." For Mr. Mayhew's part he candidly confesses he has but little faith in its virtue; for, despite these 500,000,000 tracts, our criminals and prostitutes increase yearly; he thinks that the money thus expended might be far more *wisely* laid out. But the tract world generally are guided more by their feelings than by their reason, and are consequently the most difficult of all people to *convince* of the futility of a certain line of conduct on which they have set their *hearts* rather than their minds.

The story of the poor girl above mentioned partakes of the sentimental character as detailed by W. G., but is really, when contemplated in its true light, the history of thousands of such characters. Motherless, she is brought up under the same roof with *her father's mistress* (he being what is termed "an officer and a gentleman!") Here of course, if she imbibes no bad principles, she learns, at least, no good, though to blind W. G., she makes him believe that, even in this state, she is a regular attendant at chapel! Then, *immediately on her father's death*, she is driven from his mistress's house, and goes to live with a *young woman* (apparently single), whom she accompanies *the same evening* to a theatre (immediately after her father's death, mark!), and after having retired to certain "refreshment rooms" with some *officers whom she had never seen before*, and partaken of wine with them, she becomes insensible, and is then, to use her own words, "ruined." Girls, of course, are always unwilling to attribute their degradation to their own imprudence; but assuredly the most charitable of us must allow, that this young woman was greatly to blame, and did not require over-much seducing to lead her into vicious courses. The true cause of her fall, and for which indeed she deserves our deepest pity, lies in her early career: in her want of a mother's care, counsel, and instruction, and in having a father who partook more of the attributes of the satyr than the man—so true is it, that the sins of the parents are visited upon the children, even to the third and fourth generation! There are three different classes of prostitutes, arranged according to their causes, viz., (1) those who are *driven* to adopt a vicious life; (2) those who are *bred* to it; and (3) those who *take* to it. And it is highly necessary that, in all our remedies for the evil, and attempts at reformation, we should bear these distinctions in mind, for each requires a different course of treatment. The first class is the one upon which the greatest effect can be produced; but to do much good, even here, we must begin before habit has hardened the unfortunate to practices that, at one time, she really loathed. Of the two other classes—those who are *bred* and those who *take* to prostitution, either from natural or acquired vicious propensities—it is difficult to speak in this place. It would fill a sheet of print, to set forth all the antecedents, concomitants, and consequents in connection with them. Mr. Mayhew hopes to be able to propose some new mode of mitigating this great social evil, before he has finished his inquiry, but to be called upon to propound a remedy at the commencement of his investigations, and before he has made himself acquainted with the nature and causes of the disease, is to ask him to play the quack, and prescribe a panacea without so much as knowing the character of the evils he pretends to cure. This species of moral, political, and social charlatanry is the great curse of the age. The Morrisons and Holloways are not confined to medicine alone, but pervade every part of our social system. "I would do anything but starve, to get out of this life," said the girl; "but *what can I do?*" This, after all, is the point to which we must direct our thoughts—"*What can I do?*"

ANSWERS TO CORRESPONDENTS.
[No.48, 8 NOVEMBER 1851]

Edited out:
AN EMINENT ANTIQUARIAN (ON "REREDOSS"); T.A.; W.D.M.; WURTENKRÄMER; R.W.; T.A. LIVERPOOL; G.H.; MRS R. OF HERTFORD.

W.S. finds fault and "suspects motives," &c. The gentleman can of course think has he pleases.

"Sir,

"In No. 42, page 230, of 'London Labour,' you give a table of a week's expenditure in the respective years 1845 and 1851, and I am surprised and sorry to see the unfairness of the comparison. In 1845 you charged for five loaves, but in 1851 only for four; you make a difference of one penny for tea, with which free-trade has nothing to do. You make a difference of twopence per pound on three pounds of meat, whereas your own two witnesses prove the difference to be only one penny; and in 1845 you set down a pot of beer, and in 1851 only a pint. Now, correcting these errors or misstatement, the saving is only fivepence instead of 1s. 5d., as you state the difference. You pretend to be impartial, but I fear it is not so, and I suspect your motives, which I regret, as I have been your subscriber and admirer from the beginning.

"Yours.

"W.S."

1*st October,* 1851.

The gentleman is in error. On revision, he will perceive, that the contrasted accounts went to show that the man had lost almost as much by free-trade as he had gained. If food had been cheapened since 1846, employment had become scarcer; so that he could afford to have five loaves per week before free-trade, and only four loaves per week since. Hence though the man had gained by the repeal of the corn laws one penny in every seven pence he laid out in bread, he had, nevertheless, been able to earn one loaf less per week since 1846 than he could before then, that is to say, he had gained 4d., and lost 7d. by the measure. In meat, however, he had gained 6d. a week; but then in rent he had lost 4d.; in potatoes, 1d.; in tea, 1d.; and in beer 2d. per week; that is to say, he had since 1845 been able to afford less of the three last-mentioned articles. Thus, the gains would appear to be—bread, 4d., and meat, 6d. per week, or 10d. altogether; whereas the losses are—rent, 4d.; potatoes, 1d.; tea, 1d.; beer, 2d.; and bread, 7d.; or 15d. altogether; so that there would seem to be a net loss of 5d. per week to this man since free-trade. This should have been more fully explained in the article, though the whole bearing of it inclines to the same result. Mr. Mayhew was inquiring of a man who made soldiers' trousers what he had gained by free-trade. He was one of the very poor who were to be so much benefited by the measure. Meat he *never* tasted, and his weekly consumption of bread was two loaves per week, the saving in which was 2d. His wages had not been decreased, nor was his work less, so that he was a clear gainer of 2d. in about 7s. a week, or 1d. in every 3s. 6d. of his earnings!! It would appear that those who earn about 15s. a week, and whose wages have not yet been reduced, save perhaps 1s. by the change (see the article on Street-Orderlies); and those whose wages have been reduced are, of course, considerable losers by the alteration. To the tradesman and capitalist, however, whose profits depend not, like wages, upon the price of food, the change of course is a clear gain; each pound being worth at least a guinea, since free trade.

G.W. says, Do you mean to notice "Medical Assistants" in your *exposé* of the working classes? Our twin sisters, too, the Governesses, claim a share of attention. I may be able to supply you with some information concerning the two TRADERS."

Mr. Mayhew will be happy to hear from the gentleman on both subjects.

Some reader, perhaps, will answer the following:

"Sir,

"Will you, or any of your readers, tell me to whom I can dispose of any quantity of rags (*all sorts*), brass, copper, lead, iron (cast and wrought), horse-hair, whalebone, bones, skins (*hares'* and *rabbits'*), paper (waste of all *sorts* and *sizes*). I should think some person—a buyer, for instance—would tell me. My reason for asking is this—I purpose buying such articles from hawkers and others; but before I do, I wish to be advised as to the amount I can realize for them, *and from whom I can get it.*

"I should much prefer being answered *per post*, and would gladly pay the postage or remunerate the individual for his trouble, and inclose my name for that purpose. If, however, the medium of your pages be preferred, or more practicable, let it be done so, to "News Agent."

Any letter addressed to the writer of the above, under cover to Mr. Mayhew, shall be forwarded to his address.

J. M., of Southampton, says:—

"Sir,

"Having read in your number of 'London Labour,' &c., for August 30, No. 38, a statement of the number of vehicles passing and repassing London Bridge every hour to be 13,000, thinking there must be some mistake, I would feel obliged by your giving the information."

The information was given on the authority of M. D'Arcey's Report to the French Government on the roads of London as compared with those of Paris. It will be seen, by the table printed in the present number of this work, that the amount referred to twelve hours instead of one.

The two following letters proffer information on a most important subject. The distributing of commodities is almost as important as the production of them, and any information on the subject will be most acceptable. Mr. Mayhew is much obliged to his correspondents for their promises of assistance.

"Sir,

"If you should find any difficulty in procuring information respecting the social, moral, and intellectual condition of the Drapers' Assistants, I should be most happy to give you any aid in my power, having been connected with the trade the greater portion of my life. The domestic comforts in some establishments, the bad living, shameful extortions, and tyranny in others, have so long been suffered to exist, that their magnitude has become diminished, and we rest contented under the worst form of oppression."

Letter No. 2 runs:—

"Sir,

"Having read your very excellent work, the 'London Labour and Poor,' ever since its first publication, I remember having seen in some of the back numbers an intimation to one of your correspondents that it was your intention in course of time to treat of that class of the London labour the *Drapers*. I am myself a Draper's Assistant, and having some little practical knowledge of the business, I should feel a great pleasure in giving you any information on the subject, as far as my knowledge of the peculiarities of the trade goes, if you have not already completed your inquiries; and if what little assistance I can render you in your arduous undertaking is worthy of your acceptance, I should feel the greatest pleasure in contributing my mite to the immense funds of information that you have collected. A letter addressed to me, or an answer in the next number of your 'London Labour and Poor,' stating the nature of the information you require on the subject, shall meet with my earnest attention.

"P.S. I have enclosed one of my employer's cards, to whose house, should you write, you will please address for me."

The information required upon this and, indeed, every other trade is, (1) the division of labour in the trade, citing the nature of the work performed by the different classes of workmen; (2) the hours of labour; (3) the labour market, or the mode of obtaining employment; (4) the tools employed and who finds them; (5) the rate and mode of pay of each different class of workmen, dividing the wages or salaries into two classes, the "fair" and the "unfair;" (6) the deductions from the pay in this form of fines, "rents" or stoppages of any kind; (7) the additions to wages in the shape of

perquisites, premiums, allowances, &c.; (8) a history of the wages of the trade, with the dates of increase or decrease in the pay, and the causes thereof; (9) the brisk and slack season of the trade, with statement of the causes on which they depend, as well as the number of extra hands required in the brisk season as compared with the slack; (10) the rate of pay to those who are "taken on" only during the brisk season; (11) the amount of surplus labour in the trade and the cause of it, whether from (*a*) overwork, (*b*) undue increase of the people in the trade, (*c*) change from yearly to weekly hiring, (*d*) excessive economy of labour, as "large systems" of business, (*e*) introduction of women; (12) the badly-paid trade—(*a*) the history and causes of it, (*b*) what is the cheap labour employed, or how do the cheap workers differ from those who are better paid: are they less skilful, less trustworthy, or can they *afford* to take less, deriving their subsistence from other sources? (*c*) is the badly-paid trade maintained chiefly by the labour of apprentices, women, &c., &c.? (*d*) is it upheld by middlemen, "sweaters," or the like? (*e*) are the men injured by *driving* (that is, by being made to do more work for the same money) or by *grinding* (that is, by being made to do the same or more work for less money), or are they injured from a combination of both systems? (*f*) who are the employers paying the worse wages?—are they "cutting men," that is to say, men who are reducing the men's wages as a means of selling cheap; or are they "grasping men," who do it merely to increase their profits; or small capitalists, who do it in order to live? Proofs should be given of all stated. Accounts of earnings and expenditure are of the greatest importance; also descriptions of modes of life and habits, politics, religion, literature, and amusements of the trade; estimates of the number in trade with the proportion belonging to the better and the worse paid class, and the quantity of surplus hands. If any trade and benefit society, an account of it would be desirable; if not, what do men, in case of sickness?

Can any of my etymological friends point out

the derivation of the slang term "*mort* or *mot*", a low woman, and thence a prostitute? The word *mot*, indeed, seems to be the generic term for prostitute; as a flash mot (a courtezan), a coolie's mot (a soldier's woman), a legger's mot (a sailor's woman), and so on. The prostitutes are occasionally called "marms" or "ma'ams;" this appears to be an abbreviation of "madams," which would seem to have been formerly used for "mistresses," or kept women. Can any one oblige Mr. Mayhew with proof of this, or to the contrary? Is the term mot (or mort) connected with mother? The Russian for mother is *mat;* and the Sanscrit, *mata;* the Welsh is *mam* (query, *ma'am*).

ANSWERS TO CORRESPONDENTS.
[No.49, No. VI "Those that will not Work", 15 NOVEMBER 1851, price 3d.]

Mr. MAYHEW has to acknowledge with thanks the receipt of a letter from the Registrar-General. The corrections suggested by him shall be made, and the results printed, as soon as the necessary information can be obtained.

Mr. MAYHEW has to acknowledge with thanks returns from the police authorities of the undermentioned towns as to the number of prostitutes and brothels in those localities.

Coventry.
Blackburn.
Wolverhampton.
Oldham.
Warrington.
Durham.
Saddleworth.
Eccleshall.
Bilston.
Chester.
Macclesfield.
Stockport.
Dundee.
Huddersfield.

The subjoined are the speculation of a gentleman as to some of the antecedents of prostitution:—

"*London, 6 Nov.*, 1851.
"Sir,
"Having read your letter from W.G., Jun., of Glasgow, printed in No. 47 of your work on London Prostitutes, I consider that it might not be amiss to give you the result of my experience of London during the last eleven years.

"I consider that girls, the daughters of small tradesmen and better class of mechanics, get seduced oftener from their great love of dress, and the erroneous desire to be thought *ladies*. Casinos, singing-rooms, and theatres, more especially those on the Surrey side, are frequented nightly by scores of these girls, accompanied by their sweethearts, who are generally clerks in counting-houses, shopmen, and others who are of no occupation, but only dress well. At those places a desire of gaiety is nourished in their breasts, and the glitter of the finery around them creates a longing for show of a like nature. Refreshments, of course, they must have; and these generally consist of either wine, gin-and-water, or other spirituous drinks, to which at home they are not accustomed; and, consequently, through false persuasions, promises of clothes, and to be taken again and again to these places of amusement, the minds of these girls, inflamed through the drink which they have been partaking, become an easy prey to the designer.

"Now, who is to blame most, in cases of this kind? I think decidedly the parents, for allowing daughters too much liberty of intercourse with the male sex. The parent says, My daughter is now old enough to have a beau; and one is picked, or allowed to be chosen, amongst a class rather superior in condition to themselves. The girl has every opportunity afforded of meeting her 'young man;' and the consequence is that, before many months, the girl is either seduced, or finds herself so unhappy at home that she throws herself into the arms of the first gentleman who will encourage her love of finery and pleasure. There are hundreds of girls in London, who can blush and look as modest as a maid, who are nothing but sly whores, for the love of gaiety and dress.

"How this can be cured, unless through intervention of parents, I know not; but perhaps you, from having so many instruments as you must require in the compilation of a work like 'London Labour,' may obtain knowledge and experience enough to point out a preventive to this growing evil.

"I am, Sir,

"Your obedient Servant,

"J.B.

"P.S. I may, on another occasion, renew my letter."

This is neither the fitting place nor time for expressing how a particular condition tending to produce a particular result can be presented or alleviated. All that can be attempted at present is, a short criticism on the contents of the above letter.

J.B., it will be seen, falls into the same fallacy as the Glasgow correspondent, assuming that girls are seduced through frequenting Casinos; surely the true rendering is, that they frequent such places either *because* they have been already seduced and have become shameless, or *because* they are of a *seducible* disposition. Is it compatible with the character of a modest girl, to visit a place which she knows is resorted to by women of loose character, and whither she is aware gentlemen go only to become acquainted with such people? and, even supposing her innocence led her to such a place (of which strong proof would be required), would she not, if really modest, and if she had not been previously depraved, object to dance with men whose acquaintance she had formed thus promiscuously? It would seem that we might as well believe that a girl who accompanied a man to a brothel was *seduced* by him. That there are many cases of heartless deception, no one can have the least doubt; but that modest-minded women visit Casinos, and that it requires much persuasion to induce a young lady who is in the habit of frequenting them to abandon herself to vicious practices, surely no man of common sense can believe. As was before said, girls who go to such places are

seducible, and *therefore* seduced. Nor can Mr Mayhew believe that it is *directly* a love of dress and gaiety that leads to prostitution. Prostitution is really and truly woman's crime; and the same propensity as induces men to live by thieving, cheating, or begging, rather than labouring, disposes the generality of loose women to adopt prostitution as a mode of livelihood. The Constabulary Commissioners, who are the only gentlemen that have scientifically investigated the causes of crime, have laid it down, from the testimony and experience of the most observing persons, that crime in the majority of instances arises from "a disposition to acquire property with a less degree of labour than by ordinary industry." Twist and turn the matter over as we please, we must end at this point, simply because it assumes nothing, and expresses the bare fact. Crime of all kinds, women's as well as men's, is, generally speaking, but still of course with exceptional cases, the consequence of an indisposition to labour for a living; that is to say, if a certain person possessing no property will not work for the food and comforts he or she requires in order to live, such a person in such a case can only obtain them dishonestly, or, in other words, criminally. Do not let it be understood that it is here intended to imply that such is the case universally. Heaven forbid! The meaning is, simply, that this cause of crime is the *more general* one. The love of dress is not the direct cause of prostitution, which arises rather from the disposition to obtain fine clothes other than by working for them. This is usually the *primum mobile* to vicious courses—the love of ease, and getting their wants and desires satisfied with as little difficulty and in as pleasant a manner as possible.

Nevertheless there are many other causes leading directly to the same result, and the love of admiration is necessarily one of these. What proportion of the prostitutes are led to adopt their line of life from an indisposition to earn what they require, and what proportion from the love of personal admiration, it is difficult at present to say; but, perhaps, we may even here draw this line—the prostitutes who proceed from the *poorer* classes of society become depraved because they perceive that greater creature-comforts can be obtained in our community by immoral practices than by regular industry; whereas those prostitutes who proceed from the *middle* classes are led to adopt a vicious life principally from the craving for admiration, of which the love of dress, society, and display are the consequences rather than the causes. The prostitutes of the "superior classes," on the other hand (and we must all admit there are such prostitutes), become debased purely from the love of admiration, because *they* can have no mercenary motive for pursuing such a course of conduct. The above appear to be the two prime causes of prostitution. The poorer girls take to it mainly from the irksomeness and deficient remuneration of labour among us; while those belonging to the wealthier class adopt the same course chiefly from an undue love of admiration. But this refers only to the class who *take* to prostitution, and, as was said in a previous number, there are two other distinct classes of loose women whom J.B. confounds. Those who are *driven* to prostitution, either through want or seduction, are of course the most pitiable, and at the same time the most hopeful of all the three classes; but these consist of by far the smallest number. Those who, on the other hand, take to prostitution either through an indisposition to work for their living, or from a love of admiration, as well as the third class, or, those who are *bred* to a vicious course of life, being early depraved or allowed by their parents to associate with whomsoever and go whithersoever they please, are the most difficult of all to deal with. To this latter class, it will be seen, appertain the remarks made by J.B. concerning parents' neglect of their daughters. That this is a fruitful source of prostitution—perhaps, indeed, the most fruitful of all those above mentioned—such people as have eyes in their heads and brains at the back of them must have been long convinced. How else can we explain the fact that the greater number of prostitutes belong to the humbler classes of society? In middle-class life the girl is, of course, seldom or never permitted out of her parents' sight; indeed so strict a supervision is maintained over the daughter's conduct, that no opportunity

of erring is afforded; but, among the humbler classes, it should be remembered that we have reached that state of society (the admiration of economists) which compels the wife to labour for her living; and, consequently, to absent herself from home, and to transfer her care from her children to some factory, or other place of labour. Hence, the daughters of our people are, perforce, brought up in our gutters and channels, and depraved often by vicious intercourse long ere any passion or love could have led to such a result. Gentlemen ask from their easy chairs how are we to cure this. The answer is, it never can be cured until we find a remedy for the social evils of which such things are the necessary results. In the degradation of our women we suffer for the infamy and callous selfishness of our men. Those causes of prostitution which consist in defective moral and religious training are purposely omitted here, because they have a *negative* rather than a *positive* influence on the result—such training serving simply to *check* the operation of the natural principles leading to that end, and the want of it consequently permitting them to act uncontrolled. Mr. Mayhew is much obliged to J.B. for his thoughts on the subject, and would be happy to hear from him again.

ANSWERS TO CORRESPONDENTS.
[No.50, 22 NOVEMBER 1851]

QUERY begs to know what is the true wage law, since it is asserted in 'London Labour and the London Poor,' that the law of supply and demand is untrue. To tell us, he says, that the tribute system of payment for labour *should* be the mode of remunerating the operatives is not tell us what *is* the mode, and of this he requests to be informed.

The rate of wages, Mr. Mayhew replies, is simply the ratio of the remuneration of the labourer to the quantity of work performed by him; or, in other words, the wage law is simply and self-evidently that the rate of wages is directly proportional to the quantity of work considered in connection with the quantity of pay. The gross quantity of work to be done, divided by the number of hands to do it, gives us the average quantity of *work* accruing to each workman; and the gross sum devoted to the payment for such work, divided again by the number of hands, gives us the average *remuneration* of each workman. The *ratio* of the quantity of work done to the amount of money received in remuneration for it, is the *rate* of wages or given amount of pay for a given amount of labour. This is very different from the law of supply and demand, which says that the rate of wages is determined by the quantity of work to be done and the number of hands to do it; whereas, the relation of the hands to the work can but regulate one of the necessary conditions, viz., the average amount of *work* accruing to each labourer. The above law, is, moreover, very different from the other form of the wage law of the economists, which declares that the rate of wages is determined by the proportion between the labouring population and the amount of capital devoted to the remuneration of them; for this can but regulate the average amount of *income* accruing to each labourer. Hence it is manifest, that neither of these two different forms of the "economical" wage law is alone sufficient to account for the rate of wages; for, since the *ratio* of the labourer's remuneration depends on the *proportion* that the quantity of work done by him bears to the amount of income received by him in return for it, it follows that the true wage law must be sufficient to account for *both* conditions, viz., the average quantity of work and the average quantity of pay. To illustrate this position, let us say that the gross sum annually devoted to the purchase of cloth in the metropolitan tailoring trade is two millions and a half sterling, and that there are in London twenty-five thousand operative tailors engaged in making up these materials. Thus each operative would have, on the average, 100£ worth of cloth to fashion into garments, in the course of the year. This is all the law of *supply and demand* could teach us. What remuneration each would receive for this amount of work it could not tell us, because the *fund* out of which the labourers are paid constitutes no part of that particular form of the canon. Let us, however, assume that the gross sum paid in wages to the London tailors amounts to one million and a quarter sterling, then the tailors, being twenty-five thousand in number, each would receive, on the average, 50£ in the course of the year. This would be in conformity with that phase of the economical law which says, that the payment of the labourers is equal to the proportion between the sum set aside for their remuneration and the number of the labouring population. Still it is evident that this, like the canon of supply and demand, cannot possibly determine the *rate* of wages. To arrive at the ratio of the remuneration to the work we must say, as 100£, the value of the cloth that each operative has to make up in the course of the year, is to 50£, the sum he receives for so doing so is 10s. to 1£; which is the rate at which he is paid for making up every sovereign's worth of materials.

The rate of wages, or, strictly speaking, the ratio of the remuneration to labour, is then equal to the proportion that the sum devoted to the purchase of materials bears to the sum devoted to the payment of the labourers. It is, indeed, a mere example of the "rule of three." If the circulating capital of a trade or a country equal 1,000,000£, and 500,000£ be spent upon materials, and 500,000£ upon labour, then as 500,000£ : 500,000£ = 1£ : 1£; or in other words, the rate of wages will be 20s. for every 20s. worth of materials operated upon. If, on the other hand, 750,000£ be devoted to the purchase of materials, and only 250,000£ consequently be left for the payment of the labourers then as 750,000£ : 250,000£ = 3£ : 1£; that is to say, the rate of wages in that case will be two-thirds less, or 6s. 8d. for every 20s. worth of materials made up. There is no gainsaying this fact, and yet, though it be almost as plain as the alphabet in a child's primer, the economists have been blundering all these years in the dark, vowing and protesting that the rate of wages depends on the proportion that the sum set aside for the payment of labour bears to the number of the labourers; whereas the veriest clodhopper could have told them that the rate of wages means simply *the sum received for so much work;* or, in other words, the ratio of the remuneration to the *labour*, and certainly not to the *number of people*. A schoolboy would be whipped for such gross ignorance of the "rule of proportion." The Economists' ratio is as follows:—As the sum devoted to the payment of labour is to the number of the labourers, so is the remuneration to—*the work*; but the work cannot *possibly* be determined in any such manner, since that term is in no way related to the term, number of the labourers, and there is consequently no proportion at all in the matter. The ratio of the labourers to the Wage Fund can tell us only the share of that fund accruing to each of such labourers (and this it can tell us solely on the assumption that the fund is equally distributed, *which it is not*); and most assuredly it can afford us no information as to the quantity of *work* which is given by each of the labourers in exchange for the wages he receives, and which, indeed is the whole and sole meaning of the *rate* of wages, viz., the *ratio* between the amount of the remuneration and the amount of the labour. It is positively marvellous how a man like Stewart Mill could lend himself to the propagation of such childishness as the Population and Capital rule of wages, when one minute's thought must utterly have demolished the dogma—at least if there be any truth in Cocker.

It is solely by the light of this new Wage Law that we are enabled to comprehend the difficulties of the time. The ratio of remuneration to labour depending on the proportion that the sum devoted to the payment of the labourers bears to the sum devoted to the purchase of materials, it follows that anything which tends to render labour more productive, or, in other words, enables workmen to make up more materials in a given time, must necessarily tend to the decrease of wages, by causing a larger portion of the circulating capital of the country to be spent on material, and consequently a correspondingly less sum to be spent on the labourers. If by the invention of a machine, or the division of labour, we enable the men in a trade to do double the work in the same time as formerly, then it is clear there must be twice the sum spent upon materials, and consequently four times less coming to the workmen. Here lies the great evil of the time: we are making up every year a greater quantity of materials, and

thus have less and less to pay our workpeople, so that our factories are periodically glutted with products, while the producers are in rags. How is it possible in any other way to explain this startling inconsistency? The economy of labour necessarily involves extra expenditure on materials, and it is impossible to spend a greater sum upon materials without having a correspondingly less sum left to pay to the labourers, so that the wealthy become more and more enriched at the expense of the poor. The money of the well-to-do exchanges for a greater quantity of commodities, while the workpeople get a less quantity of money to exchange. Twist and turn the matter over as you please, it must come to this:—the *circulating* capital of the country is divisible into two funds, one devoted to the purchase of materials, and the other to the payment of the labourers engaged in making up those materials. Increase the one and you must correspondingly decrease the other; for as sure as 2 and 2 equal 4, so do 3 and 1; hence to spend half as much again of the circulating capital on materials, is to change the ratio of 2 and 2 into 3 and 1, and thus, giving the labourers one-third more to do, leave them two-thirds less to receive for it; for as $2 : 2 :: 1 : 1$, even as $3 : 1 :: 1 : \frac{1}{3}$. In the same manner every decrease of wages can only induce more work by causing a greater sum to be spent on materials; and an increase in the number of labourers can only tend to reduce wages by enabling the employers to have a greater quantity of materials made up, for *without this it would of course be impossible to give employment to a greater number of labourers*.

But it may be said, granting the truth of the above exposition, how does this form of the Wage Law differ *essentially* from the economical dogma? The answer is—it differs most essentially, in not being a *natural* and *necessary* law consequent upon the ordained succession of events, and in being comparatively an *arbitrary* result dependent upon the mere will, the greed, ambition, or what you please, of the trader, who, being able to alter, in a great measure, as he thinks fit, the proportion between the sum devoted to the purchase of materials and the sum devoted to the payment of the labourers, has it thus in his power to vary the rate of wages almost at pleasure.

But the most essential difference between the Wage Law as here enunciated, and the Wage Law as propounded by the economists, lies in the remedies for low wages necessarily proceeding from the two.

According to the Wage Law of the economists there can be but two means of improving the wages of a trade—(1) by increasing the Wage Fund; (2) by decreasing the number of labourers. The increase of the Wage Fund is to be brought about either by increased accumulation of wealth, or a decrease of the number of non-productive consumers. The decrease of the number of labourers is to be effected mainly by emigration.

But if the Wage Law above propounded be true, and the capitalist has really an *arbitrary* power over the rate of remuneration for labour, then are *other* remedies required.

The questions which Mr. Mayhew has proposed as being inexplicable by the economical Wage Law are, it will be seen, easy of solution by the law here enunciated. The influence of trade societies on wages; the phenomena of the cabinet-makers and the cotton trade, as to the increase in the quantity of work (without a commensurate increase in the number of hands), being attended by a decline rather than an increase of the rate of remuneration; the depreciating effect of the relief in aid under the old Poor Law; and the extra sum paid to married labourers, as compared with single men, in the agricultural districts, are all easy of solution on the assumption of an arbitrary Wage Law; whereas, according to the economical *natural* law of Supply and Demand, they are riddles, mysteries and contradictions, confounding every unprejudiced mind.

Mr. Mayhew would be glad to receive the opinions of any gentleman who may think differently from himself on this subject, though he must request persons advancing arguments in favour of the economical law, and against the one here propounded, to refrain from citing the hackneyed reasons and illustrations of the economists with which Mayhew is already surfeited. Any new points he will be thankful for having his attention directed to.

ANSWERS TO CORRESPONDENTS.
[No.51, No.VII "Those that will not Work", 29 NOVEMBER 1851, price 3d.]

Edited out:
A READER FROM THE BEGINNING (ON REREDOSSES); J.A.W.; W.D.M.; E LE B.; J.B.; W.J. OF KENDALL;

E. F., of Islington, says:—
"The first volume of 'London Labour and the London Poor' I have had bound up, and lettered simply, '*London Labour—Vol.* 1.'

"Will you be good enough to inform me how I had better number the second volume of that subject, and the first of that on Prostitution, as it appears that I should have classed the volume that is finished as the first of that particular division of the work."

The lettering on the back of the volume should have been, LONDON LABOUR AND THE LONDON POOR—STREET-FOLK.—VOL.1. The next volume in connection with the same class will of course be similar, with the substitution of Vol. 2 for Vol. 1; while the volume upon the Prostitutes should be labelled, LONDON LABOUR AND THE LONDON POOR.—THOSE THAT WILL NOT WORK—CLASS 1—PROSTITUTES.

A Pamphlet "on the Position and Prospects of the School-Assistant, by Thomas N. Hammer," has been received. It contains curious disclosures as to the treatment of a class who are of essential service to the community, and whose remuneration is of the most inadequate character. The pamphlet will well repay perusal, especially with those who feel an interest in the class.

Mr. Mayhew has to thank Dr. T.—for "the Twelfth Annual Report of the Liverpool Benevolent Society for Reclaiming Unfortunate Females." Any further information on the subject will be of service.

The curious letter from "a Clerk in the City" will be inserted at the earliest opportunity. Mr. Mayhew has no wish to pry into matters of privacy, but the communication would be more valuable if some reference could be given as to the credibility of the writer. Mr. Mayhew does not seek to know the name of his correspondent in a case of so delicate a nature, but merely asks for some guarantee that the whole story is not pure fiction.

Returns as to the number of prostitutes have been received, and are acknowledged with thanks, from the police authorities of the following towns:—

Aberdeen.

Exeter.

King's Lynn.

A CONSTANT READER puts a curious question. He says:—

"Can you, or any of the numerous readers of 'London Labour,' explain why a police magistrate is called a *beak?*"

There are two explanations that may be given as to the meaning of the slang term "beak," but both requiring proof. The one is, that in accordance with the *metaphorical* origin of many of the words in the slang language, the term may have been formed from the beak being the organ of seizing or apprehension with birds, and so have been whimsically applied to the functionary connected with the apprehension of criminals.

The other derivation is referrible to the principle laid down by Dr. Latham, that the "lower orders" are the conservators of the Saxon part of the English language—a point which all those who have looked even superficially into the construction of their native tongue will readily admit. Assuming then the word *beak* to be of Saxon origin, we find the Anglo-Saxon term *beag* to signify, among other things, a necklace or ornament to hang about the neck, a collar of state; and when we remember that in Saxon times the aldermen were the sole magistrates (*ealdordom* means authority, magistracy), and that part of the aldermen's insignia of office consists of a chain or collar similar to this *beag*, the transition becomes easy from the emblem of the office to the office or officer himself; even as the "gold-stick-in-waiting" is the title given to the functionary occupying that post; and the policeman is called a "blue-bottle," from his blue uniform; and a soldier a "lobster," from his red coat. Hence a beak would mean simply an alderman or magistrate decorated with a *beag* or gilt collar, as indicative of the magisterial office. As was before stated, however, proof is required; and perhaps some "constant reader" may be able to cite something tending either to confirm or set aside the above suggestion.

"Waltham Cross,
"Nov. 10, 1851.

"Sir,

"Observing in your London Labour of the 8th, an enquiry as to the derivation of the word 'mot,' I take the liberty of mentioning that it is an old French word which I can only translate by '*vulva.*' You will find it so used in the '*Moyen de parvenir*' said to be written by Beroald de Verville, in 1558, or thereabouts. It is there spelt "*motte*", and the expression is still used by the French as argot, or slang, for a prostitute, as well as in the other sense.

"I am, Sir,
"Your obedient very humble Servant,"
"E.C."

The above derivation fulfils all the requirements of the dialectic process. The Italian cognate term is "*il mozzo*" which has the same double meaning as the French "*motte*". An eminent philologist suggested that the English term "*mot*" might be connected with the Norfolk word *Mawther*, a wench; but, on hearing the explanation of E.C., admitted that the matter might be considered as settled at present.

Our friend Wortenkrämer attempts to give a different origin to the term, dealing rather with the term "*mort*" which he appears to consider as the same word as "*mot*;" but this seems rather doubtful at present.

"The word, respecting the derivation of which you require the assistance of your etymological friends, appears to be '*mort*;' although commonly pronounced '*mot*'. N.

Bailey has the word, but he does not give its etymology, and he thus states it: 'a mott, a doxy or whore. Cant.' Just above he has the same word, 'a mort [*amort*, F.], a great abundance. Lincolnshire;' and, below, the phrase 'to blow a mort [hunting term] is to sound a particular air called a *mort*, to give notice that the deer that was hunted is taken and is killed or killing.' Shakspere has the word in the latter sense, in the Winter's Tale, 'and then to sigh as 't were the *mort* o' the deer.' The English dictionaries, in general, only notice the word in the latter meaning, and its derivation from '*mors*' is sufficiently plain. In Bailey-Fahrenkrüger's German and English dictionary, the word is found with the German definition thus 'mort (von *mors*) *der Stosz ins Hifthorn nach Erlegung eines Hirsches: die Menge, der Haufe* (Isl. *margr*); *ein dreijähriger Lachs; volkspr. Weibsbild, Dirne, Mädchen*. Anglice, 'derived from *mors*, the blast in a hunter's horn after the death of a stag; abundance (Icelandic, *margr*), a three-year-old salmon; popularly, a woman, a wench, a girl.' This is all I can make out from the dictionaries at my command, and it does not amount to much, but the same word with a different meaning, derived from the French '*amort*,' as above mentioned, according to N. Bailey, affords, I think, some clue to the word in question.

"It appears very probable that 'mort' is a contraction of a diminutive of *amor* or *amour*; we have the diminutive in French, in '*amourette*' and in Italian is '*amorazzo*', the letter 't' being involved in both of them [not so, they are two different affixes]; the addition of *t* to *r* is also etymologically regular, as *Μοξπὸs* from *Μόξοs* death, and the cutting off of the '*a*' at the beginning is a common case, as in Greek *μαυξόω* for '*αμαυξόω* or English mend for amend" [a is a prefix]; "we here also retain the meaning of the word. '*Amourette*' is thus defined in Laudais's French dictionary 'diminutif d'amour. *Attachement passager et sans grande passion: il a toujours quelque amourette*. The French courtezans call themselves '*filles d'amour*' and I think we must look in this direction for the derivation of *mort* rather than

to *mors* or any of its inflections, for there seems no such necessary connexion between death and harlotry, as there does between love and the sexes." [The two words, however, have evidently different origins.]

"I, at first, thought that the name '*mort*' might be a proper name, and have some such origin as the appellation '*Cyprians*' commonly given to the nymphs of the '*pavé*' because Venus was the Cyprian goddess, whose first temple was in the island of Cyprus. *Morta* was the name given by some to one of the *Parcæ*. The Greeks called the Parcæ, *Μοῖξαι* [Fates]; hence *morta*; and when we bear in mind that the Parcæ were the daughters of *Nox* and *Erebus* (night and darkness), there does seem a ground for conjecturing that the name might have so arisen; I, however, incline to the other etymology.

By-the-by you have fallen into a little error p. 183, vol. ii; '*jardin*', is not the root of our 'garden,' but '*garten*' Germ., is the root of both. Pudding is derived from '*Boudin*,' not '*Poudin*.'
"Yours obediently,
"Wortenkrämer.
"Gray's Inn."

The French *jardin* was given rather as the cognate of the English *garden* than its root, which is from the Saxon *geard*, a yard, enclosure; whence *ort-geard* and *wyrt-geard*, and our *orchard*, *wyrt* signifying a root or herb, and *wyrt-geard*, a garden or yard for fruit (Lat. *hort-us*). The term *poudin* was cited as the modern form of the old term *boudin*.[45] The term *mort* appears to be still of doubtful origin. The derivations above given are ingenious, but far from satisfactory.

The subjoined, from G.H, is etymological:—
"With regard to the derivation of the phrase 'that's the ticket' (No. 43), I venture to remark that I have always understood the complete phrase to be 'that's the ticket *for soup*.' If my reading be the original one, this slang, perhaps, has not so refined an origin as you

---

[45] A rather weak excuse as the word "Poudin" does not seem to exist in French. Pouding is the French version of Pudding.

suggest; probably some one can tell us the date of its introduction. By the way, about preserving the wrappers of your wonderful work: the Notices to Correspondents are far—very far—too good to be lost, and to bind up your title-page and the advertisements will give the book, when complete, a very awkward appearance. Can not you do something to obviate this latter feature?"

G.H. will see, by an advertisement in the present number, that some of the articles which have appeared on the wrappers of this periodical are about to be reprinted. It is most essential in a work of the character of "London Labour" that are *opinions* of a mere individual should be kept distinct from the *facts* of the subject. The latter we *must* adopt, whatever view we may take of society and governments—they *cannot but* be true; whereas the speculations of any one man *may be* untrue, and calculated to mislead. In the next volume Mr. Mayhew will endeavour to confine the Notices to Correspondents to the two last pages of each number, so that they may be bound together at the end of the volume by those who may consider them worth preserving. [*Edited out:* Mayhew's etymology of 'that's the ticket for soup.']

ANSWERS TO CORRESPONDENTS.
[No.52, 6 DECEMBER 1851]

Edited out:
WORTENKRÄMER ON BERDASH AND MAYHEW'S ANSWER; R & ISAAC C; LEWIS M.B.; A.G. & OLIM MIRATOR'S SHORT NOTICES.

—————

The subjoined is from a working tailor, who sends an account of his wages and expenditure for several years—statistics which are of the utmost possible importance, especially when the writer accompanies them with vouchers for his credibility. It were indeed to be wished that all trades would do the same; for it is only in this way that any *proof* as to wages can be arrived at. A workman's *actual* weekly wages are often so different from his *nominal* weekly wages, and his casual receipts per week frequently considerably less than his constant income, while the gains of a particular individual cannot possibly form a criterion of the general earnings of the whole trade; so that it is solely by the collection of a large number of facts any accurate and comprehensive result can be obtained. There are no less than six different kinds of wages in every trade, and it is absolutely essential that each be distinguished from the other. The two first kinds refer to a man's weekly wages. To ascertain a man's actual weekly wage, we deduct all fines and stoppages from his nominal weekly wage, or else we add to it all perquisites, allowances, and the like; the nominal wage being what he is said to receive per week for his labour, and the actual what he really does receive from his employer. To arrive at a man's constant (or average casual) wage, we must multiply his actual weekly wage by the number of weeks he has been employed, and divide by 52 (the total number of weeks throughout the year). A man whose actual weekly wages amount to 1£, and who is casually employed for six months in the year, will have had only 10s. for a constant (or average casual) wage throughout the year. The general wage of a trade is to be arrived at solely by dividing the gross amount paid for labour in the course of the year—first, by the entire number of labourers; and, secondly, by the total number of weeks in the year. The better paid journeymen tailors may earn, on an average, 1£ a week the year through; fully employed and casual men as well; and the slop-tailors, 10s. a week; and thus the general wages, as contradistinguished from the individual, will be 15s. per week. It is highly necessary for a right understanding of the wage question that each form of wage be distinguished, for one kind of wage is no guide to the other.

"DEAR SIR,

"Reading in your work, 'London Labour', No. 40, an account of wages by R.H. (though I do not quite like the way he averages it, but which supplies some information as far as it

Date.		Weekly average.	Weeks.	Highest Week.	Weeks.	Lowest Weeks.	Rent.	Firing and candles.	Bread and Flour.	Meat and Fish.
		INCOME.					*EXPENDITURE.*			
	£ s. d.	s. d.		s. d.			£ s. d.	£ s. d.	£ s. d.	£ s. d.
1841	54 13 3	21 0¼		33 0	4	Nil.	10 8 3	2 18 3	5 12 4¼	9 10 4
1842	59 1 3	22 8½	7 at	36 0	6	Nil.	10 15 0	3 4 2½	5 17 4¼	9 16 6
1843	62 13 4½	24 1¼	7 ,,	36 0	3	Nil.	11 8 3	3 10 4	5 11 10¼	10 14 0
1844	69 7 1½	26 8	1 ,,	36 0	1	Nil.	10 8 0	4 0 4½	7 3 0½	11 9 6
1845	66 18 3	25 8¾	6 ,,	36 0	3	Nil.	10 14 3	3 12 0½	7 16 10	10 12 0
1846	73 8 9	28 3	6 ,,	36 0	1	Nil.	11 1 0	3 9 0	8 5 10	12 3 4
1847	73 2 9	28 1½		35 6	2	Nil.	11 1 0	3 13 11	8 18 9	10 12 8
1848	64 5 10½	24 8½	6 ,,	36 0	2	Nil.	11 1 0	4 0 10½	8 11 10½	11 18 4½
1849	66 13 7½	25 7¾	11 ,,	36 0	4	Nil.	11 6 3	3 1 2	8 5 3½	10 18 4
1850	67 0 6	25 11½	8 ,,	36 0		1s.	11 4 3	3 15 4½	8 7 5½	10 6 7
	657 4 9	25 3¼	52		26		109 7 3	35 5 6½	74 10 8	108 1 7½

goes), I beg leave to send you an account of mine, as journeyman tailor, for the last ten years, the time I have been married (my wedding-day was Dec. 25, 1840). We have now four children, and we have buried one. My wife does nothing towards a living except look after the family, which I consider is quite plenty. I came to London on Nov. 8, 1837, and went to work at my present employer's Feb. 13, 1838, where I have worked ever since (except five months at the end of 1839, when I was in Paris). I have always made it a rule from the time I commenced as journeyman to keep an account of my earnings, and the principal items of expenditure, so you may rely on their accuracy; if you require proof you can call on me any Sunday evening, and I shall feel great pleasure in showing you the way I keep my accounts. With respect to beer, &c., in the other sheet, I keep no account of my expenditure that way, but I think 4¹/₂d. a day is as near the truth as I can come without regular accounts. My employer's name is J.—H.—, and a good master he is. I wish all were like him; but if you should make any use of any part of this paper be sure you do not mention his name. My native county is Cambridgeshire. I left home March 21, 1837, and 'tramped' to most of the principal towns in the north of England during the summer and autumn of that year, when I came to London to see the Queen go to Guildhall, on Nov. 9, 1837, and here I have been ever since, and here I suppose I am likely to remain; but I am perfectly satisfied. If I have work as I had heretofore I shall be a lucky man.

"I beg to remain

"Your obedient Servant,

"E—B—."

SOME OF THE PRINCIPAL ITEMS OF EXPENDITURE FOR THE TEN YEARS.		AVERAGE PER WEEK.	
	£ s. d.	£ s. d.	
Rent	109 7 3	0 4 2¼	
Firing and candles .	35 5 6½	0 1 4½	
Bread & flour . . .	74 10 8	0 2 10¼	
Meat, fish &c.	108 1 7½	0 4 1¾	
Soap, Soda &c.. . .	7 6 9½	0 0 3½	
Clothing for family (six persons) . . .	62 5 1½	0 2 10½	
Doctors' bills . . . (six persons)	13 12 9	0 0 6½	
Trade and benefit society and fire insurance .	45 1 2½	0 1 8¾	
Household furniture .	38 16 9½	0 1 5¾	
Beer, &c. I only suppose at 4¹/₂d. per day or £7 per annum . . .	70 0 0	0 2 8½	
	564 7 9		
Income	657 4 9		
Expenses	564 7 9		
It leaves for groceries fruit, and vegetables .	92 17 0	0 1 7¾	
Or about £9 yearly.		1 3 10	

"The above is a correct account of my income as a journeyman tailor, *in full work, at a full-priced shop, on the best work*, on the employer's premises; the average number of men about ten.

"I have not included in the above an account of a trifle I make by a little "crib" at the shop, or a few shillings by doing a job of my own, which I lay out in books; the account as I have given is for purely domestic purposes. Books by some are considered a luxury, or things that can be done without, so I did not include them; but I can vouch for the accuracy of the accounts.

"E.B."

The following explains and qualifies some of the above statements:—

"I beg leave to supply you with the other items that you require to my statement. I will take them at they stand on the cover of No. 42. 1. Am I a quick hand? I can safely say that I am quicker than the average by a good deal, when there is plenty of work. I earn more money than the rest in the shop, except one; but when it is slack time we share the work amongst ourselves as fair as we can." [E.B. should have said how much quicker he was in his work than an average hand; that is to say, how much more money he could earn than an ordinary hand in a given time at the same wages] "2. The usual hours of labour is twelve hours per day in the busy time; at other times various, according to circumstances" [What have been the average number of hours per day throughout the year?] "3. There are no manner of deductions from the wages whatever. 4. It is rather difficult in respect to reduction of wages during the period given in my accounts, for the prices paid for some garments are less than they were, but then again they are made different; other garments have more work put in, and others again something less; but I daresay the shop I work at has been reduced less in price than almost any other in the trade, that is, as far as my knowledge extends. Perhaps it is 6d. per day, or 3s. per week harder work to make up what is called full time than it was when I first went there, thirteen years ago. But as I stated

before, Mr.—is a very good master; there are indeed very few like him; he has all his work done on his premises, and he calls from the Society at present at the White Hart, Little Windmill-street. We have a clean, airy, well-ventilated shop to work in; coals and gas found us, with soap, water, and towels in the shop for our use and every other convenience.

"I beg to remain
"Your dutiful Servant,
"E—B—."

"P.S. Please not to mention any names in what you extract."

ANSWERS TO CORRESPONDENTS.
[No.53, No.VIII "Those that will not Work", 13 DECEMBER 1851, price 3d.]

Edited out:
ACKNOWLEDGED RETURNS OF THE POLICE AUTHORITIES OF: BRIGHTON. STOKE-UPON-TRENT. SUNDERLAND. GATESHEAD. WIGAN.

The following communications on the etymology of the slang term Mot, are all curious, and some very useful:—

"Albany-street,
"Dec. 2nd, 1851.
"Sir,
"It has often happened in the course of your most useful and interesting publication, 'London Labour and the London Poor,' that I have seen words used for which I could have given an explanation, but have deferred doing so till I have seen some one else come forward—then it would be needless. In the last number, in reference to the word 'mot,' your correspondent properly states it is coming from the old French word *motte*. This is the true orthography, and has reference, as he translates it, to the *vulva;* but its origin in the slang, or argot, is from *motte,* turf.

"I am, Sir,
"Yours most obediently,
"T.S.B."

[In the country the mark in quoit-playing is termed a "motte," probably from the above signification; but the slang term "mot," a low woman, is clearly another word.—H.M.]

"Sir,

"In a former number of your valuable work, 'London Labour,' &c., you made an inquiry concerning the derivation of the word 'mot,' as popularly applied to prostitutes. I did not doubt that, among the answers this inquiry would elicit from some of your numerous readers, the meaning which I have always heard abroad attributed to that term would have been mentioned; but as I do not find it in the replies of either of your two correspondents, E.C. or Wortenkrämer, I venture to suggest that this word, like so many of the same class, *argot*, or slang, adopted in our *vulgar* tongue, is derived from the Dutch, and was perhaps introduced thence by our sailors; for it is still used by the lower classes in Holland to express the same meaning as that of *mot* in English slang. Thus 'een mot' means a *low* prostitute; 'een mottekast,' a brothel (*literally*, a chest or case infested with moths). The primary and real signification of the word '*mot*,' in Dutch, is the same as *moth* in English. It is, therefore, there applied to this class of women as a vituperative term, designating them as foul agents of corruption and destruction, even as the moth is to woollen cloth.

"Etymologies, I am aware, are generally fanciful, and sometimes even border on the ridiculous. Still, when we find in so many living languages this word applied to express the same reproachful meaning in all of them, the explanation above given may not perhaps appear to you altogether improbable and unworthy of notice. *Possibly* it may be the real one.

"The French derivation given by your correspondent, E.C., seems also to point to the meaning of corruption, because the term *vulva*, or rather what it is *intended* to designate thereby, being common to all the sex, cannot in a vituperative sense be applied to the dissolute part of them exclusively, but must be intended as expressing (in a coarse manner) the

meaning of a foul and corrupt *vulva*.

"I am, Sir,
"Your obedient Servant, and
"Constant Reader,
"D.

"Upper Clapton,
"Nov. 29th 1851."

The above is useful, as giving another dialectic explanation of the term "*mot*." The question consequently becomes, are the Dutch words "mot," a moth, and "*mot*," a low woman, etymologically the same words, or do they proceed from different roots? I suspect they have *not* a common origin for the following reasons. The Saxon term *moth*, a moth, is evidently another form of the Saxon *mot*, a mote, *atomus*; and hence an insect, gnat or moth. This, again, is connected with the Anglo-Saxon *mite* and Heb., ססם moth, a little thing. The latter is probably from some root to cut, to divide; as *in-sect*, from *seco*.

Now the Dutch term *mottekast*, for a brothel, has evidently, to those who have any knowledge of the cognate languages a less fanciful origin than that supposed by D. In Anglo-Saxon, the equivalent for the Dutch *mottekast* would be *mot-hus*, that is, a moot-house, or *meeting*-house, a place of assembly; and hence a brothel, a place of assembly for men and women, a meeting or "assignation-house;" and hence *mot* would be a low woman in the habit of frequenting such places, the frequenter of brothels.

The Saxon term *mot*, or *gemot*, is an assembly, a meeting—as in the old Saxon parliament or witenagemot, i.e., the assembly (*gemot*) of the wits or wise men (*witena*). This *mot*, a meeting, was a substantive formed from the verb *metan*, to meet, meet with, find, obtain, get. Hence a "mot" would mean either a woman in the habit of frequenting a *mot-hus*, or house of assembly for men and women, a brothel; or a woman accustomed to make appointments and meet gentlemen.

The low French term *motte* signifying

vulva, and the Italian *mozzo*, are more likely to be connected with *moth* and *mote* than with *mot*, a prostitute. The derivation of *mot*, a low woman, from *mot-hus* and *mottekast*, a brothel, appears to be conclusive.

There is another term, *trull*, applied to the lower order of prostitutes. This is the Saxon term *thræl*, and old German *trulle*, a slave, one in *thraldom*. The old Dutch *drille* from the same root, is explained—*mulier vaga, levis meretrix*. The Icelandic cognate is *throell*, servus. Hence the word trull is the Saxon equivalent for the modern term *"slavey,"* the appellation given to that class of prostitutes who are, as Duchatelet [sic] expresses it, "subject to the mistress of a brothel;" that is to say, those who have to give up the whole or a portion of their gains to the bawd, in return for their board and lodging and clothes, in contradistinction to the *"femmes libres,"* or those who trade on their own account. The French term for the former class is *"esclaves,"* the English *"slavey;"* and it is curious not only that the same vile mode of traffic should be common to both countries, but that they should be expressed by the same term. The word *trull* has a similar signification to *"slavey."*

Still there is the word *mort* to be explained. Is this the same term as *mot*? I suspect not; but the following letter gives the ingenious speculations of a gentleman who has evidently paid some little attention to the subject of comparative philology.

"Ashby-de-la-Zouch,
"*Dec.* 4, 1851.

"Sir,

"I am engaged on an etymological cant or slang vocabulary, and have been hesitating whether to connect the word 'mot' with mate, a companion, &c., or with mother; I find you suggest the latter, and I have almost made up my mind to adopt it. I must confess I should be better satisfied if I could prove it from the Anglo-Saxon *maca*, a *mace*, a husband, wife, mate, or companion, or could I establish that this *a* had the broad sound; this latter circumstance would, I think, decide it, mace, make, mate, mort, mot. [The writer should

study Bopp's "Vocalismus".]

"The word mort is used in several of our dialects for a great quantity; the Anglo-Saxon for lump is *mace;* one might almost be tempted here to compare the French argot word *largue*, which means a woman, a doxy. I think, however, that the Anglo-Saxon *mace*, lump, and our *much* are connected.

"Turn now to the Sanscrit, *matar* (mother); Sclavonic, *mater;* Lithuanian, *moter* (a woman, a mother is *motina*) and Lettish, *mate;* now the broad sound being immediately given to the *a* where it occurs, and the accent being on the penultima, the last syllable would be faint and at last disappear, so that we have not much difficulty in arriving at mort, mot; and, probably, it came thus to us through the Gypsies, whether Bohemian or German." [But see the extract here appended from Borrow.] "In 'Witt's Recreation' a collection of epitaphs epigrams, fancies, &c, a Gypsy sings—

"And for the Romi-*morts*,
I know by their ports,
And there jolly resorts,
They are of the sorts
That love the true sports
Of King Ptolomæus,
Or Great Coriphæus,
And Queen Cleopatra,
The Gypsies' grand *Matra*."

"You will find in the song of the old and young courtiers, inserted in Percy's 'Reliques of Ancient Poetry,'[46] the word *madam* used for kept woman—

"'Like a flourishing young gallant newly come to his land,
Who keeps a brace of painted madams at his command.'"

"Also in 'Witt's recreation' there are some lines on a patched up "madam;" and, again, the common people in this part of the country frequently call such persons madams.

"I am, Sir, yours truly,
"T.L.L."

---

[46] Th. Percy, *Reliques of Ancient Poetry*, Vol. III, J. Dodsley, 1765.

T.L.L. will have seen that the term *mot* has a wholly different origin from that originally conjectured. The word *maca*, a mate, wife, is connected with the verb *macian*, to make, form, *match* but *mace*, a lump, is connected with Latin *massa*; *much*, on the other hand, is related to Latin *magis* and *more* with *major*, and these all with the Latin *magnus*, and the Saxon *mæg-en*, Anglice, main strength, power; whence the Saxon *mægeste*, greatest, most powerful; *maximus*, and *mæg-ester*, a master, *magister*. It is difficult to say whether these words are derivatives of *macian*, to make, or the verb derived from them. Be this as it may, however, it is manifest that from *macian*, to make, comes *mæden* (Ger. *magd*), a maiden, made, even as mate gives made in the past tense; and hence, too, the Saxon *mæg*, a relation, son, daughter, a friend, male or female, a woman: the Scotch *Mac* has the same origin. Hence, again, we have *modor*, mother, and *mater*, and the several cognates for the same word, all meaning, simply, *mactor*, a *maker*, even as *father* is from *factor*, a maker, and *author* from *auctor*. The dropping of the *c* in all these words is by no means uncommon; *c* and *g* in former times had, probably, the sound of *y*, or guttural aspirate. Blodi*g*, in Saxon, is the original of our bloody, and so, in the French, *éloigne* and *boulogne*. Thus the Latin *factum* becomes, in French, *fait*, and so our verb *make* in the *past* tense gives, *made* for *maked*, the *c*, *k*, or *g*, having a tendency first to pass into *i* or *y*, and then to disappear altogether. The ordinary derivation of *father* is from *feeder*, he who supplies the food, because *fedan*, in Saxon, is to feed, and *foeder*, a father; but the Icelandic *fœdi*, *at fœda*, is *generare*, connected with *fio*, *φυω* and *facio*. Webster strives to connect *mother* with *mud*, the earth, as when we speak of our "mother earth," but such derivations are all fanciful, and words have a far more simple and less metaphorical origin than is ordinarily believed. The word *man*, again, is from the verb to make. In Saxon *man* means—1, a man; 2, one of the human kind, a *woman* while the plat. Dutch *mäken* means a maid, maiden, so that it would appear that the word *maken* (i.e. mak+en) originally

signified any created thing, and then one of the human kind, a man or a woman; and, lastly a man proper; while the term maid, *macod*, came to be restricted to a young woman. The names Meg and Madge have the same origin, and meant, originally, merely a woman, a relation, even, as *John* means in Sanscrit, a man, and Jane, Jinny, *γυνη* a woman; all of which are connected with *γενομαι* to beget. In precisely the same manner our word *wight*, which is in Saxon *wuht*, means any created thing:—(1) a creature, wight, animal, thing; (2) aught, anything. The Dutch and German cognate *wicht*, stands for a child. All these are connected with the Anglo-Saxon weascian, to wax, grow, *nasci, fieri;* even as the Saxon *aht*, aught, something, is related to the verb *agan*, to own, have, obtain which is connected both with the Greek *εχω* and the Latin *augeo*. The relative words *what* and *it* are from this root.

To return, however, to the term *mort*. This would appear, according to Mr. Borrow, *not* to be a Gypsy term. He says, in his account of the Robber language,—

"The first vocabulary of the 'Cant Language,' or English Germania, appeared in the year 1680, appended to the life of 'The English Rogue,' a work which, in many respects, resembles the history of Guzman d'Alfarache, though it is written with considerably more genius than the Spanish novel...Amongst his other adventures, the hero falls in with a Gypsy encampment, is enrolled amongst the fraternity, and is allotted a '*mort*,' or concubine; a barbarous festival ensues, at the conclusion of which an epithalamium is sung in the Gypsy language, as it is called in the work in question. Neither the epithalamium,[47] however, nor the vocabulary, are written in the language of the English Gypsies but in the 'Cant', or allegorical robber dialect, which is sufficient proof that the writer, however well acquainted with thieves in general, their customs and manner of life, was in respect to the Gypsies profoundly ignorant. His vocabulary, however, has been always

---

[47] Poem composed at the occasion of a wedding.

accepted as the speech of the English Gypsies, whereas it is at most entitled to be considered as the peculiar speech of the thieves and vagabonds of his time. The 'cant' of the present day, which, though it differs in some respects from the vocabulary already mentioned, is radically the same, is used not only by the thieves in town and country, but by the jockeys of the racecourse and the pugilists of the 'ring'. As a specimen of the cant of England, we shall take the liberty of quoting the epithalamium to which we have above alluded.

'Bing out bien *morts*, and tour and tour,
Ring out, bien *morts* and tour;
For all your duds are bing'd awast,
The bien cove hath the loure*.

'I met a dell, I viewed her well,
She was benship to my watch,
So she and I did stall and cloy
Whatever we could catch.

'This doxy dell can cut ben whids,
And wap well for a win,
And prig and cloy so benshiply,
All daisy-ville within.

'The hoyle was up, we had good luck,
In frost for and in snow;
When they did seek, then we did creep
And plant in roughman's low.'"

The question is still whether the word *mort* is the same as mot, and if not, whence comes it?

"* This word is pure Wallachian and was brought by the Gypsies into England; it means booty what is called in the present cant language, 'swag.' The Gypsies call booty 'louripen.'"

ANSWERS TO CORRESPONDENTS.
[No.54, 20 DECEMBER 1851]

Edited out:
D.S. BIRMINGHAM; A COMMANDING OFFICER; A.C.; F.C.R.M. (M.D.).

The late remarks on machinery in connection with the increase of surplus labour have brought a small avalanche of letters down upon us. Some are from those who are known, and whose opinions are esteemed by us; while some of the writers are unknown to us, but their opinions are worthy of respect, as they have evidently been endeavouring to think out the subject for themselves. It will, perhaps, be better to give the letters seriatim, and reply to them collectively. The first refers to the use of machinery in connection with the scavaging of the streets.

"Sir,

"Having read your remarks upon machine and pauper sweeping in No. 44 [LLLP, Vol. 2, pp. 207-75] of your most interesting publication, permit me to ask you one question on the principle you advocate therein.

"You are against employing machines and paupers, because of the number of men thrown out of labour by them; for upon employing them a vast amount of labour which was formerly profitable to the community becomes unprofitable, and therefore is not employed.

"The labour in question is surplus labour, and is over and above what is required for the good of the community.

Now if individuals are employed in unprofitable labour, so that it only be innocent labour, I do not see that it matters what the nature of it is. If, then, instead of employing individuals to sweep, the machines were used, and the men thus thrown out of work were to be employed in digging holes and filling them up again, in building houses and knocking them down again, or any other work equally unprofitable, and the wages saved by the machines were expended on this, so that there would be exactly the same amount of labour employed, and the same amount of wages expended as if no sweeping-machines were used, then it seems as if it would be exactly the same as if no machines were used.

"My question, then, is this—Whether you are in favour of the community finding unprofitable labour for the surplus labourers, and paying them for the same?

"I am,

"Your obedient Servant,

"Liverpool. T.A."

The second is from a friend, and relates to the use of machinery in connection with the printing trade. It runs as follows:—

"I have been pondering a good deal at various times about your theory of the 'Wage Fund,' and am inclined to think you are mistaken in supposing that money is taken from it in order to erect machinery. Of course I look to the process in my own case as that of thousands of others. I was a hand-press printer, and made, we will say, 500£ per annum. Of this I spent 250£; 250£ I invested in 3 per cents, or bank stock, or railway shares. As a hand-press printer *I could not further extend my trade*. I could only do this by producing books at a much cheaper rate. I then, with the accumulated savings of several years, or by other means, purchase machinery; my trade increases, and, instead of discharging men, I employ a great many more. Is not this the case with the cotton and woollen manufacturers? The only difference with them was, that they throw a number of hand-loom weavers out of employ, and instead paid *a greater amount of wages* to women and children than were paid before to the men. Unless you could show that less was paid in wages after the introduction of machinery than before, you cannot prove that the 'Wage Fund' has been abstracted from and thrown into fixed capital. You will recollect that without machinery we should have little or no foreign trade."

Another refers more particularly to the use of machinery in connection with the stocking trade.

"Nov. 25, 1851."

"Sir,

"In your recent discussion on the wage law and your sweeping remarks on machinery, you seem to forget the good that machinery has done. If you look at the present time, and compare it with 50 years since—those 'good old times'— you will at once be struck with the marked improvement that has taken place. I do not deny that machinery has thrown a great many men out of employment; but you must recollect that a few must suffer for the good of the many, and that if a man is ground down by machinery, he has to pay less both for clothing and eatables. That the introduction of machinery in our manufactures has, on the whole, done more good than harm, there can be no doubt.

"You say that the machinery in England is equal in power to 600,000,000 men: in one sense so much the better; it enables the large capitalist to compete with other countries. I could adduce several instances in support of this, but will content myself with the following:—A short time ago Saxony monopolised nearly the whole of the American stocking trade; but since the recent improvements in stocking-machinery at Nottingham, we have been able to successfully compete with that country. Hoping you will excuse my freedom in writing you,

"I remain, Sir,

"Yours respectfully,

"J— C—."

Now in the above letters, it will be seen many different arguments are used in favour of machinery.

The first is, that if we can discover the means of doing a given quantity of work with fewer hands, that to employ a greater number is to employ them as fruitlessly and unprofitably as if we were to set them "to dig holes and fill them up again."

The second is, that it admits of the market being extended.

The third is, that in the cotton trade the wages of the hand-loom weavers alone have been decreased, while those of the "power" operatives have been raised.

The fourth, that it increases the foreign trade of the country, or, as one gentleman expresses it, "enables the large capitalist to compete with other countries."

These appear to exhaust the reasons above given why machinery is to be regarded as a benefit, in the present state of our social institutions. The fallacy of the whole appears to consist in ignoring the existence of the labourer, and not paying the same regard to his interests as to those of the capitalist class. This seems to be the fundamental error of all party reasoning. Each person considers the community to be made up of that class with which he is the most concerned; and when he speaks of the community being benefited, we shall find, if we probe him well, that he means merely the increase of the worldly advantages of that particular section with which he may happen to be connected. This is a natural source of prejudice; indeed, all those who have paid attention to the laws of suggestion know the tendency of every feeling to give rise to ideas and opinions in accordance with it. Hence it will be found, that when traders speak of the community being benefited, they mean, generally, that the profits of trade are to be increased; so with the landlords, when they say that the country is to derive some special advantage from a particular condition of things, the meaning is, too often, that rents are likely to be improved; and so, again, with the working men, the good of the nation signifies, in nine cases out of ten, the improvement of their own condition. Now, by the benefit of the community, we are to understand the benefit, if not of every individual member of it, at least of the greatest number. The labouring population and those who are immediately dependent upon them, necessarily make up the majority of this kingdom: the benefit of the community, therefore, involves the improvement of the condition of the labourers more particularly than that of any other section of society; and by consequence, that which tends to impoverish them, however much it may be to the advantage of any other class, must be said to inflict a national injury. A certain mode of

production may tend to increase the stock of national wealth to a considerable amount, but the increase of the riches of a country is no benefit to the people *unless those riches be distributed, and the people themselves obtain a due share of them*. The machinery question consequently resolves itself into a matter of fact—do the people, that is to say, the labouring population, become possessed of a greater amount of comforts and commodities by mechanical contrivances for the economy of labour? This must necessarily depend upon the extensibility of the market for the commodities to the production of which the machinery is applied. If there be only a definite quantity of such commodities required—as, for instance, of hearses—that is to say, if the demand for the articles be dependent on some circumstance which no cheapness could possibly influence, then of course the economy of labour in connection with the production of those articles cannot but be attended with the displacement of just as much labour as is economised; and thus, though the capitalist class would be benefited by the cheapening of the commodity, the labouring class would be injured to the extent of the economisation of the labour: for if the condition of the capitalist class depends on the quantity of commodities they can get in exchange for their capital, that of the labouring class depends on the quantity of commodities they can get in exchange for their labour;—hence the economy of labour must in all cases, where the market is circumscribed, be as great an evil to the poor as it is a gain to the rich. In other cases where the market is extensible, it must be admitted that the labourers may be benefited by the economy of labour: for since the value of those commodities the supply of which can be indefinitely extended is generally determined by the cost of production, it follows, that to economise the labour of producing such commodities is to decrease the cost of production, and so to extend the demand for them, by which means a greater quantity of labourers may be employed. There can be no doubt that a greater number of workmen are employed in producing copies of writings by means of moveable types than ever could have been employed had the scribe not been superseded by the compositor. The cause of this is to be found simply in that cheapening of the article (owing to the diminished cost of production), which has naturally induced a large increase of demand. In such a case, machinery, it must be confessed, has been a good to both classes, the producers and the consumers being equally benefited by it; but has this been the case with the cotton-manufacture? It would appear *not* by the statistics of that trade—which must be reserved till the next number—when it shall be demonstrated to all those that are open to reason, that precisely as the capitalists in that trade have been enriched, the working classes have been impoverished by it. Who can explain that the poverty and crime of this country advance at the same rate with our wealth, by any other means than that the capitalist class have learnt by the economy of labour to obtain a greater quantity of riches with a less sum paid to the labourers? Those, however, who are interested in the question, will find this part of the matter more fully discussed in the publication entitled "Low Wages" than it is possible to do here.

ANSWERS TO CORRESPONDENTS.
[No.56, 3 JANUARY 1852]

According to promise I return to the consideration of the opinions which have been forwarded to me by several correspondents in favour of machinery as applied to the purposes of manufacture in *general*. These are as follows:—

1. That if we can discover the means of doing a given quantity of work with fewer hands, to employ a greater number is to employ them as fruitlessly and unprofitably as if we were to set them to dig holes and fill them up again.

2. That machinery admits of the market being extended.

3. That in the cotton trade the wages of the hand-loom weavers alone have been decreased, while those of the "power" operatives have been raised.

4. That machinery increases the foreign trade of the country, or "enables the large capitalist to compete with other countries."

5. That the capital required for the purpose of constructing machines is not taken from the Wage Fund.

6. That the capital which is saved in wages in one trade must go to increase employment in another.

7. That labour is a curse, and consequently the saving of it must be a blessing.

8. That machinery, by diminishing the cost of production, admits of the labourer obtaining an increased supply of commodities for less money, so that even if his wages be decreased by it, he cannot be said to be a loser.

This surely is a full and fair statement of the question. The above arguments may be grouped into three classes: the first including those which uphold machinery in the abstract, on the ground that, since labour is an evil, the economy of it must be a good, and that to employ labour which can be done without is to employ it uselessly; the second class are those which uphold machinery not so much for itself as for its results, saying that it admits of the market being extended, of the increase of our foreign trade, and of the labourer obtaining increased comforts for less money; while the third class comprises those which are of a negative character, denying what has been asserted, and declaring that the capital applied to the construction of machinery is not drawn from the funds devoted to the payment of the labourers, and that the wages which are saved by mechanical appliances in one trade, go to increase employment in some other; and lastly, that the wages in the cotton trade, in particular, have not been diminished by it.

Let us first deal with the arguments which refer to machinery in the abstract. There cannot be the least doubt that labour *is* an evil, since it is that which all the world pays to avoid, and which to undergo all people require a reward of some kind as *an inducement*. Were toil, rather than ease, a pleasure, gentlemen would give a certain sum to be allowed to work, instead of parting with a portion of their wealth to servants to save them the trouble of doing the least thing for themselves. But if labour be a curse, at least it is *the means of living*—"in the sweat of thy face shalt thou eat *bread;*" and the majority of the people—the community, indeed—have no other means of subsistence. In all primitive states this is the sole means of continuing existence; nature supplies the wealth, and man has to collect it; the seeking and the gathering being then the only labour that he is called upon to perform. For this little or no capital or saving is required, provided the spontaneous productions of the earth are sufficient to enable a man in the course of each day to find and collect enough to maintain himself till the morrow. In other conditions of society, however, when or where the earth, in the common course of nature, does not yield sufficient for the support of the people located upon it, other forms of labour are obliged to be adopted, and, instead of *collection*, men then have to resort to *production* (and *extraction*, for the purpose of obtaining the minerals essential for the perfection of the productive process).

Now the difference between these several forms of labour lies in the *time* required for a return to the industry; in collection the return is almost *immediate*, the labour of each day generally yielding sufficient food for the performance of the next day's labour. In production, however, the labourer has to remain some considerable time unrewarded; he must wait until the seasons return before his exertions can meet with the least reward. But during this time he must live; hence in all productive states saving is necessary; for since the return to the labour is *not* immediate, and the necessity for food is continually recurring at short intervals, it is evident that without a stock of provisions sufficient to keep him until the earth yields him the produce of his industry, the labourer will be unable to protract his existence. But immediately society passes from a state of collection or *immediate* returns to industry, to a state of production or *deferred* returns, it necessarily changes from the condition of mere labour to one of labour and capital—for capital is simply saving with a view to production; that is to say, in the latter condition not only labour, but a sufficient stock of provisions, is required to keep the individual while labouring. And since this stock could only have been obtained by the abstinence of some of the labourers, that is to say, by their living on less than they had previously acquired, and since all men are not equally provident, it follows that some would possess such a stock, while others would be without the means of supporting themselves in the intervals of production; hence society in such a state would necessarily divide itself into two distinct classes: that of the capitalists or possessors of the stock necessary for the performance of the labour; and the mere labourers deficient of all provision for the future. The consequence, of course, would be, since the capitalists possessed the sole means of obtaining the future produce, and without which the others could not possibly prosecute their labour, that the labourers would gladly consent to allow the capitalists to share in the proceeds of their industry, provided the capitalists would allow them to share in the proceeds of their abstinence; and hence we arrive by easy gradations at the state of employer and employed, in which the capitalists possess everything, and the labourers have nothing but their labour to give in exchange for a portion of the savings of the others.

Now, the capitalists being, in such an arrangement of society, the possessors of all wealth and requiring the services of the labourers to operate on the *materials* of the future productions—whether seed to convert into crops, or wool into cloth and coats, or hides into leather and shoes, or cotton into calicoes and shirts, or wood into ships and houses and furniture, or iron into tools, weapons, and machines; of course it follows that the *less they part with* to the labourers for so doing *the greater will be their gain*, that is to say, the *more* commodities they will obtain from their materials at *less* cost. The labourers, however, having nothing to depend upon but what they receive in exchange for their labour, it equally follows, that the less they obtain for their work the worse will be their condition. The smaller the quantity of labour, therefore, that is required, or what is the same thing, the fewer the labourers that are needed to make up the materials of wealth into commodities, the less stock the capitalists will have to part with, and the more commodities they will obtain; for what they save in labour they can, of course, exchange for a greater quantity of materials, and so get a greater number of commodities at a less expense; hence anything which tends to make each of the workmen do the work of one hundred must necessarily tend to increase the gains of the capitalists as much as it does to decrease the income of the labourers in the aggregate, and to give the possessors of the stock or material one-hundredfold more articles of utility or enjoyment for the same outlay, while there must necessarily be one-hundredfold less employment for the labourers. It should be borne in mind, that the stock possessed by the capitalists is the result of saving out of the *past* produce, and consequently *cannot possibly be increased* till the next year's returns are obtained; hence this is the whole that in the interval of production can be used for the enjoyment of the capitalists, the supply of materials, and the maintenance of the labourers; so that the increase of the funds required for either of these results necessarily involve the decrease of those needed for the others, that is to say, if a larger portion of the stock be devoted to material for the future produce, there will be less left for the maintenance of the labourers; hence it follows that to enable the workmen to convert more materials into products in the same time, is to cause a greater proportion of the stock of the capitalist to be devoted to materials, and a correspondingly less proportion to be devoted to the maintenance of the labourers.

To put this clearly to those who are unused to such speculations, let us say that the national income of this country amounts to 300,000,000£, that is to say, that the whole year's produce of provisions, clothes, furniture, implements, conveyances, ornaments, &c., &c., is altogether worth that amount of money, and let us say that 100,000,000£ were paid to 4,000,000 labourers while engaged in producing the wealth; that another 100,000,000£ expressed the value of the materials—the seed, the cotton, the wool, the hides, the wood, the iron—used in the production of the various commodities. The whole of the 300,000,000£ then would, of course, belong entirely to the capitalists; 200,000,000£ going to replace the capital employed in production and 100,000,000£ being the profits on the transaction. The labourers own not one brass farthing of the produce; they have been paid for their labour in obtaining it, and are held to have no further claim upon it. Now let us suppose that by the invention of a certain machine the capitalists are enabled to convert the materials of the next year's produce into commodities with a less amount of labour, and consequently with fewer labourers, say with one-half, what must be the inevitable consequence? The result, of course, will be that only one-half the number of labourers being required, one-half less would be expended in wages, even supposing the same rate of remuneration to be paid to each (though, of course, wages would fall from the competition of those displaced), and thus the capitalists would have only 50,000,000£ to pay for the labour of the workpeople, while the workpeople, of course, would have 50,000,000£ less to live upon. But what, it may be asked, would be done with the 50,000,000£ saved? Why either it would go to increase the profits and enjoyments of the capitalists, or else it would be devoted to the purchase of an extra quantity of materials—of cotton, of wool, of silk, of wood, or what not, with the view of increasing the gross quantity of the future produce. Let us suppose the latter course to be adopted: then it follows that a certain portion of those whose labour had been superseded by the machine might be re-employed, and granting the same relation between the sum devoted to the purchase of materials and that devoted to the payment of labour, to hold good, about 17,000,000£ more might be paid for labour, and about 650,000 more labourers set to work, while the remaining 33,000,000£ would be required to obtain an extra supply of materials. Then how would the matter stand? Why, as 100,000,000£ worth of material yielded a number of commodities which were equal in value to 300,000,000£, increasing threefold, of course, 133,000,000£ expended in the same manner, would yield such an extra number of commodities as, monetarily expressed, would be equal to 399,000,000£; but the workpeople would have received only 67,000,000£ for their labour in producing them, so that the capitalists would have had their commodities and profits *increased* to the extent of 99,000,000£, while the workmen would have had their income *decreased* to the extent of 33,000,000£, and 1,350,000 of them would have been altogether deprived of their means of living. To employ these 1,350,000 people, a still further supply of materials must be obtained, and this could be done solely by further drafts upon the stock set aside for the payment of the labourers generally; so that work could be found for the unemployed workpeople solely by decreasing the remuneration of those already employed. But since, by the assumption, 100,000,000£ worth of materials are from the economy of labour rendered sufficient to give employment to only 2,000,000 people instead of double the number, it follows that to fully occupy the 4,000,000 labourers, 200,000,000£ worth of materials would be required; but this is the whole capital of the country (the other 100,000,000£ being profits); so that there would, in such a case, be nothing left wherewith to pay the labourers. The workers, however, must live in order to do their work; hence wages might and would be driven down to the point of *mere subsistence*, but could not possibly go lower. All gained by the reductions to this extent might be devoted to procuring an additional quantity of materials; still the result would be that while those who were in work got merely sufficient for the protraction of their existence from their labour, numbers would remain unemployed, and those, of course, the capitalists would have to keep either as beggars or thieves; for since it would be impossible for the displaced labourers to subsist by their labour, which would be then no longer required, and since you could not exactly do with them as Mr. Carlyle humanely recommends, "shoot them and sweep them into the dustbin," why, it follows, that an armed body of police must be instituted to keep watch day and night over the possessions of the rich, lest those who had no means of sustenance but their labour, and who could find no employment for that, sought to steal the food they could not earn. Then, as a means of decreasing the expense of keeping those who were less daring, and preferred entering the workhouse to braving a prison, a minimised and *terrible* poor law must be established under which the relief given might be just sufficient to "ward off death from starvation." The curse was, formerly, that man should get his bread by labour, but nowadays the curse is, that men can get scarcely a mouthful of bread by labouring; so that what was once considered a curse would now be looked upon as a blessing, were it *possible* for the very poor to earn their bread by the sweat of their brow.

Those who maintain that machinery in the present state of our social arrangements is a good to the labourer are urged to reflect well upon what is here stated, for it is believed that this one simple fact must force itself upon all unprejudiced minds—as you save in labour you must either employ a smaller number of labourers or else reduce wages, so as to obtain a greater quantity of materials and give employment to the same number. To reduce the matter to a formula, let C represent the capital of the country, and let this equal M, the gross sum spent on materials, and W the gross sum devoted to the payment of the labourers, then it follows that—

$$because \ C = M + W,$$
$$therefore \ C - M = W,$$
$$and \ therefore \ C - 2M = W - M;$$

or, to state the matter arithmetically, we may say let C (the gross capital of the country) $\left.\right\}$ = 200,000,000£, and M (the gross sum spent on materials) $\left.\right\}$ = 50,000,000£, and W (the gross sum spent on labour) $\left.\right\}$ = 150,000,000£,

then because 200,000,000£
= 50,000,000£ + 150,000,000£
therefore 200,000,000£ - 50,000,000£
= 150,000,000£;
and therefore 200,000,000£ - 50,000,000£ x 2
= 150,000,000£ - 50,000,000£.

Hence *as much as you increase the materials for labour, just so much must you decrease the wages of labour.* So, again, the increase of the rate of working or causing one hand to do the work of many, may be *demonstrated* to necessitate either the expenditure of a greater sum upon materials or the employment of a smaller number of operatives, thus:—since O, the gross number of operatives employed, must be regulated by M, the gross quantity of materials on which to employ them divided, R, the ordinary rate of working or quantity that each hand can manufacture in an hour, multiplied by D, the duration of the work or total number of hours employed, then

$$\text{because } \frac{M}{R \times D} = O,$$

$$\text{therefore } \frac{M}{2 R \times D} = \frac{O}{2},$$

$$\text{and therefore } \frac{2 M}{2 R \times D} = O;$$

and because C – M = W,
therefore C – 2M = W – M.

or, reduced to figures, we should say let O (the number of operatives) = 1,000,000, R the rate of working or quantity of materials made up by each operative per week . . . . $\left.\right\}$ = 1£;

and D (the duration of the labour, or number of weeks work done in the course of the year . . . $\left.\right\}$ = 50;

$$\text{then because } \frac{50,000,000£}{1£ \times 50} = 1,000,000£,$$

$$\text{therefore } \frac{50,000,000£}{(1£ \times 2) \times 50} = \frac{1,000,000}{2} = 500,000,$$

$$\text{and therefore } \frac{50,000,000 \times 2}{(1£ \times 2) \times 50} = 1,000,000,$$

and because 200,000,000£ - 50,000,000£
= 150,000,000£,
therefore 200,000,000£ - 50,000,000£ X 2
= 150,000,000 - 50,000,000£.

Hence we see, that as the rate of working is increased so must either workmen be thrown out of employment or more money be spent on materials, and the more money there is spent on materials the less there must be left to pay the labourers.

I shall return to this subject in the next number of this portion of "LONDON LABOUR," for the economy of labour is the main difficulty of the time.

ANSWERS TO CORRESPONDENTS.

[No.57, No.X "Those that will not Work", 10 JANUARY 1852, price 3d.]

Edited out:
A.B.; G.H.

The whole of the back numbers are now reprinted, and maybe had of any newsman or bookseller. Some correspondents complain that they occasionally do not obtain their copies of "London Labour" till three weeks after the date. The fault lies with the bookseller or newsman serving them, as the numbers are invariably published on the day of their date.

On the 1st of January, 1852, an extra part was published; so that the subscribers who receive their copies monthly may be supplied up to the current number. This is a necessity of the difference between the lunar and the calendar month; and were any other plan adopted, the price of the parts would be continually varying.

Several inquiries have been made for the index and title-page of Volume II.; but it will be seen, on reference to the paging of the alternate numbers of "London Labour," that two distinct volumes are in the course of publication. Neither of these will be completed for some weeks yet, when the proper titles, indices, and directions to the binder, will be issued. It is proposed to publish, as soon as convenient, an extra part in connection with each subject, so that the respective volumes may be made up with as little delay as possible.

The following letters, requiring no comment, are printed verbatim, with the grateful acknowledgment of the Editor:—

"Sir,

"Although brought up, in early life, in the school of *Irish Orangeism*, and sincerely opposed to many doctrines of the Church of Rome, as I am still more to the nondescript doctrines of the Tractarian party, a sense of justice constrains me to say I think many very unjust charges have been preferred against the English Roman Catholics; and I am pleased to find you do justice, in your work on 'London Labour and the London Poor,' both to their zeal and charity, and the sense of religion and chastity, which, with all their many faults, the poor Irish Roman Catholics for the most part evince in the metropolis.[48]

"At Hammersmith, the nuns of the Convent of the Good Shepherd, twenty in number, take charge of about eighty professed female penitents, and endeavour to train them in habits of virtue, order, and industry. Of course they sometimes, as may be expected, fail, and meet ingratitude and calumny; but this can only cause surprise to such as are utterly ignorant of the depravity of the poor unfortunates whom they seek to reclaim. I believe the Convent of the Good Shepherd originated some 20 or 25 years ago, with two wealthy French ladies.

"Not very long since, Signor Palliano, formerly master of the Sabloniere Hotel, Leicester-square, brought over six nuns from Brittany, and hired a house at Brook-green,

Hammersmith, in which they received a few poor old women, whom they supported by soliciting food and clothing from the charitable. The establishment has since been transferred to Great Windmill-street, Golden square, as larger premises became needful.

"I should feel greatly delighted if, when your present labours terminate you would take up the cause of the Agricultural Labourers. The publications of the Society for promoting the welfare of the industrious poor (The Labourers' Friend Society) give ample details of the means by which crime and pauperism have been propagated in the rural districts; but we still want some popular serials on the subject.

"The educational establishments and charities of the Moravians, Quakers, and Roman Catholics, and the cooperative industry of the Moravians at Fulneck, Ockbrook, &c., are worthy of notice.

"Trusting you will excuse this liberty,

"I have the honour to be,

"Sir,

"Your most obedient Servant,

"JNO. A. W."

Mr. MAYHEW purposes an inquiry into the condition of the Agricultural Labourers at the earliest opportunity.

"Sir,

"I have lately met with a passage in Jeremy Taylor's 'Holy Living' the introduction to the chapter on Chastity, which seems to me so well suited to be a motto to your publication on Prostitution, that I cannot forbear calling your attention to it. As you may not have the book at hand, I will transcribe the sentences I refer to on the other side.

"I am, Sir,

"Your attentive Reader and

"obliged humble Servant,

"———."

"Lincoln's-inn,

"Dec. 26, 1851.

"'Reader, stay, and read not the advices of the following section unless thou hast a chaste spirit, or desirest, to be chaste, or at least art apt to consider whether you ought or no. For

[48] 1851 was marked by the agitation against Catholics following the re-establishment of a Catholic clergy in Britain with its centre at the Westminster archbishopric.

240

there are some spirits so atheistical, and some so wholly possessed with a spirit of uncleanness, that they turn the most prudent and chaste discourses into dirt aud filthy apprehensions; like choleric stomachs, changing their very cordials and medicines into bitterness, and, in a literal sense, turning the grace of God into wantonness. They study cases of conscience in the matter of carnal sins, not to avoid, but to learn ways how to offend God and pollute their own spirits; and search their houses with a sunbeam, that they may be instructed in all the corners of nastiness. I have used all the care I could in the following periods, that I might neither be wanting to assist those that need it, nor yet minister any occasion of fancy or vainer thoughts to those that need them not. If any man will snatch the pure taper from my hand, and hold it to the devil, he will only burn his own fingers, but shall not rob me of the reward of my care and good intention.'—Jeremy Taylor."[49]

The following contains much truth, and evidences not only good feeling, but nice observation:—

"Sir,

"Considering it the duty of every well-disposed person to render you every assistance in their power, however trifling that may be, in your endeavour to investigate the habits and mode of life of the prostitute class, with a view to the mitigation of this giant social evil, I take the liberty of mentioning a few facts which have come under my own observation, as a young man living in London, and having for some ten years seen more or less of the class in question.

"We must all agree with your remarks on the letter of W. G., Jun. published in No. 47. He saw and heard nothing more than what every man who walks the streets of this town after dark must see and hear, but I fear much, even from his own narrative of the girl's story, that he was imposed upon. The tale is an old one,

and what in the slang of the fast men would be called the 'officer dodge,' and I think had W.G. made the same inquiries of a dozen different women in the Casino, he would have heard the same story repeated, of course with variations, several times; at least I have myself; but it is quite impossible to place reliance on one word these women say, at all events until you have known them for some time, and had the opportunity of judging for yourself what degree of confidence can be placed upon their word. I have found them, without a solitary exception, utterly regardless of the truth in their assertions; but this cannot be wondered at.

"While on the subject of W.G.'s letter, I would call attention to the girl's words, 'I have had no Bible these four years,' merely to remark that I have been surprised at the number of cases in which I have found Bibles, Prayer Books, and other serious works in their rooms, and I may say the almost total absence of indecent prints and books. It is true some of the 'dress lodgers' and 'French women' make use of the allurement of 'pretty pictures,' &c., to induce young men to accompany them home; but I believe, in most cases, they would be disappointed when they got there, as none would be forthcoming. Lying, swearing, and drinking, are the three common vices of the prostitute, and from these or some of them none of the class are altogether free; they begin with their first fall, and lead to every other vice; but obscenity or indecency of language or action I do not think, on the whole, general amongst them, and kindliness of feeling and attention to one another in case of illness exist, I think, to a considerable extent, where not interrupted by jealousy, or the ill-will springing from a sense of rivalry.

"I am led to think that superstitious ideas are more than usually prevalent amongst them, and that they are, in a great measure, the support of the fortune-tellers and so-called astrologers, who haunt the low neighbourhoods in and about London.

"A woman to whom I recently spoke on the subject, told me she had been to most of these fortune-tellers of any 'note,' either alone or with

[49] J. Taylor, *The Rule and Exercise of Holy Living*, Roystem, 1650. This classic text of the religious literature had many editions and was part, for example, of Bohn Standard Library in 1846.

other women, and had seen as many as a dozen 'gay women' waiting to have their fortunes told; that cards were usually used for the purpose, and the fee varied from 1s. to 2s. 6d. Others have told me much to the same effect, generally adding that they did not believe a word told them, but still—sometimes something came true, and—in short, they went again.

"If I recollect rightly, there is in the then rather celebrated 'Tom and Jerry; or, Life in London,' published many years back, a print of two courtezans having their fortunes told by an old woman.

"If this be so, what reason can be given? Is it that these poor creatures, their hearts not entirely deadened, seeking for some hope in the future, take refuge in the miserable tissue of falsehoods and absurdities uttered by these women?

"I have already trespassed too long on your time, and can only plead as an excuse, the wish to be of the slightest use to you; and if the publication of any part of this letter on the wrapper of your periodical induces other young men to communicate to you the results of their observations, I think it may be of some little service, as it is the experience of those by whom the class is supported, and by the majority of whom, I verily believe, the system is as much detested as it is by, Sir,

"Your obedient Servant,
"E.J.B."

The next treats of the causes and remedies of prostitution.

"Sir,

"In whatever light we may view the fearful increase of female criminality, we are equally baffled in our endeavours to find a remedy for so overwhelming an evil. The refined morality of the present day is not calculated to arouse and set in motion the higher and more virtuous feelings of human nature, but rather to produce a lethargic and inactive spirit of false pride and exclusiveness inimical to the best interests of humanity. If we look at the social position of women, the estimation in which they are held by the opposite sex, their treatment and helpless condition from infancy upwards, the limited choice of a profession, and the scandalous remuneration for their services, and last, but not least, the almost worthless education they receive, so ill-adapted to the requirement and bitter realities of everyday life,—how many of us, with natures less susceptible and confiding, placed in their position, would have fallen! To mitigate this crying evil we must raise women socially and physically, we must find a legitimate sphere of action adapted to their moral and physical capacities, and remove every obstacle and unjust oppression, in the way of living honourably and respectably in their several callings or pursuits. For we must bear in mind that few would chose a life that must bring ruin and disgrace upon them, and be but of short duration, were they not impelled to it as a last resource to escape aggravated distress and sometimes utter destitution.

"I am, sir, with much esteem,
"Yours respectfully.
"A.C."

The subjoined is from a former correspondent, treating of the same subject:—

"London, Nov. 14, 1851,
"Sir,

"I have been encouraged to accept your kind request to hear again from me (see your remark upon my letter of the 6th inst., published in No. 49 of your excellent work upon 'London Labour,') in the hope that it may induce others, more able than myself, to take up the various branches of the causes of prostitution, and thereby contribute to the suppression of that evil which it is the purpose of your work to expose and put down.

"In my last I attributed 'dress and love of gaiety' as some of the antecedents on seduction, and I quoted the frequenting of casinos and theatres, &c., as giving openings for the seduction of the daughters of small tradesmen and of mechanics of the better sort.

"It is quite true, as you say, that girls frequenting casinos must either have *been seduced* or be of a *seducible disposition:* with regard to the latter, *too many* are to be found amongst the class I then alluded to, and can it be wondered at!

Children of small tradesmen and mechanics are generally comparatively uneducated, and their religious duties are very little impressed upon them. Now in my opinion nothing tends more to form a 'seducible disposition' than the want of moral education, and if parents allow their uneducated daughters to walk out with 'sweethearts,' or 'young men,' as they are called, and attend such places, it is, I think, not at all surprising that they fall a prey to the seducer.

"I may instance a case which came within my own knowledge, of two sisters, aged then about 16 and 17 years of age respectively, who were allowed to go out in the way before described. They some years ago went to one of those nuisances called a fair, near Camberwell, entered a dancing booth with their 'young men,' and what between dancing, refreshments, and amorous dalliance, when they left the fair they did not return to their parents' house till after they had been persuaded to sojourn on the way, viz., at a brothel. One of these girls keeps a brothel now, and the other is in 'splendid misery,' living with a gentleman.

"Now, in this case had the parents done their duty (and they could afford to look after their girls), such a misfortune would not, perhaps, have occurred; and if there were not such openings as dancing-rooms, fairs, &c., permitted, many girls in a similar class as the two above alluded to might be in a respectable position in society, and, instead of being the seducers of youth and inexperience, might have been the promoters of virtue and honour.

"I fear I have intruded too much upon your patience at this time, and shall conclude by wishing you every success in your endeavours to expose and lessen the prostitution in London.

"J.B."

The last communication tells one a tale of deep suffering and misery. Mr. Mayhew will be happy to furnish any subscriber who may desire a tutor for the French, German, or Dutch languages with the name of the writer of the following:—

"Sir,

"A young man, of highly respectable family, takes the liberty to address you a few lines. Perhaps you may consider it bold of me, respected Sir, I am so free to write to you, but the most dreadful distress makes me resolve to use those means. I am a native of Holland, and am born of Jewish parents. I had the privilege to get a most excellent education, and it pleased the Lord to let me come, eight year ago, to the conviction of the truth that the Lord Jesus Christ is the Saviour of the world. I was baptized February 17th, 1850, at Liverpool. I returned March 4th, 1850, to Holland, but was there so dreadfully persecuted by all my relations and the whole mass of the Jews, that I was obliged to fly, so that I went to New York. There I was till December 4th of last year, but I suffered also there the most dreadful privations. I arrived December 26th at Liverpool, and February 28th at London, and should have undoubtedly been admitted into the Hebrew College or Jewish Operative Converts' Institution, but for illness. I am now established as a Professor of Languages, but all my endeavours have till this time shipwrecked in getting a living. I am literally without bread, and exposed to the most dreadful hunger and cold. I am every day on the point of being turned out by my landlord, as I owe this gentleman already 1£ 14s. I happened to see your work 'London Labour and the London Poor,' and as I saw how much you do for suffering mankind, I made bold enough to address you those lines. Believe me, highly respected Sir, no trouble will be too great for me to get an honest living, and wherever you might think fit to place me in, all will be accepted by me with a thankful heart, and I shall always remember you have saved me from my ruin. In name of humanity, in name of the blessed Lord Jesus Christ, I pray and beseech you to help me in the one or other way, and you will not only have the satisfaction of having saved an unhappy young man of starvation, but also of having rendered him to human society. In the hope you may do something for me in the one or other way, I sign most respectfully,

"Your obedient Servant,

"S.M.B."

"I am ready to furnish very high references, if required."

The letters of the "City Clerk" and the "Commanding Officer" will be printed in the next number of "Those that Will Not Work."

ANSWERS TO CORRESPONDENTS.
[No.58, 17 JANUARY 1852]

I RETURN to the consideration of the effects of machinery, or economy of labour, upon the condition of the labourers.

In No. 56 it was demonstrated that in the present arrangement of society it was physically impossible that machinery in the abstract could benefit the labourer. To perceive this clearly and unmistakeably, we have but to imagine the mechanical appliances carried out to the utmost, and *all* manual labour superseded, with the exception of such as is needed to keep the machines in repair and construct new ones, for even the tending of them appears to be an imperfection which superior science may ultimately remove, as we have already had self-acting steam-engines which supplied their own boilers and fed their own fires. All that the labourers are at present required to do, is to convert the capitalists' material into commodities; and if this can be done by mechanical power instead of manual, surely there can be no necessity for workmen; and when human operatives are rendered obsolete, will capitalists consent to feed *them* any more than they feed horses when displaced by the railway? A new element has been introduced into society within the last century—a labourer of brass and iron, one that knows no fatigue, and, consequently, requires no rest; one that cannot possibly "strike," or refuse to do his master's bidding; one that requires only coals and water, instead of bread and beer, to set him working. Six hundred millions of these steam-labourers have been created within the last 75 years; they have been made to compete with creatures of flesh and blood, and the consequence is, that the human labourer is being driven out of the field. *The steam engine gets his share of the wage-fund*, it should be remembered; the capital that formerly went to find the muscular man and his family in bread, and to reinvigorate his frame, now goes to supply the steam man with fuel, and to pay for wear and tear. Those who are pleased with puzzles can amuse themselves by inventing some form of society in which the steam-engine and other mechanical contrivances for superseding human labour shall confer an equal amount of benefit upon the labourer as upon the capitalists. This is the great problem that requires to be solved. A Liverpool correspondent justly observes, that by the invention of a particular machine a vast amount of labour, which was formerly profitable to the community, becomes unprofitable, and therefore is not employed, and we consequently might just as well employ the labourers in digging holes and filling them up again, or building houses and knocking them down again, or any other useless occupation, so long as the same wages were paid for the unprofitable as for the profitable employment. If we can, by means of a machine, sweep the streets with 100 instead of 400 men, then, argues he, to employ the extra 300 is to waste so much labour. There is no gain saying this point. But surely this wasting of labour regards only the capitalists, or the possessors of the entire stock of the country; to get this stock converted into commodities with as little labour as possible, and, consequently, at as little cost as possible, is the greatest possible good to them, seeing that the same capital under such circumstances yields them a greater number of products. But how about the labourers? That which is the greatest good to the possessors of the stock is the greatest evil to the labouring class—those who possess nothing, and merely live by working up the materials of the others. The less labour there is required, and the less that is paid for it, the less, of course, they have to live upon. Hence we perceive that the unprofitable employment of workmen who would otherwise be unemployed, though the greatest evil to the capitalist class, is no evil at all to the labouring class, seeing that without it they could obtain no portion of the riches of the country. "Are you," says T.A. of Liverpool, "in favour of the community finding unprofitable employment for the surplus labourers, and paying them for the same?" Here we see that the general term community is used simply for the capitalist portion of it, and, consequently, the unprofitable employment of the surplus labourer must be admitted to be an evil, if regarded solely in that light; but it must also be admitted to be a good if considered with regard to the labourer; seeing that if it does not tend to increase the stock of riches, at least it does to distribute them, and distribution is often as great a good as production. But what moral right have we to deprive a number of labourers of their only means of living? The good of the community, is the "economical" answer. But in the case of railways, and improvements which are regarded as national benefits, we do not allow a private wrong to be done for a public good. Compensation is required to be made to every individual injured by the improvement. In the case of labour, however, we know no "rights of property." A man may have been all his life acquiring a certain kind of skill which a particular mechanical contrivance may render utterly valueless, and what recompense has he? Did he possess a park, a house, or even a business, and this had been in the least damaged by some projected public benefit, the amount of injury done would be valued by a jury of conscientious men, and adequate recompense awarded. The labourer, however, is beggared without a single voice being raised in his favour. His labour has, in the struggle to live, been rendered superfluous, and he may maintain himself as best he can. There is the workhouse open, for as yet economists do not admit the right of the "community" to wring the necks of the superseded labourers; and since the law of the kingdom still declares that every man, if unable to maintain himself by his own industry, is entitled to live upon the wealth of others, it is clear, if you deprive a labourer of the power of living by his labour, you must be prepared to keep him as a pauper. But

supposing every inventor of a machine that superseded a particular class of labourers was bound to make the displaced workmen a yearly allowance out of the profits, by way of compensation to them—even if such an arrangement were in any way practicable— what kind of compensation could possibly be made to the future children of the labouring class—those who are born with no spoons at all, instead of silver ones, in their mouths, and have nothing to look forward to but their own labour as their means of life? How could they be recompensed—save by the workhouse? If there were no labourers and labourers' children to keep, then machinery and economy of labour might be a national blessing, but so long as society *will* permit labourers to have children—so long as the "painless extinction" of every poor man's child, as soon as born, which Mr. Carlyle advocates "in grim earnest!" is not part and parcel of the law of the land— so long must the invention of machinery and the economy of labour be a national curse instead of a blessing—that is to say, if the capitalists have been in the habit of paying 150,000,000£ a year as wages for the conversion of the materials of wealth into commodities, and they are ultimately enabled, by mechanical contrivances or otherwise, to do with two-thirds less labour, and consequently to reduce the sum spent in wages from 150,000,000£ to 50,000,000£—surely it must be apparent to all but those who mistake the welfare of this one class for the welfare of the whole country, that the majority, or indeed the people generally, cannot have benefited by the change? And if we can conceive the economy of labour to extend thus far, why not much farther, till the sum spent in wages is reduced to a mere fraction, and the whole of the quondam working class have become inmates of either our workhouses or our prisons. "By the year 2000," says an American paper, "it is probable that manual labour will have utterly ceased under the sun, and the occupation of the adjective 'hard-fisted' will be gone for ever. They have now, in New Hampshire, a potato-digging machine which drawn by horses down

245

the rows, digs the potatoes, separates them from the dirt, and loads them up into the cart, while the farmer walks alongside, whistling 'Hail, Columbia,' with his hands in his pockets."

In the next number I shall speak of the special application of machinery in connection with the cotton and other trades.

The following communication makes known a gross wrong:—

"I was last year employed as a canvasser for signatures to a petition to Parliament in respect of the total abolition of the duty on paper. The secretary of the 'Association,' who is also secretary of a Freehold Land Society, not far from Beaufort-buildings, Strand, gave as a return for that labour 2s. a day, the enormous sum of 12s. a week. Most of the canvassers were married men, and all highly respectable, and of course of good address and good appearance, otherwise they would not have been eligible for the employment. For that paltry sum I had to obtain at least 30 or 40 signatures, genuine ones of course. You are aware how long it would take to obtain that number of respectable business men's signatures. Some conversation, of course, was necessary, and knowledge of the subject; and, therefore, the illiterate and uneducated would have been useless. This, in the absence of all other chance of work, I performed for that sum of 12s. weekly. That being finished, this kind, humane individual said he would give me further employment in the office. I, of course, having a family, was forced to accept of it. But as he was now employing me as a clerk, I of course never thought but that I should have 1£ a week at the least.

"But no, although employed in writing letters, circulars, &c., from nine till seven, he, at the end of the week, put down half-a-sovereign and 2s. 6d., telling me to return the 6d. on the Monday. I ask did that man deserve to be treated honestly? I answer, certainly not. I remained there about six weeks, of course. Although *obliged* to have respectable exterior, I was, with my wife and family, starving and

getting into debt. Now, sir, is not such treatment as this calculated to arouse feelings of hatred and contempt for those who will so inhumanly oppress their fellow man?

"But, in conclusion, I must inform you that this gentlemen (*so he* terms himself) was merely paying me and others out of a fund contributed for the purpose, receiving a *good* salary himself, and expected by the committee to *properly* and adequately pay those he employed.

"Of course he charged them with about 4s. a day, and paid me 2s. *O tempora! O mores!* I consider, sir, this man robbed me and mine. Any one would think so. But I had almost forgotten this cruel treatment, had it not been that I called there the other day looking for employment, when this sage, sagacious, and humane 'gentleman,' in answer to my question, replied, 'No; *all* those who were employed last year on the paper duty must go and help the Kaffirs; they want all the money.' There was a kind, considerate reply to a man soliciting employment—to a man, who although now brought low and in poverty, had been brought up in a sphere of life and received an education far superior to his own.

"I should greatly wish to expose this heartless robber of the poor and industrious. Should this be unfit or too long for your publication, perhaps you would be kind enough to intimate to me how I could best publicly hold up this 'gentleman' to shame.

"I am, Sir,

"Yours respectfully,

"J.R."

"P.S. I am at present out of employment with *good* reference."

The following corroborates Wortenkrämer's derivation of Haberdasher:—

"Sir,

"If I am not too late I gladly forward you the following solution (if it is one) of a controversy about the word 'Haberdasher,' that I read in your excellent papers of 'London Labour and London Poor.' It is extracted from the *People's Advocate*, a New South Wales (Australia) Paper, of the date Feb. 1st, 1851:—

"'A "Berdash" was a name given anciently in

England to a sort of neck-dress, and the person who made or sold such neck-dresses was called a "Berdasher," now corrupted into "Haberdasher."'

"As to the origin of the word 'berdash,' I am quite ignorant. Hoping the enclosed may prove useful to your correspondents on that head, and wishing you every possible success.

"I am, Sir,

"Yours most respectfully,

"LEWIS M.B."

ANSWERS TO CORRESPONDENTS.
[No.61, No.XII "Those that will not Work", 7 FEBRUARY 1852, price 3d.]

The letter here appended is of so curious a character that Mr. Mayhew was induced before printing it to request some voucher for the truth of its statements. The answer is appended. The letter professes to be written with the object of showing that all the public women are not so "bad" as certain correspondents have endeavoured to make them appear—a proposition which none can doubt. The writer seeks to prove the "goodness" of these characters by the sacrifices they make for the man to whom they become attached, and there are certainly many noble actions to be told concerning them in this respect. This, indeed, is but natural; for being shunned by the whole world, and feeling doubtlessly a supreme disgust and contempt for the sensualists who purchase their favours, of course they are easily "taken" with those who exhibit any real sympathy for them. Unfortunately, however, the "fancy men" of such characters are usually of the lowest possible stamp—though this would seem to be a necessity of the circumstances, for none other, of course, could bear to be the companions and dependents of prostitutes. Such men must necessarily be dead to all moral sense and deprived of all social position. It is peculiar, as showing that the love of woman to man is

caused mainly by a feeling of her own weakness and consequent need for protection, that the fancy men of the prostitutes always belong to the powerful or reckless class of individuals, such as prize-fighters, thieves, cabmen, soldiers, sailors, and the like; these are by far the most usual characters, and all, it will be seen, are connected with some expression of boldness—either a disregard of danger, the pursuit of some perilous calling, or the possession of a certain amount of physical strength. The proverbial love of servant maids for policemen is to be explained only in the same manner. The admirable with woman would thus appear to be the powerful rather than the sensuously beautiful; they seem to prefer bravery to symmetry. This, as it was before stated, seems to be a necessity of the weakness and timidity of the feminine nature, and the consequent craving for a protector. Of course, this feeling takes different expressions in different classes. Fashionable ladies admire officers, naval and military, noblemen, fox-hunters, and indeed any of those classes who are distinguished either for the *disposition* or *power* to protect them. Women of a lower grade, on the other hand, approve of a lower grade of characters; but all remarkable for the same qualities. In the class of fancy men such attributes are found associated with the most despicable characters, but still they all show that the disposition or the power to protect constitutes the admirable with the female sex, whether high or low, chaste or unchaste. And fallen as are the class of women of whom we are here treating, still the same devotion and the same self-sacrifice is found in their love as marks the affection of the sex generally. Among the public women, however, this one gleam of beauty appears the brighter and the more admirable from the many loathsome qualities with which it is contrasted. The love of woman, indeed, is seen in all its perfection of disinterestedness and devotion among those who appear to be destitute of all such qualities. This will, in a future number, form a most extraordinary chapter in the history of prostitution, perhaps the most extraordinary

THE ESSENTIAL MAYHEW

of all. The men, however, who are the object of this love are naturally the most degraded and the most brutal of human beings. Why they *must* be so, it is unnecessary to say here; the reasons will suggest themselves spontaneously to every rightly-constituted mind, and common honesty requires that the writer of the following letter should be included in this class.

"London.

"Sir,

"Allow me to offer a few remarks on behalf of the unfortunate women in London and elsewhere. As none of your correspondents have yet been able to find good qualities in them, my experience may, perhaps, show they are not so bad as they seem.

"Some three years back I went to the Casino to have a look about me, and after I had been sitting upstairs for about half an hour, and was about to leave, a nicely-dressed good-looking woman came up and asked me if I would go home with her. I told her I could not. She said she had suddenly felt an insurmountable passion for me, and was determined to take me away with her. I told her flatly I could not go with her, and amongst other things said I had no money, upon which she gave me such a spurning look of contempt, and immediately walked away. I did not take any particular notice of this, and was walking out of the place, when she came up to me and said, 'Never you mention such a thing as money to me again,' and, taking my arm, walked out with me, when immediately a dashing brougham and pair came up, in which we got and drove off to her house in—place, where there was a good supper laid out. On leaving in the morning she gave me her address, and begged of me to come and see her again as often as I liked, saying that if I wished to be good friends with her I must never allude to money in her presence. After seeing her three or four times, of course I thought I must make some little return, and bought a bracelet to present to her. Judge of my astonishment, after giving it to her, to see her throw it behind the fire, saying that if I thought I must pay for her favours she did not want to see me, or words to that effect.

"I left off visiting for about a month, and, happening to go to a ball, met her with her friend. Immediately she saw me she left him and came to me. I declined dancing with her, nor would she by any persuasion of mine leave me. Her friend, seeing this, came up and told her she need not trouble herself any more about him, and left the room. When we reached her house the key would not open the door, and as London is pretty full of accommodation houses we were not* long in finding out one. I imagined what might be the consequence the next day, and appointed to meet her about two o'clock, whilst she went to her house. When she got there she found all her dresses packed up, and the servant had orders, directly she got there, to call a cab, put her and her things in it, and drive to where she pleased. In the meantime, I had taken apartments, where we repaired to, and from that time to this we have lived happily together in a quiet way, and still do so—she improving her mind by reading. I have taught her to write, play the piano, and various little things. I perfectly believe her to be true to me, and can only say we are living as happily together, though not married, as any man could wish to live with his wife. She is not fond of dress or show; is punctual in all her payments, for which I give her money; keeps an account of all she spends, inviting my inspection of it; and is as good a companion to me as a wife could be, nor am I ashamed of being seen anywhere with her.

"Your correspondents should not condemn all by the many, but have the charity to suppose that there are a few good amongst so many bad. With many apologies for thus trespassing on your time, and trusting you will make what use you please of this,

"I am, Sir,

"Your obedient Servant,

"A CLERK IN THE CITY."

"'A Clerk in the City,' whilst acknowledging the validity of Mr. Mayhew's remarks on his communication, thinks it will be sufficient if he states that his father was a well-known merchant in the City, keeping a good account at Messrs. Glyn's bank, and that two of his brothers are still carrying on the same business. Mr. M. can reject the communication (positively true) if he thinks fit, or only quote extracts from it relative to the fact of a 'woman' living quietly and respectably with one man. The object of the writer was merely to say something good of women whom Mr. M.'s correspondents seem to think so bad of, and to show that, though all are bad, all are not equally so, and that there are a few good, comparatively speaking."

The City Clerk will doubtless be exceedingly wrath at being ranked among the fancy men of the metropolis, but common sense compels it. If he object to the position, he has it in his own power to remedy it; let him make the same sacrifice for the woman he degrades by living with as she has made for him. "She is," he says, "as good a companion to me as a wife could be." Then what a mere lump of selfishness he must be not to make a wife of her. Let him read his own letter calmly over, and then ask himself whether, if he possess the faintest spark of honour, he can do otherwise to one who has sacrificed for his sake all for which she once debased herself. For the character of his own sex it is to be hoped that the next letter from the City Clerk will contain an account of his marriage with the woman he here speaks of.

Here follows a letter that should have been inserted long ago:—

"Sir,

"I purchased Part 12 of 'London Labour' at a railway station, and read it on my journey.

"Do you really give credit to the statement of W.G. jun., of the seduction of a child, the daughter of an officer?

"In the first place, no commanding officer of a regiment, or other officer, would permit an officer to keep a mistress with the regiment.

"An officer might do so, privately and unknown to his brother officers for a short time, but it is impossible he could do so for a month without it coming to the knowledge of some of the officers, and consequently to the ears of the commanding officer, when he would immediately order the officer offending to send away the woman.

"And in so gross and beastly a case, as an officer keeping a mistress with his young daughters, he would have the offer of 'leaving the regiment' or a court-martial.

"It is not two years ago an officer was brought to a court-martial by his commanding officer for even bringing a prostitute into the barracks, and dismissed the service by its sentence.

"And sir, do you suppose, if a brother officer's family were left in a state of destitution, as W.G. states this child to have been, the officers of the regiment would not have provided for her, at least for a time? And only consider the seduction. A brother officer dies, leaving a daughter only fifteen, pretty and well-disposed, in a state of destitution. She is seduced by officers of the regiment (as the father, from his destitute state, must have been with the regiment) immediately after the father's death, in the barracks, and *kept* by the officer as long as the regiment remained there.

"If the officers did not bring this offender to a court-martial, the non-commissioned officers and privates would.

"What, an officer seduce or keep a child of fifteen, the daughter of a brother just dead!

"I am fully persuaded my denial that such a case is possible, that it could have happened in any regiment, will have little weight with you, as you have inserted the statement; but your examination of the persons you are writing of must have made you careful of dissecting their evidence, to sift what is probable and true from the improbable and false. I think, therefore, you ought to have been more cautious of giving credence to W.G., particularly as you see in what part of his statement 'he was over zealous.'

"Although a commanding officer, I have paid great attention to the state of the poor, from being generally quartered in manufacturing towns, and also having a considerable estate; and I read your statements with interest, until I came to this story of seduction, which I knew must be false. Others may see in other statements what they also know to be false.

"Thus discredit will be thrown upon the whole of your writings, which otherwise not only would incite the interest of those able to return it, but who would be ready to do so.

"Yours obediently,

"A COMMANDING OFFICER."

The commanding officer (who forgets to send his name) is under a mistake. No credence was given to the story, as indeed was stated at the time; and the letter of W.G. was inserted merely as an example, not only of the gullibility of a well-intentioned class of gentlemen, but also of the tendency of the women of the town to lay the odium of their position on any person's shoulders rather than their own.

The following is from an esteemed correspondent:—

"Ashby-de-la-Zouch, Jan. 7, 1852

"Sir,

"Where shall we find *mót-hús* with the meaning of brothel? I have searched and cannot find it; but that the verb *metan* is the root of *mot* I think very probable, notwithstanding our method of arriving at it may be somewhat different; for since writing my last to you I have made the following notes from various sources.

"Anglo-Saxon, *metan*; Mœso-Goth., *mot-jan*; Belg., *mœten, occurrere, concurrere, invenire;* hence past participle *gemet, gemœt, aptus, conducens;* and so our *mate* and *mot*—one exactly answering the wishes of another—one fit for some particular purpose, or to a thing—one matching another. Compare Alemannic, *mate, maes;* Icelandic Suio-Gothic, *mat, maet;* Teutonic, *maed, maet,* and modern German *maat, socius sodalis equalis;* and presuming that the Dutch *motte,* in *mottekast* has the same Gothic verbal origin, then *mottekast* may equal a mating-house, or a house where mates may be had; and that mate is applied to a female, see Chester plays (the 'Creation'); nor do I consider that it is absolutely necessary to suppose that the word *mot* was always accepted in a bad or low sense, as at present. Compare the words lewd, imp, villain, knave, harlot, quean, this last being connected with γυνη and so with Sanscrit *g'ani*

and the verbal root *g'an,* to be born.

"You know Horne Tooke's derivation of *trull,* could not the Dutch *drille* have come from the root he has selected? Again, is Mr. Borrow right, when he says the first cant vocabulary appeared in 1680? Harman's 'Caveat' first appeared in 1566; Rowland's 'Martin Mark-All' was published in 1610, and 'Dekker's Bellman,' and also the 'Bellman's Second Night Walk,' appeared before 1613.[50]

"I have, I fear, trespassed too long and been very tedious, but I cannot conclude without thanking you for your several hints in your comments on the different speculations respecting the word *mot.* You have, I think, furnished me with a key to the etymon of *meg des megs;* the French *ayot,* word for *Dieu;* and I may say, in the words of Horace:—

——"'Ergo fungor vice cotis acutum
Reddere qua ferrum valet, exsors ipsa
secundi.'   R.55,81.

"I am, Sir,

"Yours Truly,

"T.L.L."

If T.L.L. will turn to Bosworth's "Anglo-Saxon Dictionary" (p.47, col.G), he will find the following:—"*Mot,* a moot, an assembly, v. *gemot; mot-bell,* a bell used to call an assembly, L. Edw. Conf., 35; *mot-ern,* a place of meeting, a moot-hall, C. Jn. 18, 28; *mot-hus,* moot-house, a house of assembly, R. 107; *mot-stow* a meeting-place, R. 55, 81."

Surely this will convince T.L.L. that the verbal element *mot,* as here given, is directly from the verb *metan,* to meet, and only indirectly connected (if at all) with the word *mate,* which is from *maca* and *macian* to make match (Icel., *maki,* an equal, a wife).

T.L.L. appears to be a little too much inclined to run into fanciful etymologies (he must pardon the remark), and hasty

---

[50] Thomas Harman, *Caveat or Warning for Common Cursetors Vulgarly Called Vagabones,* 1566, 100 copies of a reprint of the 1573 edition were issued in 1814, Triphook, London. Thomas Dekker, *The Bell-man of London* and *Lanthern and Candlelight or the Bell-man's Second Nights Walke,* John Busbie, 1608.

generalizations constitute the absurdities of all science. Horne Tooke, whom T.L.L. quotes, is utterly valueless as an etymologist, for his philological conceits. There are but two modes of derivation, be it observed, for the third time, the *historic* and the *dialectic*. Words that are not composed of any root within the language in which they exist must be looked for in some other tongue, and there found differently spelt (generally, if not invariably), but meaning the same thing. This is the dialectic form of derivation, in which the difference of spelling, that is to say, the changes of letters, must conform to regular laws—those laid down by Grimm for the consonants, and Bopp for the vowels.[51] Words, on the other hand, the elements of which exist within the language, generally differ in meaning from those elements, but are similarly spelt, if we except the addition of certain prefixes and affixes. This is the historic mode of derivation, and is the simplest form of the two. The historic is indeed the intrinsic, and the dialectic the extrinsic method of deriving words, and uncertainty belongs chiefly to the latter form. [Follows a series of examples: thunder-storm, blood-y, whit-en, dis-may &c. edited out.]

[51] Grimm's work was not translated into English by 1850, while Bopp's only translated work was *A Comparative Grammar of the Sanskrit, Greek, Latin, Lithuanian, Gothic, German and Slavonic languages*. Translated by H. Eastwick, Vol. III., H.A. Wilson, 1845-1850.

INDEX

This index includes themes and names. It only includes the name of authors explicitly discussed in the text and footnotes. References to *London Labour and the London Poor* are between brackets: [Vol. p.]

A'Beckett, George A., 3, 9
account books, 23, 29, 89, 226-8
Acton, William, 54, 79-80
agricultural labourers, 240
Agnes M., see needlewomen
Ainsworth, Harrison, 16, 70
alcohol, consumption of, and temperance, 40, 98-9, 109, 154-5, 156, 206-8
Alloway, Charles (crippled street seller), 11, 134, 160, 174-5
Answers to Correspondents, 23-6, 119, 157, 187-8, 226
apprenticeship, 89, 92, 154
aristocracy, 90, 146
Arkwright, Richard, 132
Art-Union Journal, 164
Association for the Relief of the Poor of the City of London, see City Kitchen,
Athenaeum Club, 113
Australia, 163
autobiographies, diaries and journals, 4, 28-30, 37

Babbage, Charles, 33, 42, 113, 133, 140-1
Bailey and Fahrenkrüger (German and English Dictionary), 170, 180, 227
ballast heavers, 40, 94, 109
Banfield and Weld, *Statistical Companion*, 175
Barnett, John, 9
Barthes, Roland, 74
Beard, Richard, 66
Beauclerc, 163
Bible and Gospel, 54, 136, 187,

213, 241
binding and plans for *LLLP*, 20, 25, 85-6, 109, 119, 144, 158, 163, 185-6, 223, 239-40
Binny, John, 4
Birkenhead, 139
Birmingham, 169
Bishop's Dog Bill [Vol. 2: 48-50], 174
blind needle sellers [Vol. 1: 340-1], 155-6
blind boot-lace seller [Vol. 1: 393], 159
Bogue, David, publisher, 3
Bohemians, 9, 13, 20, 66
Bolt Makers Trade Society (Manchester), 41, 158
Bolton, 166
book sellers, 159
Booth, Charles, 5, 50
Bopp, Franz, 46-8, 51, 180, 230, 251
Bosworth, *Anglo-Saxon Dictionary*, 250
Bradford, 166
brewing industry, 206-8
bricklayers, 103, 109-10
Briggs, Jeremiah, 94, 107-8, 209-10
British Ladies for the Promotion of Reformation of Female Prisoners, 196
British Library and Museum, 12, 25, 187
British Penitent Female Penitentiary, 196
brothels, see prostitution
Brougham, Henry P., 196-7

bunmaree, etymology of, 45, 101, 170

cabinet makers: Society of, 88; trade of, 34, 111, 117, 133, 148-9, 162-3, 172, 191
calico, 106, 172, 184
cant, 52, 56, 79, 157-8, 202, 224-5, 228-32, 250
capital, capitalism, capitalists, 40-1, 95, 106, 109-12, 114-15, 125-44, 148-54, 161, 166, 172, 203-5; penny capitalists, 43, 161, 171-2
Carlyle, Thomas, 43, 238, 245-6
Carpenter, William Benjamin, 98-9
casinos, 56, 80, 212-13, 218-19, 242-3, 248
Catholic Church institutions, 180, 240
Chadwick, Edwin, 17, 71, 171
charity and philanthropy, 4, 11, 19, 30, 89, 92, 94, 98, 144-5, 164-5, 172
Chartier, Roger, 22, 28, 45, 73
chartism, 17-18, 33, 38, 40, 71, 97, 197
Cheshire, 167
cholera, 17-18
Christian Socialists, 20, 34, 40, 43, 76-7
Church: of England, 95, 124; Missionary Society, 95
City: Kitchen, 30, 102; Police Bill, 121-2
class struggle and war, 21, 178, 238

classes dangereuses, 55, 71, 94
classification of *LLLP*, 19, 36, 87-8, 111
clergymen, 24, 51, 95, 97-8, 119, 162
Clerk in the City, 56, 224, 247-9
clerks, 23, 26, 51, 186, 246-7
Clickers, Society of, 88
Cobbett, William, 43
Cocker, Edward, 100, 125
coker, 120, 129
coffee stalls, 94
Coleridge, Samuel T., 105
corruption, old, 49, 55-6
community, 42, 234-5, 245
Conolly, *On the Construction and Government of Lunatic Asylums*, 164
consumers, 95
consumption, 103, 106, 139-41, 166-9
co-operative labour and co-operation, 39, 43, 97, 121,161
Conan Doyle, Sir Arthur, 7
Contagious Diseases Acts (1864-9), 57, 80
corn laws, 34, 42, 103, 109, 205
Corbin, Alain, 71
Cornhill, 206
Cornhill Magazine, 10
costermongers, see street pedlars
cotton spinning and weaving, 105-6, 117, 130-3, 141-3, 153, 162, 167, 172, 175-7, 181-2
Covent Garden, 178-80
Cries of London, 18
crime: causes of, 71, 90, 99, 178-9, 188-90, 238, 242-3; reformed, Ticket-of-Leave-men, 11, 200; thieves [Vol. 1: 418-19], 29, 197; maps of, 189-90
crippled street seller of nutmeg-graters [Vol. 1: 330-3] see Alloway, Charles
Crosby, Christina, 78
Crystal Palace, 19, 37, 50, 196
Cruikshank, George, 3, 66
Cruikshank, R.J., 5
Cyder Cellars, 100

Darwin, Charles, 48
Davy, Humphry, 13

Daylye Oratour, 187, 211
Deas, Malcolm, 45
Dekker, Thomas, 250
De Quincey, Thomas, 42, 170
Devon, 167
Dickens, Charles, 5-7, 9-10, 20, 24, 44; *Our Mutual Friend*, 5, 20
docks, 109, 139
Dodd, G., 132
drapers, 26, 103, 180, 185, 216-17
Dublin Commercial Journal, 88
Dundee, 94
Durham, 167
Dutch: 52, 101, 187, 229, 231, 250; and German and French Tutor, 243

Eco, Umberto, 26
Economist, The, 44, 152, 173
Edinburgh Review, 104, 136
education, 13-17, 21, 23, 31, 70, 111, 119, 120-1, 184-6
Edwards, E., *The Disease and the Remedy*, 88
Elias, Norbert, 45
emigration, 162-3, 190
engravings, 10-11, 66-7, 102, 134, 155, 159
errata of *LLLP*, 49, 103, 145, 216, 225
Essex, 166
ethnology, ethnologists, 16, 19, 21-2, 31, 48, 51, 54, 58
Evans Late Joy, 100
Exeter, 169

F.B.B., Bedford-square, 103-5
Figaro in London, The, 3, 9
flower selling, 56, 92, 99
Fleet Street, 8, 10
food, 98-100, 105, 130-1, 207-8, 244; adulterated, 182-3
Forman, W.H., 91
Foster (harp player), 22, 30, 99, 120, 159
Foucault, Michel, 46, 78
France, 22, 52, 78
Franklin, Benjamin, 13
free trade, 36-7, 109, 175-9, 215-16
Frégier, Henri, 18, 55, 71
Freud, Sigmund, 7

Gagnier, Reginia, 75
gambling, 113-14
Gardener, 91
Germany, 12, 48, 78, 101
Glasgow, 32, 56, 211-13
Godwin, George, 147
Governess, Lucy L., 23-4, 93
G.P., Edinburgh, 32, 94
Gravesend, 205
Great Exhibition, 35-7, 103, 155
Great Grimsby, 139
Great World of London, 3, 4, 8, 76, 102
Greatest Plague in Life, 14
Grey, Sir George, 109
Griffin, Bohn and Co., 4, 9
Grimm, Jakob, 47-8, 180, 251
Grimm, Wilhelm, 48
Grub Street, 10
Guildhall, 25
Gypsies, 231-2

haberdasher, 45, 155, 162, 169-70, 180-1, 187, 196, 246-7
Hackney, 205
Hall, Marshall, 99
Halliday, Andrew, 4
Hammer, Thomas N., *On the Position and Prospects of School Assistants*, 223
Hammersmith, 240
handloom weaving, 42, 109-18
Harman, Thomas, 250
Hargreaves, James, 132
harp player, see Foster
hatters trade, 208-10
Haymarket, 211
Hebrew, 181, 201
Hemyng, Bracebridge, 4
Herbert, Sidney, 190
Himmelfarb, Gertrude, 6, 18, 64
history, 27-8, 48, 58, 198
Hoggart, Richard, 64
Holborn, 174
Holloway, 215
Horne Tooke, John, 49-50, 78, 180-1, 196-7, 251
hosiery goods, 107
hot cross buns, 188
house of call, 156
Household Words, 10
Howden, John, publisher, 92-4, 120, 134

Hughes, John, [Vol. 1: 279-80], 24, 156, 158-9
Humpherys, Ann, 6, 65
Hunt, Leigh, 72
Hyams and Co., 94, 109
Hyde Park, 155

Illustrated London News, 11, 14
India, 9, 78
Ingestre, Viscount, 19
Ingram, Herbert, 10
Iron Times, The, 11

Jane W., see needlewomen
Jerrold, Douglas, 9, 10-11, 20, 66
Jerrold, Mathilda, 11
Jew(s): and antisemitism, 43, 94, 109, 145, 191, 209-10, 243; fence, 43, 96, 176, 192, 202; Jewish Operative Converts' Institution, 243
Johnson, Samuel, 50, 180
Journal of Industry, 88
Joyce, Patrick, 45
J.T. *(Who Pays the Taxes?)*, 88
justice and fairness, 34-7, 42, 96, 103-4, 111, 160-1, 191-3

Keeling and Hunt Ltd., 120, 128-9
kingfisher's nest, 182
Kingsley, Charles, 20

labour market, see wages
Lancashire, 166
Lancet, The, 183
Landais, Napoléon, 170, 225
Latin, 52, 181, 196, 231
Leclaire, 112, 164
Leeds, 166
Lemon, Mark, 10
Lepenies, Wolf, 65
Lincoln, 166
Liverpool: 166, 169, 203; Benevolent Society for Reclaiming Unfortunate Females, 223
Lloyd's Weekly London Newspaper, 10, 66
loan fund: 39-40, 92, 101-2, 158, 163, 164-5, 171; account sheet, 23, 164-5
lodging houses: 119; Edinburgh,

123; model, 145-7 and lodgers, 23, 145-7; landlord, 145-6; low [Vol. 1: 254-8, 408], 20, 145-6
Logan, William, 54, 80
London: coal-whippers and their journal, 95-7; Female Penitentiary, 196; saw mills, 42, 162; shopmen, 103; traffic [Vol. 2: 184-5], 216. See also under separate areas, e.g. Holloway, Holborn
Loughborough, 107-8
low wages, 7, 19, 25, 31-2, 43, 113-14, 125-44, 157, 238-9
Luddism, 38, 161
Ludlow, John, 20
Luther, Martin, 13

machinery, 35, 42, 108, 117, 125-43, 152-3, 161-2, 166-9, 173-4, 232-9, 244-6
McCulloch, John Ramsay, 91, 103, 120, 150
Mackenzie, Charles, 155
Malthus, Thomas R., 7, 33, 37-9, 103-5, 114-15
Manchester, 166, 169, 173
Manchester School of Economics, 41, 103-6, 152, 161-2, 166-9, 175-6, 181, 203-5
market and distribution, 104-6, 129-34, 166-9
marriage and divorce, 58, 173, 179-80
Martineau, Harriet, 9, 29, 33, 75
Marx, Karl, 6, 18, 36-8, 43
Mass Observation, 5, 63
masters, small, 23-4, 89-90, 161
Mayhew, Athol, 11-12
Mayhew, Amy, 11
Mayhew, Augustus, 9, 20, 62, 65
Mayhew, Edward, 9
Mayhew, Henry, biography of, 3, 9; complete works of, 3, 8, 68-9; novels, 13-14; portrait of, 154
Mayhew, Horace, 9-10
Mayhew, Jane (*née* Jerrold), 11
Mayhew, Joshua, 9
Mayhew, Thomas, 9, 65
Maxwell, Richard, 64
medical: gentleman, 173; assistants, 216

melodrama, 20-21, 31, 56
Midlands counties, 107
Middlesex, 167
Mill, John Stuart, 33, 42, 50, 74, 105, 114, 131, 132-3, 135, 140, 172, 178, 222
milliners, 160
Milton, John, 15, 173, 182
Montgomery, the Rev. Robert, 97-8
Moravians, 240
Morning Chronicle: 6, 8, 17, 24-7, 30, 56, 88, 91, 92, 98, 121, 128, 164, 206; censorship of, 18, 42, 109, 176-7
Morrison, 215
Moses inc., 94, 109, 191
mot (prostitute), etymology of, 45-6, 51-2, 218, 224-6, 230-2
Müller, Max, 46
Murger, Henri, 66
music (collecting street ballad tunes), 157, 188
mutual: investment society, 40, 93; assistance, 102

national: income, 105-6, 115-16, 131-44, 150-2, 234-5; Philanthropic Association (Mackenzie Sec.), 155
Neale, Edward Vansittart, 184
needlewomen, Agnes M. and Jane W., 17, 23, 30, 40, 55-6, 88, 91-2, 120, 124, 154
nestie man, 182
Nicol Brothers, 17, 94, 109, 116, 128, 153
Nightingale, Florence, 5, 63
Norfolk, 166
Norman yoke, 49
Norwich, 169
nurses, 124

O'Connor, Feargus, 161
O'Day, Rosemary, 63
Officer, 24, 249-50
omnibus conductors, and Clapton lines, 201-2, 205-6
oral history, 6
Orangeism, 240
Orwell, George, 5
Owen, Sir Richard, 12, 67

Parent-Duchâtelet, Alexandre, 54, 63, 113, 230
Paris, 9-10, 66, 227
paupers, 90, 99, 166-8
Paved with Gold, 20, 62
pawn shops, 171-2, 199
pedlar, etymology of, 157
Peel, Robert, 17
penny gaff, 100
Percy, Th., 230
petition to Parliament, 246
People's Advocate (New South Wales), 246
philanthropy, see charity
philology, 8, 45-52, 56, 58, 119-20, 157, 162, 169-71, 174, 180-1, 184, 187, 196-7, 201-2, 224-6, 228-32; Philological Society, 46, 77
phrenologists, 98
Pickwick's Papers and Advertiser, 24
Pimlico Society of Carpenters, 88
Plotkin, Cary, 46
plumber's trade, 91
Plymouth, 169
police, 56-7, 94, 121-2, 155, 195-6, 200-1, 219, 224, 238
political economy, 33-7, 103-6, 114-18, 125-44, 148-154, 191-4, 221-3
politics, see also Chartism, 29-30, 97, 118
poor: poet, see John Hughes; Law (old and new), 20, 34, 38, 91, 95, 166-7, 172, 191, 238
Poor Man's Guardian, 9
Prichard, W.B., 188-9
Prince, William, 119
printing trade, 88, 108, 190-1, 210-11, 233
property rights, 39, 175-7, 198-9, 245
prostitution: 47, 52-8, 99, 113, 120, 173, 185-6, 202, 213-15, 218-20, 243; brothels, 195, 213-15, 218-20, 229; fancy men, 56, 81, 214, 248-9; and fall, 8, 55-56, 173, 211-13, 218-20; French, 211, 241; statistical inquiry, 57, 184, 195-6
protectionism, 97, 177
Proudhon, Pierre Joseph, 39, 43
Provident Society at Manchester,

114
public baths, 88
Punch, 3, 10, 17
Pusey, E.B., 120
purity, 8, 47

Quakers, 240
Queen's Theatre, 3, 9
Quennell, Peter, 5
Quételet, L.A.J., 191-2

ragged schools, 94
rags, 216
railway(s), 109, 136-9, 176; mania, 109-10, 126; spring makers (committee of Sheffield), 203-5; workers and navvies, 109-10
rational recreation, 124, 155, 157
Reach, Angus, 17
refuge for the destitute, 196
Regent Street, 211-13
registrar general, 181, 218
Religious Tract Society, 214
rent, 107-8
Reynolds, George W., 16
R.H. 175-9, 184, 191-2, 208-9
Rhine, 11, 16
Ricardo, David, 33, 41-2, 74, 131, 172
Richardson, Charles, *New English Dictionary*, 50, 180, 196
Rousseau, Jean-Jacques, 13
Rowntree, Benjamin S., 5
R.T., Edinburgh, 102
Ryan, Michael, 54

St. John, Horace, 19, 53-6, 60, 79
St. Katherine's, 139
Sala, George A., 10
Salt, *Facts and Figures*, 175
Samuel, Raphael, 6
Sanskrit, 47, 202, 218, 229-30
Saussure, Claude, 27, 74
Saxon language 50-1, 53, 170, 181, 202, 225, 229-30, 250
Saxony, 233
self-help, 24, 30, 39-40, 75, 89, 102, 145-6
sempstresses, 161
sewers, 54
Shakespeare, 15, 225
Sheffield, 39, 203-5

Shops of London, 81
sick-fund, 102
silk weaving, 34
slang see cant
Smiles, Samuel, 33, 75
Smith, Adam, 33, 43, 118, 172, 179, 191, 199
Smith, Olivia, 45
Smith, Sidney, 184
soap (alkali and tallow), 130
socialism and communism, 39, 97, 104-5, 121, 197
Society of Cabinet Makers, 88
Society of Clickers, 88
sociology, early, 6-8, 21, 31, 50, 59
Solomon, Ikey, see Jew fence
Song of the Shirt, The, 17
spectacles, worn in workshops, 154
Spielmann, Marion H., 66
Staffordshire, 167
Standard Library Cyclopaedia, 101, 172
statistics, 29, 89, 142-3, 157, 178-9, 185, 189, 192
steam engines and power, 37-9, 104-5, 109-10, 130, 166-9, 233-5, 244
Stedman-Jones, Gareth, 45
Steedman, Carolyn, 74, 78
stocking frames, 107-8
Stockport, 32
Stockport Advertiser, 88
street: Act, 94-5, 201; art, 84, 118, 170; artizan, 87; blind, 87, 159; book seller, 159-60; buyer, 87; folk, 19, 122; Gipsies, 87; Irish, 87; Italians, 87; Jews, 87; pedlars, 19, 44, 94-5, 100, 129, 144, 155; performer 87; poets, 169; sellers (Edinburgh), 94-5, 102-3, 121-2; showman, 122, 134; style and rhetoric, 13-17, 28, 47-8
Suffolk, 166
Sunday work, 89, 155
supply and demand, 42, 97, 103-6, 111-12, 114-18, 148-54, 161-2, 172-4, 175-9, 191, 197-9, 220-3
Swansea Herald, 88

sweaters and sweatshops, 35, 37-8, 89, 94, 109, 115-17, 153-4, 191-3

tailor(s) and tailoring: master [Vol. 1: 340-1] Allen and Co., 155-6; collective reading among, 120; trade, 34, 128, 136-9, 140, 154, 226-8
Taylor, Secretary of the Provident Society at Manchester, 114
Taylor, Jeremy, 240-1
taxes, 176-8
temperance, see alcohol
Thackeray, William M., 9, 20
Thames, 169
Thompson, Edward P., and Yeo, Eileen, *The Unknown Mayhew*, 6, 27, 64
Thompson, Noel, 33, 75
Times, The, 10, 154, 163
Tinsley, William, 10
Tractarian Party, 240
trade(s): information on, 89-90, 217; societies and unions, 39-40, 89-90, 109, 158, 161,

203-5, 223; and traders, middlemen, 37, 76, 96-7, 139-41, 161, 182-4, 191
Training Institution for Nurses, for Hospitals, Families and the Poor (St. John's House, Fitzroy Square), 124
travel literature, 17, 27, 54
Tuckniss, William, 4
Tweedie, William, 206-8

Universal Anti-Truck Society and Act, 39, 94, 107-8, 209-10
Unitarians, 181
Utilitarianism, 35

Verville, Béroald de, 224
vice: business of, 54, 57-8; vicious habits, 54, 100
Victoria Theatre, Gallery of [Vol. 1: 15,18,19], 91
Villefosse, Monsieur de, 35, 111, 141-2
Vizetelly, Henry, 10

wages: 34-40, 233-5; aid to, 89,

120; rates of, 109-10, 117-18, 196-7, 226; laws, 103, 109-2, 114-17, 125-44, 148-54, 191-5, 209-11, 220-3
Wales, 3, 189-90
watercress girl, 31, 74, 92
Webster's dictionary, 196
Wedgwood, Hensleigh, 48
Welsh language, 218
Westminster School, 3, 9
What to Teach and How to Teach It, 13
Wicks, Thomas, 119
Williams, Karel, 4, 7, 35, 76
Williams, Raymond, 77
Witt's Recreation, 230
workhouses, 30, 92, 122, 196, 245
W.G., Glasgow, 32, 56, 211-13
W.H., Manchester, 166-8, 172
Wortenkrämer, 170, 174, 224-5, 246-7
W.R., a farmer of Bury St. Edmund's, 99-100

Yorkshire (West Riding), 167